Tourism and Hospitality: ICT Tools and Applications

Tourism and Hospitality: ICT Tools and Applications

Editor: Elise Baker

NY RESEARCH PRESS

New York

Published by NY Research Press
118-35 Queens Blvd., Suite 400,
Forest Hills, NY 11375, USA
www.nyresearchpress.com

Tourism and Hospitality: ICT Tools and Applications
Edited by Elise Baker

International Standard Book Number: 978-1-64725-443-8 (Hardback)

Cataloging-in-publication Data

Tourism and hospitality : ICT tools and applications / edited by Elise Baker.
p. cm.
Includes bibliographical references and index.
ISBN 978-1-64725-443-8
1. Tourism--Information technology. 2. Hospitality industry--Technological innovations. 3. Tourism--Technological innovations. I. Baker, Elise.
G155.A1 T68 2023
338.479 1--dc23

Contents

Preface

Travel and tourism technology can be described as the application of information and communications technology (ICT), e-commerce, and other technology solutions in the field of tourism, travel and hospitality. There are various emerging technological developments such as contactless payments, virtual reality, AI chatbots, cybersecurity measures, Internet of things (IoT), artificial intelligence and augmented reality in the field of tourism and hospitality. The implementation of recognition technology in tourism industry has several advantages such as increased security, service non-transferability, and a higher level of efficiency. There are four major types of recognition technologies, namely, face recognition, voice recognition, fingerprint recognition and eye scanning. Face recognition technology assists in automated check-in into hotels and flights. The system of contactless payments is another prominent technology used in travel that has made the process of payments and receipts less time-consuming and safer. This book outlines the applications of ICT tools in tourism and hospitality industry in detail. A number of latest researches have been included to keep the readers up-to-date with the global concepts in this area of study.

This book has been the outcome of endless efforts put in by authors and researchers on various issues and topics within the field. The book is a comprehensive collection of significant researches that are addressed in a variety of chapters. It will surely enhance the knowledge of the field among readers across the globe.

It gives us an immense pleasure to thank our researchers and authors for their efforts to submit their piece of writing before the deadlines. Finally in the end, I would like to thank my family and colleagues who have been a great source of inspiration and support.w

Editor

COVID-19

1

Building Resilient Smart Cities for Sustainable Urban Tourism in Africa Post-COVID-19 Pandemic

Erisher Woyo[1(✉)] and Dandison Ukpabi[2]

[1] Tourism Research in Economic Environs and Society, North-West University, Potchefstroom, South Africa
[2] University of Jyväskylä, Jyväskylä, Finland
dandison.c.ukpabi@jyu.fi

Abstract. This paper contributes to the knowledge by examining the role of smart tourism technologies in destination resilience amidst the COVID-19 pandemic. Considering tourism in the COVID-19 crisis as an emerging stream of research, the study also explores how African cities deployed smart tourism technologies and how effective it has been in creating resilient and safe destinations. Data were collected through a semi-structured online interview from destination managers in Ghana, Kenya, and South Africa. The findings pose critical lessons for city destinations and how they need to transition into smartness to create safe spaces for travellers during and post-COVID-19. Our study makes novel contributions to literature and practice. Theoretically, our study fills the void identified in the relationship between STTs and COVID-19. Our study also offers practical recommendations that will accelerate African destination reset strategies.

Keywords: Smart cities · Smart technologies · Post-COVID-19 · Urban tourism · African cities

1 Introduction

As the world reels from the effect of COVID-19, different industries have structurally rebalanced their operations to remain competitive. Banks now mostly serve their customers via digital channels; the same is true for groceries and educational institutions [2]. The tourism industry is not an exception. Destinations are increasingly deploying virtual and augmented reality to connect with tourists [1, 21 pp. 1]. While these measures are essential for the short term, COVID-19 will be with us for a long time [28]. This requires destinations to strategically implement more digitally sustainable programmes to be resilient from the effects of the pandemic and remain competitive in the long term. The adoption of smart tourism technologies (STT) by tourist destinations has gained popularity in recent years [14, 24]. STTs imply various technologies embedded at destinations to enhance value-added to the people [4]. Studies have found that STTs are integral to tourists' satisfaction at destinations and their intention to revisit [13; 14]. STTs are also linked to urban resilience [9].

Resilience from COVID-19 is critical for the survival and competitiveness of destinations. However, literature is not clear on the role of STTs on resilience from the effect of COVID-19.

The United Nations World Tourism Organisation reported an increase of above 7% and 2% on international tourist arrivals and receipts, respectively, in Africa in 2018 [27]. COVID-19 threatens the upward trajectory of this growth. Interestingly, there is a lack of empirical studies that have explored the nexus between STTs and resilience from COVID-19, especially from a developing country context. Using Africa as a case in point, the objective of this study is to examine the role of STTs in destination resilience amidst the COVID-19 pandemic. Specifically, this study explores (a) how different African destinations deploy STTs, (b) how effective has these STTs been in fostering destination resilience amidst COVID-19, and (c) what strategic implications STTs have for the future of African tourism.

Our study makes novel contributions to literature and practice. Theoretically, our study fills the void identified in the relationship between STTs and COVID-19. Furthermore, it builds the importance of smart technologies for African destinations generally deemed authoritative and unwilling to support national-level technologies. Our study also offers practical recommendations that will accelerate African destination reset strategies.

2 Literature Review

2.1 Smart Cities and Smart Tourism Technologies/Destination

The concept of smartness is a multidisciplinary term with several definitions depending on the context [4]. The smartness of a city implies interconnecting different information and communication technologies to enhance value for different stakeholders [14]. The proliferation of different ICTs has also created avenues for city administrators to creatively use them to enhance living and social services. In today's complex scenario, the role of the smart cities as leading actors to face Covid-19 and future pandemics cannot be overemphasised. Similarly, these ICT tools provide various value-enhancing experiences for tourists. Destination managers have used them to enhance tourists' experiences and increase destination competitiveness [4].

Smart tourism technologies (STTs) constitute general and specific ICT tools employed by destinations to enhance tourists' experiences and value [12, 14]. While there are different variants of STTs, the most popular ones identified in literature includes social network sites, augmented reality, smartphones, beacons, the internet of things (IoT), cloud computing, sensors, mobile apps, Google maps, etc. [4, 13, 14]. The harmonious operation of these tools in creating, managing, and sustainably integrating them to enhance the touristic experience gives rise to the smart tourism ecosystem [11]. The literature identified such destinations as smart destinations [13].

Shafiee et al. [24] categorized smart tourism destinations under five components: stakeholders, structure, process, technology, and policies. Per stakeholders, these comprise the public and private sectors. Public sectors include national governments, while private sectors comprise active enterprises in smart tourism, information technology companies and other tourism organisations. For structure, they argue that it comprises strategic-communicative level, instrumental level, and applied level. Processes are value-creating process, decision-making process, digitization, and information exchange. The technology component comprises those as listed above. Lastly, policies deal with data access, privacy and security of customers' data, and personal data generated by smart devices.

On the other hand, smart tourism technologies possess four key attributes essential to their usability in each destination: informativeness, accessibility, interactivity, and personalization [13, 14]. Informativeness implies the quality of the information from the STTs. Accessibility has to do with how tourists can easily access information from the destination via the STTs. On the other hand, interactivity implies how tourists can communicate effectively and obtain feedback via the STTs. Finally, personalization implies how tourists can obtain specific and relevant information suitable to them from the STTs.

Scholars have conducted empirical studies that examined the application of STTs on destinations and their effects on attractiveness and revisit intention. Huang et al. [13] found a positive association between the explorative use of STTs and travel experience satisfaction. Similarly, Jeong and Shin [14] found that the three key attributes of STTs (informativeness, interactivity and personalization) are positively associated with travellers' memorable experiences. In the same study, the memorable experience was also found to positively influence satisfaction and travellers' intention to visit.

2.2 Resilient Smart Cities in Post-COVID-19

Pandemics such as the current COVID-19 pose varying levels of challenges to cities and their inhabitants. Thus, the concept of resilience implies the "ability of a city to understand and prevent the disaster risks, mitigate those risks, and respond in such a way as to minimize loss of or damage to life, livelihoods, property, infrastructure, economic activity and the environment" [12 pp. 97]. Foreseeing risks and preparing adequately for them greatly enhances cities' ability to withstand those risks and equips them to bounce back immediately [23, 29].

Tourism is one of the most affected sectors due to the ongoing COVID-19 pandemic. Geographically, cities were significantly affected by the COVID-19 pandemic as they were hotspots for transmitting the virus [18]. However, as many destinations lift travel restrictions, sound recovery strategies are pertinent to remain competitive post-COVID-19. Scholarly evidence suggests that smart solutions are linked to urban resilience, such as community disaster resilience [9], emergency management [15], crime prevention [20] and disaster recovery [25, 30]. Thus, research notes that cities are becoming more resilient to crises due to their adoption of smart technologies, including IoT, artificial intelligence (AI) and big data [18]. For instance, the use of contact tracing apps could help check COVID-19 transmissions among tourists. The app could easily identify and alert relevant authorities where they are found [22, 26]. Though STTs have strongly been linked to post-COVID-19 recovery strategies, research investigating their adoption in urban contexts have largely been done in cities in China and Western democracies [18], leaving African cities relatively understudied.

This study foresees an uptick in adopting STTs by destinations as part of COVID-19 recovery strategies. Tourists' perception of post-COVID-19 destination attractiveness would be hinged on the availability of accessible digital technologies. For instance, while social distancing and lowered mobility may continue post-COVID-19, augmented reality could be a critical technology to offer tourists deep, unique, context-specific, and memorable experiences [21]. Even at the destination, the functionalities of STTs such as the internet, free Wi-Fi access points, big data and various social networking apps afford tourists up-to-date information on possible areas to avoid due to crowd and opportunities for information sharing.

3 Methodology

Smart tourism is an underexplored concept in Africa as a tourist destination. A qualitative methodology that followed an exploratory research design was employed in this study to examine the smart solutions implemented in East, West and Southern Africa cities as a response to building resilient cities post-COVID-19. Data were collected using a semi-structured interview guide. This instrument was chosen to allow participants to communicate how cities use smart solutions to create safe tourist spaces during the pandemic [7]. The instrument was designed based on a comprehensive review of literature on smart tourism and technology. We pretested the instrument before data collection, and unambiguous wording was revised accordingly. The interview schedule contained the following questions:

1. Do you think your destination or city has the networked infrastructure that enables informativeness and accessibility of tourism resources needed to support urban tourism development post -COVID-19?
2. What policies are available to support business-led urban development and creative industries to promote resilient urban tourism growth?
3. Your comment on the social inclusion of various urban stakeholders, including residents and social capital in urban tourism development for a safe and resilient post-COVID-19 city environment?
4. Are there any smart plans that your destination is currently pursuing to create resilient and safe tourist environments? They are hinged on what? Does your plan utilise any technologies? If yes, which ones?
5. Which technologies are you using as a destination to make the destination COVID-19 safe and resilient?
6. Does the destination offer free internet, Wi-Fi access points, or other big data or open data technologies to enhance tourist experiences?
7. Do you think the official tourism website of the destination was created to be present throughout the tourist Lifecycle? Explain your answer?
8. Does your destination use QR codes? If yes, explain what they are used for?
9. As a destination, are you able to do data-driven marketing and base your decisions on data? Have you been able to collect data on the impact of smart solutions on the experiences of tourists?
10. Are tourists aware of any smart solutions in your destination?

A combination of purposive and snowball sampling approaches was utilised in selecting participants. Destination managers recruited to participate in this study were from Kenya, Ghana, and South Africa. We used our professional networks to recruit participants using WhatsApp and emails. These platforms were used to confirm availability and consent to participate in the study. The messages sent to participants outlined the purpose of the study and its nature and explained why the participants' opinions were being sought. Furthermore, the participants were also informed of their right to participate and withdraw at any time during the research. No financial incentives were offered for participation. Destination managers were eventually invited to refer the researchers to other managers in their respective countries and cities. Data were collected until saturation, and the anonymity of the participants was guaranteed.

Participants were interviewed between June and July 2021 using MS Teams and Zoom facilities, and each interview lasted approximately 30 min. Interviews were conducted in English. Creswell [6] recommended conducting between 5 to 25 interviews to reach data saturation. In this study, data saturation was reached after 9 interviews. All the interviews were done synchronously, and the details are summarised in Table 1. Interviews were conducted, transcribed, and analysed using thematic analysis. Data analysis started with full data transcription, data familiarisation, codes identification, searching, reviewing, defining themes, and generating results. Coding was performed manually through repeated reading of and making notes on interview transcripts.

Table 1. Participants' profile

Participant ID	Gender	Location
DM1	Male	Nakuru, Kenya
DM2	Female	Accra, Ghana
DM3	Male	Tshwane, South Africa
DM4	Female	Accra, Ghana
DM5	Male	Nairobi, Kenya
DM6	Male	Nairobi, Kenya
DM7	Female	Accra, Ghana
DM8	Male	Johannesburg, South Africa
DM9	Male	Johannesburg, South Africa

4 Findings

Based on the analysis of the interviews, it was possible to examine and categorize smart solutions being used by the destination to create safe and resilient cities for a post-pandemic era. The findings of the study are organised based on the objectives, namely (1) how different African cities deployed STTs during the COVID-19 pandemic, (2) how effective has these STTs been fostering safe and resilient cities amidst COVID-19 and (3) the strategic implications STTs in creating safe and resilient tourism cities in Africa.

4.1 Deployment of STTs in African Cities During COVID-19

To achieve greater resilience during COVID-19 for the travel industry, cities need to implement a range of smart technologies [10]. Such technological interventions are critical given that currently, anything that involves touch is frowned up. A destination manager from Nakuru City in Kenya argued that "*digital cities are important, as they give tourists a perception of safety*". This view is consistent with past research that advocated for developing digitalized cities as a fundamental concept of smart tourism [3, 19]. Further data analysis shows more smart technologies deployment during COVID in Kenya than in South Africa and Ghana. This could be explained by the commitment of the Kenyan government, as summed up by this quote:

> *"There is a greater government involvement in enabling the utilisation of technologies. For instance, there was a creation of the Data Protection Commission of Kenya, to help with data breaches".*

The South African government has made similar efforts that saw the Presidential Commission on Fourth Industrial Revolution being established to drive the smartness concept. Table 2 provides a range of smart technologies deployed to create safe spaces for tourism in Ghanaian, Kenyan, and South African cities during COVID-19. Key among the interventions was promoting mobile payments, reducing data bundles, using drones, and contact tracing apps. The aspect of mobile money payments was already in existence in Kenya but was magnified during the pandemic. These findings are consistent with earlier studies [16, 31] that argued that using such technologies is critical in decreasing contact among tourists and contagion.

Table 2. Interventions and STTs deployed during COVID-19 in African cities.

Intervention(s)	Location	Objective
Portals; Interactive dashboards, toll-free lines, and WhatsApp channels (in multiple languages)	Ghanaian, Kenyan, and South African cities	To disseminate reliable information on the pandemic as well as enable citizens to report suspected cases
Digital platforms	Ghanaian, Kenyan and South African cities	Remote learning; working from home; service providers such as health, banking, and entertainment
Cashless payments	More pronounced in Kenyan cities; Ghana, and South Africa	To reduce contagion and transactional fees were waived
Doubling internet speeds	Kenya (Google Loon)	To enhance universal 4G coverage and connectivity in the country for people working from home. Speeds were doubled at no extra costs

(*continued*)

Table 2. (*continued*)

Intervention(s)	Location	Objective
Contact tracing apps	Kenyan cities of Nairobi and Kisumu (Msafari); Ghana (GH COVID-19 Tracker App), and South Africa	To track passengers on public transport
Drones	Ghana, Kenya, and South Africa	To ferry medicines, blood, vaccines and share information about the pandemic
Promotional of work from home data bundles	Kenya	Campaign to educate the public on the pandemic
QR codes	Kenya and South Africa	For online ordering, virtual queues in restaurants, hospitals and reducing restaurant visits

Before COVID-19, there was a huge convergence of disruptive effects in the form of new technologies. As a result, this resulted in the proliferation and consolidation of smart cities. However, with consumer concerns for more sustainable, resilient, and safer spaces, technologies in the African cities of Accra, Nairobi, Nakuru, Cape Town, and Johannesburg are at the heart of city development and the tourism sector. There was a consensus among participants from all the cities that COVI-19 has increased the need for a smart technological solution to safer tourism. The participants noted an increased usage of STTs in cities, tourism establishments, hotels, and restaurants to manage the spread of COVID-19. Most of the cited technologies used are aimed at decreasing tourist contacts.

4.2 STTs' Effectiveness in Fostering Safe and Resilient Cities Amidst COVID-19

The study sought to establish how effective STTs were in creating safe and resilient tourism cities during the COVID-19 pandemic. Participants from Kenya and South Africa pointed out coordinated efforts between the government and other stakeholders in creating safer and resilient cities during the pandemic. This was evidenced by the creation of the Data Protection Commission of Kenya. Though there was a huge drive for technological solutions in South Africa pre-COVID-19, through the formation of the Presidential Commission on the Fourth Industrial Revolution (PC4IR), destination managers from South Africa argued that efforts to create smart tourism in the city of Tshwane, Johannesburg and Cape Town appears to be slower. Past research has long identified these aspects as critical in developing smart cities for enhanced tourism competitiveness [8].

"I think due to the effort of the government of Kenya, smart technologies have been effective in making our cities safe and resilient."
"In South Africa, the pace before COVID-19 was amazing. However, more could be done to create safe and resilient urban spaces".
"The government of Kenya has a full-fledged ICT, Innovation and Youth Affairs ministry driving smart innovations to reduce transmission during COVID-19".
"Data Protection Commission of Kenya is responsible for dealing with complaints about the data breach, and this is a critical step in creating safe and resilient spaces for tourists in Kenya."

Based on the narratives received from participants in Kenya, it appears that STTs were more effective in fostering safe and resilient cities amidst the COVID-19 pandemic. This could be attributed to government policy and innovative digital culture. Regarding Ghana, the participants noted that the digital innovation aspect is rather silent, and therefore, the notion that STTs are thus not driving more from the government. However, one destination manager from Ghana noted that "*more recently, the ministry of health has been distributing COVID-19 vaccines to remote areas as a means of speeding up its vaccination campaign, and this is a right step in ensuring that cities in Ghana are safe for tourism purposes*".

There are currently no public policy plans in Ghana to direct the implementation of smart technological solutions, as is the case in Kenya and South Africa. The use of drones in delivering vaccines is a welcome solution. This could be more meaningful if the government put policies to promote the usage of smart technologies.

4.3 Implications of STTs in a Post-pandemic City Environment

One of the key attributes of STTs is to ensure that tourism products and services are accessible. Due to COVID-19, participants from all three countries noted that the demand for STTs was high, given its implications on tourist safety. [21] argue that using STTs during and post-pandemic must also ensure aspects of uniqueness, accessibility, personalisation, context-specific, memorable experiences among travellers. The data analysis shows that Kenyan tourism is currently implementing several smart technologies to build decision support systems of the destination to deepen travellers' experiences.

A destination manager from Kenya mentioned that "*building an information hub is necessary though current efforts around that are currently fragmented*". Most participants in Kenya and South Africa argued for the need to develop regulated and coordinated information hubs. This was argued as critical in ensuring that information about COVID-19, COVID-19 guidelines, visas, and attractions is widely accessible for tourists during and post-pandemic. Participants mentioned that using STTs such as drones, GIS, and QR codes is crucial in providing thematic maps to help cities with smart elements of accessibility and informativeness. One destination manager from South Africa added that "*using smart technologies is critical in helping tourists during COVID-19 understand the destination comprehensively*". This view is consistent with past literature that argues that such provision of smart technologies is imperative for enhancing visitors' experiences [21].

"Technologies are crucial in enhancing the promotion of Kenya tourism to domestic and international travellers during and post-pandemic."
"We are currently implementing smart solutions that help tourists identify and find the best tourism spots here in Kenya. QR codes are widely used in Kenya for this aspect".
"South Africa, at the beginning of the pandemic, has been using drones and geospatial technologies. This should continue in the future to provide timely information about COVID-19".
"Mapping of existing and potential tourism facilities, services, infrastructure, resources, and attractions using smart technologies is important in displaying the well-known tourism products and opening the underutilized regions."

Most of the technologies used in Kenya and South Africa are aimed at digital mapping as a strategic response. The study also found that South Africa, just like Kenya, has been using GIS and location technologies to provide real-time visualizations, identify hotspots, and update current progress on its national dashboards. A study on smart cities in South Korea showed that through technologies, firms, citizens, and the government could flatten the curve during the COVID-19 pandemic without closing their borders [17]. In this case, the proactive exchange of information allowed tourists to form a shared comprehension of the context while complying with the rules and security measures adopted to increase trust in the institution's ability to manage the crisis.

This is critical in enhancing the informativeness attribute for smart tourism and the creation of safe tourism cities. Tourist maps have also been known to play vital roles in identifying and locating tourist attractions and have essential roles in the effective and efficient management of tourism resources. The creation of smart tourism cities, thus, depends on the availability of information that comes with spatial representation. This enables the analysis of the virus patterns and helps tourists to make informed decisions.

"In Kenya, we recently launched a digital mapping of tourism resources using drones, and it is a strategy that aims to enhance smart conservation".
"All wildlife in Kenya is set to be counted using drones in the next six months. Geographical Information System (GIS)".
"The use of GIS and location technologies during the pandemic has been very helpful for South Africa in creating safe spaces by helping travellers identify hotspots and be aware of current progress".

Though mapping will be important in promoting safe and resilient tourism cities in Africa post-COVID-19, the role of the government in implementing smart solutions is relatively limited in the empirical context of Ghana. However, these findings show that smart tourism among African cities will be integral in the post-pandemic era, given their ability to provide tourists with an enhanced public health environment.

5 Conclusion

The study examined the smart technologies adopted by African cities in Ghana, Kenya, and South Africa to create safe, and resilient smart tourism cities. The findings show that cities in Kenya, Ghana and South Africa differ significantly in adopting smart technologies to create safe cities. In Kenya and South Africa, the findings show that the government actively coordinated and controlled the narrative of smart technologies based on initiatives such as the Data Protection Commission of Kenya and the

Presidential Commission on the Fourth Industrial Revolution in South Africa. However, cities in Ghana seem to lack coordination efforts with the national government to create safe spaces using smart technologies. Overall, the usage of smart technologies differed significantly.

Unlike research that focuses on the negative impacts caused by the pandemic, this paper focuses on evaluating actions and strategies based on the adoption of smart technologies in the respective countries to face the pandemic. The study highlights those smart technological responses are useful in dealing with an ongoing pandemic, even in a continent that often disregards such technologies as a means of wielding political power. Thus, instead of suppressing the consumption of smart technologies, African governments may gain full control over a situation by adopting a techno-driven approach when faced with a pandemic. Furthermore, the contribution of this study lies in bringing a perspective of developing countries in the African region. However, there is an overall concern that governments in Africa, generally known to be authoritative, may take advantage of the Covid-19 to reinforce technological visioning on citizens beyond controlling the pandemic.

African cities must fully benefit from these technologies to ensure that stakeholders increase smart governance and equitable data distribution [5]. Furthermore, based on Kenya's findings, there is a need for continued government participation, especially in creating an enabling environment crucial for creating sustainable smart cities.

References

1. Akhtar N et al (2021) Post-COVID 19 tourism: will digital tourism replace mass tourism? Sustainability 13(10):5352
2. Baig A, Hall B, Jenkins P, Lamarre E, McCarthy B (2020) The COVID-19 recovery will be digital: a plan for the first 90 days. McKinsey Digital 14
3. Bassano C, Barile S, Piciocchi P, Spohrer JC, Iandolo F, Fisk R (2019) Storytelling about places: tourism marketing in the digital age. Cities 87:10–20
4. Boes K, Buhalis D, Inversini A (2015) Conceptualising smart tourism destination dimensions. In: Tussyadiah I, Inversini A (eds) Information and communication technologies in tourism 2015. Springer, Cham, pp 391–403. https://doi.org/10.1007/978-3-319-14343-9_29
5. Choi J, Lee S, Jamal T (2021) Smart Korea: governance for smart justice during a global pandemic. J Sustain Tour 29(2–3):541–550
6. Creswell JW (1998) Qualitative inquiry and research design: choosing among five traditions. SAGE Publications, Thousand Oaks, CA, Thousand Oaks, CA
7. Creswell JW, Creswell JD (2018) Research design: qualitative, quantitative, and mixed methods approaches, 5th edn. SAGE Publications, Los Angeles, Los Angeles
8. Dredge D, Phi G, Mahaderavan R, Neehan E, Popescu ES (2018) Digitalisation in Tourism: in-depth analysis of challenges and opportunities. Low value procedure GRO-SME-17-C-091-A for Executive Agency for Small and Medium-sized Enterprises (EASME) virtual tourism observatory. Aalborg University Copenhagen (2018)
9. Dufty N (2012) Using social media to build community disaster resilience. Australian J Emerg Manag 27(1):40–45
10. Gretzel U, Koo C (2021) Smart tourism cities: a duality of place where technology supports the convergence of touristic and residential experiences. Asia Pac J Tour Res 26(4):352–364

11. Gretzel U, Werthner H, Koo C, Lamsfus C (2015) Conceptual foundations for understanding smart tourism ecosystems. Comput Hum Behav 50:558–563
12. Hernantes J, Maraña P, Gimenez R, Sarriegi JM, Labaka L (2019) Towards resilient cities: a maturity model for operationalizing resilience. Cities 84:96–103
13. Huang CD, Goo J, Nam K, Yoo CW (2017) Smart tourism technologies in travel planning: the role of exploration and exploitation. Inf Manag 54(6):757–770
14. Jeong M, Shin HH (2020) Tourists' experiences with smart tourism technology at smart destinations and their behavior intentions. J Travel Res 59(8):1464–1477
15. Ji Z, Anwen Q (2010) The application of internet of things (IOT) in emergency management system in China. In: 2010 IEEE international conference on technologies for homeland security (HST), IEEE, pp 139–142
16. Jiang Y, Wen J (2020) Effects of COVID-19 on hotel marketing and management: a perspective article. Int J Contemp Hosp Manag 32(8):2563–2573
17. Jo W, Lee J, Park J, Kim Y (2020) Online information exchange and anxiety spread in the early stage of the novel coronavirus (COVID 19) outbreak in South Korea: structural topic model and network analysis. J Med Int Res 22(6):e19455
18. Kummitha RKR (2020) Smart technologies for fighting pandemics: the techno-and human-driven approaches in controlling the virus transmission. Govern Inf Q 37(3):101481
19. Kunzmann KR (2020) Smart cities after COVID-19: ten narratives. disP – Plann Rev 56 (2):20–31
20. Lee JS, Park S, Jung S (2016) Effect of crime prevention through environmental design (CPTED) measures on active living and fear of crime. Sustainability 8(9):872
21. Mohanty P, Hassan A, Ekis E (2020) Augmented reality for relaunching tourism post-COVID-19: socially distant, virtually connected. Worldwide Hosp Tour Themes 12(6):753–760
22. Munzert S, Selb P, Gohdes A, Stoetzer LF, Lowe W (2021) Tracking and promoting the usage of a COVID-19 contact tracing app. Nat Hum Behav 5(2):247–255
23. Poku-Boansi M, Cobbinah PB (2018) Are we planning for resilient cities in Ghana? An analysis of policy and planners' perspectives. Cities 72:252–260
24. Shafiee S, Ghatari AR, Hasanzadeh A, Jahanyan S (2021) Smart tourism destinations: a systematic review. Tour Rev 76(3):505–528
25. Suri N et al (2018) Exploiting smart city IoT for disaster recovery operations. In: 2018 IEEE 4th world forum on Internet of Things (WF-IoT), IEEE, pp 458–463
26. Ukpabi D, Olaleye S, Karjaluoto H (2021) Factors influencing tourists' intention to use covid-19 contact tracing app. In: Wörndl W, Koo C, Stienmetz JL (eds) Information and Communication Technologies in Tourism 2021. Springer, Cham, pp 504–516. https://doi.org/10.1007/978-3-030-65785-7_48
27. UNWTO (2019) International tourism highlights. World Tourism Organisation. Madrid
28. World Health Organisation (WHO) (2020) WHO Director-General's opening remarks at the media briefing on COVID-19. https://www.who.int/director-general/speeches/detail/who-director-general-s-opening-remarks-at-the-media-briefing-on-covid-19–22-april-2020. Accessed 19 Aug 2021
29. Woyo E (2021) The sustainability of using domestic tourism as a post-COVID-19 recovery strategy in a distressed destination. In: Wörndl W, Koo C, Stienmetz JL (eds) Information and Communication Technologies in Tourism 2021. Springer, Cham, pp 476–489. https://doi.org/10.1007/978-3-030-65785-7_46
30. Yao F, Wang Y (2020) Towards resilient and smart cities: a real-time urban analytical and geo-visual system for social media streaming data. Sustain Cities Soc 63:102448
31. Zeng Z, Chen PJ, Lew AA (2020) From high-touch to high-tech: COVID-19 drives robotics adoption. Tour Geogr 22(3):724–734

2

Communicating to Tourists during and Post-COVID-19: What do they want (need) to hear?

Laura Zizka(✉), Meng-Mei Chen, Effie Zhang and Amandine Favre

Ecole Hoteliere de Lausanne//HES-SO University of Applied Sciences and Arts Western Switzerland, Lausanne, Switzerland
{Laura.ZIZKA,Maggie.CHEN-HOLLERAN,Effie.ZHANG2, Amandine.FAVRE}@ehl.ch

Abstract. Swiss tourism relies heavily on international clientele to book rooms and purchase goods and services. However, from March to June 2020, due to the COVID-19 pandemic, travel and subsequent bookings slowed and, in some cases, stopped altogether. Based predominantly on Situational Crisis Communication Theory (SCCT), this paper investigates Swiss hotels' messages on their official Facebook pages and the SCCT strategies they employed during this crisis. The findings from 48 independent four- and five-star hotels show that the *Victimage* strategy was the most often employed when communicating about the COVID-19 pandemic in general. Further, most hotels published positive messages during this period (68%) and strongly emphasized their roles as victims at this time. Only 5% of the messages posted were negative messages. Hotels 'blamed' the government and the sanitary measures for their closing or reduced services. The findings presented here contribute to the literature by offering a pattern of crisis responses from Swiss hotels in the early period of the pandemic. These results are currently being updated with the messages communicated in the 12 months since the beginning of this study. The findings of this crisis communication during an early stage of the pandemic will be used to make concrete recommendations for the strategies that should be implemented in the future if the COVID-19 crisis continues or when faced with other crises.

Keywords: Swiss hotels · COVID-19 · Facebook · Situational Crisis Communication Theory (SCCT) · Crisis communication strategies

1 Introduction

Tourism in Switzerland is a lucrative business. The tourism industry is one of the largest export industries in Switzerland with 4.4% of export revenue [1], providing many jobs to the local communities and contributing significantly to the local economy in general. According to the 2019 official statistics, Swiss tourism includes 28 985 hotel and restaurant establishments that generate CHF 44.7 billion in total revenue, CHF 16.6 billion from foreign tourists in Switzerland [2].

The 2019 tourist season was a profitable time for Swiss tourism. The expectations for 2020 were equally positive until late December 2019, when news of the COVID-19 pandemic and its potential to spread globally was shared.

As word of the COVID-19 pandemic spread, the Swiss tourism industry experts began making ominous predictions regarding the 2020 tourism season, and early statistics confirmed those predictions. According to a press release from the official Swiss Federal Statistical Office (FSO) on Feb. 2, 2021- "In 2020, the Swiss hotel sector registered 23.7 million overnight stays. This represents a fall of 40.0% (−15.8 million overnight stays) compared with 2019. The exceptional context of COVID–19 explains this unprecedented fall at a level not seen since the end of the 1950s. Foreign demand registered 7.3 million overnight stays, i.e., a decline of 66.1% (–14.3 million). Swiss demand fell less drastically (–8.6%/–1.5 million) to 16.4 million overnight stays." (para.1) [3].

Previous studies have examined crises in the hospitality industry, and Swiss hotels have remained relatively unscathed from previous crises. Nonetheless, with the COVID-19 pandemic, Swiss tourism was significantly affected. In the period examined in this study (March through June 2020), Swiss tourism saw foreign demand fall by 68% in March and overnight stays by Swiss guests by 55% [3]. The number of Swiss guests declined further in April 2020 (by −86%) and rose slightly in May 2020 (−54%) [3]. With the relaxation of some of the COVID-19 restrictions, domestic rose slightly to only 23% less than the previous year's statistics [3].

This study aims to investigate the messages that Swiss hoteliers provided to their clients on their official Facebook pages. As many clients use social media, particularly Facebook, to gather information before traveling, this communication channel was selected as the most appropriate for analyzing the SCCT strategies these hotels employed. The overarching objective is to establish the strategies used and gauge their effectiveness in communicating during a crisis, namely, the COVID-19 pandemic. These results can be used to communicate 'better' when the next crisis hits the hospitality industry.

2 Literature Review

2.1 Crisis and Situational Crisis Communication Theory (SCCT)

Crises have been defined as unpredictable events that can disrupt an organization's operations, impact their performance and, potentially, generate negative feelings toward the organization leading to reputational damage [4]. While an organization is concerned about its reputation, public safety and keeping customers safe comes first [5]. The COVID-19 pandemic is a crisis where the organization has little to no responsibility or control over the circumstances. This type of crisis is categorized by stakeholders as a Victim crisis, as the organization could do nothing to prevent its occurrence [6]. With this global pandemic, all industries were affected, but some industries fared better than others. For the tourism industry, COVID-19 had significant consequences. In this paper, one part of the broader tourism industry, i.e., hotels, will be examined to gauge how they faced the pandemic.

According to Coombs Situational Crisis Communication Theory (SCCT), when the organization has been attributed weak responsibility or has been identified as a Victim crisis such as COVID-19, the organization should implement an ethical base response. This base response consists of *instructing* information (i.e., explaining the crisis to the stakeholders) and *adjusting* information (i.e., helping stakeholders cope with the crisis) [7]. This is the overarching strategy that should be used in the case of any crisis. However, organizations can choose to employ other strategies as well based on the crisis. For example, they could include SCCT strategies such as *ingratiation* (i.e., praising stakeholders for efforts they have made), *victimage* (i.e., confirming that the organization is a victim of this crisis), or *reminder* (i.e., telling stakeholders the good things you did in the past) [8]. These are part of the crisis communication strategy cluster known as *bolster* [9]. Other crisis communication strategy clusters include *instructing* and *adjusting* (i.e., the base response of all crisis messages), *deny*, *diminish*, and *rebuild* [9]. Depending on the type of crisis, the attribution of responsibility, and the intensifying factors, organizations will choose which response or which combination of responses best fits the crisis at hand.

The research has evolved to include crisis communication strategies consisting of enhancing, scapegoating, and transferring. *Enhancing* is defined as telling stakeholders about current good works the company is doing) [10]. *Scapegoating* occurs when companies shift the blame to another group outside of the organization [11]; this is part of the deny cluster [9]. *Transferring* entails naming a credible third party as part of the crisis response [10]. This paper examines how Swiss independent hotels communicated crisis responses on their official Facebook pages during 3 months in 2020.

2.2 Crisis Communication in the Hospitality Industry

Researchers have examined how and what companies communicate with their stakeholders in times of crisis. In the hospitality industry, specifically, researchers have examined the messages posted on social media platforms such as Twitter or Facebook during crises. Tourism organizations are encouraged to use social media to communicate during crises as many tourists turn to social media to seek information about the destination or property [12]. After all, their stakeholders are using social media and often post on their own social media accounts while on vacation [SAME]. However, studies have shown that the hospitality industry, in particular, has not been proactive and does not take advantage of the reach that social media has during crises [8]. Further, some hospitality organizations have given inappropriate responses in times of crisis [11]. The hospitality industry must become less averse to social media and embrace it as a potential channel for crisis communication. As Switzerland is dependent on international travel for their tourism, particularly for hotel occupancy, this study will analyze the crisis communication strategies used on the official Facebook pages and address the following two research questions:

RQ1: What crisis communication strategies were employed most frequently during the first wave of COVID-19 by Swiss hoteliers?

RQ2: What sentiment were the Swiss hoteliers trying to communicate to their clients during this first wave of COVID-19?

3 Methodology

This paper examines the messages during and after the first wave and first confinement of 48 Swiss four- and five-star, independent hotels to analyze the crisis communication strategies they employed during this period. Their messages posted on their official Facebook pages are measured against Situational Crisis Communication Theory (SCCT). Both content analysis and a sentiment analysis of their messages were conducted to establish the strategies they used and the emotion they created in doing so. This paper concludes with the implications of effectively using crisis communication strategies during the COVID-19 pandemic and future crises.

To examine the messages posted on Swiss hotel Facebook pages, a list of 222 independent hotels (four- and five-star independent hotels in Switzerland) was created. Of the original 222 hotels, only 96 had Facebook pages. Of the 96 remaining hotels, those that were part of a group (though not a chain) and hotels that were closed during this period were eliminated. The remaining 48 hotels were used in this study, and a comparison between their Facebook traction in 2019 versus 2020 was made. The Facebook comments were tracked from mid-crisis when many hotels were closed (March 13, 2020) to June 13, 2020, again, when many of the hotels reopened. The same dates were used in 2019 as well. Some hotels were preparing to open their doors when this study was conducted, while others communicated the reopening date. This study analyzes the crisis communication strategies employed by Swiss hotels during this first de-confinement stage.

The research team collected all posts and calculated descriptive statistics, including means and standard deviations. Two research assistants independently coded all comments based on the SCCT strategies and recorded the frequencies. Their results were compared to seek differences. Any differences were discussed until a final agreement was reached. A sentiment analysis was conducted by inserting each post to the sentiment analysis tool available at Monkeylearn.com. For each post, Monkeylearn.com classifies it as positive, negative, or neutral and provides its confidence level. The closer the confidence level is to one, the more reliable the result. The research team recorded the sentiment classification, frequencies, and confidence level.

4 Results

4.1 Descriptive Statistics Results

The means and standard deviations for the numbers of posts are 23.85 (S.D. 24.46) and 1.98 (S.D. 1.54) for 2019 and 2020, respectively. The two tail t-test result ($t(47) = 6.296$, $p = 0.000$) confirmed the significant difference between 2019 and 2020. While the literature suggests that communication during a crisis should be frequent, timely, and consistent [7], the lack of communication from Swiss hoteliers seems to indicate the opposite. They posted quite infrequently, particularly in comparison with the same period in 2019. One explanation could be that the hotel business is quite competitive; thus, hotels post their special offers to attract clients during their busiest seasons. In the case of COVID-19, there was nothing new to post and nothing to offer.

Further, international tourists who could not travel due to sanitary restrictions, quarantines, or lockdowns would not search for hotel information on Facebook. The typical exchanges on social media, i.e., travel stories or photos, were not posted during this period.

4.2 Hotel Official Facebook Comments – Frequency of SCCT Strategies

The Swiss hotels examined in this study are located in various regions in Switzerland. Thus, many of the messages are communicated in the local language. Switzerland has four official languages, French, German, Italian, and Romansch, but, as an international travel destination, Swiss hotels are obliged to provide messages in English as well. In this study, we focused on all the messages communicated in English. On Table 1, the frequency of the types of SCCT strategies employed by the hotels are analyzed. The only SCCT strategy that was not employed was *apology*; this result could be expected as all hotels were victims of this crisis.

Table 1. Frequency of SCCT strategies employed by Swiss hotels

Strategies	Number of times employed	Frequency
Scapegoat	11	12%
Justification	8	9%
Apology	0	0%
Compensation	7	8%
Endorsement	2	2%
Enhancing	5	5%
Ingratiation	10	11%
Reminder	3	3%
Victimage	46	49%
Transferring	1	1%
Total	93	100%

From the results, only one strategy, *victimage*, was used in 49% of posts communicating about the Covid-19 situation. All the other strategies were employed less than 12% of the time, such as *scapegoat* (12%), *ingratiation* (11%), *justification* (9%), and *compensation* (8%), *enhancing* (5%), *reminder* (3%), *endorsement* (2%), and *transferring* (1%). To further investigate these strategies, a sentiment analysis was conducted with all the posts. Table 2 displays those results. As seen in the literature, *ingratiation* and *victimage* derive from the *bolster* crisis communication cluster.

4.3 Hotel Facebook Comments and Sentiment Analysis

The 93 messages on Facebook were also examined through sentiment analysis. As seen on Table 2, the vast majority of the messages posted were classified as positive messages. Nonetheless, there were examples of positive, negative, and neutral in the data.

The confidence levels for positive messages ranged from .4 to .99 indicating a strong relationship between the words and the sentiment as the closer to one, the more reliable the result. For negative messages, the confidence levels ranged from .56 to .80 and, for neutral messages, from .40 to .94.

Table 2. Sentiment analysis and frequency of communication strategies

Sentiment	Positive		Negative		Neutral		Total	
Strategies	#	In %	#	In %	#	In %	#	In %
Scapegoat	0	0%	1	1%	10	11%	11	12%
Justification	3	3%	1	1%	4	4%	8	9%
Apology	0	0%	0	0%	0	0%	0	0%
Compensation	3	3%	0	0%	4	4%	7	8%
Endorsement	1	1%	0	0%	1	1%	2	2%
Enhancing	2	2%	1	1%	2	2%	5	5%
Ingratiation	9	10%	1	1%	0	0%	10	11%
Reminder	2	2%	0	0%	1	1%	3	3%
Victimage	43	46%	1	1%	2	2%	46	49%
Transferring	0	0%	0	0%	1	1%	1	1%
Total	63	68%	5	5%	25	27%	93	100%

Overall, comments classified as positive were the most frequent in the study at 68%, followed by neutral (27%) and negative (5%). This finding indicates that under difficult times, hoteliers still wanted to create positive sentiments. Neutral responses were relatively common which could be explained by the need to give 'distressing' information while still holding a positive attitude. Only five messages were categorized with negative sentiment. Nonetheless, these results can be explained by the SCCT strategy adopted.

Based on Table 1, victimage and scapegoat are the most adopted strategies. Table 2 demonstrated that different strategies could be applied in positive, negative, or neutral tones. Victimage was the dominant strategy employed by Swiss hotels and was primarily executed in positive tones but could be in negative, or neutral tones. For example, a positive sentiment analysis phrase for victimage read: 'We wish you a lot of energy for the coming weeks and are already looking forward to welcoming you again in the summer' (confidence level = .67). A neutral sentiment analysis of victimage stated: 'The hotel is closed at this due to Corona measures' (confidence level = .50). The negative example of victimage was: 'Finally it starts again today Wednesday, and we will see you again after a long break' (confidence level = .56).

For comments with negative sentiment analysis, five SCCT strategies were used equally: Justification, victimage, ingratiation, enhancing, and scapegoat. Nonetheless, the negative category had the least comments (one per category), which could explain this even spread. Justification, victimage, and scapegoat may be explained by the need to 'blame' someone outside of themselves or to justify the measures they have taken against their will. As these decisions were imposed on the hotels, they may have felt obliged to communicate this to their clients. The only other strategies used with negative sentiment analysis were enhancing and ingratiation.

For neutral sentiment analysis comments, eight SCCT strategies were employed. The least frequent strategies were reminder, endorsement, and transferring (once each), enhancing and victimage (twice each), and justification and compensation (four times each). Scapegoat was the most commonly used strategy (10 times). The latter could be explained by the hoteliers' need to blame someone else for their situation; it appeared simpler to identify an enemy, i.e., COVID-19, than to admit a fault that was clearly not their own.

By conducting both the SCCT strategy analysis and sentiment analysis, this research advances the SCCT research in the hospitality industry to another level.

As shown in Table 2, the SCCT provides a general guideline, but these strategies can be executed in different tones. For example, victimage, justification, and enhancing appeared in positive, negative, and neutral sentiment analysis results. Practitioners are encouraged to explore the different sentiment tones when implementing the SCCT strategies.

5 Discussion

As mentioned in the literature review, The COVID-19 pandemic was not a unique crisis affecting an individual property or region; instead, this crisis affected all hotels and regions equally. There was minimal responsibility attribution allocated to the hotels; thus, their response could be justifiably minimal as well. Many establishments could have posted only a base response, i.e., *instructing and adjusting* information without communicating further. In some cases, hoteliers did not need to communicate about the sanitary measures if their establishment was closed or had only limited business; thus, even the base response was unnecessary. Nonetheless, from this study, it can be seen that many Swiss hoteliers chose to offer more than the base response. Further, they attempted to communicate positively despite the dire circumstances and immediate bleak season in sight.

RQ1: What crisis communication strategies were employed most frequently during the first wave of COVID-19 by Swiss hoteliers?

When they communicated via Facebook, Swiss hoteliers predominantly employed the *victimage* strategy, i.e., reminding customers that the hotels are victims of this crisis as well as the clients. In this way, it is a shared victim status that could, in theory, bring customers and hoteliers together for a common cause. While seemingly contradictory, a *victimage* strategy is not negative in the case of a crisis; instead, it shows that the stakeholders do not attribute blame to the company, i.e., the company could do nothing to avoid this crisis. Of the other strategies, *scapegoat*, *ingratiation*, *justification*, and *compensation* were used in fewer than 12% of the messages. No apologies were offered as the pandemic was not a crisis that was in their control.

RQ2: What sentiment were the Swiss hoteliers trying to communicate to their clients during this first wave of COVID-19?

As seen from the sentiment analysis, Swiss hoteliers preferred to focus on positive messages to convince the clientele that the opportunity to return to their properties had finally arrived. These messages did not inform the guests that the experience could potentially be different from previous stays; instead, the messages focused on getting the clients back. Swiss hoteliers did not post daily updates on the COVID-19 pandemic nor the status of their hotels. While they may have missed an opportunity to show compassion or empathy, as the literature advises, their strategy revolved around the better days to come.

6 Conclusion/Implications

Coombs outlines the importance of preparing strategic messages that align with a company's crisis and applying the appropriate SCCT strategies to communicate these key messages. Based on the SCCT theory, crisis communication teams can brainstorm potential crises for their industry and proactively prepare crisis communication templates for the different communication channels they use. The COVID-19 pandemic was the latest in a long line of health crises that the hospitality industry has endured. However, the extent of the COVID-19 pandemic and its long-lasting effect on the industry has yet to be seen. While some hotels have reopened, closed, and opened again, others have suffered lay-offs and, in some cases, closures.

The COVID-19 pandemic placed all hotels (and their guests) in the position of the victim. This could explain why the *victimage* strategy was employed in their Facebook posts. Swiss hoteliers preferred to state the facts, i.e., "we are closed due to COVID-19", followed by frequent communication about the ever-changing COVID-19 status or regulations, i.e., "guests must wear masks in the public areas" or "hand sanitizers are available in all public spaces." With the vaccine and the falling number of new COVID-19 cases, hoteliers need to take strategic decisions on how to reopen safely and sustainably without putting themselves, their guest, or their reputations at risk.

As the sanitary conditions improve and more guests and employees are vaccinated, Swiss hotels can begin reflecting on how well they dealt with the COVID-19 crisis and communicated about it during this unprecedented crisis. While many hotels reduced their Facebook posts, there may have been a better strategy to use. These hotels could have opened a dialogue with their customers to entice them to return once the situation improved. Swiss hotels could have proactively promoted next season's opportunities or offers instead of waiting until they were open.

7 Limitations/Future Studies

This study had several limitations. Firstly, the hotels were limited to four- and five-star Swiss independent properties that posted messages from March to June 2020 on their official Facebook page. Future studies could evaluate other social media platforms or other periods. Secondly, this study focused on Swiss hotels. Comparative studies against other countries could be preferable in the future to identify best practices in communicating about a crisis on an industry level. Thirdly, the messages in this study derived uniquely from the hotels' official Facebook pages. A further study should investigate the comments posted by the other stakeholders as well. Finally, while the

SCCT strategies and their sentiments were analyzed in this paper, there was a lack of discussion on the influence of these messages on their clients. A future study could examine the relationship of these strategies with the public's response or emotions.

When this ENTER2022 conference occurs in January 2022, the tourism industry will have opened, closed, and opened again, with restrictions being relaxed only to return to lockdown. Now that the base of SCCT strategies has been established during this time frame, a study is currently being undertaken to analyze the messages posted on social media for the nine months that followed. Examining a full year of crisis messages will inform tourism professionals of the best practices to employ when a future crisis arrives. In the end, a complete picture of what Swiss hoteliers communicated through the various phases of the COVID-19 pandemic will be examined to gauge which strategies were used and their overall effectiveness.

References

1. Swiss tourism in figures 2018 (2019) Structure and industry data. https://www.stv-fst.ch/sites/default/files/2019-07/STiZ_2018_EN_Web.pdf
2. Swiss hotel industry enjoyed record year in 2019. https://www.swissinfo.ch/eng/tourism_swiss-hotel-industry-enjoyed-record-year-in-2019/45583872
3. Record drop in overnight hotel stays in Switzerland in 2020 (2021). https://www.bfs.admin.ch/bfs/en/home/statistics/tourism.assetdetail.16044296.html
4. Coombs WT, Holladay SJ (2002) Helping crisis managers protect reputational assets: initial tests of the situational crisis communication theory. Manag Commun Q 16:165–186
5. Coombs WT (2007) Protecting organization reputations during a crisis: the development and application of situational crisis communication theory. Corp Reput Rev 10(3):163–176
6. Claeys A-S, Cauberghe V, Vyncke P (2010) Restoring reputations in times of crisis: an experimental study of the situational crisis communication theory and the moderating effects of the locus of control. Pub Relat Rev 36:256–262
7. Coombs WT (1995) Choosing the right words: the development of guidelines for the selection of the 'appropriate' crisis response strategies. Manag Commun Q 8:447–476
8. Barbe D, Pennington-Gray L (2018) Using situational crisis communication theory to understand Orlando hotels: Twitter response to three crises in the summer of 2016. J Hosp Tour Insights 1:1–18
9. Scheiwiller S, Zizka L (2021) Strategic responses by European airlines to the Covid-19 pandemic: a soft landing or a turbulent ride? J Air Transp Manag 95:1–10
10. Cheng Y (2018) How social media is changing crisis communication strategies: evidence from the updated literature. J Conting Crisis Manag 26(1):58–68
11. Ki E-J, Nekmat E (2014) Situational crisis communication and interactivity: usage and effectiveness of Facebook for crisis management by Fortune 500 companies. Comput Hum Behav 35:140–147
12. Schroeder A, Pennington-Gray L, Donohoe H, Kiousis S (2013) Using social media in times of crisis. J Travel Tour Mark 30(1–2):126–143

3

An Exploratory Study of Consumers' Travel-Related Concerns about COVID-19

Wenqi Wei(✉) and Irem Önder

University of Massachusetts, Amherst, MA 01002, USA
wenqiwei@umass.edu, ionder@isenberg.umass.edu

Abstract. This study explores consumers' travel-related concerns about the COVID-19 pandemic via YouTube comments. Drawing on the risk perception theory and adopting a Markov Chain approach, this study demonstrates the topics that consumers discussed and empirically illustrates perceived risk in the tourism and hospitality industry via sentiment analysis across four sectors: recreation and entertainment, accommodation, transportation, and food and beverages. Results indicate discussion regarding travel-related videos is not only limited to travel-related topics but also includes a broad perspective of social, political, and historical topics. For instance, hotels have a new function as quarantine facilities with effective disease control procedures and social responsibility for public health. Additionally, health, performance, financial, social, and psychological risks are identified. Whereas the presence of travelers is typically regarded as positive, travelers during the crisis are regarded as "irresponsible" and "selfish" individuals who spread the virus and endanger public health. This shift of perception calls for both the industry and academia at large to educate people about the importance of disease control and rebuild travelers' image and reputation. Recommendations to reduce the perceived risk in each sector are also provided.

Keywords: Risk perception · Sentiment analysis · Markov chain · YouTube comments · User-generated content

1 Introduction

Even though the outbreak of Covid-19 imposed extraordinary uncertainty and crisis in the hospitality and tourism industry, the World Tourism Organization (UNWTO) has announced to switch the direction towards reopening and restarting tourism [1]. Because the pandemic-related restrictions are gradually lifted and COVID-19 vaccination doses have been widely administered in U.S. [2], people are heading back to restaurants and travel destinations [3]. Based on the report released by [4], the level of the seated customers in restaurants has reached the pre-pandemic levels in the U.S.

Following the devasting impact and forthcoming recovery in the hospitality and tourism industry, numerous studies are calling for theoretically driven, and systematic research about how customers perceived travel-related activities and correspondingly perceived risk and concerns [1–4], so that the hospitality and destination managers can develop the coping strategy to reduce the perceived risk and recover the whole industry [5].

However, the majority of current studies about perceived risk are conducted in designed questionnaires [5–7], which constrained the capability that consumers can freely speak out their perceived risk. In fact, it calls for an exploratory study related to COVID-19 in tourism and hospitality, instead of fully grounded in the existing literature [5]. Considering the outbreak of Covid-19 pandemic created an unprecedentedly social and economic environment, people are likely to have unpredictable behaviors and feelings, which makes the validity of existing knowledge under the new normal much more challenging and questionable [6].

Given the identified research gap, this study explored the consumers' travel-related concerns about the crisis of the Covid-19 pandemic. Drawing on the risk perception theory, this study adopted the Markov Chain text mining method to identify the topics discussed by consumers and empirically illustrated the perceived risks in the overall tourism and hospitality industry and four sectors respectively. Results show that when consumers are watching travel-related and Covid-19 related videos, what they are discussing is not constrained in travel-related topics, but include a broad perspective of social, political, and historical topics. Noticeably, hotels are assigned a new function, the quarantine facilities, which require hotel businesses to develop effective disease control procedures and shoulder more social responsibility for public health. Additionally, health risk, performance risk, financial risk, social risk and psychological risk are all identified. Different from the previous that travelers are regarded as positive image, travelers during the crisis are regarded as "irresponsible" and "selfish" who spread the virus and danger the public health. It calls for both the industry and the academia to educate the importance of disease control and rebuild travelers' image and reputation. Practically, this study can benefit policymakers and managers to understand customers' beliefs and behaviors under the crisis as well as consumers' expectations towards the post-pandemic, which is crucial for designing and operating actionable policies and coping strategies.

2 Literature Review

2.1 Risk Perception

Perceived risk refers to the potential future loss that may happen if a particular decision has been made [8]. People perceive risk since the uncertainty may potentially trigger negative outcomes. Perceived risk has been widely recognized as the critical factor that have an effect on consumers' decision-making and behavior [8–10]. There are a variety of perceived risks that have been identified in destination marketing [11], food delivery [12], and service industry [13]. Performance risk refers to the expectation may not be satisfied after the service is delivered [14–16]. Financial risk refers to the potential financial loss that the service has to be replaced, fixed or compensated [17, 18]. Psychological risk refers to the psychological discomfort (e.g., regret, worry) caused by the service experience [11, 19]. Social risk is linked to the probability of a customer's buying behavior that can influence another customer's opinion and perception [20–22]. Health risk reflects the situation that the consumption of the service can trigger an unprecedented hazard to the customer's health [15, 23].

Perceived risk from COVID-19 is very critical since it has severely negative impacts on revisit intention for hotels [24]. However, most of the studies are supported by primary data [5–7], which constrained the capability that consumers can freely speak out their perceived risk [25]. This study adopted the User-Generated Content, specifically, YouTube comments, to explore consumers' travel-related concerns in the inductive way.

2.2 User-Generated Content

User Generated Content (UGC) is regarded as the creative work that is published on accessible and public platforms and usually has no direct linkage to commercial profits or monetary interests [26]. Customers are more likely influenced by the UGC with negative valence [27]. Novelty, reliability, understandability, and interestingness embedded in UGC would influence consumers' selection of destination [28]. Since Covid-19 is the first pandemic most of us faced, the repercussions for the travelers are not researched before. This study aims to explore the risk perception of travelers via YouTube comments, classify the risks based on different tourism sectors, and understand the sentiment of these comments. YouTube comments were selected since this platform features genuine debates on controversial issues and has been regarded as a significant public space for engaging in debate and exchanging opinions [29]. For many less active social users are the observers, their attitudes and intentions may be influenced by being exposed to YouTube comments [30], highlighting the significance of exploring them as a textual corpus of study.

3 Method

3.1 Sample

This study employed YouTube Comments as the sample. First, we designed a list of keywords that includes both Covid-19 related words and tourism and hospitality related words. Next, we scraped the YouTube videos whose titles include any of the keyword. Finally, we exported the comments below each of the video and complied all the comments as the sample of this study. The data sample includes 521 YouTube videos and 9,727 unique comments. The data were collected on October 5, 2020. At that time, the videos that include the keywords were relatively limited. Since the perception from consumers is the research objective in this study, the producers and origins of the videos were not collected.

3.2 Contribution of Sentiment Words

Sentiment analysis was used to not only understand the opinions and attitudes delivered in the comments, but also capture which words with emotional and opinion information are critical in the text. Considering the exploratory nature of this study, we didn't assess the sentiment scores in traditional way but explore the most significant sentiment words according to the frequency of the word.

3.3 Popular Bigrams

We further examined the relationship between words by Markov Chain. Markov Chain, the common model in text mining, was selected as the approach for visualization [31]. Markov chain theory refers to the adjacent characters sequences are employed to generate the probabilities transition matrices. In the linguistic field, Markov Chain has been widely used in identifying malicious attack [32], predicting the geo-location of Twitter users [33], evaluating digital document authentication [34]. In fact, Markov Chain have been used in tourism literature to forecast tourist arrivals [35] or model the spatial and temporal movement of tourists [36] but rarely used for text analysis [37]. This study innovatively used Markov Chain to visualize the topics that consumers discussed about the travel-related concerns. Markov chain in this study is used to identify the words are more likely to follow others immediately or to co-occur within the same document. Specifically, we tokenized the text into pairs of two consecutive sequence of words to explore how often word A is followed by word. This process is called "bigrams" [38].

3.4 Sector of Hospitality and Tourism

In order to capture the dynamics of each sector underlying the hospitality and tourism industry, we categorized the YouTube Videos in the sample into five groups based on the sector of hospitality and tourism industry, including accommodation, food and beverage, entertainment and recreation, transportation, and others [39–41]. Tables 1 and 2 and demonstrate the process of classifying the YouTube Videos.

Table 1. Keywords for classifying videos based on four sectors.

Sector	Keywords
Recreation and entertainment	Travel, tour, beach casino, park, Las Vegas, Florida, Disney, holiday, wedding, Halloween, gym, vacation
Accommodation	Hotel, motel, Airbnb
Transportation	Airplane, airport, flight, fly, train, bus, car
Food and beverages	Restaurant, bar, food, dining

Table 2. Descriptive information about the sample.

Sector	Number of Video	Percentage	Number of Comments	Percentage
Recreation and entertainment	186	35.70%	3630	37.32%
Accommodation	78	14.97%	1157	11.89%
Transportation	39	7.49%	1024	10.53%
Food and beverage	36	6.91%	603	6.20%
Others	182	34.93%	3313	34.06%
Total	521		9727	

4 Results and Discussion

4.1 Sentiment Contribution

There are 2,441 unique sentiment words identified in the dataset, including 1,656 negative words and 785 positive words. Table 1 demonstrates the top 20 Words that contribute to negative and positive sentiment. The results in Table 3 demonstrate three types of risk, including health risk as the direct outcomes of the Covid-19 ("die", "infect", "sick", "symptom", "outbreak", "cold", "kill"), the psychological risk as the cognitive perception of Covid-19 ("bad", "risk", "fear", "hard", "scare", "lost", "sad") and social risk as the skeptical behavior towards the related information ("lie", "fake", "stupid", "wrong", "blame"). As anticipated, health risk is the most salient risk, which is consistent with current study that there is significant interaction between perception of coronavirus pandemic and perceived health risk besides non-pharmaceutical intervention [42].

Table 3. Top 20 words contributing to negative and positive sentiment.

Negative sentiment	Positive sentiment
Virus, die, bad, infect, risk, sick, symptom, lie, fear, fake, stupid, hard, scare, lost, outbreak, wrong, sad, cold, kill, blame	Safe, love, protect, clean, free, healthy, nice, healthy, nice, glad, happy, cure, support, enjoy, trust, beautiful, top, freedom, amazing, bless, fine, luck

Table 3 illustrates the top 20 positive words that contributed most. Consumers are very concerned about the disease protocol issues in the travel process, including "safe", "protect", "clean", "healthy", "cure", "support", and "trust". At the same time, consumers still anticipate the travel experience with "love", "nice", "glad", "happy", "enjoy", "beautiful", "amazing", "fine". It indicates consumers concerned about the performance risk and are very likely to expect both high level of precautions and positive travel experience at the time same, which presents a significant challenge for practitioners to satisfy consumers' expectations.

Figure 1 demonstrates the most popular bigram that occurred more than 10 times, which reflects the consumers' travel-related concerns from a comprehensive point of view. The largest cluster of the bigrams is represented by "covid-19", which includes the testing and spreading process as well as the negative consequences of Covid-19. "People" represents the second cluster, which focuses on the self-protection activities, including mask wearing and staying home. Next came the cluster called "quarantine", which demonstrated the 14-day requirement endorsed by CDC. Noticeably, "hotel industry", "hospitality", "airlines" and "restaurant" are closely related to this cluster, indicating our industry, especially hotels, are assigned new function as the quarantine facilities during the pandemic. Another representative cluster is "travel", which strongly tied with "travel ban" and "travel restrictions". The topic related to politics cannot be ignored, including nations and government (e.g., "china", "uk") and political figures (e.g., "trump", "prime minster", "johnson boris"). Consumers can also consult historical event to understand this pandemic, including "spanish flu", "1984". Media plays an important role to introduce the practice of social distancing, but the creditability of the media is questioned as "fake news". Additionally, medical experts and organization are regarded as the authority to provide relevant information, including "fauci", "morris", "john", "richard" as the medical professionals and "nih", "nlm", "ncbi" as the medical organizations and departments.

Fig. 1. Common bigrams showing those that occurred more than 10 times.

Table 4 summarizes the positive words and negative words in each sector separately. In order to explore consumers' idiosyncratic concerns towards four sectors of tourism and hospitality industry respectively, we excluded the words that have already included in Table 3. First, the Recreation and Entertainment Sector includes "selfish", "crowded", "nervous", "hoax", "ignorant", "correct", "peace", "ready", "worth", "fun". Different from normal time that travelers are regarded as people with positive personality, such as adventurous, empathetic and curious, travelers during the pandemic are perceived as "selfish", "hoax", "ignorant", which reflect the social risk that an individual's traveling behaviors will influence another people's opinion. In terms of the performance, people are concerned the travel destination is "crowded" and whether the discase control procedures are "correct" or "ready" to let people enjoy the travel experience with "peace" and "fun". Additionally, people are concerned about the psychological risk as "nervous" and financial risk as "worth".

Table 4. Sentiment words in each sector.

Sector	Negative	Positive
Recreation and entertainment	Selfish, crowded, nervous, hoax, ignorant	Fun, worth, ready, peace, correct
Accommodation	Expensive, cheap, disgusting, collapse, recession	Smart, fair, refund, approve, affordable
Transportation	Useless, selfish, cheap, expensive, contagious	Brave, comfortable, ease, accurate, appreciated
Food and beverage	Idiots, carp, panic, irresponsible, destroy	Effective, fast, backbone, benefits, fresh

Next, Accommodation Sector includes "expensive", "cheap", "disgusting", "recession", "collapse", "affordable", "refund", "approve", "fair", "smart". Financial risk is the most salient risk in this sector. People are worried about the price (e.g., "expensive", "cheap", "affordable") and also the change or cancel of the booking can be "refunded" successfully. At the same time, people are worried about the cleanness of the accommodation (e.g., "disgusting") as the performance risk. Interestingly, people are aware the loss and challenge that the accommodation sector are facing right now and worried about the overall social and economic condition as "collapse" and "recession". We recommend hotel companies and Airbnb need to clarify the coronavirus related changes, in terms of cancellation policies and price policies on booking websites to reduce perceived financial risk. It is also necessary to circulate positive industry news to boost the overall confidence. For example, SoftBank's is investing $1.7 billion in Yanolja, the company that provides AI-powered hotel software and contactless services for guests. The endorsement of SoftBank represents a wave of travel-related optimism [43].

In the Transportation Sector, people as usual are concerned about the punctuality (e.g., "accurate") and on-board experience (e.g., "ease" and "comfortable") as the performance risk. Consistent with the accommodation sector, people are concerned about the financial risk ("cheap" and "expensive") and social risk (e.g., "selfish"). Noticeably, consumers are concerned the health risk considering the virus can spread in the close environment with the interaction with people (e.g., "contagious"). We recommend airlines companies should highlight the coronavirus change and cancellation policies on booking websites to decrease perceived financial risk. It is also critical to strictly follow the CDC guidelines and demonstrate the efforts on social media platforms.

Last, in the Food and Beverages Sector, social risk is the most salient risk since drinking in bars and similar activities are regarded as "idiots", "crap" and "irresponsible". While people feel "panic" as the psychological risk, they still anticipate the food and beverage service can be "fresh", "fast", "effective", which can reflect the performance risk. We strongly recommend restaurants and bars strictly follow the CDC guidelines, including preparing adequate supplies (masks, soap, hand sanitizer and disinfectant wipes) and maintaining healthy environment by cleaning and disinfecting regularly [44]. Additionally, social media can be used to communicate how restaurants and bars strictly implement the strategies, considering social media is an critical tool in crisis communication and crisis management plan [45]. We suggest restaurants and bars can reduce customers perceived social risk and psychological risk by demonstrating the process of executing the relevant protocols on various social media platforms.

5 Discussion and Conclusion

Drawing on the risk perception theory, this study explored the travel-related concerns about the outbreak of Covid-19 by automated text analysis. It is the first study which employed YouTube comments as the sample to conduct tourism research. Sentiment analysis of the overall tourism and hospitality industry indicates that the health risk is most concerned by consumers, showing that people are highly aware of their health in terms of the general travel activities. By drawing the most popular bigrams by Markov Chain, this study found that when consumers are watching travel-related videos, what they are discussing is not constrained in travel-related topics, but include a broad perspective of social, political, and historical topics. At the same time, this study explored consumers' idiosyncratic concerns towards four sectors of the tourism and hospitality industry and provides practical recommendation to reduce the perceived risk.

Despite its contribution, this study has some limitations. First, this study focused on the UGC in English language. Considering the Covid-19 is a global crisis and is devesting the worldwide industry, Asian customers may perceive travel risks drastically different from American and European customers [46], which is calling for future research to explore this topic in different language settings (e.g., Chinese, Spanish and Korean etc.). Also, policymakers need to consider different approaches for dealing with the pandemic among different regions [47]. Second, this study adopted YouTube comments as the sample, but the comments are highly associated with the specific videos [48]. Future research can explore UGC from other social media platforms in order to understand a comprehensive picture of the travel-related concerns. Third, this is an exploratory study focusing on the descriptive findings. Future studies can empirically conduct relational analysis, for example, particular risks or concerns are related to demographic variables.

References

1. Godovykh M, Pizam A, Bahja F (2021) Antecedents and outcomes of health risk perceptions in tourism, following the COVID-19 pandemic. Tour Rev 76:737–748. https://doi.org/10.1108/TR-06-2020-0257
2. Huifeng P, Ha H-Y, Lee J-W (2020) Perceived risks and restaurant visit intentions in China: do online customer reviews matter? J Hosp Tour Manag 43:179–189. https://doi.org/10.1016/j.jhtm.2020.04.005
3. Volgger M, Taplin R, Aebli A (2021) Recovery of domestic tourism during the COVID-19 pandemic: an experimental comparison of interventions. J Hosp Tour Manag 48:428–440. https://doi.org/10.1016/j.jhtm.2021.07.015

4. Elhoushy S, Elbayoumi Salem I, Agag G (2020) The impact of perceived benefits and risks on current and desired levels of outsourcing: hotel managers' perspective. Int J Hosp Manag 91:102419. https://doi.org/10.1016/j.ijhm.2019.102419
5. Villacé-Molinero T, Fernández-Muñoz JJ, Orea-Giner A, Fuentes-Moraleda L (2021) Understanding the new post-COVID-19 risk scenario: outlooks and challenges for a new era of tourism. Tour Manag 86:104324. https://doi.org/10.1016/j.tourman.2021.104324
6. Bae SY, Chang P-J (2021) The effect of coronavirus disease-19 (COVID-19) risk perception on behavioural intention towards 'untact' tourism in South Korea during the first wave of the pandemic (March 2020). Curr Issues Tour 24:1017–1035. https://doi.org/10.1080/13683500.2020.1798895
7. Qiu RTR, Park J, Li S, Song H (2020) Social costs of tourism during the COVID-19 pandemic. Ann Tour Res 84:102994. https://doi.org/10.1016/j.annals.2020.102994
8. Stone RN, Grønhaug K (1993) Perceived risk: further considerations for the marketing discipline. Eur J Mark 27:39–50
9. Han H et al (2019) Halal tourism: travel motivators and customer retention. J Travel Tour Mark 36:1012–1024. https://doi.org/10.1080/10548408.2019.1683483
10. Quintal VA, Lee JA, Soutar GN (2010) Risk, uncertainty and the theory of planned behavior: a tourism example. Tour Manag 31:797–805. https://doi.org/10.1016/j.tourman.2009.08.006
11. Chew EYT, Jahari SA (2014) Destination image as a mediator between perceived risks and revisit intention: a case of post-disaster Japan. Tour Manag 40:382–393
12. Choe JY, Kim JJ, Hwang J (2021) Perceived risks from drone food delivery services before and after COVID-19. Int J Contemp Hosp Manag 33:1276–1296. https://doi.org/10.1108/IJCHM-08-2020-0839
13. Pappas N (2016) Marketing strategies, perceived risks, and consumer trust in online buying behaviour. J Retail Consum Serv 29:92–103. https://doi.org/10.1016/j.jretconser.2015.11.007
14. Horton RL (1976) The structure of perceived risk: some further progress. J Acad Mark Sci 4:694–706
15. Huang H, Liu SQ, Kandampully J, Bujisic M (2020) Consumer responses to scarcity appeals in online booking. Ann Tour Res 80:102800
16. Kim M, Roehl W, Lee SK (2020) Different from or similar to neighbors? An investigation of hotels' strategic distances. Tour Manag 76:103960
17. DeFranco A, Morosan C (2017) Coping with the risk of internet connectivity in hotels: perspectives from American consumers traveling internationally. Tour Manag 61:380–393
18. Matzler K, Teichmann K, Strobl A, Partel M (2019) The effect of price on word of mouth: first time versus heavy repeat visitors. Tour Manag 70:453–459
19. Roehl WS, Fesenmaier DR (1992) Risk perceptions and pleasure travel: an exploratory analysis. J Travel Res 30:17–26
20. Choi M, Law R, Heo CY (2018) An investigation of the perceived value of shopping tourism. J Travel Res 57:962–980. https://doi.org/10.1177/0047287517726170
21. Dayour F, Park S, Kimbu AN (2019) Backpackers' perceived risks towards smartphone usage and risk reduction strategies: a mixed methods study. Tour Manag 72:52–68. https://doi.org/10.1016/j.tourman.2018.11.003
22. Murray KB, Schlacter JL (1990) The impact of services versus goods on consumers' assessment of perceived risk and variability. J Acad Mark Sci 18:51–65. https://doi.org/10.1007/BF02729762
23. Sheng-Hshiung T, Gwo-Hshiung T, Kuo-Ching W (1997) Evaluating tourist risks from fuzzy perspectives. Ann Tour Res 24:796–812. https://doi.org/10.1016/S0160-7383(97)00059-5

24. Yu J, Lee K, Hyun SS (2021) Understanding the influence of the perceived risk of the coronavirus disease (COVID-19) on the post-traumatic stress disorder and revisit intention of hotel guests. J Hosp Tour Manag 46:327–335. https://doi.org/10.1016/j.jhtm.2021.01.010
25. Denscombe M (2006) Web-based questionnaires and the mode effect: an evaluation based on completion rates and data contents of near-identical questionnaires delivered in different modes. Soc Sci Comput Rev 24:246–254. https://doi.org/10.1177/0894439305284522
26. Lu W, Stepchenkova S (2015) User-generated content as a research mode in tourism and hospitality applications: topics, methods, and software. J Hosp Mark Manag 24:119–154. https://doi.org/10.1080/19368623.2014.907758
27. Sparks BA, Browning V (2011) The impact of online reviews on hotel booking intentions and perception of trust. Tour Manag 32:1310–1323. https://doi.org/10.1016/j.tourman.2010.12.011
28. Chen Y-C, Shang R-A, Li M-J (2014) The effects of perceived relevance of travel blogs' content on the behavioral intention to visit a tourist destination. Comput Hum Behav 30:787–799. https://doi.org/10.1016/j.chb.2013.05.019
29. Thelwall M, Sud P, Vis F (2012) Commenting on YouTube videos: from guatemalan rock to El Big Bang. J Am Soc Inf Sci Technol 63:616–629. https://doi.org/10.1002/asi.21679
30. Jin S-AA, Phua J (2014) Following celebrities' tweets about brands: the impact of twitter-based electronic word-of-mouth on consumers' source credibility perception, buying intention, and social identification with celebrities. J Advert 43:181–195. https://doi.org/10.1080/00913367.2013.827606
31. Al-Anzi FS, AbuZeina D (2018) Beyond vector space model for hierarchical Arabic text classification: a Markov chain approach. Inf Process Manag 54:105–115. https://doi.org/10.1016/j.ipm.2017.10.003
32. Gao Y-X, Qi D-Y (2011) Analyze and detect malicious code for compound document binary storage format. In: 2011 International conference on machine learning and cybernetics, pp 593–596
33. Ahmed A-F, Mohamed R, Mostafa B, Mohammed A-S (2015) Authorship attribution in Arabic poetry. In: 2015 10th international conference on intelligent systems: theories and applications (SITA), pp 1–6
34. Shen JJ, Liu KT (2014) A novel approach by applying image authentication technique on a digital document. In: 2014 international symposium on computer, consumer and control, pp 119–122
35. Sun X, Sun W, Wang J, Zhang Y, Gao Y (2016) Using a Grey–Markov model optimized by Cuckoo search algorithm to forecast the annual foreign tourist arrivals to China. Tour Manag 52:369–379. https://doi.org/10.1016/j.tourman.2015.07.005
36. Xia J, Zeephongsekul P, Packer D (2011) Spatial and temporal modelling of tourist movements using Semi-Markov processes. Tour Manag 32:844–851. https://doi.org/10.1016/j.tourman.2010.07.009
37. Yan Y, Chen J, Wang Z (2020) Mining public sentiments and perspectives from geotagged social media data for appraising the post-earthquake recovery of tourism destinations. Appl Geogr 123:102306
38. Wang S, Manning C (2012) Baselines and bigrams: simple, good sentiment and topic classification. In: Proceedings of the 50th annual meeting of the association for computational linguistics (volume 2: short papers). Association for Computational Linguistics, Jeju Island, Korea, pp 90–94
39. Leiper N (1990) Tourist attraction systems. Ann Tour Res 17:367–384. https://doi.org/10.1016/0160-7383(90)90004-B
40. Mill RC, Morrison AM (2002) The tourism system. Kendall Hunt

41. Novak P. What are the 4 segments of the hospitality industry | By Peter Novak (2017). https://www.hospitalitynet.org/opinion/4082318.html
42. Foroudi P, Tabaghdehi SAH, Marvi R (2021) The gloom of the COVID-19 shock in the hospitality industry: a study of consumer risk perception and adaptive belief in the dark cloud of a pandemic. Int J Hosp Manag 92:102717
43. Hamlin K (2021) SoftBank checks in early for post-Covid hotel boom. https://www.reuters.com/breakingviews/softbank-checks-early-post-covid-hotel-boom-2021-07-21/
44. CDC. Community, work, and school (2021). https://www.cdc.gov/coronavirus/2019-ncov/community/organizations/business-employers/bars-restaurants.html
45. Liu B, Pennington-Gray L, Klemmer L (2015) Using social media in hotel crisis management: the case of bed bugs. J Hosp Tour Technol 6:102–112. https://doi.org/10.1108/JHTT-08-2014-0036
46. Uğur NG, Akbıyık A (2020) Impacts of COVID-19 on global tourism industry: a cross-regional comparison. Tour Manag Perspect 36:100744. https://doi.org/10.1016/j.tmp.2020.100744
47. Farzanegan MR, Gholipour HF, Feizi M, Nunkoo R, Andargoli AE (2021) International tourism and outbreak of coronavirus (COVID-19): a cross-country analysis. J Travel Res 60:687–692. https://doi.org/10.1177/0047287520931593
48. Khan ML (2017) Social media engagement: what motivates user participation and consumption on YouTube? Comput Hum Behav 66:236–247. https://doi.org/10.1016/j.chb.2016.09.024

Special Track on the Sharing Economy in Travel and Tourism: Experiences and Social Networking

4

Using Machine Learning Methods to Predict Demand for Bike Sharing

Chang Gao[1(✉)] and Yong Chen[2(✉)]

[1] Boston University, Boston, MA 02215, USA
changgao@bu.edu

[2] Ecole Hôtelière de Lausanne, HES-SO, University of Applied Sciences Western Switzerland, Rte de Cojonnex 18, 1000 Lausanne, Switzerland
yong.chen@ehl.ch

Abstract. We applied four machine learning models, linear regression, the k-nearest neighbors (KNN), random forest, and support vector machine, to predict consumer demand for bike sharing in Seoul. We aimed to advance previous research on bike sharing demand by incorporating features other than weather - such as air pollution, traffic information, Covid-19 cases, and social economic factors- to increase prediction accuracy. The data were retrieved from Seoul Public Data Park website, which records the counts of public bike rentals in Seoul of Korea from January 1 to December 31, 2020. We found that the two best models are the random forest and the support vector machine models. Among the 29 features in six categories the features in the weather, pollution, and Covid-19 outbreak categories are the most important in model prediction. While almost all social economic features are the least important, we found that they help enhance the performance of the models.

Keywords: Machine learning · Data mining · Bike sharing · Demand prediction · Seoul

1 Introduction

Over the past two decades sharing economy has not only revolutionized the organization of economic activity but also unleashed the consumption and production potentials of a variety of tourism and hospitality businesses. These businesses include but are not limited to sharing accommodation exemplified by Airbnb, sharing transportation pioneered by Uber and Lyft, as well as various online booking platforms such as Booking.com and OpenTable. There are even more localized sharing businesses, such as bike sharing provided by private enterprises or governments as an alternative to the so-called "last-mile" public transportation. Bike sharing has been popular in many countries, due to the fact that environmental proception organizations proposed environmental sustainability transportation methods such as electric vehicles and bicycles [13]. Bike sharing provides benefits in various aspects and is achieving world-wide popularity [20]. For instance, the number of renters in US was larger than 28 million in 2006 [33]. All these businesses share one commonality, for which consumer demand is upon request. Namely, suppliers need to immediately, if not instantaneously, deploy goods and services as soon as demand is generated. On the one hand, the success of sharing economy lies at such on-demand features; on the other hand, this requires supplies to predict consumers demand on various occasions as accurately as possible in the first place, thereby diverting goods and services to consumers as efficiently and timely as possible.

One telling example is Uber's surge pricing. Uber is capable of striking immediate balance between demand and supply through detecting riders' request in different periods of time, especially when demand fluctuates drastically in small geographical region [8]. In this case and many others, conventional econometric modeling in predicting demand would become less useful because it relies on predictors that usually do not change in the short run. For instance, it is extremely rare, if at all, to model consumer demand on a daily or hourly basis through using social or economic indicators. Of course, both economic indicators, such as income and price and a wide range of social demographics have compelling explanatory power in predicting long-term demand because they are grounded on sound economic theories. They would become useless in predicting instantaneous demand, such as in the case of Uber's surge pricing in which demand changes in a course of a few hours. The reason is that these predictors are constant on a daily basis not to mention on an hourly basis, which renders conventional economic modeling and forecasting obsolete. For this reason, machine learning has gained momentum in predicting demand in these contexts.

While studies using machine learning techniques to predict consumer demand are proliferating in tourism and hospitality, there are very few devoted to predicting demand for bike sharing. A wealth of studies that indeed addressed bike sharing are primarily from the field of computer sciences [5, 14, 26, 27, 34]. In fact, modeling tourism demand is disproportionately devoted to predicting tourist arrivals using either machine learning or a combination of machine learning and search query data [3, 9, 10, 23–25, 30]. However, sharing economy has not only changed the way we model tourism demand but also extended what is modeled to reflect the nature of sharing economy in various areas. In this regard, we aim to use machine learning techniques to predict consumer demand for bike sharing. We also aim to advance previous research on bike sharing by incorporating a wide range of features other than weather to increase prediction accuracy.

2 Literature Review

Machine learning and big data have been increasingly applied to model and predict tourism demand in various domains. This strand of research bifurcates evidently between enhancing the performance of econometric models through incorporating machine learning techniques and using search engine data in prediction algorithms [1, 3, 6, 9, 10, 30, 35]. As a matter of fact, tourism research has focused on predicting tourist arrivals through using both conventional econometric models and machine learning techniques [1, 3, 9, 10]. For instance, Akın [1] used Neural Network models to predict tourist arrivals in Turkey while using conventional econometric techniques, such as autoregressive integrated moving average (ARIMA), as a benchmark. Claveria et al. [9] used machine learning algorithms such as the support vector regression,

Gaussian process regression, and neural network models to predict tourist arrivals in Spain. Similar to Akin [1], they found that machine learning methods improved forecasting performance against the autoregressive moving average (ARMA) model as a benchmark.

On the other hand, researchers have started to realize the importance of big data in predicting tourism demand. In particular, search engine data provides researchers a viable substitute for conventional economic variables as predictors in modeling and forecasting tourism demand. In this respect, search engine data have been extensively used to predict tourism demand and tourist arrivals in particular [23–25, 30, 35]. Sun et al. [30] used kernel extreme learning machine (KELM) models and search results generated by Google and Baidu to forecast tourist arrivals in China. Xie et al. [35] fed search query data (SQD) generated from Baidu to a least squares support vector regression model with gravitational search algorithm (LSSVR-GSA) to predict cruise tourism demand. Many studies concluded that using machine learning coupled with search query data increases the forecasting performance and robustness of the models [25, 30, 35]. This perhaps explains why various search engine data were also used to model and predict tourist arrivals [23, 24], which used to be addressed in conventional econometric models.

One of the advantages of using machine learning is to predict micro-level tourist demand and the facet of demand, such as network effects on the Internet, that cannot be accounted for by conventional economic indicators. This advantage also enables researchers to narrow down the prediction horizon, thereby modeling short-term demand patterns. However, demand modeled in many studies is conventional tourism consumption, such as park attendance, cruise demand, and tourist arrivals [23, 24, 35]. The overriding objective was to improve prediction accuracy through using machine learning techniques. Hence the focus is a matter of model selection while having little to do with modeling on-demand economy, such as car or bike sharing. In fact, bike-sharing modeling entails short-term even almost instantaneous demand prediction. On the other hand, machine learning models need to take into account stational-level variance in bike demand, which would allow suppliers to deploy bikes efficiently across destination to ensure supply. Such deployment requires modeling and forecasting demand across different docking stations on an hourly basis depending on the degree of demand fluctuation.

There is a great deal research devoted to forecasting bike demand in various cities [5, 27]. A majority of these studies modeled bike demand on an hourly basis, aiming to provide policy implications for deploying bikes in a timely manner [14, 32]. For this reason, the features that were used to predict bike demand were exclusively weather conditions, ranging from precipitation, humidity to wind speed and temperature in the course of 24 h. We aimed to predict bike demand by extending the scope of features on a daily basis. Indeed, some studies have shown that the geography of bike-docking stations has impacts on bike demand, which has a lot to do with social and economic situations in which these stations are located. Obviously, hourly-based models with weather conditions as the primary predictors are insufficient to account for such difference. Insofar as policy is concerned, this study can provide implications for the supply of bikes in different districts and the deployment of bikes across stations.

3 The Data

We retrieved the counts of public bike rentals in Seoul of Korea from January 1 to December 31, 2020 from Seoul Public Data Park website [21]. This data set consists of hourly bike rentals recorded from 2,148 docking stations in 25 districts of Seoul. Note that 55 stations that were not functioning in the study period were discarded from the analysis. We ended up identifying a total of 2,093 stations that were active during the whole study period. We aggregated hourly data to compile daily rental counts, giving rise to a total of 9,111 observations, with a daily average of 2029 bike rentals in Seoul in the year 2020.

To predict bike rentals in Seoul, we identified a total 29 features in six categories: (1) weather, (2) air pollution, (3) traffic accidents, (4) Covid-19 outbreak, (5) social and economic factors, and (6) seasonality. These data are retrieved from the website Seoul Open Data [21]. These 29 features are the potential features influencing bike sharing demand. When weather or air quality is bad, people might be reluctant to rent a sharing bike. On the other hand, when traffic is bad, renting a bike will be more efficient. We also suspect that Covid-19 cases and other social economic factors might also influence the demand of bike renting. Note that Covid-19 confirmed cases and deaths were analyzed with a one-day time lag since their influence on bike demand, if any, would take at least one day to emerge. The reason that we delayed one day confirmed and deaths cases is that residents need time to process the news information produced. They might not realize the disease cases immediately after the release of the news on media, and they need some time to process the information. Since the new cases counts updates each day, the case number delayed by one day is more applicable. We aimed to pinpoint the most important features that can accurately predict bike demand.

4 Methods

We performed four machine learning algorithms to predict bike rentals, which are linear regression, the k-nearest neighbors (KNN), random forest, and support vector machine. All of these models were performed on R studio. Since these four models were developed based on different assumptions for identifying the relationships between independent and dependent variables, it is a convention in machine learning to use them complementarily for prediction.

4.1 Algorithms

Linear regression. Linear regression is the most widely used and simplest method to predict demand in various contexts. Due to its simplicity and straightforward economic intuition in explaining the relationship between predictors and the outcome, we use linear regression as a benchmark against which other more advanced models are compared for their predictive power. The linear regression model is given as

$$y = \beta_0 + \sum_{i}^{n} \beta_i x_i + \varepsilon \tag{1}$$

where β_i is the coefficient of feature x_i, β_0 is the constant, and ε is the random error [28].

K-Nearest Neighbors (KNN). The k-nearest neighbors (KNN) is a machine learning algorithm used for both classification and prediction. The KNN is a nonparametric technique which provides solution for the curve fitting of unknown shape, and has an advantage for data mining, because it does not assume specific forms of regression functions [2]. For both classification and prediction, explanatory variables take into account the k (a positive integer) closest instances. The parameter k needs to be tuned before modeling and it is crucial for non-parametric regression performance [2]. The calculations of the KNN are based on distances between an instance to its neighbors. The distances used for continuous variables are the Euclidean distance. The Euclidean distance d between two n-dimensional vectors $(p_1, p_2, \ldots, p_n)$ and $(q_1, q_2, \ldots, q_n)$ is given by:

$$d = \sqrt{\sum_{i}^{n} (p_i - q_i)^2} \tag{2}$$

The prediction of an observation is the mean of the values of k neighbors that are the nearest when implementing the KNN as the regression model in prediction.

Random Forest. Random forest is a almighty tool which ensembles decision trees and bagging [4].The base learner of random forests is a binary tree constructed by recursive partitioning (RPART) and then developed using classification and regression trees [7]. Binary splits of the parent node of a random forest splits data into two children's nodes and increases homogeneity in children nodes compared to parent nodes. Note that a random forest does not split tree nodes based on all variables; instead, it chooses random variable subsets as candidates to find the optimal split at every node of every tree [7]. Then the information from the n trees is aggregated for classification and prediction [7]. Random forests also provide the importance of each feature by accumulated Gini gains of all splits in all trees representing the variable discrimination ability [19]:

$$impor_j = \frac{1}{\#trees} \sum_{v \in x_j} Gain(x_j, v) \tag{3}$$

where $Gain(x_j, v)$ is the gain of the Gini index of feature x_j combined with node v [32].

Support Vector Machine. Support vector machine (SVM) is a machine learning technique for classification and regression [11]. SVM is suitable for general relationships between explanatory variables and responsive variables. The basic idea of SVM is to map nonlinear explanatory vectors onto a high dimensional space in order to find a linear decision hyperplane. The solution of SVM regression is given as:

$$f(x) = \sum_{i=1}^{n} (\alpha_i - \alpha_i^*) K(x_i, x) + b \tag{4}$$

where $K(x_i, x)$ is the kernel function that satisfy Mercer's conditions, where α_i and α_i^* are the dual variables larger than or equal to 0 and smaller than or equal to the hyperparameter C [31]. We use the radial basis function (RBF) kernels with the corresponding Kernel equation of

$$K(x_i, x) = \exp(-\gamma||x - x_i||^2) \tag{5}$$

in which γ is the kernel parameter. The RBF kernel provides solutions when the relationship between features and responsive variables is nonlinear and is computationally easier than polynomial kernels [12].

4.2 Feature Selection

We split the 9,111 observations into a training set with 75% of the cases, or 6,235 observations, while 25% as a test set, or 2,276 observations. The training set was used for feature selection, hyperparameter tuning, and prediction. The test set was used for evaluation and prediction for bike rentals. Prior to selecting features, we explored the Pearson correlation coefficients between the number of bike rentals and the features in each of the six categories. Major findings are summarized here. Most of the pollution features except CO are positively correlated with bike rentals. Covid-19 cases and deaths are negatively correlated with bike rentals. All but two social economic factors, namely the number of markets (−0.09) and number of stores (−0.06), are positively correlated with bike rentals. The population in a district has the strongest correlation with bike rentals (0.35). The number of traffic accidents is positively correlated with bike rentals (0.20). Visibility and humidity are most correlated with bike counts (0.29). Visibility is positively correlated to the number of bike rentals, while humidity, precipitation, and wind speed are negatively correlated with bike rentals.

We proceeded to use Boruta and recursive feature elimination (RFE) to select features. Boruta is a wrapper approach to determine the relevance of features through implementing a random forest classifier. A shadow attribute is created for each feature, and classification is performed based on the feature importance by using all attributes and shadow attributes. These shadow attributes help reduce the distracted impact of random fluctuations [22]. Even though Boruta uses random forest as the base algorithm, this will not increase the accuracy of random forest since the testing set was never exposed to the algorithm. Figure 1 shows the result of the Boruta feature selection on all 29 features but districts and rented bike counts because it is the dependent variable. The blue boxes represent the shadow attributes, green ones are the accepted or confirmed attributes while red attributes are rejected. Thus, the number of deaths in the category of traffic accidents is rejected, so this feature will not be entered in the regression models. Binary variables of traditional holidays and leisure holidays are not as important as expected, and this result indicates that bike renting demand was not strongly influenced by the indicator holiday. We suspected that most residents rent bikes for many other reasons instead of holiday leisure activities.

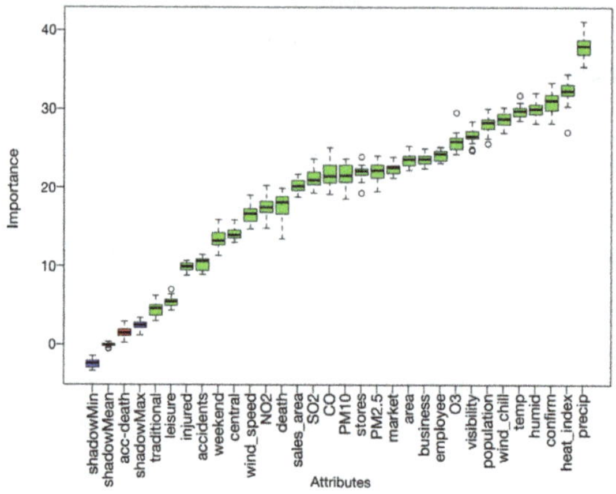

Fig. 1. Boruta feature selection.

While the Boruta algorithm can indicate what features will be accepted or not based on their performance, it does not state the variable's root mean squared error (RMSE). To retrieve lower RMSE, we further used the recursive feature elimination (RFE) to select features that can minimize the RMSE [15]. Like Boruta, RFE is also based on random forests in terms of method of implementation. RFE was implemented along with cross validation repeated three times for training to increase prediction performance. Like Boruta, no testing set instances had been exposed to the RFE algorithm. We identified the threshold number of features with the lowest RMSE is 25. Thus, the first 25 confirmed features are selected, and the excluded features are the number of injuries in the category of traffic accidents and holidays in the category of seasonality.

4.3 Model Development

We used hyperparameter tuning to optimize the performance of each of the four models. Hyperparameters are crucial to the result of machine learning algorithms and can affect the performance of the models [34]. There are several hyperparameter tuning methods, such as manual tuning, random search, and grid search, which can be applied in different contexts. We performed grid search for it is widely implemented and requires less experience and computational efforts. Grid search iteratively assesses over potential hyperparameter values, which are the number of neighbors (k). Figure 2 shows that a search on k value between 1 and 30 is computed, and the optimal k value with the highest coefficient of determination (R-squared) is 12. We identified two hyperparameters: *ntree* and *mtry* of the random forest. *ntree* is the number of trees to grow in the model and *mtry* is the number of variables that are selected as candidates at liberty during each split [18]. We set *ntree* as the default value of 500, which is large enough to produce stable models and *mtry* in the range from 1 to 15 in the tune grid. Figure 3 shows that 10 is the optimal value of *mtry*.

The support vector machine (SVM) has two essential hyperparameters, sigma and cost, to be tuned. The tune grid of cost ranges from 0 to 120 with the step of 10. The tune grid of sigma uses 0.1, 0.01 and 0.001 as these three values are the conventional learning rate of SVM models. Figure 4 shows that the optimal combination with the highest *R*-squared is a cost of 120 with sigma equal to 0.01.

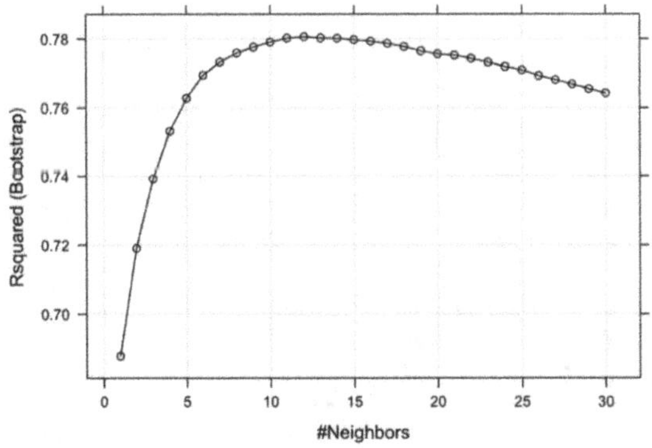

Fig. 2. Grid search of KNN.

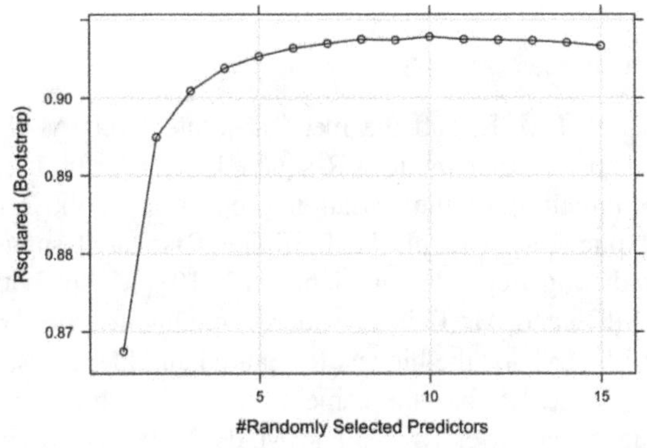

Fig. 3. Grid search of random forest.

5 Results and Discussion

All prediction models were implemented using10-fold cross-validation process repeated for three times during training, which generated a total 30 results for each model. Cross-validation is an approach to increase the performance of the proposed models [29]. The K-fold cross-validation separates the data set randomly into k subsets and one subset is used for testing while the other k-1 subsets are used for training. The whole process of randomly separating, splitting, training, and testing is repeated several times and the optimal one is identified as having the minimum RMSE.

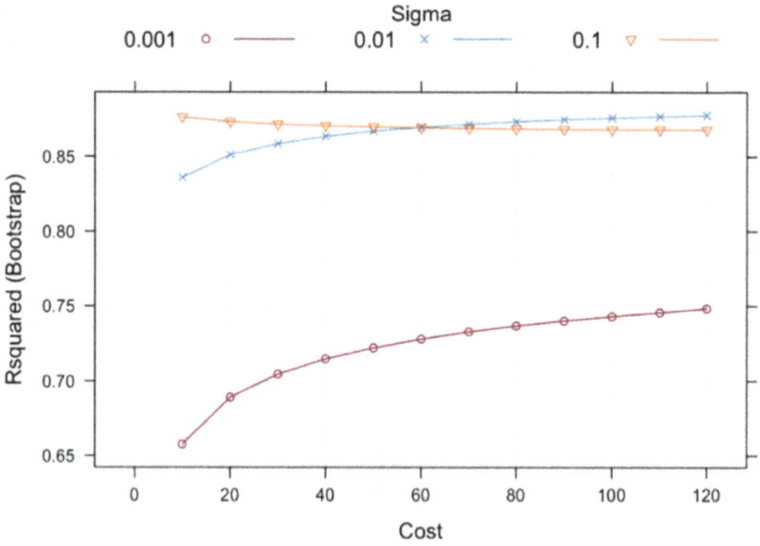

Fig. 4. Grid search of support vector machine.

5.1 Model Performance

We use the R-squared, RMSE, and the mean absolute error (MAE) to evaluate the performance of each of the four models. R-squared is a statistic measure (also called coefficient of determination) of the variation proportion in the responsive variable predicted by the explanatory variable [16]. Higher R-squared suggests better model performance in predicting dependent variable [17, 19]. Model with the highest R-squared, lowest RMSE and MAE is considered having the best predictive power. Table 1 shows that SVM yields the highest R-squared and the lowest RMSE and MAE in the training set. While RF has the same R-squared in training set (0.92), SVM outperforms RF due to its lower RMSE and MAE. However, when it comes to the testing set, RF outperforms SVM in terms of both R-squared and RMSE and MAE values. RF performs slightly better in the testing set than in the training set. Comparing prediction performance in the training and testing sets, RF's R-squared in the testing set is 0.93 while 0.1 lower in the training set. This result suggests that the RF model performs even better in the testing sets. The R-squared of KNN in the testing set decreases by 0.4 than in the training set which is the largest decrease compared with other models. The LM has the worst performance in both the training and testing sets, indicating that the relationship between bike rentals and the explanatory variables is nonlinear.

Table 1. Results of regression algorithms.

Models	Training			Testing		
	R^2	RMSE	MAE	R^2	RMSE	MAE
LR	.48	1065.12	778.87	.46	1062.37	796.30
KNN	.85	589.95	408.74	.81	641.82	448.22
RF	.92	442.25	274.04	.93	399.21	264.40
SVM	.92	415.45	252.40	.90	457.88	306.21

Note: LM = Linear regression, KNN = *k*-nearest neighbors, RF = Random Forest, SVM = Support vector machine, R^2 = *R*-squared, coefficient of determination, RMSE = Root mean squared error, and MAE = Mean average error.

5.2 Feature Importance

As shown, the random forest model performs the best in terms of R-squared, RMSE, and MAE. Figure 5 shows the feature importance of the RF model. As we can see, precipitation is the most important feature in predicting daily bike rentals, followed by Covid-19 confirmed cases and the O3 level of air pollution. Heat index and the levels of PM10 and PM2.5 are also strong predictors. The least important predictor for bike rentals is the number of traffic accidents. The most important social-economic feature is population while the rest are not salient. Table 2 shows the average of the feature importance in different categories of variables for the RF model. The category with the highest average feature importance is Covid-19 (50.37) while the lowest average feature importance category is traffic accidents (14.56). Air pollution and weather have similar average feature importance.

Table 2. Average feature importance by category of RF

Feature category	Average importance of features
Weather	40.31
Air pollution	41.70
Covid-19 outbreak	50.37
Traffic accidents	14.56
Social economic	21.86

Although the SVM has lower performance than RF, the evaluation matrices of SVM is also superior. The SVM in this study implemented RBF kernel. Unlike linear kernel, since RBF does not directly provide feature importance, the relative feature importance is composed by the weight of weight vectors. Features with higher weights indicate higher importance. Figure 6 shows the feature importance generated by the SVM model. The level of O_3 has the highest weights, followed by wind chill temperature, visibility, temperature, and population. The feature for the number of stores in the district has the least weight. The level of PM10, weekend or not, the number of business and number of employees in the district also have low weights. It is worth noting that the features that are important in RF are not necessarily important in the SVM model, for instance PM10 level and heat index. The number of markets, business and employees are not the strong indicators in both RF and SVM models.

We also calculated the average feature importance in each of the six categories of the variables. Table 3 shows that weather has the highest weight, followed by Covid-19 outbreak and traffic accidents. Social economic features have the lowest weight. Comparing the feature importance of the RF model and SVM model, features in weather and Covid-19 are important in both models. Features in the Social-economic category have less importance in the RF and SVM models. In the RF model, the category of air pollution is more important than traffic accident, while in SVM model, air pollution is less important than traffic accidents. In both models, the level of O_3 ranks top 5 for the feature with high importance or weights.

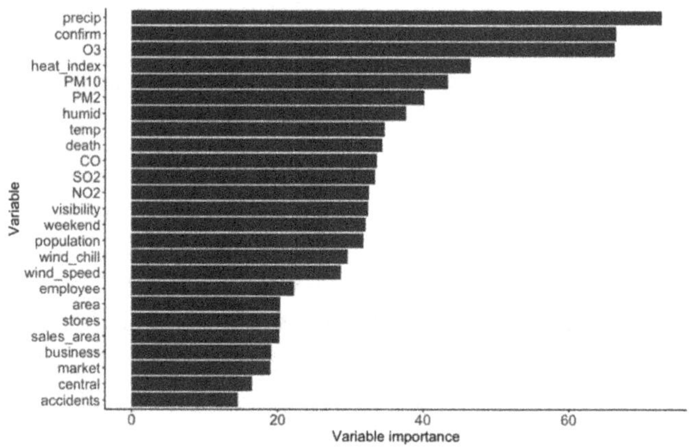

Fig. 5. Random forest model feature importance.

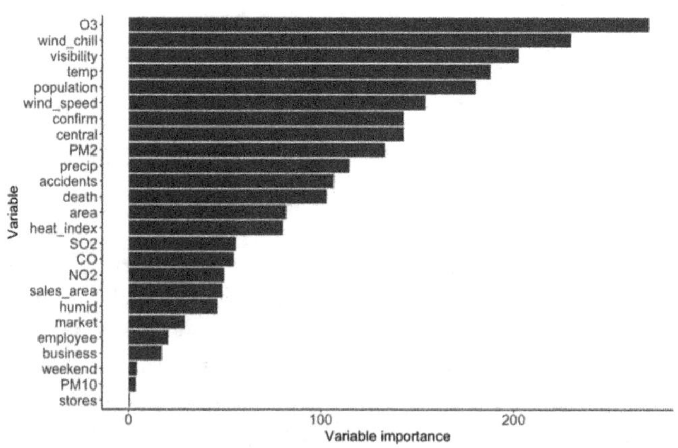

Fig. 6. SVM model feature importance.

Although social-economic features are not important, they did increase the predictivity of both the RF and SVM models. A subset without social-economic features was taken from the data set and implemented in RF and SVM models. Table 4 shows that the RF and SVM models without social economic factors have substantially lower evaluation matrices. For the RF model, the *R*-squared of the model without social economic features decreased by 0.39 in the training set and 0.38 in the testing set compared to the evaluation matrices with the features. As for the SVM model, the *R*-squared of the model without social economic factors also decreased drastically in both the training (0.34) and testing sets (0.37). This result suggests that social economic features are crucial to increase prediction accuracy, even though they may not have high feature importance values on their own right.

Table 3. Average feature importance by category in SVM

Feature category	Average importance of features
Weather	144.77
Air pollution	94.30
Covid-19 outbreak	122.58
Traffic accidents	106.33
Social economic	53.93

Table 4. Results of the RF and SVM models with and without social economic factors

Models	Training			Testing		
	R^2	RMSE	MAE	R^2	RMSE	MAE
RF	0.92	442.25	274.04	0.93	399.21	264.40
RF w/o	0.53	1019.77	722.62	0.55	972.90	693.26
SVM	0.92	415.45	252.40	0.90	457.88	306.21
SVM w/o	0.58	982.13	615.05	0.53	1018.03	649.37

6 Conclusion

While machine learning models are completely data driven, we have attempted to incorporate social economic variables in the models to predict bike sharing demand. Despite the fact that these variables are barely useful in explaining and predicting short-term bike demand because they are constant, they did reveal demand differences between docking stations that are characterized by different social economic conditions. The roles that these variables play are to reveal population and economic activity that may differ across districts where bike docking stations are located. In this regard, bike sharing demand at the station level could perhaps be divided into basic demand, which is determined by social economic factors and induced demand, which changes with weather, pollution as well as a wide range of features that vary in the short term or even instantaneously. We advanced studies conducted by V E et al. [32] and E and Cho [14] in predicting bike demand in Seoul in the sense that they only addressed the induced demand for bike sharing on a daily basis.

The best model is the random forest model in our study, and the most important features are precipitation, the number of Covid-19 cases, the level of O3, heat index, and the level of PM10. The most important categories of features for the random forest model are Covid-19 outbreak, followed by air pollution and weather. Almost all social economic features are the least important, however they played a role in enhancing the performance of the models. The SVM is also an acceptable model. The features in the categories of weather, Covid-19 outbreak and traffic accidents have highest average weights. These results indicate that weather features such as precipitation, temperature, heat index, wind chill temperature as well as Covid-19 outbreak have huge impacts on bike sharing demand in Seoul. Further research can focus on many other potential features that influence bike sharing demand and many other machine learning algorithms such as Multilayer Perception Model.

References

1. Akın M (2015) A novel approach to model selection in tourism demand modeling. Tour Manage 48:64–72. https://doi.org/10.1016/j.tourman.2014.11.004
2. Altman NS (1992) An introduction to kernel and nearest-neighbor nonparametric regression. Am Stat 46:175. https://doi.org/10.2307/2685209
3. Bi J-W, Han T-Y, Li H (2020) International tourism demand forecasting with machine learning models: the power of the number of lagged inputs. Tour Econ. https://doi.org/10.1177/1354816620976954
4. Breiman L (2001) Mach Learn 45:5–32. https://doi.org/10.1023/a:1010933404324
5. Chang P-C, Wu J-L, Xu Y, Zhang M, Lu X-Y (2017) Bike sharing demand prediction using artificial immune system and artificial neural network. Soft Comput 23(2):613–626. https://doi.org/10.1007/s00500-017-2909-8
6. Chen K-Y, Wang C-H (2007) Support vector regression with genetic algorithms in forecasting tourism demand. Tour Manage 28:215–226. https://doi.org/10.1016/j.tourman.2005.12.018
7. Chen X, Ishwaran H (2012) Random forests for genomic data analysis. Genomics 99:323–329. https://doi.org/10.1016/j.ygeno.2012.04.003
8. Chen Y (2021) Economics of tourism and hospitality a micro approach. Routledge, New York, NY
9. Claveria O, Monte E, Torra S (2016) Combination forecasts of tourism demand with machine learning models. Appl Econ Lett 23(6):428–431. https://doi.org/10.1080/13504851.2015.1078441
10. Claveria O, Monte E, Torra S (2018) Modelling tourism demand to Spain with machine learning techniques. The impact of forecast horizon on model selection. Revista de Economia Aplicada, **24**(72):109–132
11. Cortes C, Vapnik V (1995) Support-vector networks. Mach Learn 20:273–297. https://doi.org/10.1007/bf00994018
12. Dong B, Cao C, Lee SE (2005) Applying support vector machines to predict building energy consumption in tropical region. Energy Build 37:545–553. https://doi.org/10.1016/j.enbuild.2004.09.009

13. Dora C, Phillips M (2000) Transport, environment and health. World Health Organization, Regional Office for Europe, Copenhagen
14. Sathishkumar VE, Park J, Cho Y (2020) Using data mining techniques for bike sharing demand prediction in Metropolitan City. Comput Commun 153:353–366. https://doi.org/10.1016/j.comcom.2020.02.007
15. Fan C, Xiao F, Wang S (2014) Development of prediction models for next-day building energy consumption and peak power demand using data mining techniques. Appl Energy 127:1. https://doi.org/10.1016/j.apenergy.2014.04.016
16. Friedman J, Hastie T, Tibshirani R (2001) The elements of statistical learning (Vol 1, No 10). Springer, New York, NY. https://doi.org/10.1007/978-0-387-84858-7
17. Glantz SA, Slinker BK (1990) Primer of applied regression and analysis of variance. McGraw-Hill, Health Professions Division
18. Han S, Kim H (2021) Optimal feature set size in random forest regression. Appl Sci 11:3428. https://doi.org/10.3390/app11083428
19. Hastie T, Tibshirani R, Friedman JH (2009) The elements of statistical learning: data mining, inference, and prediction. Springer, New York, NY. https://doi.org/10.1007/978-0-387-84858-7
20. Hulot P, Aloise D, Jena SD (2018) Towards station-level demand prediction for effective rebalancing in bike-sharing systems. In: Proceedings of the 24th ACM SIGKDD international conference on knowledge discovery & data mining. https://doi.org/10.1145/3219819.3219873
21. Seoul Open Data. http://data.seoul.go.kr
22. Kursa MB, Rudnicki WR (2010) Feature selection with the boruta package. J Stat Softw 36:11. https://doi.org/10.18637/jss.v036.i11
23. Law R, Li G, Fong DK, Han X (2019) Tourism demand forecasting: a deep learning approach. Ann Tour Res 75:410–423. https://doi.org/10.1016/j.annals.2019.01.014
24. Li H, Hu M, Li G (2020) Forecasting tourism demand with multisource big data. Ann Tour Res 83:102912. https://doi.org/10.1016/j.annals.2020.102912
25. Li X, Li H, Pan B, Law R (2020) Machine learning in internet search query selection for tourism forecasting. J Travel Res 60:1213–1231. https://doi.org/10.1177/0047287520934871
26. Li Y, Zhu Z, Kong D, Xu M, Zhao Y (2019) Learning heterogeneous spatial-temporal representation for bike-sharing demand prediction. Proc AAAI Conf Artif Intell 33:1004–1011. https://doi.org/10.1609/aaai.v33i01.33011004
27. Liu J et al (2015) Station site optimization in bike sharing systems. In: 2015 IEEE international conference on data mining. https://doi.org/10.1109/icdm.2015.99
28. Saud S, Jamil B, Upadhyay Y, Irshad K (2020) Performance improvement of empirical models for estimation of global solar radiation in India: a k-fold cross-validation approach. Sustain Energy Technol Assess 40:100768. https://doi.org/10.1016/j.seta.2020.100768
29. Sun S, Wei Y, Tsui K-L, Wang S (2019) Forecasting tourist arrivals with machine learning and internet search index. Tour Manage 70:1. https://doi.org/10.1016/j.tourman.2018.07.010
30. Vapnik V (1999) The nature of statistical learning theory. Springer, Berlin. https://doi.org/10.1007/978-1-4757-3264-1
31. Sathishkumar VE, Cho Y (2020) A rule-based model for Seoul bike sharing demand prediction using weather data. Europ J Rem Sens 53(sup1):166–183. https://doi.org/10.1080/22797254.2020.1725789
32. Wang Z, Sun Y, Zeng Y, Wang B (2018) Substitution effect or complementation effect for bicycle travel choice preference and other transportation availability: evidence from US large-scale shared bicycle travel behaviour data. J Clean Prod 194:406–415. https://doi.org/10.1016/j.jclepro.2018.04.233

33. Wong J, Manderson T, Abrahamowicz M, Buckeridge DL, Tamblyn R (2019) Can hyperparameter tuning improve the performance of a super learner? Epidemiology 30:521–531. https://doi.org/10.1097/ede.0000000000001027
34. Xie G, Qian Y, Wang S (2021) Forecasting Chinese cruise tourism demand with big data: an optimized machine learning approach. Tour Manage 82:104208. https://doi.org/10.1016/j.tourman.2020.104208
35. Xu T, Han G, Qi X, Du J, Lin C, Shu L (2020) A hybrid machine learning model for demand prediction of edge-computing-based bike-sharing system using Internet of Things. IEEE Internet Things J 7:7345–7356. https://doi.org/10.1109/jiot.2020.2983089

5

Window to the Destination: Tourists' Local Experience via "Online Experiences" on Airbnb Amid the Pandemic

Junjiao Zhang(✉) and Hanqin Qiu

Nankai University, Tianjin 300350, China
{junjiao.zhang,qiuhanqin}@nankai.edu.cn

Abstract. This study aims to explore the composition of virtual guided tour experience on Airbnb and to develop a formation process of virtual guided tour experience. A case study based on the qualitative analysis was conducted with a dataset of online reviews towards an Online Experience in Beijing, China. A three-stage process of virtual guided tour experience was concluded, including experience encounter, experience evaluation, and behavioral intention. Experience encounter describes the experience composition from four dimensions: interpretation quality, host credibility, tourist-host social contact, and peer interaction; Experience evaluation is involved with benefits mainly gained from the enhanced understanding of local culture and the satisfaction attributed by the sense of telepresence; Further, behavioral intention covers both online and offline willingness to recommend or repurchase the virtual tour, or visit the destination in person after the pandemic. Theoretical and practical implications in navigating tourism recovery were discussed.

Keywords: Local experience · Staycation · Airbnb · Online experiences · Tourist-host social contact · The COVID-19 crisis

1 Introduction

Due to the restrictions on travel especially international air travel, staycations are becoming the alternatives for travel to the destinations amid the COVID-19. Despite that, the changing travel patterns generate new growth opportunities to independent service providers [1]. For instance, to navigate the business recovery, Airbnb released the "Online Experiences" program as the virtual tour activities without leaving home, switching the engaging activities designed by the locals to online tours or classes. Understanding the new growth space in sharing economy for coping with the pandemic crisis is therefore essential since adversity breeds innovation. The composition and its consequences of the virtual guided tour experience, however, are still ambiguous. Although sharing platforms such as Airbnb have attracted increasing attention in the industry and academics, the majority focus in previous studies is still limited in the issues of short-term rentals. On the other hand, researchers have confirmed the role of Airbnb in creating authentic tourism experiences by connecting the tourists directly with the locals [2, 3]. Yet how tourists understand and evaluate their experience in virtual tours guided by the locals remains unknown. To address the knowledge gaps, two research questions were raised: 1) what is the composition of consumer experience in virtual guided tours hosted by the locals? and 2) what is the formulation process of consumer experience of virtual guided tours?

2 Consumer Experience and Virtual Guided Tour

Consumer experience framework in hospitality and tourism was developed by [4] based on the diverse theoretical underpinnings of consumer experience. It postulates that consumer experience is formed by the core experience values (emotive, cognitive, extraordinary, ordinary) with the impact of the peripheral factors related to physical and human interaction dimensions (individual characteristics, physical experience, human interaction, and situation factors). Accordingly, the composition of virtual guided tour experience can be multidimensional and can transpire as the peripheral factors elicit the core experience values. However, given the contextual nature of consumer experience, there is still much to know about tourists' local experience through the involvement of virtual tours guided by the locals in the specific times of the pandemic.

Virtual tour guided by the locals is a new type for users on sharing platforms to share their underutilized services (i.e., information or knowledge of the destination). Scholars have extended the research on local experience to food-sharing services and advanced our understanding of meal-sharing experiences with local foods [5, 6] and peer-to-peer dining experiences [7]. For instance, [5] identified a five-component construct of street food experience in local-guided tour, including "local guide's attributes, perceived food authenticity, local culture, perceived cleanliness, and novelty." They further found social interaction, awe, and servicescape can also be the key components of meal-sharing experience with local foods [6]. Such forms of tours are unique with more authentic engagement in the destination because the local experiences are cocreated by the residents (hosts) and visitors [7]. That is, social interaction is at the heart of consumer experience to the tours designated and organized by the locals. However, the standstill of traveling brought by the COVID-19 prevented these peer-to-peer social interactions, leading the industry and tourists to embrace the alternative models of traveling such as virtual tourism and online experiences [8]. Although it was noted that consumers' experience in virtual tours amid the pandemic significantly increase their visit or purchasing desire [9], a critical gap exists in the understanding of consumer experience in the new service, virtual tour guided by the locals.

3 Methodology

A qualitative approach following the interpretive paradigm was utilized because the phenomenon can be understood from the perspective of individual experiences. Tourists' online reviews about their virtual tours were adopted for the sake of generating primary and insightful data. Three selection criteria were employed to confirm the eligible virtual tours: organized by the locals, available during the pandemic, merge the experience with the local culture. Finally, one of the most popular Online Experiences uploaded in August 2020 and led by a Beijing native on Airbnb was selected. It is focused on experiencing Great Wall from its different sections and history and the host has visited Great Wall for many times. This 45-min activity costs 120 CNY (per tourist) with maximum bookings of 10 persons each time. The listing of the reviews from August 2020 to July 2021 was ordered based on relevance, helpfulness, and length. 190 reviews were obtained and read through, among which 39 reviews in Chinese or other language were translated into English. 21 reviews that have no meaningful units or cannot form a complete sentence were filtered out. The qualitative data selection was ended when no new meaningful understanding on the virtual local experience was read. Finally, 135 reviews (11–150 words) were collected for further analysis.

The narrative information was interpreted with a thematic and paradigmatic data analysis approach. The multidimensional framework of consumer experience proposed by [4] guided the procedure. Given the contextual nature of consumer experience, the distinction in contexts (online vs. offline) and situations (normal vs. non-normal) were particularly addressed when capturing the meaningful units and formulating key themes about tourists' local experience via the virtual tour amid the pandemic. NVivo 12 was applied to code and examine the texts. Trustworthiness of data analysis was confirmed after being checked by an expert in the field of sharing service.

4 Findings and Discussion

Three stages embedded in tourists' local experience via virtual tours were concluded, delineating experience encounter, experience evaluation, and behavioral intention (Fig. 1). Experience composition covered four dimensions of the virtual tour experience, namely interpretation quality, host credibility, tourist-host social contact, and peer interaction. Each dimension was further determined by particular factors. Interpretation quality was composed of information quality, orchestration quality, and display quality of the virtual guided tour. A successful interpretation was mainly characterized by informative and insightful understanding of the destination, well-designed orchestration based on story, culture, and gamification, as well as the immersive audio-visual enjoyment; Host credibility was understood through five factors, among which appetency and ardent love to local culture were revealed as the unique reasons that bring praise to the hosts; Tourist-host social contact was qualified by instant Q&A, relationship maintenance, service recovery, and special care from the hosts before, during, and after the virtual tour; Peer interaction mainly occurred between friends or families members and was enhanced by the increasing intergenerational conversation and social bond.

Experience evaluation came from tourists' benefits and satisfaction gained from the virtual tour. Besides the educational function similar to other tourism types, virtual guided tours could offer unique tips to navigate tourist trips after the pandemic, bond their social network during the staycation time, and could also make some tourists recall the wonderful past visits to the same destinations. Tourists' satisfaction was assessed through the comparison to their expectation and their feeling in the past visits in person. It is worthy to note that tourists' sense of telepresence, "feeling like visiting the destination for real with the hosts," became the majority motive of their satisfaction.

Tourists' behavioral intention illustrated behavioral tendencies both online and offline. Tourists tend to recommend or repurchase the virtual tours organized by the same host, or plan to attend other virtual tour activities in the future. The virtual tour experience can also catalyze tourists' offline tour after the pandemic by facilitating them to visit the destination in person whether guided or not guided by the host.

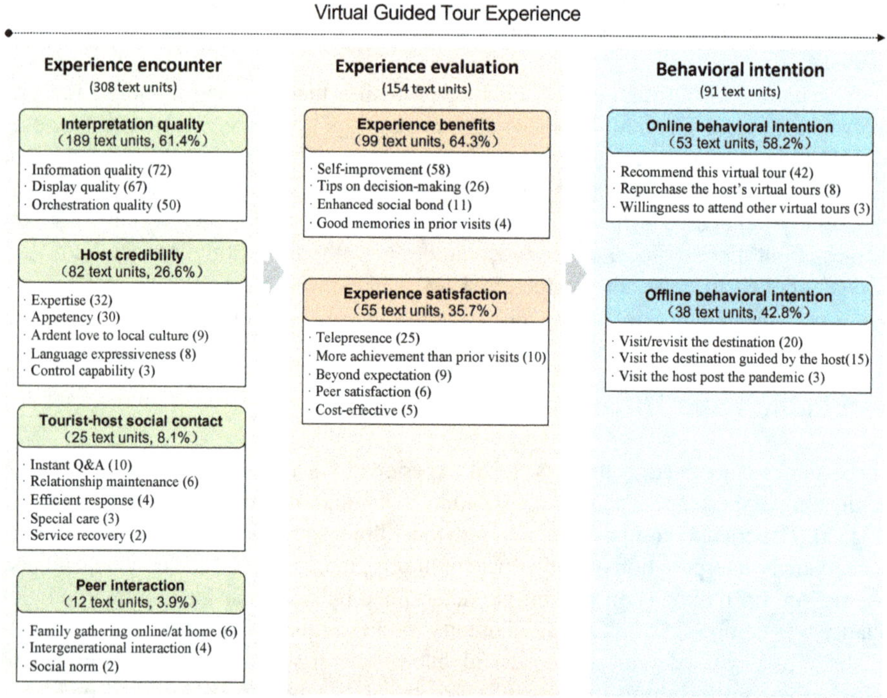

Fig. 1. Conceptual framework of virtual guided tour experience process

Findings of this study revealed that tourists can feel a solid space beyond the plane screen through the immersive experience based on culture and story-based interpretation supported by the local hosts. The consequences of such experiences can accelerate tourists' willingness to recommend or repurchase online experience activities, which may further switch into a real visit or revisit the destinations after the pandemic. Accordingly, a formation process of the virtual guided tour experience for tourists is developed by identifying the constructs and stages of consumer experience (Fig. 1). This process suggests that sociability and interactivity of the virtual guided tours, to a certain extent, satisfy the consumers' desires for travel amid the pandemic and induce the travel desire post-COVID-19. Despite that virtual guided tour is less likely to be substitutes of conventional travel, it can advance the innovation of travel activity by designing high-quality local experiences with the wisdom of the locals.

5 Implications

This study enriched the knowledge on virtual tours and sharing economy by developing a conceptual framework of tourists' local experience via virtual tour guided by the locals; it accounted for determinants and consequences specific to the immersive experience of the destination with experience encounter, experience evaluation, and behavioral intention. It also identified the factors constituting tourists' online local experience, which provides a comparison agenda to distinct and understand the differences between virtual tours guided by the locals and conventional tours. More importantly, this study contributed a marketing strategy to navigate tourism crisis recovery by co-creating values between the sharing platform and the locals, which will be helpful for destination marketers, small tourism operators, especially for the small independent operators. Also, it suggested that the virtual tour providers should pursue an immersive experience combining their understanding of the local culture with a high level of interactivity and sociability in designing.

6 Limitations and Future Research

Considering virtual tours' diversity, findings in this study are necessary to be further examined in other themes of experience activities guided by the locals, such as online classes about cooking, writing, dance, or other arts. Quantitative approach is need in future to test the feasibility of the proposed virtual guided tour experience process.

References

1. Jones P, Comfort D (2020) The COVID-19 crisis and sustainability in the hospitality industry. Int J Contemp Hosp Manag 32(10):3037–3050
2. Tussyadiah IP (2016) Factors of satisfaction and intention to use peer-to-peer accommodation. Int J Hosp Manag 55:70–80
3. Guttentag D (2018) Commentary on authenticity and the sharing economy: which Airbnb are we talking about? Acad Manag Discov 4(3):373–375
4. Walls AR, Okumus F, Wang YR, Kwun DJW (2011) An epistemological view of consumer experiences. Int J Hosp Manag 30(1):10–21
5. Cifci I, Atsız O, Gupta V (2021) The street food experiences of the local-guided tour in the meal-sharing economy: the case of Bangkok. Br Food J 123(12):4030–4048
6. Atsız O, Cifci I, Rasoolimanesh SM (2021) Exploring the components of meal-sharing experiences with local foods: a netnography approach. Curr Issues Tourism 1–18
7. Lin PMC, Ok CM, Ching Au W (2021): Peer-to-peer dining: a motivation study. J Hosp Tourism Res 1–26
8. Sigala M (2020) Tourism and COVID-19: impacts and implications for advancing and resetting industry and research. J Bus Res 117(117):312–321
9. Wen H, Leung XY (2021) Virtual wine tours and wine tasting: the influence of offline and online embodiment integration on wine purchase decisions. Tourism Manag 83(2):104250

6

A Framework of Resilience for Peer-to-Peer Accommodation Hosts under COVID-19

Yu-Hua Xu[1], Shihan (David) Ma[2(✉)] and Xin-Yue Li[2]

[1] Arizona State University, HNU-ASU International Tourism College, Haikou, People's Republic of China

[2] School of Management, Zhejiang University, Hangzhou, People's Republic of China

mashihan@zju.edu.cn

Abstract. The pandemic has hit the tourism industry in various ways. P2P accommodation (P2PA) is one of most disrupted sectors. Different types of P2PA hosts are confronting different levels of challenges. From an angle of social equity, the study adopted a resilience model to examine the resilience of P2PA hosts' business during the first COVID outbreak in Florida, USA. Statistical results show P2PA hosts' business resilience negatively associates with their housing liability and hosting experience. Social superiority in owning more assets can be a defect in coping with COVID crisis. P2PA operators need to maintain an appropriate level of financial flexibility when faced with the threat of COVID outbreaks. We suggest the government and industrial organizations to distinguish the types of P2PA operators when carrying out rescue plans for the industry.

Keywords: P2P lodging · Financial resilience · Social equity · Pandemic recovery

1 Introduction

With the ongoing COVID-19 pandemic and the emergence of new variants of the virus upgrading the unpredictability of the global lodging market, recovering from the constant outbreaks and strengthen financial resilience of accommodation business has become one of the most urgent topics in hospitality industry.

Compared with corporational hotel businesses, small lodging establishments like Peer-to-Peer accommodations (P2PA) experiences a higher level of operational vulnerabilities and business fragilities [1]. While traditional "sharing economy" assumes the sharing of personal idle resources for non-essentially profit purpose, the burgeoning professional P2PA hosts own multiple properties and operate their business in a similar way as full-time hoteliers. Who are more resilient and adaptive in the pandemic disturbing? These professional players fully dependent on accommodation investment for living, or those with only individual listed property? Given the potential government subsidies for small establishments in the hospitality industry, there is an urgent need to understand the mechanism of resilience and examine the resilience status of different types of hosts in the P2PA industry.

The study is first to testify to an adapted resilience model to examine financial resilience in P2PA industry; Second, we aim to examine the level of resilience among different types of P2PA hosts based on our proposed model.

2 Theoretical Background

Resilience was defined as the ability of a system to return to equilibrium after a shock [2]. Despite the variability in definitions of social/human-related resilience, many address the interplay between social vulnerability and the adaptive ability, and how the human network reorganizes and transforms during disturbances and shocks. Briguglio et al. [3] proposed a risk model which distinguished the character of vulnerability and resilience in an economic context, where vulnerability was considered as an inherent factor, while resilience played as a nurtured factor that can ease the risk. The subtraction between vulnerability and resilience equals the risk. This static model refers "risk" as the endogenous odds of being exposed to external shocks, rather than an external factor that is independent from the entity under observation. As a result, it is difficult to operationalize the "risk" factor and evaluate its effect in empirical cases.

Martin [4] proposed a spatial-economic resilience model to describe socio-economic system's adaptive power to regional economic hysteresis. The conceptual model put that how much a system can absorb depends on its intrinsic vulnerability and resilience features. Based on Briguglio's and Martin's work, we proposed our framework to measure resilience as in Eq. 1:

$$\text{Resilience} = \text{Adaptability} - (\text{Vulnerability} + \text{Shock}) \quad (1)$$

Three research questions were consequently developed from the research goals:

Question 1: How could the pandemic shock affect the resilience of P2PA business?
Question 2: How could adaptability affect the resilience of P2PA business?
Question 3: How could vulnerability affect the resilience of P2PA business?

The concept of social equity has been widely used in tourism and economy domain [5], especially to explain the dynamics in the interactions between hosts and tourists [6]. Yet another possible dyadic inequity, the imbalance and contradiction between smaller operators and large asset owners, is equally noteworthy but has been largely neglected. During the pandemic, small operators may have suffered disproportionate challenge because of their financial inelasticity [1]. The supply side of hospitality industry has long been dominated by perspectives of industrial development, and there is an urgent call for a scrutiny of the possible imbalance among different scales of P2P accommodation hosts.

Based on the discussion of social equity, the last research question was developed:

Question 4: Do hosts with social superiority possess higher business resilience?

3 Research Design

3.1 Conceptual Framework

We proposed a model to measure the financial resilience of P2P accommodation during the pandemic (Fig. 1) based on the abovementioned resilience framework.

The severity of the COVID represents the level of external shock, which is operationalized as the number of COVID-19 infected cases. We used both ***Overall Shock (OS)*** (monthly new reported case number of Florida) and ***Local Shock (LS)*** (reported cases on county level, weighted by the room scale of the property situating within the county) for measurement.

Adaptability is represented by a series of variables regarding host capability, business scale/feature and operational experience, including ***Host Experience (HE)*** (the length of a host's experience in P2PA business), ***Property Scale (PS)*** (total number of operating properties under one host), ***Room Scale (RS)*** (total number of available bedrooms under one host) and ***Business Level (BL)*** (average room rate from January 2008 to February 2020, indicating the targeted market of a host's P2PA properties).

Vulnerability is gauged by the financial liability in maintaining the properties. ***Maintenance Cost (MC)*** is the monthly housing expense including utilities, property tax, and mortgage; ***Housing Burden (HB)*** is the ratio calculated by the MC over regional household income.

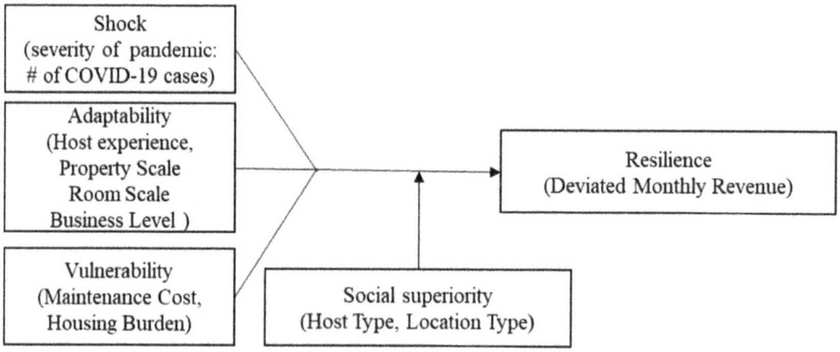

Fig. 1. Conceptual model

The Dependent Variable (DV), resilience, is represented by ***Deviated Monthly Revenue (DMR)***. It is calculated by the difference between the monthly revenue year-on-year, where month ranges from March 2020 to September 2020. A positive DMR indicates vigorous performance and strong resilience of the business hosts, and vice versa.

Finally, we introduce two Control Variables (CVs) to represent the construct Social Superiority. ***Host Type (HT)*** reflects hosts' individual social superiority based on their owned properties scales. HT is an ordinal variable with "Single" represents hosts with one property, "Small" for two to three properties, "Medium" for four to five properties), and "Large" for over five properties. ***Location Type (LT)*** reflects the social superiority of a host' neighborhood. It was calculated by the median housing value of the community where the properties are located.

3.2 Data Preparation and Preprocessing

We took the State of Florida as the study site for the research. The primary data was purchased from AirDNA (www.airdna.co). The time span of the data ranged from early 2008 to September 2020. The reported COVID case data was retrieved from the New York Times (NYT) Coronavirus Data in the United States. The financial cost data for vulnerability-dimension were obtained from American Community Survey (ACS) data. The NYT and ACS datasets were later integrated to the primary dataset by either zip-code or county labels.

The completed dataset was structured by monthly entries of host performance during the COVID pandemic. We finally collected 138,138 entries from 43,935 hosts after data preprocessing. During the observed period, 4,550 hosts shutdown their business and the remaining 39,385 survived at the end of September 2020. We further removed the data points with missing values and outliers, retaining a final dataset of 112,597 monthly entries from 29,114 hosts for analysis.

4 Preliminary Results and Conclusion

The conceptual model was tested with OLS linear regression with a decent explanation power ($R^2 = 0.24$) (see overall model in Table 1).

Both overall shock (OS) and local shock (LS) are significant factors influencing host resilience. OS (standardized beta = −0.46, $p < 0.01$) has an overwhelmingly negative impact, arguably the strongest, on revenue performance. This indicates that the majority of the P2PA business suffer from the external shock of the pandemic. Interestingly, LS has a slight positive effect (beta = 0.03), albeit largely overshadowed by the powerful negativity from OS. The plausible explanation is that the hotspots of the first peak of the pandemic in Florida concentrates on those top tier destinations with crowds of visitors and likely better revenue performance, yet inevitably causing a higher number of infected cases at the local level. Regardless of the positive effect from LS on DV, the overall travel flows to Florida have shrunk significantly, as the OS has devastatingly influenced tourists' willingness to travel and play a more crucial role in the performance of P2PA industry during the pandemic.

Adaptability variables like host experience (HE) (beta = −0.08), room scale (RS) (beta = −0.04), property scale (PS) (beta = −0.27) and business level (BL) (beta = −0.12) turned out to be significant negative impact factors on resilience. Contrary to our assumptions, this result means that P2PA hosts with more properties/rooms and higher business levels were not as flexible as smaller practitioners in terms of adaptation to the COVID. This finding resonated with the result from control variable host type (HT), where medium operators were fiercely strained in recovery (beta = −0.50,) while single operators and small operators were not as significant.

Both vulnerability variables, maintenance cost (MC) (beta = −0.13) and housing burden (HB) (beta = −0.02) were a significant hindrance to resilience performance. Hosts with higher liability or debt level were more vulnerable in the pandemic and might struggle to make ends meet in maintaining their properties.

Finally, the control variable location type (LT) indicated that hosts with properties in more affluent communities were more likely to recover.

Table 1. Regression model results

Constructs	Variables	Overall model	Model (Mar–Jun)	Model (July–Aug)
	Constant	0.02* (−0.01)	−1.00*** (−0.02)	−2.02*** (−0.08)
Shock	Overall shock	−0.46*** (0.00)	−1.98*** (−0ṇ.03)	0.39*** (−0.04)
	Local shock	0.03*** (0.00)	0.05** (−0.02)	0.03*** (0.00)
Adaptability	Host experience	−0.08*** (0.00)	−0.08*** (0.00)	−0.07*** (−0.01)
	Room scale	−0.06*** (0.00)	−0.06*** (0.00)	−0.19*** (−0.02)
	Property scale	−0.10*** (−0.02)	−0.10*** (−0.02)	−0.02 (−0.02)
	Business level	−0.12*** (0.00)	0.01*** (0.00)	−0.38*** (−0.01)
Vulnerability	Maintenance cost	−0.13*** (−0.01)	−0.11*** (−0.01)	−0.17*** (−0.02)
	Housing burden	−0.02*** (0.00)	−0.03*** (0.00)	0.0037 (−0.01)
Social superiority	Host type [Single]	0.01 (−0.01)	−0.08*** (−0.01)	1.00*** (−0.04)
	Host type [Small]	0.01 (−0.01)	−0.08*** (−0.01)	0.63*** (−0.04)
	Host type [Medium]	−0.50*** (−0.01)	−0.34*** (−0.02)	0.23*** (−0.03)
	Location type	0.07*** (−0.01)	0.06*** (−0.01)	0.08*** (−0.02)
	Adjusted R-square	0.24	0.17	0.26
	Observations	112597	68354	30350

Dependent Variable: Deviated Monthly Revenue
Standard errors in parentheses
* $p < 0.1$, ** $p < 0.05$, ***$p < 0.01$

5 Discussions, Limitations and Future Directions

Linking back to our proposed resilience model, the following constructs agreed with our assumptions: 1) vulnerability negatively associates with the resilience of revenue. Housing Burden (HB) turns out to be a valid indicator to examine vulnerability of households. 2) the level of overall shock exhibits a negative relationship with the resilience of revenue, while the county-level local shock shows a positive relationship. This interesting paradox may be explained by spatial heterogeneity. This indicates the existence of spatial variances in the P2PA resilience at a regional level. Adopting a spatial approach can help explain the pattern of local variance in resilience.

Two of the constructs exhibit different results compared with our assumptions: 3) adaptability shows a negative association with resilience. Using host experience (HE) to represent hosts' resourcefulness in dealing with crisis may be reasonable, but the statistical results remind us that there could be disturbance when using HE. The longer experience a host has, the higher odds that the P2PA investment as their major income. Such over-dependency on tourism-related industry has leveraged hosts' financial vulnerability. 4) Social superiority shows negative associations with resilience. This can be explained by the hosts' level of dependency on P2PA business. In addition, owning more P2PA properties during a crisis can cut short the cash flow of a host, thus reduce hosts' marketing and operational budget. This may be the cause for the downshift of revenue among those hosts with higher social superiority.

When faced with the threat of COVID outbreaks, P2PA operators should maintain an appropriate level of financial flexibility. We suggest the government and industrial organizations to distinguish the types of P2PA operators when carrying out rescue plans for the P2PA industry. The periodic outbreak and remission of COVID indicates the necessity to examine the pattern of P2PA hosts' business in a temporal perspective. Models in separate stages have been conducted, yet the results have not been fully addressed in the short paper. Ideally, a lengthened observation timeframe is encouraged to detect temporal patterns with robustness and carry out a potential time-series model. Extended data collection and analysis are expected in the full-paper version to complement current findings.

Theoretically, this paper examined an adapted resilience model and operationalized constructs like adaptability, vulnerability, and shock in different ways in P2PA industry. However, further examinations are needed to improve the reliability of this framework in tourism field.

References

1. Rivera M, Kizildag M, Croes R (2021) Covid-19 and small lodging establishments: a break-even calibration analysis (CBA) model. Int J Hosp Manag 94:102814. https://doi.org/10.1016/j.ijhm.2020.102814
2. Pimm SL (1984) The complexity and stability of ecosystems. Nature 307:321–326. https://doi.org/10.1038/307321a0
3. Briguglio L, Cordina G, Farrugia N, Vella S (2009) Economic vulnerability and resilience: concepts and measurements. Oxford Dev Stud 37:229–247. https://doi.org/10.1080/13600810903089893
4. Martin R (2012) Regional economic resilience, hysteresis and recessionary shocks. J Econ Geogr 12:1–32. https://doi.org/10.1093/jeg/lbr019
5. Jamal T, Camargo BA (2014) Sustainable tourism, justice and an ethic of care: toward the just destination. J Sustain Tour 22:11–30. https://doi.org/10.1080/09669582.2013.786084
6. Burrai E, Font X, Cochrane J (2015) Destination stakeholders' perceptions of volunteer tourism: an equity theory approach. Int J Tour Res 17:451–459. https://doi.org/10.1002/jtr.2012

7

Platform Stress in Hospitality – Focusing on the Technology dimension

Jae Eun (Francesca) Park, Namho Chung and Chulmo Koo(✉)

Smart Tourism Education Platform, Kyung Hee University, Seoul, South Korea
{francesca.jep,nhchung,helmetgu}@khu.ac.kr

Abstract. For the emergence of platform business, it is important to manage the stress that hosts receive from the business. Considering the characteristics of the platform business, stressors arise from social and technology dimension. In the global platform business (e.g., Airbnb), social dimension stressors mostly arise from the relationships among stakeholders, and technology dimension stressors arise from the system they utilize. This research aims to define this combination of social and technology stress as "Platform Stress." Especially focusing on the technology dimension, this research empirically verified the relations of techno-stressors, burnout, and switching intention. Further, mediating effects of burnout in between the relationships demonstrates the importance of investigating the hosts' stress. Exploring the platform stress from the technology-usage perspective, this research provides theoretical and managerial implications.

Keywords: Platform stress · Platform business · Technostress · Airbnb

1 Introduction

Disruptive development of Information Communication Technologies (ICTs) over the last decade generated the new type of business model: platform business [1]. Among the various platform businesses in overall industries, Airbnb is a typical example in the hospitality, especially accommodation industry [2].

Much research has been conducted regarding the platform businesses focusing on the relationship in it [3, 4]. However, most of these studies aim at guests whereas insufficiently aimed at hosts [5]. Furthermore, although the platform businesses have been growing fast in various industries, few research has investigated the strain hosts go through. Particularly, stress from the platform business is unique in that it is caused by both social and technological issues considering the peer-to-peer service-providing and at the same time technology-based characteristics of the business.

This work was supported by the Ministry of Education of the Republic of Korea and the National Research Foundation of Korea (NRF-2019S1A3A2098438)

2 Literature Review

2.1 Platform Business and Its Complaints

Platform business is made upon the relationships between stakeholders (e.g., in case of Airbnb, guests, peer hosts, and employees of the platform company) who make transactions and the ICTs that make the online transactions possible. It can be said that platform is composed of two dimensions: social dimension and technology dimension.

In the social dimension, hosts may perceive the relationship with the headquarters, customers, and peer hosts as stressors [6]. In addition, hosts may feel the transformations relatively abrupt and perceive it as stressor since individuals have to learn such things by themselves.

Against this backdrop, we define this specific stress that occurs from the social and technology dimensions of the platform business as "platform stress." In this research, we focused on the technology dimension and the further will be discussed below.

2.2 Platform Stress in the Technology Dimension - Technostress

Technology gave pressure to users, in our research hosts, who are not accustomed to the technology and thus have difficulty in handling it. This adaptation problem "caused by and inability to cope with the new computer technologies" was coined as "technostress" [7]. From the various previous study, researchers categorized these stressors mentioned above into 5 types: work-overload, complexity, uncertainty, job-insecurity, and job-invasion [8]. In this research, we focused on the first 3 factors since the platform business if far from job-insecurity and job-invasion, and rather created the opportunity on the basis of technology (Table 1).

Table 1. Definition of independent variables

Variable	Definition
PTC	The state which technology makes users feel inadequate and forces them to spend time and effort in learning and understanding it [8]
PTU	The state which technology continues to changes and upgrades and makes users unsettle and create uncertainty [8]
PWL	The state which the technology force users to work faster and longer [8]

Meanwhile, the technology dimension from platform stress is not the same with technostress. Platform stress is the specific burnout that service providers in the P2P platform business experience due to the relational and technological issues. Therefore, the former indicates the burnout that platform service providers (e.g., Airbnb hosts) experience and it may be the trigger for service providers to leave the platform whereas the employees experiencing the latter might not leave their organization since they are not individual business runners.

3 Research Model and Hypotheses Development

Technology as a stress factor causes hosts to feel burnout, which may ultimately make them leave the platform. Thus, we hypothesized as following:

H1a-3a: Platform technology complexity, -uncertainty, and -work overload is positively related to burnout.
H1b-3b: Platform technology complexity, -uncertainty, and -work overload is positively related to switching intention.

When employees feel a sense of strain, they no longer want to stay in the organization and instead hope to leave, which can be interpreted that the employees' burnout affects their switching intention [9]. Accordingly, people who work in stressful conditions are more likely to undergo burnout, and this burnout arises switching intention [10]. Therefore, we hypothesized as following (Fig. 1):

H4: Burnout is positively related to switching intention.

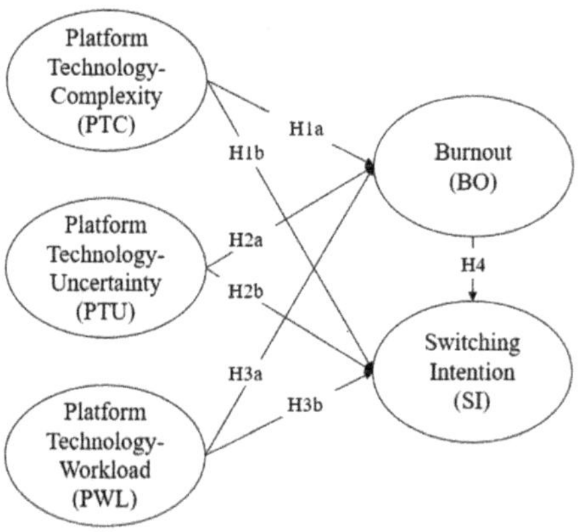

Fig. 1. Research model

4 Research Methodology

4.1 Data Collection

Measurement items were taken from prior literature, and content validity was checked to identify ambiguous definitions or questions that are difficult to answer. The survey was conducted through the online survey platform Qualtrics to the members of Airbnb hosts' internet community (Feb 23, 2021–Mar 07, 2021). Considering the statistical technique employed, the sample size was checked based on G*Power [11]. According to this, testing the proposed model required a minimum sample of 110 individuals for a statistical power of 0.95. Therefore, it can be safely concluded that the sample size used (157) was acceptable for the purposes of our research. Descriptive details such as gender (Male 47.13%, Female 52.87%) and age were almost equally distributed, whereas in location Seoul, the capital city, took half of the percentage (51.6%).

4.2 Results

Through partial least squares SEM (PLS-SEM) analyses using SmartPLS 3.0 [12], Cronbach's alpha and composite reliabilities all exceeded the threshold value of 0.70, all indicator loadings and all AVE values exceed each threshold value of 0.60 and 0.50 cut-off, supporting convergent validity. Fornell and Larcker criterion and the factor loading were confirmed supporting discriminant validity.

As Table 2 shows, hypotheses regarding the relations of each stressor and burnout are all supported, whereas relations of switching intention are all rejected. In addition, the relations of burnout and switching intention is supported. It demonstrates that stressors do not directly provoke platform switching intention but do indirectly provoke when burnout mediates in between. Further, the R^2 values for dependent variable burnout and switching intention were 0.53 and 0.32, respectively.

Table 2. Result of hypotheses testing

Hypothesis	Path	β	P	Result
H1a	PTC → BO	0.284	0.001**	Supported
H1b	PTC → SI	0.029	0.788	Rejected
H2a	PTU → BO	0.243	0.003**	Supported
H2b	PTU → SI	0.161	0.184	Rejected
H3a	PWL → BO	0.352	0.000***	Supported
H3b	PWL → SI	0.220	0.062	Rejected
H4	BO → SI	0.274	0.013*	Supported

4.3 Mediating Effects

To further examine the mediating effects of burnout, our research conducted VAF analysis through PLS-SEM bootstrapping technique [13]. Table 3 shows the result that burnout has partial mediating effects on the relationships between each of PTC, PTU,

Table 3. Result of mediating effects testing

Path	Coeff of P1	Coeff of P2	Coeff of P3	VAF	Result
PTC → BO → SI	0.284**	0.274*	0.029	0.729	Partial mediation
PTU → BO → SI	0.243**		0.161	0.293	Partial -
PWL → BO → SI	0.352***		0.220	0.305	Partial -

Note: P1 = independent variable(iv) → mediator(m), P2 = mediator(m) → dependent variable(dv), P3 = independent variable(iv) → dependent variable(dv); VAF = (βiv-m * βm-dv)/(βiv-m * βm-dv + βiv-dv), More than .80 = full mediation; .20–.80 = partial mediation; Less than .20 = no mediation.

PWL and SI. It can be interpreted that while stressors of platform technology complexity, -uncertainty, and -work overload do not directly arise switching intention, it merely does when mediated by burnout.

5 Conclusions

We tried to explore the new type of stress and newly defined it as "Platform Stress." This research especially focused on the technology dimension, reflecting the dependency technology dimension, and highlighting the importance of it. Theoretical implication is provided by extending the understanding of technostress and proposing the concept of platform stress. Managerial implication is provided by suggesting that not only stressors themselves, but also controlling burnout is essential to keep hosts from leaving the platform. Limitations of the research are found in restricted platform (Airbnb), market (South Korea), and industry (accommodation). Future research is expected to be conducted in more diverse platform, market, and industry.

References

1. Wirtz J, So KKF, Mody MA, Liu SQ, Chun HH (2019) Platforms in the peer-to-peer sharing economy. J Serv Manag 30(4):452–483
2. Pînzaru FM, Mitan A, Mihalcea AD (2018) Reshaping competition in the age of platforms: the winners of the sharing economy. In: Vătămănescu E-M, Pînzaru FM (eds) Knowledge management in the sharing economy, vol 6. KMOL. Springer, Cham, pp 19–38. https://doi.org/10.1007/978-3-319-66890-1_2
3. Lin PM, Fan DX, Zhang HQ, Lau C (2019) Spend less and experience more: understanding tourists' social contact in the Airbnb context. Int J Hosp Manag 83:65–73
4. Park S, Tussyadiah IP (2020) How guests develop trust in hosts: an investigation of trust formation in P2P accommodation. J Travel Res 59(8):1402–1412
5. Lee H, Yang SB, Koo C (2019) Exploring the effect of Airbnb hosts' attachment and psychological ownership in the sharing economy. Tour Manage 70:284–294
6. Shaukat R, Yousaf A, Sanders K (2017) Examining the linkages between relationship conflict, performance and turnover intentions: role of job burnout as a mediator. Int J Conf Manag 28(1):4–23. https://doi.org/10.1108/IJCMA-08-2015-0051
7. Brod C (1982) Managing technostress: optimizing the use of computer technology. Pers J 61 (10):753–757
8. Tarafdar M, Tu Q, Ragu-Nathan BS, Ragu-Nathan TS (2007) The impact of technostress on role stress and productivity. J Manag Inf Syst 24(1):301–328
9. Shi X, Gordon S, Tang CH (2021) Momentary well-being matters: Daily fluctuations in hotel employees' turnover intention. Tour Manag 83:104212
10. Sonnentag S, Fritz C (2007) The recovery experience questionnaire: development and validation of a measure for assessing recuperation and unwinding from work. J Occup Health Psychol 12(3):204
11. Faul F, Erdfelder E, Lang AG, Buchner A (2007) G* power 3: a flexible statistical power analysis program for the social, behavioral, and biomedical sciences. Behav Res Methods 39 (2):175–191

12. Hair JF, Ringle CM, Sarstedt M (2011) PLS-SEM: indeed a silver bullet. J Market Theory Pract 19(2):139–152
13. Hair Jr JF, Hult GTM, Ringle CM, Sarstedt M (2021) A primer on partial least squares structural equation modeling (PLS-SEM). Sage publications

8

Identifying the Elements of Great Online Customer Encounters

Johanna Heinonen[1(✉)] and Juho Pesonen[2]

[1] LAB University of Applied Sciences, Lappeenranta, Finland
Johanna.heinonen@lab.fi
[2] University of Eastern Finland, Joensuu, Finland
juho.pesonen@uef.fi

Abstract. Customer service is a major factor in the success of digital marketing. This study examines the service encounters between tourists and service providers, in this case, Visit Helsinki. The goal is to understand what are the dimensions of service quality in online chat discussions between tourists and DMO personnel and what elements in these discussions support the co-creation of great customer experiences. Altogether 123 chat discussions in June 2020 were downloaded and analysed using qualitative content analysis and statistical tests. The results show that great customer experiences are the result of extensive effort from the customer service agents where they go beyond just providing a satisfactory solution for the customer. The results are managerially important for destinations and tourism businesses around the world and increase the theoretical understanding of the moment of truth concept and its different elements in online service encounters.

Keywords: Customer service · Online service · Customer satisfaction · Customer value · Chat service

1 Introduction

1.1 Background

One of the most critical elements in producing services is the customer encounter, a situation where the customer and the service provider meet each other [1]. This service encounter is increasingly happening online. Furthermore, the challenge is not only to provide high-quality services as such but also to communicate with customers in such a manner that the service exceeds their expectations. This does not only improve customer satisfaction but also helps the company to improve its processes more effectively, motivate its personnel and build the company image and reputation successfully [1]. When encountering a customer in an online medium, the company finds itself in a situation where the old face-to-face service procedures do not work anymore. Without gestures, mimes, and tone of voice, the written context becomes essential as well as the technical elements like speed and visual design [2].

The demand for online services has increased during the past years [3–6]. Already in 2015 fifty-seven per cent of customers preferred to contact companies online [7] and the number has not at least decreased. Customers are often found complaining about bad online service that is the result of, for example, unanswered questions [6], unpolite customer service agents [5], or unkept promises [6].

Research of online customer service has focused on technical issues, like information quality, website design, social media, and the role of chatbots or self-service [8], among others. Several researchers [e.g. 8, 9] have suggested more research on the moment of truths in technology-mediated encounters and thus improve the understanding of the critical elements in online customer service.

The purpose of this study is to increase understanding of the elements of great service in customer online service encounters. The study is inspired by Bitner and Wang [10], who encouraged researchers to study the prerequisites of good service in micro-level conversations in technology-mediated encounters. This study first identifies the elements of service quality in online chat discussions and then analyses how they support or undermine a great customer online service experience.

2 Theoretical Framework

2.1 Customer Service Encounter

Customer encounter can be considered as the core competence of a service business [11]. However, the concept of customer service is complex. Depending on the perspective and the author, it can be seen as a momentary interaction, as an offering – a package – of services, [12] or as a longer process [13] that is affected by actors not visible in the service event or outside of it, i.e. other customers and online reviews. Traditionally, service has taken place in direct customer encounters, usually in the face-to-face meetings between the customer and the service provider [14]. In a service encounter, a customer and a service provider interact and participate actively [12] in core service, i.e. in a moment of truth [9, 10], a unique situation, in which the perceptions of customers are tested.

Many companies have realized the meaning of service encounters online and invested in more effective customer–technology interactions in the moment of truth [8]. These interactions can happen in many channels. Customer's capabilities, the availability of technology and, also, the co-creative role customer plays, determines which channel the customer chooses. Today, service encounters can be divided into three different types: remote encounters, phone encounters, and face-to-face encounters [15]. ICT-mediated service encounters are part of the remote encounters.

Larivière et al. [16] talk about service encounter 2.0 which they define as follows: "any customer-company interaction that results from a service system that is comprised of interrelated technologies (either company-or customer-owned), human actors (employees and customers), physical/digital environments and company/customer processes." These service encounter 2.0s are increasingly important in the tourism field and a much better understanding of these encounters is needed to provide customers with the service that they expect and that even might delight them.

2.2 Online Service Encounters and Service Quality

Service quality depends on how customers' experiences are equivalent to customers' expectations, i.e. the customer is always the one who decides how the service experience was and this judgment can vary from one customer to another [12, 17] The main issue in producing high-quality services is to fulfil customers' expectations or even exceed them [15]. Service quality is traditionally defined through five variables: tangibles, reliability, responsiveness, assurance and empathy [17–19]. *Tangibles* include the place where service is produced, the equipment that is used as well as written materials. With *reliability* researchers refer to a company's capability to perform the service it promises to its customer's. *Responsiveness* means the company's ability to give customers the help they need to provide the demanded service. *Assurance* is an outcome of employees' professionalism, knowledge and polite behaviour as well as the way they create trust and confidence. *Empathy* includes listening and personal, tailor-made attention to each separate customer [18].

These traditional elements are further defined and developed by Jawardheena [19], Ansari [20], Miceli [21], and Immonen [22] in the online setting. Most of these are adapted from the traditional model with specific emphasis on challenges caused by the technology environment. Quality elements in an online setting are called Effectiveness, Responsiveness, Politeness and Personalization by the researchers [19–22]. *Effectiveness* is defined as the ability to answer customer requests fast without delays. Also, if delays should appear, it is mentioned that customers should be informed of them and their length instantly. *Responsiveness* is characterized by solving customer problems and fulfilling customer expectations. *Politeness* refers to service providers professionalism, trustfulness and polite behaviour and can be analysed through thanking, apologising and way of greeting customers. With *personalization,* each customer gets tailor-made service, targeted especially to him to answer his questions and solve his problems [19–22]. Also, the length of the text, its structure and readability are important factors in online encounters [23], but precise effects of these on customer online experience in tourism are still largely unexplored.

Figure 1 builds upon the aforementioned literature to form a framework for analysing service quality elements. In addition to the traditional service quality elements, the online context adds several new perspectives that need to be accounted for.

Studies from online shopping have shown some central flaws in encounters causing dissatisfaction [24]. These are a failure in technology, failure in processes or failure in customer interaction. Also, slowness, easiness, competence and attitude were considered important factors. Customers wanted the service or the service agent to "get it done" while the service should be easy, effortless and enjoyable for the customer. This can be considered as part of the Responsiveness element.

Many authors [25–27] have stated that web 2.0 has not only a great effect on customer experience but also plays a major role in creating them. Thus digital service encounters should be taken into account during every step of the customer journey. Requirements for successful online presence during the customer journey lies in the understanding of the customer and his or her needs [28]. In all steps, it is important to activate the customer and create an interactive, collaborative and continual atmosphere online [29].

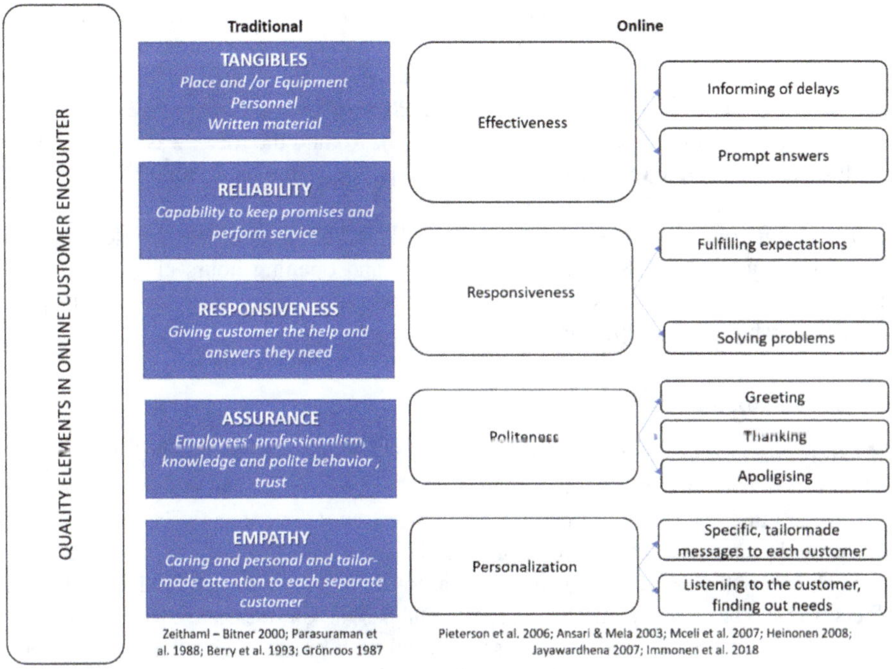

Fig. 1. The adapted framework of service quality elements

The service value, and thereby also the customer experience, has its grounds in either the tangible benefits customer experiences by participating in the service co-creation or the emotional benefits [22, 30]. This is also supported by the concept of customer engagement, which describes customers mental state and conviction when she or he feels committed and safe in a co-creative customer relationship [29]. Thus an important element to study is also Customer responses.

3 Research

3.1 Target Group and Data Collection

In this study, the framework presented in Fig. 1 is used to study online customer encounters and improve our understanding of the online service quality elements. We focus on understanding how the service quality elements contribute to customer service that exceeds customer expectations. Distinguishing great service from satisfactory service provides an even deeper understanding of the customer encounters online.

Data for this study were collected during June 2020 among Visit Helsinki chat users. Visit Helsinki is one of the biggest DMOs (Destination Management Organisation) in Finland. Chat users included both Finnish (domestic) and foreign customers asking for information about services and attractions in Helsinki. Two service agents from Visit Helsinki responded to all these discussions.

In total, data included 123 discussions that lasted 18 min on average and included 1623 lines in total (including both service agents' and customer's lines). Even though this might sound like a proper amount of data, it is still limited to the COVID-19 situation all over the world during summer 2020.

Data were analysed as anonymous with SPSS 27.0 and the focus was merely on the discussions and service quality elements in them. Due to the anonymity, it is assumed that all 123 discussions had a different, unique customer.

The main topics in these discussions involved different events in Helsinki (20 discussions), activities (18), opening hours (15) and opening hours (11 discussions). Surprisingly, there were also quite a many customers asking about jobs, entrepreneurship and co-operation in Helsinki (13 in total).

3.2 Methodology

The study can be described as abductive [31], since it starts with everyday observations and descriptions concerning online customer service, and then moves for deeper analysis and understanding of them based on literature. Content analysis was chosen as the research approach as it allows a holistic view and generalisation of the chat material, but at the same time, it provides a possibility for a deeper understanding of effects [32]. The cornerstone in content analysis is on messages. It provides an objective and systematic way to analyse material with preset, theory-based categories. Its nature is descriptive, not explanatory [32].

The analysis involved coding and categorizing the data first into four main service quality elements, based on the framework presented in Fig. 1: Effectiveness, Responsiveness, Politeness and Personalization. Each discussion was carefully read and each line from the text-based chat data was placed underneath a suitable category. Delays and lengths were calculated and the appearance of analysis elements was quantified as 0 (not existing) or 1 (existing).

For a deeper understanding, the service elements were divided into subcategories, with help of which the qualitative data was modified in a quantified form, which enables to better distinguish the connection between the elements and customer satisfaction.

Effectiveness included two sub-categories: length of delay in minutes and information on whether the customer was informed of the delays. *Responsiveness* refers to service agents' response and action, and whether the discussion fulfilled the expectations and solved the problems of the customer. Also, during the analysis of data, two extra subcategories for analysis of Responsiveness arose. These were "Giving alternatives and links" and "Providing the customer further contact information". *Politeness* was studied based on phrases the service agent used. Phrases like greeting and thanking and apologizing were interpreted as polite. *Personalization* was analysed based on whether the service agent asked further questions to find out the needs of a customer and whether he showed effort for fulfilling the needs.

Visit Helsinki did not have any satisfaction measurement system in place in their online chat. To define the outcomes of the customer discussions were analysed and 19 cases where the customer praised the encounter or the customer service agent at the end of the encounter (see Example 1) were identified These cases were coded as great customer service encounters and the differences between these and the other encounters were analysed using statistical methods (Table 1). Even though it is possible that in some additional cases customers experienced great service, the 19 cases selected surely belonged to that category as customers took additional actions to praise the service. The quantified topics in the discussions were based on the framework presented in Fig. 1.

Example 1.

10:47:20 | Visitor	*Heippa! Onko siellä joku paikalla? :) /Hi! Anyone there?*
10:47:50 | XX	*Moikka! Täällä ollaan :) / Hello! Here we are*
10:47:54 | Visitor	*Mahtavaa! Hei, minulla on tällainen kysymys: / Great, I have this kind of question*
	...
11:17:51 | Visitor	*OHHHHH <3 <3 <3 <3*
11:17:59 | Visitor	*täydellistäääää / Perfect*
	...
11:30:02 | Visitor	*Mihin voin kannella tästä erinomaisesta palvelusta :D / Where can I tell about excellent service?*

3.3 Findings

In total there were 123 discussions from 22 days in June 2020. The majority of the discussion was in Finnish (83) and the rest (41) in English. Most of the discussions concerned topics like events (20), opening hours (15), activities (18), cooperation with Visit Helsinki (10), attractions (11) and cooking places (7).

The first element of service quality (Table 1), *Effectiveness*, shows that in great service, the customer service agents (SA) kept the customer better on track about what is happening by informing them about delays and wait times. Delay times and lengths of discussions were longer in services resulting in a great service experience. It could be that long delays in a discussion can be alleviated by keeping the customer on track with what is happening. With longer delays, the discussions took longer in great online service encounters than in other discussions. In these great customer encounters the SAs used considerably much more lines than in other discussions, even though the customers messaged equally much in both cases.

Responsiveness analysed whether the customer's problem was solved and whether the customer expectations were fulfilled. Based on our analysis, 67% (83) of discussions solved the problem and 28% (35) fulfilled expectations. All the customer encounters resulting in customers praising the service were coded as fulfilling expectations and solving problems, as these encounters probably even exceeded expectations.

When analysing *Politeness*, we can see that in great service encounters SAs greeted and thanked the customers more than in normal customers encounters. Also, SAs used more emoticons in encounters resulting in great experiences compared to normal encounters.

Table 1. Comparing effects of service elements on great online customer service

Variables	Normal service (n = 104)	Great service (n = 19)	Statistically significant difference
Effectiveness			
Informing of delays and waiting			$X^2 = 12.03$, df = 2, p = 0.002
0 times	51.9%	36.8%	
1 time	44.2%	36.8%	
2 or 3 times	3.8%	26.3%	
Prompt answers			
Delay in minutes	8.2 min (SD = 6.8)	14.7 min (SD = 10.4)	Mann-Whiteny U-test p = 0.003
Length of discussion in minutes	20.0 min (SD = 21.7)	27.1 min (SD = 16.0)	Mann-Whiteny U-test p = 0.013
Number of SA lines in the discussion (mean)	6.9 (SD = 3.6)	16.0 (SD = 11.0)	Mann-Whiteny U-test p < 0.001
Number of customer lines in the discussion (mean)	4.9 (SD = 5.5)	5.0 (3.2)	n.s.
Responsiveness			
Fulfilling expectations	15.4%	100%	
Solving problems	61.2%	100%	
Customers repeating themselves in discussion	4.8%	0%	n.s.
Politeness			
SA greeting the customer			$X^2 = 9.44$, df = 2, p = 0.009
1 time	19.2%	5.3%	
2 times	49.0%	26.3%	
3 or 4 times	31.7%	68.4%	
SA thanking the customer			$X^2 = 10.45$, df = 2, p = 0.005
0 times	46.2%	21.1%	
1 time	46.2%	47.4%	
2 times	7.7%	31.6%	
SA apologising from the customer			n.s.
0 times	93.3%	94.7%	
1 time	4.8%	5.3%	
2 or 3 times	2.0%	0%	
Number of emoticons used by the customer (mean)	1.6 (SD = 0.8)	1.9 (SD = 1.3)	n.s.
Number of emoticons used by the SA (mean)	1.6 (SD = 0.8)	3.7 (SD = 2.4)	Mann-Whiteny U-test p = 0.015

(*continued*)

Table 1. *(continued)*

Variables	Normal service (n = 104)	Great service (n = 19)	Statistically significant difference
Personalization			
SA asking for further information	22.1%	57.9%	Fisher's Exact Test $p < 0.001$
SA giving an effort for finding the best solution	11.5%	52.6%	Fisher's Exact Test $p < 0.001$
Links per discussion in average	1.2 (SD = 1.2)	3.3 (SD = 2.6)	Mann-Whiteny U-test $p < 0.001$

In *Personalization,* the results show that the efforts SAs put into the service encounter matters significantly. The more information they find and the better the solution solves the customer problems, the more likely it is that the customer encounter is great from the customer perspective.

4 Discussion and Conclusions

The purpose of the research was to find out how service quality elements are represented in online chat discussions and how they support achieving a great service experience. A framework for elements was created based on the literature [17–22] and divided into four main elements: Responsiveness, Effectiveness, Politeness and Personalization. The framework was partially adapted from the traditional service quality literature. In the data analysis, some elements were added and also customer response part was included. The four elements with added customer response information are suitable to analyze online discussions. Naturally, the online environment adds specific elements like emoticons and sending links to the service encounters, which were also included in this study.

Based on the data, we can see great customer service online is provided with the same elements as it is in a live situation. Solving the customer's problem and even exceeding his expectations is the key in an online chat environment [6]. While lacking mimes, tone of voice and gestures of face-to-face encounters, online customer encounters have other ways to create great service experiences.

It is important to inform them about changes and what is happening. This concerns as well the delays as the change of service agent. The findings of this study are in accordance with Meuter et al. [33] and van Dolen et al. [34] and indicate dissatisfaction among customers when delays were long without any notice. It might also indicate distrust when a customer is facing a new person without warning. The results show that taking a long time to answer questions does reduce the quality of online service if the customer is updated with what is happening and gets the information they seek in the end. This is also supported by Jayawardhena [19] and even mentioned in the traditional framework [17]. When customers do not see what is happening on the other side very few customers wait or respond to the delayed answers, which can be considered as a sign of unsatisfaction [6].

Also, the style of communication was important in data. Personalized, polite and trustful experiences do not include mass messages. Thanking the customer is essential.

Based on these elements, we can provide an answer for Bitner and Wang's question "What precisely is good service in micro-level conversations in technology-mediated encounters?" It is caring about the customer and showing him that with elements from politeness like thanking, greeting, using emoticons and asking questions. Great customer service is also created when the service agent invests in the customer and goes to great lengths to solve his problem. This does not happen by merely posting links or giving telephone numbers and email addresses, it requires more personal touch and more extensive communication of information.

To conclude, service quality is always the customer's subjective experience. To provide superior service, a company must think and act from the customer perspective [7]. However, experiential customer service needs still some sharpening. From the destination marketing point of view, this is most likely something in common for many destinations. Great customer service needs resources to allow customer service agents to spend enough time to craft detailed, personalized and effective communication. It is possible to solve customer problems with fewer resources, but great service encounters typically need more time and effort. This is also the managerial implication of this paper.

Since the literature on online customer service quality and experiences in service encounters is more concentrated on technical and structural elements of service, this study elaborates on the complexity of achieving a competitive advantage in online customer service. It also tests the elements from the literature and brings some deeper understanding to them. The results demonstrate that many caveats can result in non-satisfied customers. Satisfaction can be considered as the minimum level to achieve and to build upon. The next step would be to create unique, experiential customer service to gain a competitive advantage, i.e. to have great customer service. However, more research on this topic is needed.

Figure 1 demonstrates that experiential aspects of online customer service are still missing from the literature. The findings of this study demonstrate that tourism organizations can have difficulties in reaching satisfactory customer service levels. As a result, cases, where online customer services can be considered experiential, are difficult to find and analyse. For further studies, it is important to deepen the research to the emotional state and thus analyse the discussions with the emotional and sentimental elements. It is also worth studying the customer point of view to ensure the proper interpretations.

References

1. 2021 Customer Expectations Report: What Customers Expect From a Modern Online Shopping Experience. Gladly. https://www.gladly.com/reports/2021-customer-expectations-report/. Accessed 15 Oct 2021
2. Lennon R, Harris J (2002) Customer_service on the web: a cross-industry investigation. J Target Meas Anal Market 10(4):325 338

3. Januszewska M, Jaremen DE, Nawrocka E (2015) The effects of the use of ICT by tourism enterprises. Serv Manag 2(16):65–73
4. Ficarelli S, Sendra S, Ferrando L, Lloret J (2013) Effects of web technologies on tourism industry in some southern European countries. In: quaestus multidisciplinary research journal. Proceedings of WEB 2013: the first international conference on building and exploring web based environments, pp 49–56
5. Sehgal H Customer Experience Statistics Which Will Impact Your Business in 2016. https://www.ameyo.com/blog/customer-experience-statistics-which-will-impact-your-business-in-2016. Accessed 18 Oct 2021
6. 2020 CGS Customer Services Preferences in Times of Distress Survey. https://www.cgsinc.com/en/resources/customer-service-in-crisis. Accessed 18 Oct 2021
7. Customer Service Stats for 2020. https://www.customerthermometer.com/customer-service/customer-service-and-satisfaction-statistics-for-2020/. Accessed 18 Oct 2021
8. Buhalis D (2019) Technology in tourism-from information communication technologies to eTourism and smart tourism towards ambient intelligence tourism: a perspective article. Tour Rev **75**(1), 267–272
9. Voorhees CM et al (2017) Service encounters, experiences and the customer journey: defining the field and a call to expand our lens. J Bus Res 79:269–280
10. Bitner MJ, Wang HS (2014) Service encounters in service marketing research. In: Rust RT, Huang M-H (eds) Handbook of service marketing research. Edward Elgar Publishing Limited: Massachusettes
11. Carson D, Cromie S, McGowan P, Hill J (1995) Marketing and entrepreneurship in SMEs: an innovative approach. Prentice-Hall International, Great Britain
12. Grönroos C (2000) Creating a relationship dialogue: communication, interaction and value. The Market Rev No 1:5–14
13. Surprenant CF, Solomon MR (1987) Predictability and Personalization in the Service Encounter. J Market 51(2):86–96
14. Normann R (1991) Service management strategy and leadership in service businesses, 2nd edn. John Wiley and Sons, Chichester
15. Zeithaml V, Bitner J, Gremler DD (2013) Services marketing: integrating customer focus across the firm. McGraw-Hill, New York. 6th ed. -Item scale for measuring consumer perceptions of service quality. Journal of Retailing. 64, Spring, pp 12–40
16. Larivière B et al (2017) Service encounter 2.0: an investigation into the roles of technology, employees and customers. J Bus Res 79:238–246
17. Parasuraman A, Zeithaml V, Berry LL (1988) SERVQUAL: a multiple-item scale for measuring consumer perceptions of service quality. J Retail **64**(1), 12–40. Spring
18. Berry L, Parasuraman A, Zeithaml VA (2002) Ten lessons for improving service quality. marketing science institute's working paper series, Report 93-107. In: Witkowski TH, Wolfinbarger MF. (eds.) Comparative service quality, German and American ratings across service settings, Journal of Business Research 55, pp 875–881
19. Jayawardhena C (2007) Outcomes of service encounter quality in a business-to-business context. Ind Mark Manage 36(5):575–588
20. Ansari A, Mela CF (2003) E-customization. J Mark Res 40:131–145
21. Miceli G, Ricotta F, Costabile M (2007) Customizing customization: a conceptual framework for interactive personalization. J Inter Market **21**(2):6–25
22. Immonen M, Sintonen S, Koivuniemi J (2018) The value of human interaction in service channels. Comput Hum Behav 78(2018):316–325
23. Mihalcescu C, Sion B, Marginean A (2016) The development, success and impact of electronic tourism in the digital age. J Inf Syst Operat Manag Bucharest **10**(2), 416–424

24. Ranaweera C (2005) A model of online customer behavior during the initial transaction: moderating effects of customer characteristics. Mark Theory 5(1):51–74
25. Mihajlović I (2014) ICT and new trends in consumer behaviour - new experiential knowledge. Opportunities or challenges for intermediaries. J Market Manag **2**(1):43–46
26. Buhalis D, Law R (2008) Progress in information technology and tourism management: 20 years on and 10 years after the Internet—The state of eTourism research. Tour Manage 29 (4):609–623
27. Neuhofer B, Buhalis D, Ladkin A (2014) A typology of technologyenhanced tourism experiences. Int J Tour Res 16:340–350
28. Cohen AS, Prayag G, Moital M (2014) Consumer behaviour in tourism: concepts, influences and opportunities. Curr Issue Tour 17(10):872–909
29. Ge J (2014) Tourism marketing communications on a chinese social media platform. In: eProceedings of the ENTER 2014 PhD workshop - information and communication technologies in tourism 2014, pp 11–19
30. Collier JE, Barnes DC (2015) Self-service delight: exploring the hedonic aspects of self-service. J Bus Res 68(5):986–993
31. Kovalainen A, Eriksson P (2015) Qualitative methods in business research. Sage, A Practical Guide to Social Research
32. Neuendorf KA (2004) Content analysis: a contrast and complement to discourse analysis. Qual Methods Spring 2004:33–36
33. Meuter ML, Ostrom AL, Roundtree RI, Bitner MJ (2000) Self-service technologies: understanding customer satisfaction with technology-based service encounters. J Mark 64 (3):50–64
34. van Dolen W, de Ruyter K (2002) Moderated group chat: an empirical assessment of a new e-service encounter. Int J Serv Ind Manag 13(5):496–511

Special Track on Big Data and Smart Tourism

9

Destination Image of DMO and UGC on Instagram

Roman Egger(✉), Oguzcan Gumus, Elza Kaiumova, Richard Mükisch and Veronika Surkic

Salzburg University of Applied Sciences, Salzburg, Austria
{roman.egger, ogumus.imte-m2019, ekaiumova.imte-m2019, rmuekisch.imte-m2019, vsurkic.imte-m2019}@fh-salzburg.ac.at

Abstract. Social media plays a key role in shaping the image of a destination. Although recent research has investigated factors influencing online users' perception towards destination image, limited studies encompass and compare social media content shared by tourists and destination management organisations (DMOs) at the same time. This paper aims to determine whether the projected image of DMOs corresponds with the destination image perceived by tourists. By taking the Austrian Alpine resort Saalbach-Hinterglemm as a case, a netnographic approach was applied to analyse the visual and textual posts of DMO and user-generated content (UGC) on Instagram using machine learning. The findings reveal themes that are not covered in the posts published by marketers but do appear in UGC. This study adds to the existing literature by providing a deeper insight into destination image formation and uses a qualitative approach to assess destination brand image. It further highlights practical implications for the industry regarding DMOs' social media marketing strategy.

Keywords: Machine learning · Instagram · Destination image

1 Introduction

The rise of social media has changed the process of information creation and communication, which affects consumer behaviour, marketing strategies, and brand image [1]. Social media further fosters the production of user-generated content (UGC), referring to any content created by consumers online [2]. Meanwhile, UGC has become a more critical source of information for consumers due to its richness, diversity [3], and authenticity [4] compared to traditional advertising and official sources. One industry that relies heavily on communication technologies is tourism. Since UGC can influence brand image creation and consumer behaviour [3, 5], social media is earning a leading role in the multiphasic travel stages, from pre-, during-, to post-travel experiences, for information gathering and sharing [1]. Recent literature further reinforces that a destination's online image positively affects consumer behaviour in increasing one's intention to visit, revisit, or recommend the destination [5–7]. Notably, destination image has become a multifaceted concept by considering both the attributes of a destination as well as the sum of beliefs and impressions a tourist has [8]. Seeing that official information provided by destination marketing organisations (DMOs) no longer has absolute control over image creation [5], DMOs are suggested to be aware of tourists' perception of the destination in order to develop quality marketing campaigns [2]. This can be determined through UGC analysis, which enables marketers to view destinations from tourists' perspectives and discover what they are most interested in [9]. Yet, despite the importance of image congruence [10], scholars in the field of destination marketing mainly analyse the image created by tourists [2] *or* DMOs [11] rather than comparing both contexts at the same time [12].

To close the aforementioned research gaps, this study aims to identify destination image on social media by analysing both UGC and content published through official tourist board channels. With a particular focus on Instagram, one of the many channels heavily used by (young) tourists [3], this study adopts the destination Saalbaach–Hintergelmm in the Alpine region of Austria as its research context. Specifically, through the use of netnography supported by machine learning approaches, this paper evaluates whether tourists' image of the destination corresponds to the image the DMO attempts to promote. Meanwhile, this study also examines how UGC can be used to plan and develop social media marketing activities for DMOs. Shaping destination image is vital for official institutions in order to attract tourists, consumers, events, and investors [2]. This study advances methodological approaches by using machine learning techniques to shed light on the differences between projected and perceived destination image on Instagram. By outlining the textual and visual content analysis, this research contributes to tourism marketers optimising social media storytelling and marketing strategies.

2 Literature Review

The ubiquity of communication technologies and social media has changed users' attitudes and behaviours, and provides everyone with an opportunity to generate online content. Social media platforms such as Instagram, Facebook, and Snapchat involve common instances of UGC in tourism, where users can create their own content in the form of texts, images, comments, or messages [10]. In the tourism industry, UGC not only reflects the preferences, beliefs, and emotions of tourists regarding their travel experience [13], but it also shapes the image of a destination. As tourists actively look for inspiration and explore other users' experiences, the association of images delivered through pictures or texts on social networks plays an important role in influencing visitor satisfaction and future behaviour [14].

Due to globalisation and increasingly fierce competition, various branding strategies are now being developed in most destinations [15]. One way to position a destination better is to adapt to the development of online communication tools. More specifically, seeing that social media has weakened the traditional role of DMOs as a leading source of information for visitors [16], marketers nowadays are inclined to include social platforms in their marketing activities. In doing so, DMOs can co-create content with tourists so as to maintain competitiveness and gain online visibility [17, 18]. The significance of DMOs' social platforms is evidenced by the fact that it is embedded in tourist activities' planning processes [19]. The delivered content can support visitors during their travel [18], thereby reinforcing the need for DMOs to optimise social media marketing strategies and to face high competition in the tourism industry [20].

Amongst the various available channels, Instagram has not only been embraced by tourists as a trendy platform [4] but is also well-liked by marketers to create compelling marketing strategies [11, 21]. Characterised as a highly visual platform, approximately 1 billion monthly active users and 95 million photos shared per day on Instagram were recorded, as of 2020 [22]. In tourism marketing, the implication of online photography is to shape a positive perception of a particular destination. Moreover, this platform offers a space where the projected and perceived destination image are intertwined. The UGC as an agent of perceived destination image formation is a key factor in the destination choice process. Thus, it is crucial to consider the effect of UGC on the destination image when setting up marketing strategies.

A number of studies focus on comparing the destination image positioned by official sources with the destination image perceived by users of various kinds of social media, by applying content analysis. For example, the studies conducted by Stepchenkov and Jean [23] and Tussyadiah [24] compared images gathered from the DMO website and Flickr, while Song and Kim [25] contrasted the image of Guangzhou, positioned by the DMO on Twitter, with its image on Pinterest. The relevance of the comparison between the promoted destination image and the destination image revealed from the UGC has been proved by Jiménez-Barreto et al. [6] and Chang J-H, Wang S-H [26]. These studies confirmed that congruence between the projected and perceived destination images decreases the possible deviation of expectation from reality, thus affecting brand credibility, tourist satisfaction, and visit intentions.

Despite the fact that the destination image has been the subject of debate since the last century [27], content analysis for destination image marketing insights is fairly novel. The current study complements the body of work on this topic by applying content analysis combined with the use of machine learning.

3 Methodology

To explore destination image presented by DMOs and tourists on Instagram, this study applied netnography as a research method. Additionally, the Alpine resort Saalbach–Hinterglemm in Austria was chosen as the research context. The following section outlines the data collection and analysis procedure.

3.1 Data Collection

Data was collected from public posts shared on Instagram using *Phantombuster*, an automated data crawling software. Figure 1 outlines the data collection process. For the collection of UGC, posts captioned with the hashtag #saalbachhinterglemm were extracted. Although the destination Saalbach–Hinterglemm has a notable summer and winter season, this study was narrowed down to include solely the posts from the 2019/2020 winter season so as to compare the posts published by users and the DMO within a defined time frame. In addition, only posts written in English were considered. The language recognition was performed in Python using the langdetect module.

Next, *Phantombuster* was used to obtain publicly available information about Instagram users who published the collected set of posts. This step was to filter out business accounts, whose posts might have been of commercial nature. The filtering process included the removal of profiles with the words "*saalbach*", "*hinterglemm*", "*leogang*", and "*fieberbrunn*" in the profile name or the bio, and the removal of profiles with an enlisted business email. Because the neighbouring villages Leogang and Fieberbrunn are parts of the same ski resort, those keywords were included. Ultimately, the filtering process resulted in a final set of 1,448 posts. A similar procedure was performed to obtain the Instagram posts published by the DMO in which a total of 2,091 posts shared via the official Tourist Board Saalbach-Hinterglemm account (@saalbach_com) were retrieved. Likewise, the posts were filtered to include the winter season and posts written in English, reaching a final number of 85 posts.

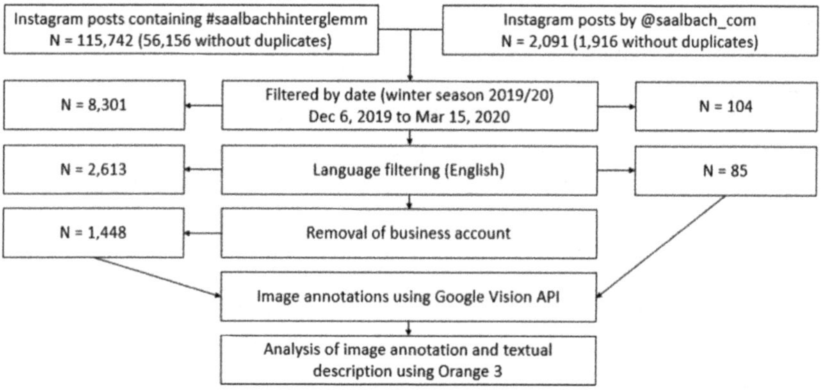

Fig. 1. Data collection process for UGC (left side) and DMO (right side) Instagram posts.

3.2 Data Analysis

For further analysis, both the DMO's and the users' Instagram posts were split into two elements (*images* and *textual description*), and the data was organised into four datasets: (1) DMO image annotations, (2) UGC image annotations, (3) DMO textual description, and (4) UGC textual description. The textual description refers to the caption of a post. To analyse pictorial content, Google Vision API was used to retrieve textual annotations of the images.

The annotations and the textual description were analysed with *Orange 3*, an open source machine learning software that enables textual data to be converted into features (i.e., vectors) [28]. In this research, the textual description and annotations of the images were treated as documents. As such, document embedding, which generates a vector for the document by embedding the words in the document [29], was applied using the pre-trained *fastText* model [31]. K-means clustering was then applied to group similar data points (vectorised annotations or vectorised textual descriptions) into clusters [32]. This method in particular was chosen to examine whether the posts could be divided into distinct clusters according to their content.

When applying the k-means algorithm, silhouette scores were calculated to identify an optimal number of clusters and to assure the reliability of the content analysis results. After obtaining the clusters, t-SNE dimensionality reduction was used for cluster visualisation in a scatter plot. The scatter plot thus presents the size and layout of the clusters in addition to which DMO posts overlap with the ones published by tourists, and, more importantly, where the DMO lacks posting coverage. The entire process was performed in the same manner for each of the four datasets mentioned above.

Subsequently, content analysis was carried out to identify emerging themes amongst the posts. A classical NLP pipeline [33] with lowercasing, removing stop-words, lemmatizing etc. was applied to pre-process the corpus. It included naming and categorising all the obtained clusters for both DMO and UGC annotations and textual descriptions based on TF-IDF (term frequency–inverse document frequency) weighting. Although state-of-the art NLP approaches such as BERT are available for text representation, studies show that for simple classification and clustering tasks conventional methods such as TF-IDF provide equivalent results [34]. Specifically, TF-IDF quantifies a word in the documents that implies the significance of a word to a document in the corpus. The results of each cluster were visualised with word clouds to gain a better understanding of data interpretation. Finally, the cluster categories were compared to find similarities and differences between the DMO and UGC Instagram posts. In this way, it was possible to assess the extent to which the DMO presentation on social media matched those of the users' destination image.

4 Results

4.1 Comparison of the DMO and UGC Image Annotations

The results suggest 8 clusters for the DMO image annotation and 3 clusters for the UGC annotation according to the silhouette scoring. Each of the 8 identified DMO clusters were named and categorised based on TF-IDF (i.e., words contributing to a cluster the most) as the following: *Mountainous winter landscape (5 clusters); Winter sports (1 cluster), and People and events (2 clusters)* (see Table 1). However, the clusters vary in size; clusters 1, 2, and 3 are more extensive than other clusters. Thus, the primary number of images represents the *winter mountain setting and the slopes*, whereas a smaller number of images portray *a person or a group engaged in winter activities*. Therefore, it can be concluded that the DMO concentrates mostly on creating a *winter mountain ambience*.

The same procedure was conducted for UGC annotations. Although UGC images' sample size is larger, the content seems to be more homogeneous. Thus, only 3 clusters were obtained. The clusters were named as follows: *People enjoying winter sports*; *Winter sports*; *Mountain landscape* (see Table 1). Compared to the amount of nature represented on the DMO images, the UGC images feature mainly *people*.

Table 1. Categorisation of clusters for DMO and UGC annotations.

Cluster	Words with the highest TF-IDF	Name	Category
DMO image annotations			
1	Snow Winter Sky Mountainous Landforms Mountain Geological Phenomenon Freezing Slope Mountain Range Glacial Landform	Mountainous landscape	Mountainous winter landscape
2	Snow Sky Winter Nature Geological Phenomenon Tree Cloud Freezing Atmospheric phenomenon mountain	Winter atmosphere	Mountainous winter landscape
3	Snow Winter Mountain Mountainous landforms Piste Hill station Geological phenomenon Slope Ridge Atmospheric phenomenon	Winter slopes	Mountainous winter landscape
4	Cable car Snow Cable car Winter Transport Geological phenomenon Sky Slope Hill station Vehicle	Cable car	Mountainous winter landscape
7	Sky Blue Pink Purple Cloud Red Winter Snow Violet Evening	Magical winter colours	Mountainous winter landscape
5	Skier Winter sport Recreation Slalom skiing Speed skiing Skiing Ski Ski Equipment Sports equipment Para-alpine skiing	Ski equipment	Winter sports
6	Crowd People Performance Rock concert Sky Concert Light Music venue Event Stage	Events / Crowd of people	People and events
8	Red Crowd Font Event Recreation Graphic design Team Art	Promotional posters	People and events
UGC image annotations			
1	Cool Friendship Selfie Fun Snapshot Black hair Photography Music venue Night Party	People enjoying winter sports, happy faces, ski wear	People and events
2	Skier Snow Freestyle skiing Sports Skiing Ski Winter sport Recreation Winter Sports equipment	Winter sports	Winter sports
3	Snow Mountainous landforms Mountain Winter Sky Mountain range Alps Hill station Cloud Recreation	Mountain landscape (nature, ski resort and infrastructure)	Mountainous winter landscape

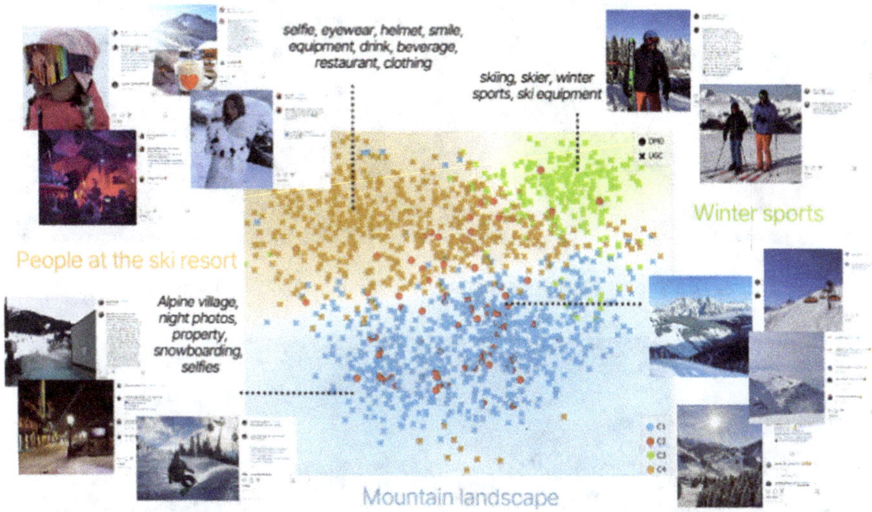

Fig. 2. Scatter plot of DMO and UGC overlaying images.

Next, this study visualises cluster layout/overlays (see Fig. 2) to which the scatter plot revealed 4 clusters. The cluster marked in red refers to the DMO image annotations, whereas the other 3 clusters reflect the UGC annotations. The plot indicates that the red dots representing the DMO posts overlap across the 3 UGC clusters, suggesting that the photos from the DMO match pictures posted by tourists. Yet, because several DMO photos in the orange and the green cluster do not overlay with UGC, further analysis was conducted to see which photos posted by tourists are not covered by DMO.

Cluster 4 (orange) represents the UGC content of *People at the ski resort*. Since the area involving cluster 4 does not overlay with cluster 2 (red colour), this was analysed further. The findings show that these photos refer to *leisure*, *entertainment,* and *people*, with the most prominent annotations being *selfie*, *eyewear*, *helmet*, *smile*, *equipment*, *drink*, *beverage*, *clothing*, etc. In other words, this sub-cluster represents the photos of people in their ski clothing taking pictures during their refreshment break at the restaurants and ski-huts on the slopes (see Fig. 3).

Cluster 3 (green) relates to *winter sports*, with photos depicting people during their skiing activities or engaging in other winter sports. The analysis of the DMO photos has similar categories (*Winter sports*; *Ski equipment*), meaning that the DMO posts also encompass this category. This is confirmed by the overlaying cluster 2 (DMO) and cluster 3 (UGC). However, the scatter plot implies that the photos in this category are represented to a far lesser extent by the DMO posts than the UGC posts.

Cluster 1 (blue) represents the UGC posts that overlay the most with those from the DMO (see Fig. 4). These photos represent the *mountain landscape* and show mostly mountainous panoramas and skiing resorts in a winter setting. The sub-clusters with no overlaying DMO posts are mostly photos of the *Alpine village* or the *property and accommodation*, especially *during the night hours*, as well as *snowboarding* and *selfies*, or photos of the *people on the slopes* in the *skiing equipment* doing *winter sports*.

Fig. 3. Examples of UGC images not overlaying with DMO images.

Fig. 4. Examples of overlaying UGC and DMO images.

5 Comparison of the DMO and UGC Textual Image Description

The comparison of DMO and UGC textual image description was conducted in the same manner as described for DMO and UGC annotations. Overall, key topics for the DMO include *winter* and *snow*, the promotion of *Salzburgerland* and *Skicircus* areas, the slogan '*Home of lässig*', and the events *FIS Alpine World Cup* in Saalbach and the *Freeride World Tour*. UGC has a broader topic of *a winter wonderland and the mountains*, *snowboarding* and *skiing activities*, and a seemingly well-accepted slogan of the ski resort '*Home of lässig*'. Overall, the results reveal a 5-cluster solution for the DMO and a 2-cluster solution for UGC. Similar to image annotations, there is a lower number of clusters for UGC textual content than DMO's, implying that UGC is more homogeneous and random, whereas the DMO posts are rather structured and planned.

The following categories for the DMO clusters were revealed: *The view from the local mountaintops*, *Nice conditions & invitation to come*, *Promotion of the FIS World Cup* and *the Freeride World Tour*, *A perfect day* (see Table 2). Cluster 2 (*Nice conditions & invitation to come*) is the largest and represents most of the DMO's content when it comes to textual descriptions. Cluster 3 contains a single post with no significant difference in the content; thus, it was assigned to cluster 2.

The two clusters from the UGC textual descriptions are approximately equal in size with the following categories: *Appreciation of nature and the winter activities during the winter holidays at the destination* and *Fun with friends and family* (see Table 2). Similar to the analysis with the image annotations, the DMO textual descriptions highlight nature and landscape, while UGC focuses more so on activities and people.

Table 2. Categorisation of clusters for DMO and UGC textual description.

Cluster	Content example	Cluster name
DMO textual description		
1	Today's view from the Schattberg down to Saalbach #saalbach #homeoflässig	The view from the local mountaintops
2	"Simply unbelievable what the @freerideworldtour athletes showed at yesterday's competitions in the @skicircus! We have some highlights for you. 😲 #saalbach #homeoflässig #skicircus #fieberbrunn #fwt20 #freerideworldtour 📷 fwt ddaher/jbernard"	Nice conditions, invitation to come, featuring a part of the ski resort; promotion of the destination and the events
3	The Audi Fis Ski World Cup in Saalbach Hinterglemm is on. 🥇🥈🥉We wish all the best for the racers! 🍀⛑ #saalbach #worldcupsaalbach #homeoflässig #fisalpine	Promotion of the FIS World Cup and the Freeride World Tour
4	morning rides 🌞 the perfect start into a beautiful day on the slopes #homeoflässig #saalbach #hinterglemm #skicircus @skicircus	A perfect day
UGC textual description		
1	Happiness is first tracks in fresh snow ❄🏂 #travel #happiness #saalbachhinterglemm #wintervacay #ski #traveldiary #travelgram #saalbach #austriaAT #skiislife #skyphotography #saalbach_com #saalbachhinterglemmleogangfieberbrunn #snow #winterwonderland #travelphotography #tagsforlikes #instadaily #instalike #photooftheday #naturelovers #photography📷 #skicircussaalbachhinterglemmleogangfieberbrunn	Appreciation of nature and the winter activities during the winter holidays at the destination
2	"Back at the slopes of #saalbachhinterglemm. Sunny weather and good company. ❄⛰🌞❤ #lovethemountains #skiing #fun #outsideisfree #austria 📷"	Fun with friends and family

6 Discussion

This study aims to compare the extent to which the marketed destination image corresponds to tourist experiences on Instagram. Specifically, UGC suggests topics such as *fun, social interaction, casual environment, outdoor activities,* and *winter sports*. These themes indicate that tourists perceive the resort as a relaxing and casual destination. In comparison, some other ski resorts build an image of a high-end resort, party destination, or family resort.

This study presents congruency between the projected and perceived destination image. Hence, this research affirms the importance of tourists' destination brand image, as mentioned in previous literature [6, 10, 12]. If tourist experiences correspond to the stories delivered by DMO, the brand credibility increases and consequently, user intentions to visit, revisit, or recommend the destination also increase [6]. Moreover, tourists create an emotional bond with a destination according to its personality by choosing the brands or destinations that fit their own style [18]. Destination personality is usually described using human characteristics based on the brand experience, such as *cool* or *exciting* [35].

This research reveals tourists' acceptance of the destination's logo *Home of lässig* [Home of *cool*]. The critical aspect of the DMO's social media activities is communicating the values that determine the destination's personality and thus facilitating this emotional bond with the visitors [30]. In this case study, the communication of the destination's personality can be seen in the DMO's activity and posts. Moreover, the positive response of the users to such communication can be witnessed. Thus, this research confirms the impact of destination's personality communication so that visitors can identify with a destination.

Furthermore, the comparison of the DMO with users' posts reveals that the DMO generally delivers mostly *nature* and *landscape*-related content, whereas tourists tend to include both *nature* and *people* in their posts. The images for both UGC and DMO could be categorised into three themes: *winter mountain atmosphere*, *winter sports*, *people*. However, the majority of the DMO posts presented the *slopes* and the *snowy mountains* in the first category. A great deal of UGC posts relates to images of *socialising*, be that either selfies, people during winter activities, or people at a restaurant, bar, or in the street. Such content could be interpreted the following way: tourists come to the resort not only to enjoy winter sports but to also experience the immersion into a warm and cosy environment; to enjoy social activities with friends and family, take selfies, enjoy contemporary accommodation facilities, and visit trendy restaurants where they can talk about various topics and try delicious dishes. Undoubtedly, the main reason to visit a ski resort is to engage in winter sports, but without these add-ons, customers would be missing out on a peak experience [36].

7 Conclusion

This work provides deeper insights into destination image creation and user behaviour on social media and contributes to understand the effect of social media on DMO marketing strategy development. According to existing literature, social media marketing efficiency has been measured by user involvement: their interaction, influence, and intimacy [6]. DMOs most commonly measure the return on investment of social media effectiveness by counting the number of 'followers', 'likes', and the rate at which those numbers increase [1, 6]. Typically, netnographic research provides no insights on how the brand positioning strategy should be conducted. Thus, this study incorporates a qualitative analysis instead of the measurements mentioned above, thereby offering an alternative approach to the destination brand image assessment. This attempts to provide an in-depth insight into consumer behaviour on social media.

The findings suggest values and beliefs embedded in the posts instead of the quantifiable interacting aspects. In that case, market research, such as a visitor survey combined with a netnographic study, might be helpful.

Furthermore, this study provides several implications for DMOs by analysing similarities and differences between the Instagram posts created by tourists and the DMO. Although the projected image highly matches tourist experiences, not all the UGC posts' themes are covered by marketers, and vice versa. Such insights indicate opportunities for the improvement of a DMO's marketing strategy regarding their storytelling. A DMO could utilise the study's findings and adjust their marketing strategy by promoting the services and content appearing in the visitors' posts. For instance, an image of a cup of coffee amidst a winter scenery with an attractive caption could influence a prospective visitor by creating anticipation of fulfilling this desire [9].

Including and highlighting additional activities the destination has to offer aside from primary ski activities would be a strategic decision regarding the DMO's marketing activities promote the destination. For example, an additional offer may refer to ski huts, local dishes or activities such as night tobogganing.

Further managerial implications include promoting properties on the DMOs social media channels. The importance of a professional marketing strategy lies in the fact that DMO's social media activities influence the destination image and the intention to visit [7]. Essentially, this research presents deeper insights into tourist experiences at the destination and confirms their impact on adding value to the destination image.

However, this research is, naturally, not without its limitations. First, the analysis was not incorporated through the most commonly used performance indicators (e.g., user engagement), nor did it provide quantifiable data (e.g., the exact percentage to which the perceived user image corresponds to the projected destination image). For future research, we encourage an assessment of user engagement in regard to DMO and UGC matching content. Similarly, a quantitative measurement of destination image perception and intention to visit regarding content congruence is recommended. Saalbach-Hinterglemm has a clear, one-dimensional profile as a ski destination. For more diverse destinations, future studies could perform multilingual text analysis utilizing BERT in order to provide deeper insights. Despite its exploratory nature, this study offers valuable insights into the role of UGC on destination brand image.

References

1. Hays S, Page SJ, Buhalis D (2013) Social media as a destination marketing tool: its use by national tourism organisations. Curr Issue Tour 16:211–239
2. Arefieva V, Egger R, Yu J (2021) A machine learning approach to cluster destination image on Instagram. Tour Manage 85:104318
3. Yu J, Egger R (2021) Color and engagement in touristic Instagram pictures: a machine learning approach. Ann Tour Res 89:103204
4. Yu C-E, Sun R (2019) The role of Instagram in the UNESCO's creative city of gastronomy: a case study of Macau. Tour Manage 75:257–268
5. Huertas A, Marine-Roig E (2015) User reactions to destination brand contents in social media. Inf Technol Tourism 15(4):291–315. https://doi.org/10.1007/s40558-015-0045-9

6. Jiménez-Barreto J, Rubio N, Campo S et al (2020) Linking the online destination brand experience and brand credibility with tourists' behavioral intentions toward a destination. Tour Manage 79:104101
7. Molinillo S, Liébana-Cabanillas F, Anaya-Sánchez R et al (2018) DMO online platforms: image and intention to visit. Tour Manage 65:116–130
8. Baloglu S, Henthorne TL, Sahin S (2014) Destination image and brand personality of Jamaica: a model of tourist behavior. J Travel Tour Mark 31:1057–1070
9. Urry J, Larsen J (2011) The Tourist Gaze 3.0. SAGE Publications Ltd, London
10. Fatanti MN, Suyadnya IW (2015) Beyond user gaze: how Instagram creates tourism destination brand? Procedia Soc Behav Sci 211:1089–1095
11. Yu C-E, Xie SY, Wen J (2020) Coloring the destination: the role of color psychology on Instagram. Tour Manage 80:104110
12. Huerta-Álvarez R, Cambra-Fierro JJ, Fuentes-Blasco M (2020) The interplay between social media communication, brand equity and brand engagement in tourist destinations: an analysis in an emerging economy. J Destin Market Manag 16:100413
13. Conti E, Lexhagen M (2020) Instagramming nature-based tourism experiences: a netnographic study of online photography and value creation. Tour Manag Perspect 34:100650
14. Kim H, Chen JS (2016) Destination image formation process. J Vacat Mark 22:154–166
15. Beritelli P, Laesser C (2018) Destination logo recognition and implications for intentional destination branding by DMOs: a case for saving money. J Destin Mark Manag 8:1–13
16. Li SC, Robinson P, Oriade A (2017) Destination marketing: the use of technology since the millennium. J Destin Mark Manag 6:95–102
17. Mariani MM, Di Felice M, Mura M (2016) Facebook as a destination marketing tool: evidence from Italian regional Destination Management Organizations. Tour Manage 54:321–343
18. Lalicic L, Huertas A, Moreno A et al (2020) Emotional brand communication on Facebook and Twitter: are DMOs successful? J Destin Market Manag 16:100350
19. Xiang Z, Gretzel U (2010) Role of social media in online travel information search. Tour Manage 31:179–188
20. Roque V, Raposo R (2016) Social media as a communication and marketing tool in tourism: an analysis of online activities from international key player DMO. Anatolia 27:58–70
21. Daxböck J et al (2021) The implicit and explicit motivations of tourist behaviour in sharing travel photographs on Instagram: a path and cluster analysis. In: Wörndl W, Koo C, Stienmetz JL (eds) Information and Communication Technologies in Tourism 2021. Springer, Cham, pp 244–255. https://doi.org/10.1007/978-3-030-65785-7_22
22. Brandwatch (2020) 126 Amazing Social Media Statistics and Facts. https://www.brandwatch.com/blog/amazing-social-media-statistics-and-facts/. Accessed 15 Apr 2020
23. Stepchenkova S, Zhan FZ (2013) Visual destination image of Peru: comparative content analysis of DMO and user-generated photography. Tour Manage 36:590–601. https://doi.org/10.1016/j.tourman.2012.08.006
24. Tussyadiah IP (2010) Destination promoted and visitor-generated images–do they represent similar stories? In: Burns P, Lester J, Bibbings L (eds) Tourism and Visual Culture. CABI, Wallingford, pp 156–168
25. Song S, Kim D (2016) A pictorial analysis of destination images on Pinterest: the case of Tokyo, Kyoto, and Osaka, Japan. J Travel Tour Mark 33(5):687–701. https://doi.org/10.1080/10548408.2016.1167384
26. Chang J-H, Wang S-H (2019) Different levels of destination expectation: the effects of online advertising and electronic word-of-mouth. Telemat Inform 36:27–38

27. Echtner CM, Ritchie JRB (1993) The measurement of destination image: an empirical assessment. J Travel Res 31:3–13. https://doi.org/10.1177/004728759303100402
28. Duque T (2020) How to turn text into features: a comprehensive guide into using NLP for machine learning. https://towardsdatascience.com/how-to-turn-text-into-features-478b57632e99. Accessed 18 Nov 2020
29. Godec P (2020) Documents embeddings and text classification without coding. https://towardsdatascience.com/documents-embeddings-and-text-classification-without-coding-e274b4e191e9. Accessed 18 Nov 2020
30. Jabreel M, Moreno A, Huertas A (2017) Semantic comparison of the emotional values communicated by destinations and tourists on social media. J Destin Mark Manag 6:170–183
31. Grave E, Bojanowski P, Gupta P, et al (2018) Learning Word Vectors for 157 Languages
32. Garbade MJ (2018) Understanding K-means clustering in machine learning. https://towardsdatascience.com/understanding-k-means-clustering-in-machine-learning-6a6e67336aa1. Accessed 18 Nov 2020
33. Egger R (2022) Text representation and word embeddings. In: Egger R (ed) Applied Data Science in Tourism. Interdisciplinary Approaches, Methodologies and Applications. Springer, Cham
34. Marcińczuk M, Gniewkowski M, Walkowiak T, Będkowski M (2021) Text document clustering: Wordnet vs. TF-IDF vs. word embeddings. In: Proceedings of the 11th Global Wordnet Conference. pp 207–214
35. Usakli A, Baloglu S (2011) Brand personality of tourist destinations: an application of self-congruity theory. Tour Manage 32:114–127
36. Pine BJ, Gilmore JH (2011) The Experience Economy. Harvard Business Press, Boston

10

Understanding Preferences in Tourism Email Marketing

Elide Garbani-Nerini, Elena Marchiori, Rossella Reale and Lorenzo Cantoni

Università della Svizzera italiana, Via Buffi 13, 6900 Lugano, Switzerland
elide.garbani.nerini@usi.ch

Abstract. Nowadays, advanced tools allow the personalization of email communication with tourism clients or prospects based on explicit (e.g. name, age, language, country) and implicit indicators (e.g. ranking of activity in the opening rate of the newsletter, browsing preferences, online preferences provided by cookies, etc.). However, knowing how audiences react to emails allows Destination Marketing Organizations (DMOs) to create content clusters for personalized communication. The purpose of this study is to empirically investigate the preferences on tourism email marketing of different audiences based on a specific explicit indicator, namely the language chosen by users to receive communications by a DMO. A content analysis on a longitudinal dataset based on 131 newsletter messages sent between 2018 and 2021 to more than 50′ 000 contacts by a DMO in Switzerland was performed. Results show that content should be adapted to different audiences speaking different languages instead of providing just a translation. Specifically, the German-speaking audience seems to be more inclined to messages that focus on winter sports and hiking, the Italian-speaking audience to news about hiking and information on COVID-19, the French-speaking audience to news about promotions, while the English-speaking audience to contents on discounts and COVID-19-related. These results provide an important contribution to studies on tourism personalization of communication in the context of email marketing, suggesting the role of content adaptation according to the language and cultural background of the audience. DMO managers can also benefit from this research in understanding how to address a similar study on their datasets and compare the emerged content clusters.

Keywords: Email marketing · Tourism personalization · Tourism preferences · Customer value creation

1 Introduction

Email is an important communication channel in marketing and is still one of the most commonly used by many industries, including tourism, and, in this specific case, DMOs. The main reasons for that, as highlighted by many authors in the literature, is its cost-efficiency and its speed, in terms both of reaction by customers/prospects and of development of marketing campaigns [1–4]. Generally, in email marketing campaigns, success is determined by using specific metrics such as open rate (OR), i.e. the percentage of addressees who have opened the message, and click-through rate (CTR), i.e. the percentage of those who have clicked on at least one link out of the people who had received the email [5]. Clicking on a link represents the voluntary act of interest/curiosity that addressees show towards the sender of the message as they select topics that they are interested in learning more about. In the industry, email marketing is usually managed using special tools (such as the popular tools named Mailchimp, MailUp, Salesforce). These tools provide statistics on campaign performances and audiences, allowing for a first customer segmentation. Extending this analysis could bring interesting insights on how to segment customers more efficiently. DMOs have in fact access to several data when it comes to email campaigns and audiences and this makes it interesting to study the potential to develop this channel with personalization to improve communication practices. However, few companies and DMOs are willing to share such performance data, as they represent a competitive and strategic asset. Thus, the lack of studies in this area can be related to this limited access to data. This study emphasizes the importance of studying email marketing performance by bringing insights from a longitudinal study on newsletters in tourism. Results underline how to identify more personalized content clusters for different audiences thanks to the analysis of a specific explicit indicator, namely the language chosen by users to receive communications by a DMO in relation with an implicit indicator, namely click behavior.

2 Literature Review

2.1 Segmentation in Email Marketing

Studies on email marketing consider audience segmentation as key to a successful interaction with clients, reflected with high open, click-through and conversion rates [3, 4, 6–8]. In particular, Mailchimp, an integrated marketing platform, compared the results of its users' segmented campaigns with those of the same users' non-segmented campaigns: segmented campaigns performed better, with higher open, unique open, and click rate, and lower bounces and unsubscriptions [6]. There are several methods for customer/audience segmentation that have been studied in the literature. There are methods that use customer details [8] such as demographic and lifestyle data, others use data product, others customer/audience behaviors - the most popular models being the RFM model, clustering customers according to their purchase's "recency", "frequency" and "monetary" value, and the customer lifetime value (CLV) model, which determines customers' importance level based on a calculation of the net cash flow generated by the customers [4, 9]. The market standards with respect to how to classify contacts can be divided into two main approaches: i) explicit indicators on users/audience (e.g.: name, age, language, country), that is information voluntarily provided by users; and ii) implicit indicators on users/audience (e.g.: ranking of activity in the opening rate of the newsletter, browsing preferences, online preferences provided by cookies, etc.), that is information that can be inferred from users' interaction with emails and connected web pages. In general, different data sources can be used and combined to create more efficient segmentations and consequently more efficient communication [8].

Segmentation is the foundation for personalized email marketing campaigns, one of the main trends in email marketing [10], as the format and content of messages can be adapted to different segments and eventually for a given individual. Similarly to segmentation, personalized emails have been found to increase campaign performance [11, 12].

2.2 Personalization in Tourism

Personalization has been defined by Jackson [13] as "a way of doing things. Personali [z]ation derives customer information to provide consistent, timely and relevant individuali[z]ed interactions and offers to each customer across all touchpoints that increases customer loyalty and lifetime value" (p 26). In general, however, personalization is not always easily applied and, above all, univocally understood and interpreted [14]. In tourism, personalization has been studied and applied to different areas, such as travel planning and recommender systems. Existing recommender systems have been analyzed in the literature [15, 16], and new ones have been proposed: Missaoui S. [17] presented the mobile app LOOKER, a recommender system based on a user generated content-based filtering algorithm; Amer-Yahia et al. [18] developed an interactive framework that generates customized travel packages for individuals or for groups of travelers; De Carolis et al. [19] analyzed the potential of social robots in providing effective tourism recommender systems; Wang [20] proved how including data on online behavior of potential travelers can improve personalized recommendations systems; Ravi et al. [21] worked on an algorithm- and hybrid user clustering-based travel planning system for personalized point of interest recommendation; Choi et al. [22] presented a recommender system to help tourists create a personalized travel plan based on collaborative and constraint satisfaction filtering; Chen et al. [23] developed a method to design personalized travel routes for tourists by combining user clustering, improved genetic, and rectangular region path planning algorithms. Personalization can be used also to provide specific information to tourists with particular needs, as proposed by Ribeiro et al. [24] with their personalized system to assist mobility disabled tourists during their visit and activities.

In cultural tourism, personalization can help enhance the dialogue between culture providers and cultural tourists. Ross [25]'s study on Alentejo in Portugal showed that more personalized individual-based guiding activities can be used in co-creating experiences by cultural tourism providers to deliver more meaningful experiences also appealing to visitors with alternative sets of beliefs and motivations. Konstantakis et al. [26]'s work demonstrated that it is possible to provide higher quality and more relevant cultural recommendations when including information regarding the cultural background of tourists. In the context of audio tours, Shilov et al. [27] proposed automatically generated personalized audio tours based on the context and tourists' preferences. Specifically to museum visits, Kaghat et al. [28] advanced an adaptive and personalizable gesture-based audio augmented reality system.

Personalization can have an impact also in the hospitality domain: Neuhofer et al. [29] proposed a model for personalized experience co-creation between a hotel's staff and its guests, while Piccoli et al. [30] studied the benefits brought by IT-enabled customer service systems to service personalization, customer service perceptions, and hotel performance.

The point of view of tourists has been analyzed by Volchek et al. [31], who highlighted how personalization plays an important role but does not automatically guarantee a positive tourist experience.

In the context of tourism-related online communication, research has been conducted on the one hand, on the effectiveness of DMO's websites [32, 33] and, on the other hand, on how personalization can have a positive impact on tourism e-commerce websites, in terms of revenue [34] and customers' loyalty [35]. A lack of studies has been found for what regards email communication and marketing, more specifically newsletters, both in terms of effectiveness of the tool and personalization. Newsletters are very relevant and extensively used in the tourism domain and more and more a tool for email personalization; hence, they should be further studied. This paper wants to contribute to this gap by analyzing different audience's preferences in email marketing, as a starting point to understand how to better personalize content in DMO's newsletters making them more effective.

3 Research Method

The case study used for this research has been provided by Agenzia Turistica Ticinese (ATT), a regional Destination Marketing Organization active in the southern part of Switzerland. ATT has a mailing list including 50′239 contacts (data updated in April 2021). The mailing list has been shared with the researchers ensuring the anonymity of the contacts: all were shared with an anonymous ID (erasing personal data such as name and surname and email address of the contact). The indicators shared were the language that users had chosen to communicate with the DMO and their country of residence.

Table 1. Distribution of languages and related countries of the analyzed mailing list.

		CH	DE	I	FR	UK	USA	Other	Total
DE	Count	16316	5206	233	195	61	416	10560	32987
	%	49.5%	15.8%	0.7%	0.6%	0.2%	1.3%	32.0%	100.0%
EN	Count	3833	169	1324	79	33	113	1875	7426
	%	51.6%	2.3%	17.8%	1.1%	0.4%	1.5%	25.2%	100.0%
IT	Count	1266	32	5	230	2	10	581	2126
	%	59.5%	1.5%	0.2%	10.8%	0.1%	0.5%	27.3%	100.0%
FR	Count	1306	253	169	66	976	1296	3634	7700
	%	17.0%	3.3%	2.2%	0.9%	12.7%	16.8%	47.2%	100.0%
TOT	Count	22721	5660	1731	570	1072	1835	16650	50239
	%	45.2%	11.3%	3.4%	1.1%	2.1%	3.7%	33.1%	100.0%

Table 1 presents the distribution of languages and related countries of the analyzed mailing list. Contacts were classified according to four languages with a majority of contacts having selected German as language to communicate with the DMO, followed by English, Italian and French. Looking at the residence country: the majority of the contacts were from Switzerland, followed by Germany, Italy and France. The particular linguistic characteristics of Switzerland must be considered: in the country, there are three official languages – German, French, Italian, and a fourth national minority language: Romansh. The latter was not considered in this study as it is not a language in which ATT's newsletter is available.

In order to empirically investigate the preferences on tourism email marketing of different audiences, the following available indicator has been used: the language chosen by users to receive communications with a DMO. Language and geographical variables are indeed a criterion for customer segmentation [36, 37] and, as research suggests, online tourism promotion is not culturally neutral and should rather take into account cultural differences [38]. More precisely, studies conducted on web communication have shown the importance of studying content adaptation to the language and culture of the various audiences [39, 40]: websites that are culturally and linguistically adapted have been found to be more effective [41–43]. For these reasons, language was selected as segmentation criteria. It is important to note that in this study languages are not representing a specific country.

Email is among the main tools of direct marketing communication used by the DMO. Specifically, ATT regularly sends a newsletter to its contacts using the popular email marketing tool Mailchimp. The newsletter is sent at the beginning of each month to its mailing list and it is translated in the four languages, keeping the same structure and content for the four versions. Figure 1 presents a screenshot of part of a newsletter, where the header, main story and content module are visible. In addition to header and footer, the main body of the newsletter is generally structured as follows:

- Character story module: consists of image/video with link, title and text, call to action with link. The module is dedicated to interview stories with a local person, artisan, producer, guide, host, sport instructor, etc. presenting a peculiar activity in Ticino.
- Content modules: each module consists of an image with link, title with link and a text. On average, six content modules are present in every newsletter message.
- Event modules: not present in every newsletter, consist of images with link, title with link to upcoming events.

The links in the newsletter refer to the correspondent content pages on ATT's website, which provide more information on the topic. The links in each module are the same, for image/video and call to action in the story module and image and text in the content modules.

Fig. 1. Screenshot of part of a newsletter by ATT

For this study, it was possible to analyze the newsletters sent to ATT's mailing list from April 2018 to February 2021 in the four languages for a total of 131 analyzed newsletters (note that newsletters were never sent in January; in May 2020, three newsletter were sent; there was no data recorded for the following newsletters in the DE version: October 2018, August 2019, April 2020, in the FR version: April 2020, and EN version: April 2020). The average OR of ATT's newsletters is 30.2% (with a min. OR of 18.3% and max. of 49.1%), which is above the tourism and hospitality industry average of 17.70% [44]. Table 3 shows the average performance of ATT's newsletter divided per language segments. In order to identify preferences in the content promoted within the newsletters, the top 10 newsletters for each language, namely the 10 newsletters with the highest OR for each language were considered (Table 2). This allowed focusing on the newsletters that received the most attention. A total of 40 newsletters were analyzed.

Table 2. OR of the top 10 newsletters for each language

Newsletter	DE OR (%)	EN OR (%)	IT OR (%)	FR OR (%)	Avg. OR
April 2018	25.0	**23.3**	**37.7**	32.8	29.7
May 2018	24.0	**22.5**	32.5	37.3	29.1
June 2018	24.3	21.7	32.6	**38.8**	29.4
July 2018	**27.9**	21.6	36.6	36.9	30.8
August 2018	22.7	**22.3**	34.6	35.9	28.9
Sept. 2018	21.3	**22.6**	**37.1**	33.5	28.6
April 2019	26.4	20.8	**38.6**	35.9	30.4
May 2019	21.6	21.7	**37.2**	37.3	29.5
March 2020	24.1	20.4	**38.7**	**39.7**	30.7
April 2020	NA	NA	**42.1**	NA	42.1
4 May 2020	**32.7**	**27.0**	**42.2**	**49.1**	37.8
11 May 2020	**31.0**	**24.0**	**38.2**	**44.4**	34.4
18 May 2020	**31.0**	**27.8**	**36.9**	**44.4**	35.0
June 2020	**29.4**	**22.2**	36.6	**42.5**	32.7
July 2020	**26.8**	22.0	32.4	37.7	29.7
August 2020	**29.0**	**23.6**	36.0	**42.2**	32.7
Sept. 2020	**28.4**	21.0	34.1	**39.3**	30.7
Oct. 2020	26.1	21.1	33.1	**39.7**	30.0
Dec. 2020	**27.0**	**24.4**	32.5	37.7	30.4
Feb. 2021	**29.2**	21.7	**38.9**	**40.3**	32.5

Table 3. Statistics of ATT's newsletter performance per language compared to industry average 2021 [44]

	OR (%)	Bounce rate (%)	CTR (%)	Unsubscriptions/Successful deliveries (%)
Industry average 2021	17.7	–	2.0	0.2
Newsletter DE	25.7	1.3	4.1	0.6
Newsletter EN	21.5	1.7	1.8	0.6
Newsletter IT	36.1	1.5	6.9	0.4
Newsletter FR	37.8	0.9	6.6	0.6

The following content analysis was performed on the 40 identified top newsletters in order to understand which topics were considered as the most interesting and whether there was a difference depending on the language of the newsletter:

- The topics related to the links in the newsletter were listed, until saturation was reached.
- For each newsletter, the three most clicked links with their click rates (CR), and related topics were identified (note: images and titles have the same link in ATT's newsletter). As CR, it is here intended the percentage of clicks that a specific link in

the newsletter has received out of all total clicks of the same newsletter (the data is provided by Mailchimp).

- The position and type of these links were also analyzed (text, photo or video) in order to understand whether there was an incidence of the link's visual characteristic, in other words, whether the most clicked links were those positioned on top of the newsletter and/or anchored to video/photo.
- For each language, the average CR of the most clicked links for each topic was calculated. The topics with the highest value were identified for each language.

4 Results

From the content analysis 19 topics emerged and are presented in Table 4. For each topic and for each language the average CR of the three most clicked links in the 40 newsletters analyzed is indicated. Highlighted are the three highest CR per language.

Table 4. Most clicked topics per language

Topic	Avg. CR of top 3 links DE	Avg. CR of top 3 links EN	Avg. CR of top 3 links IT	Avg. CR of top 3 links FR
Ideas Ticino (top to dos/must-sees)	**29.6**	**33.1**	**35.8**	**39.9**
Ideas Christmas				
Character Story	20.9	22.7	14.6	**27.5**
City-attraction excursion		23.1		
Nature: discover a place	22.2	15.3	17.4	17.1
Nature: excursion	19.1	20.8	19.9	21.5
Campaign: for hotels	24.3	**32**		**28.2**
Campaign: COVID-19-related	24.1	**27.2**	**28.7**	25.5
Campaign: create postcard				
Offer: discount on accommodation	25.7	20.9	16.5	21.7
Offer: families			15.6	
Food: recipes	17.6	27.1	13.7	
Products (magazine, poster)	18.1	23.4	26.9	17.2
Events	11.6	13.9	18.2	17.5
Sport: hiking	**29.7**		**31.3**	19
Sport: biking				
Sport: winter	**30.9**		22.8	27.2
Sport: trail running				
Sport: water		14.8		

In general, the topic “Ideas Ticino” (top to dos and must-sees) is the only one that had a high CR for all the languages: 29.6% for the German-speaking audience, 33.1% for the English-speaking audience, 35.8% for the Italian-speaking audience and 39.9% for the French-speaking audience. This type of content seems to be of interest throughout the different segments. With regard to the other topics, results show the presence of specificities for the different audiences divided by language in the interaction with newsletters sent by the DMO. In particular:

- For the German-speaking audience, the topics with the highest interest were winter sports (CR of 30.9%) and hiking (29.7%).
- For the English-speaking audience, the topics with most interest were those containing information about discounts on accommodation (32%) and COVID-19 related campaigns (27.2%).
- The audience indicating Italian as the language of interaction with the DMO showed a greater interest in content connected to hiking (31.3%) and information related to the campaign COVID-19 (28.7%).
- The French-speaking audience appeared to be interested in content regarding discounts on accommodation (28.2%) and the character story (27.5%).

It is also interesting to note that not all the topics appeared in the top three links of the different audiences. For example, content on city attractions was top content only for the English-speaking audience, while offers for families were top content only for the Italian-speaking audience.

Regarding the position of the most clicked content, the results suggest an incidence of link positions in the top news: the position might indeed influence users’ click behavior. Results show, indeed, that the content that was placed in the first part of the newsletter, and hence required less scrolling to be visualized, was clicked more than the content in the lower part of the newsletter.

5 Discussion

Several insights emerged from this study. First, there is a need for case studies in tourism email marketing: the lack of literature in the tourism domain demonstrates a need for more studies for comparisons and insights on the topic. While other topics might be perceived as more “trending” or new, the role newsletters play within the everyday activities of tourism destinations call for further attention and larger studies. Second, analyses over time allow to outline trends associated with segments grouped by specific variables, in this case by language factor. In fact, while language is the considered factor here, due to the concerned DMO’s practices, and due to an actual declaration of users themselves, it opens up insights on specific customers/prospects’ groups. The analysis might go further and explore the drivers that attract Italians to Ticino vis-à-vis of the ones, which attract people from northern Switzerland and Germany (or Austria), or those interesting for French travelers. Moreover, info needs might be somehow disclosed also through the proxy of language: for instance, one might assume that information about COVID-19-related regulations were quite clear to Swiss travelers/prospects, while others needed to understand if travelling internationally was still possible, and under which conditions. Third, the actual choices related to content production and formatting can facilitate (or not) analytics. In this case, the presence of links that are divided by topic is a good way to facilitate the identification of preferences in the audience.

This study has implications also for personalization practices: such a research shows a good first step for audience segmentation and preferences' analysis in order to provide more personalized communication. The results show, indeed, that by segmenting your audience (in this case it was done according to the audience's language), different click behaviors can emerge which can be indicators of different preferences among the different segments. This study also has implications for the tourism industry: it shows the importance of implementing audience clusters in email marketing messages in order to make messages more personalized. The methodology used in this study can be applied to analyze and segment an audience, and to understand the content preferences of the different segments drawing from click behavior. This study could also be replicated using different explicit and implicit indicators for audience segmentation.

The study presents some limitations that set the stage for future research: i) the language factor is not representative of a specific region. Therefore, future research should also analyze results coming from the analysis of the country of residence to see if there are socio-cultural aspects typical of a specific region; ii) a comparison with other cases should be conducted in order to generalize results. Furthermore, having identified the 19 topics, it would be interesting to analyze who the specific audiences are for each topic. Studies on the title of the newsletters could also be conducted in order to understand whether there are different audience preferences in terms of title formats and length. Lastly, A/B tests will be conducted personalizing the content for different audiences in order to verify and validate the results of this study.

Acknowledgment. The work described in this paper was funded by the DESy (Digital Destination Evolution System) Interreg Italy-Switzerland Project.

References

1. Chaffey D, Ellis-Chadwick F, Mayer R, Johnston K (2009) Internet Marketing: Strategy, Implementation and Practice, 4th edn. Pearson Education Limited, Harlow
2. Vasudevan R (2010) E-mail marketing. J Contemp Res Manag 5(3):37–42
3. Bawm ZL, Nath RPD (2014) A conceptual model for effective email marketing. In: 17th International Conference on Computer and Information Technology (ICCIT). IEEE, Dhaka, pp 250–256
4. Morandini FS, Dobrinić D (2018) The role of segmentation in e-mail marketing. Int. J. Market Sci 1(1):145–156
5. Mailchimp: About Open and Click Rates. https://mailchimp.com/help/about-open-and-click-rates/. Accessed 11 Aug 2021
6. Mailchimp: Effects of List Segmentation on Email Marketing Stats. https://mailchimp.com/resources/effects-of-list-segmentation-on-email-marketing-stats/. Accessed 09 Aug 2021
7. Hiziroglu A (2013) A neuro-fuzzy two-stage clustering approach to customer segmentation. J Market Analyt 1(4):202–221
8. Punhani R, Arora VPS, Sabitha S, Shukla VK (2021) Application of clustering algorithm for effective customer segmentation in E-commerce. In: 2021 International Conference on Computational Intelligence and Knowledge Economy (ICCIKE). IEE, Dubai, pp 149–154

9. Hiziroglu A, Sengul S (2012) Investigating two customer lifetime value models from segmentation perspective. Procedia Soc Behav Sci 62(2012):766–774
10. Litmus: State of Email Report 2020. The data, trends, and innovations that shape successful email programs in 2020- and the decade to come. https://www.litmus.com/resources/state-of-email/. Accessed 09 Aug 2021
11. Campaign Monitor: The Power of Email Personalization to Reach Humans (Not Just Inboxes). https://www.campaignmonitor.com/resources/guides/personalized-email/. Accessed 09 Aug 2021
12. Phan QAH (2019) Personalization in Email Marketing – Case Study: Debic Brand at FrieslandCampina. Karelia University of Applied Sciences
13. Jackson TW (2007) Personalisation and CRM. Datab Market Cust Strategy Manag 15 (1):24–36
14. Vesanen J (2007) What is personalization? A conceptual framework. Eur J Mark 41 (5/6):409–418
15. Chen X, Liu Q, Qiao X (2020) Approaching another tourism recommender. In: 2020 IEEE 20th International Conference on Software Quality, Reliability and Security Companion (QRS-C). IEEE, Macau, pp 556–562
16. Ricci F, Rokach L, Shapira B (eds) (2015) Recommender Systems Handbook. Springer, Boston. https://doi.org/10.1007/978-1-4899-7637-6
17. Missaoui S, Kassem F, Viviani M, Agostini A, Faiz R, Pasi G (2019) LOOKER: a mobile, personalized recommender system in the tourism domain based on social media user-generated content. Pers Ubiquit Comput 23(2):181–197
18. Amer-Yahia S, Borromeo RM, Elbassuoni S, Omidvar-Tehrani B, Viswanathan S (2020) Interactive generation and customization of travel packages for individuals and groups. In: Proceedings of the 25th International Conference on Intelligent User Interfaces Companion (IUI 2020). Association for Computing Machinery, New York, pp 69–70
19. De Carolis B, Lops P, Cataldo M, Semeraro G (2020) Towards a social robot as interface for tourism recommendations. In: Proceedings of the Workshop on Adapted intEraction with SociAl Robots, cAESAR 2020, Cagliari, pp 28–33
20. Wang X (2020) Personalized recommendation framework design for online tourism: know you better than yourself. Ind Manag Data Syst 120(11):2067–2079
21. Ravi L, Subramaniyaswamy V, Vijayakumar V, Jhaveri RH, Shah J (2021) Hybrid user clustering-based travel planning system for personalized point of interest recommendation. In: Sahni M, Merigó JM, Jha BK, Verma R (eds) Mathematical Modeling, Computational Intelligence Techniques and Renewable Energy, vol 1287. AISC. Springer, Singapore, pp 311–321. https://doi.org/10.1007/978-981-15-9953-8_27
22. Choi Y, Ryu YU, Kim JK (2021) A recommender system based on personal constraints for smart tourism city. Asia Pacific J Tour Res 26(4):440–453
23. Chen C, Zhang S, Yu Q, Ye Z, Ye Z, Hu F (2021) Personalized travel route recommendation algorithm based on improved genetic algorithm. J Intell Fuzzy Syst 40(3):4407–4423
24. Ribeiro F, Metrôlho J, Leal J, Martins H, Bastos P (2018) A mobile application to provide personalized information for mobility impaired tourists. In: Rocha Á, Adeli H, Reis LP, Costanzo S (eds) WorldCIST'18 2018, vol 746. AISC. Springer, Cham, pp 164–173. https://doi.org/10.1007/978-3-319-77712-2_16
25. Ross D (2020) Towards meaningful co-creation: a study of creative heritage tourism in Alentejo, Portugal. Curr Issues Tour 23(22):2811–2824
26. Konstantakis M, Alexandridis G, Caridakis G (2020) A personalized heritage-oriented recommender system based on extended cultural tourist typologies. Big Data Cognit Comput 4(2):12

27. Shilov N, Kashevnik A, Mikhailov S (2018) Context-aware generation of personalized audio tours: approach and evaluation. In: Karpov A, Jokisch O, Potapova R (eds) SPECOM 2018, vol 11096. LNCS (LNAI). Springer, Cham, pp 615–624. https://doi.org/10.1007/978-3-319-99579-3_63
28. Kaghat F, Azough A, Fakhour M, Meknassi M (2020) A new audio augmented reality interaction and adaptation model for museum visits. Comput Electr Eng 84:106606
29. Neuhofer B, Buhalis D, Ladkin A (2015) Smart technologies for personalized experiences: a case study in the hospitality domain. Electron Mark 25(3):243–254. https://doi.org/10.1007/s12525-015-0182-1
30. Piccoli G, Lui T, Grün B (2017) The impact of IT-enabled customer service systems on service personalization, customer service perceptions, and hotel performance. Tour Manag 59:349–362
31. Volchek K, Law R, Buhalis D, Song H (2019) The good, the bad, and the ugly: tourist perceptions on interactions with personalised content. e-Rev Tour Res 16(2/3), 62–72
32. Park YA, Gretzel U (2007) Success factors for destination marketing web sites: a qualitative meta-analysis. J Travel Res 46(1):46–63
33. Drosopoulou C, Malama E-I, Patsioura F, Vlachopoulou M (2015) Evaluating destination marketing organizations' websites: conceptual and empirical review. In: Information Resources Management Association (ed.) Hospitality, Travel, and Tourism: Concepts, Methodologies, Tools, and Applications. IGI Global, pp 250–262
34. Khai DL, Das D (2020) Data mining and personalization for smart travel management. J Crit Rev 7(3):66–73
35. Martínez-González JA, Álvarez-Albelo CD (2021) Influence of site personalization and first impression on young consumers' loyalty to tourism websites. Sustainability 13(3):1425
36. Hughes AM (2006) Strategic Database Marketing, 3rd edn. McGraw-Hill, New York
37. Kotler P, Keller KL, Martinović M (2012) Marketing Management, 14th edn. MATE, Zagreb
38. Mele E, Cantoni L (2017) Localization of national tourism organizations websites: the case of ETC members. In: Schegg R, Stangl B (eds) Information and communication technologies in tourism. Springer, Cham, pp 59–71
39. Cappelli G (2008) The translation of tourism-related websites and localization: problems and perspectives. In: Baicchi A (ed) Voices on Translation. RILA Rassegna Italiana di Linguistica Applicata. Bulzoni Editore, Roma, pp 97–115
40. Achkasov VA (2015) Words under pressure: translation in the context of search engine optimization. J Siberian Federal Univ Human Soc Sci 8(2):200–208
41. Tixier M (2005) Globalization and localization of contents: evolution of major Internet sites across sectors of industry. Thunderbird Int Bus Rev 47(1):15–48
42. Singh N, Fassott G, Chao M, Hoffmann J (2006) Understanding international web site usage: a cross-national study of German, Brazilian, and Taiwanese online consumers. Int Mark Rev 23(1):83–98
43. Baack DW, Singh N (2007) Culture and web communications. J Bus Res 60(3):181–188
44. Campaign Monitor: Ultimate Email Marketing Benchmarks for 2021: By Industry and Day. https://www.campaignmonitor.com/resources/guides/email-marketing-benchmarks/. Accessed 12 Aug 2021

11

Understanding Hotel Employees'and Guests' Perceptions of Smart Hotels using Q Methodology

Ye Shen(✉)

California Polytechnic State University, San Luis Obispo, CA 93407, USA
yeshen@calpoly.edu

Abstract. Nowadays, hotels are adopting high technologies to improve the quality of their facilities and services to build competitive advantages. Although smart hotels are an emerging trend, no known studies have investigated hotel employees' and guests' perceptions of this kind of hotel. This research will investigate how hotel employees and guests perceive the benefits and drawbacks of smart hotels using Q methodology.

Keywords: Smart hotel · Q methodology · Perception · Hotel guest · Hotel employee

1 Introduction

A smart hotel is "an intelligent hotel with a range of information technologies working together to let the guests have an honorable and convenient vacation environment" [1] (p. 42). Different technology innovations, such as service robots, Artificial Intelligence (AI), and the Internet of Things (IoT), have been implemented by certain hotels to enhance customer experiences. Opened in December 2018, Flyzoo Hotel in China is the world's first full-featured smart hotel that allows customers to enjoy its intelligent experience and facilities. Hilton Hotels have collaborated with IBM and used an AI robot, Connie, to provide guests with concierge service and travel suggestions. Hôtel Monville in Montreal is the first hotel in Canada using autonomous delivery robots for room service. As hotels adopt high technologies to improve the quality of their facilities and services to build competitive advantages, smart hotels are an important trend to watch out for.

Although smart hotels are an emerging trend, no known studies have investigated hotel employees' and guests' perceptions of this kind of hotel. Hotel employees and guests are two important stakeholders for a hotel. The stakeholder theory reveals that business operation needs to balance the benefits of every related group [2]. From a managerial perspective, the stakeholder theory shows that managerial decision-making will be influenced directly by the various groups [3]. Therefore, there is a need to understand how hotel employees and guests evaluate smart hotels, which will impact the development and adoption of technologies in hotels.

Q methodology is a qualitative research approach to explore attitudes, beliefs, and opinions of different stakeholders. This research method is especially useful for understanding new phenomena [4]. It analyzes shared subjectivity among people based on inter-correlated and factor analysis, resulting in several potential factor solutions. The Q-factor analysis can cluster participants into different groups and have insights into the relationships between the characteristics of the participants and each factor [5]. As "a method for the scientific study of human subjectivity" [6] (p. 12), Q methodology has been widely used to explore different stakeholders' subjectivity, such as visitors' and locals' tourism experiences [7] and Chinese and Canadian perceptions of photographic images of travel destinations [8].

The goal of this research is to understand hotel employees' and hotel guests' attitudes towards smart hotels. The Q methodology will be used to understand employees' and guests' perceptions. This study will answer the following research questions: (1) What are the benefits and drawbacks of smart hotels from the perspectives of hotel employees and guests? (2) What is the typology of the smart hotel employees and smart hotel guests? (3) What are the characteristics of each group?

2 Methodology

To conduct a Q methodology, the first step is to develop Q-sort statements (Fig. 1). This research has reviewed the literature related to people's perceptions of smart hotels, including perspectives from both hotel employees and guests. There are pros and cons associated with smart hotels. Smart hotels can shorten customer waiting times [9], provide seamless experiences [10], enhance service quality [10], and improve service efficiency [11]. However, others have argued that smart hotels lack personal interactions, raise privacy issues, and have potential technological failure [12].

In addition, hotel guests' reviews on the smart hotel, including Flyzoo Hotel, Hôtel Monville, and Hilton McLean in Virginia (Connie), will be analyzed to further develop Q-sort statements. Choosing these three hotels is because they have a good number of guest reviews on TripAdvisor and Booking.com. It will allow researchers to collect adequate data to further understand guests' attitudes towards the smart hotel. Additionally, in-depth interviews will be conducted to understand hotel employees' and residents' perceived benefits and drawbacks of smart hotels. A total of 15 hotel employees working at a smart hotel and 15 hotel guests who have stayed in a smart hotel will be invited to an interview. The transcripts will be analyzed in NVivo to add or revise the Q-sort statements derived from the literature review and content analysis. It is estimated that this research will develop around 30 statements.

The Q-sort statements are the concourse of the attitudes of both hotel employees and guests. For example, hotel employees may be more likely to judge the smart hotels regarding maintenance and work replacement, while hotel guests may focus on the aspects of excitement and fun. The statements in this research will include both different views of employees and guests. It will allow researchers to better understand how employees rate the benefits that smart hotels could bring to the hotel guests. It will also give insights into how hotel guests evaluate how the technology can benefit hotel employees.

In the data collection, participants (i.e., hotel employees and hotel guests) will be asked to rank the Q-sort statements based on their agreement levels (Fig. 2). And then, a post sorting interview will be conducted to understand why participants ranked the statements in that way and their attitudes towards smart hotels. In addition, the demographic information of the participants will be collected. As a large sample size may negate complexities and slight distinctions, 80 is deemed a valid number. Therefore, this research will recruit 40 hotel guests who have stayed in a smart hotel and 40 hotel employees who worked in a smart hotel.

Data will be analyzed in PQMethod to compare the different factor solutions. The most appropriate factor-solution will be selected based on correlation matrix, the total variance explained, and the number of subjects that loaded on factors [5].

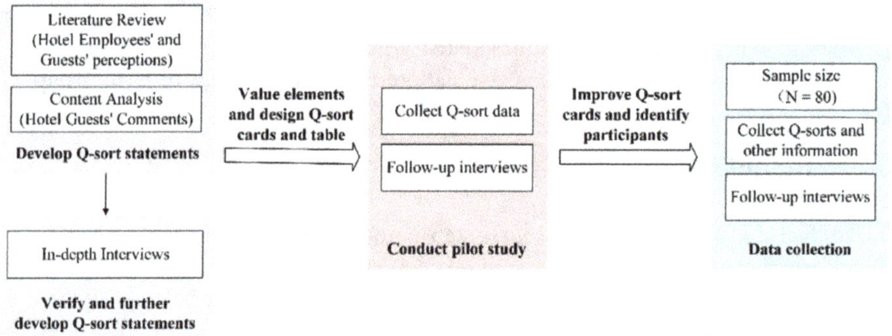

Fig. 1. Data collection process

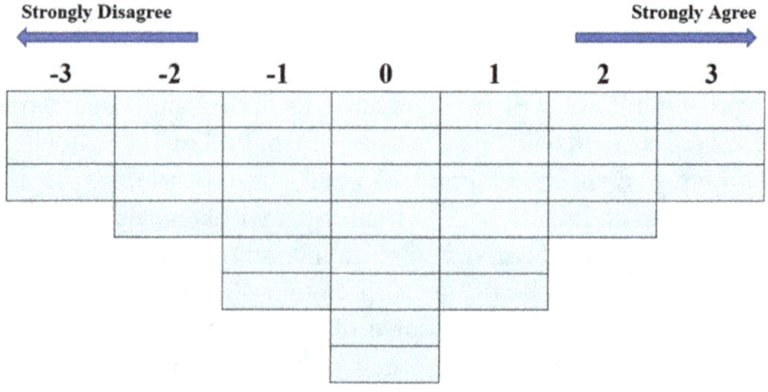

Fig. 2. Fixed distribution used for the Q-sort statements

3 Expected Results and Contributions

First, this research will summarize the benefits and drawbacks of smart hotels from the perspectives of hotel employees and guests. Second, the typology of smart hotel employees and smart hotel guests will be developed. Third, the characteristics of the employees and guests will be analyzed along with the typology.

This research will give insights into the benefits that hotel guests most value. Since building or converting to a smart hotel is costly, both hotel employees' and guests' perceptions will have implications for the development of smart hotels. Additionally, the perceptions will be categorized into several factors based on Q-factor analysis, resulting in a typology of perceptions. Additionally, the characteristics of the participants loaded on the factors will give insights into how to better attract potential smart hotel guests and mitigate hotel employees' potential resistance to smart hotels. The benefits that perceived across different groups will shed light on marketing strategies and human resources practices: These benefits could be advocated in marketing messages for customer acquisition or embedded in training materials to enhance employees' support for smart hotel features (e.g., service robots, AI, and IoT).

References

1. Wu H-C, Cheng C-C (2018) Relationships between technology attachment, experiential relationship quality, experiential risk and experiential sharing intentions in a smart hotel. J Hosp Tour Manag 37:42–58
2. Freeman RE (1984) Strategic management: a stakeholder approach. Pitman, Boston
3. Jones TM (1995) Instrumental stakeholder theory: a synthesis of ethics and economics. Acad Manag Rev 20(2):404–437
4. Hunter WC (2011) Rukai indigenous tourism: representations, cultural identity and Q method. Tour Manag 32(2):335–348
5. Shen Y, Choi HC, Joppe M, Yi S (2020) What motivates visitors to participate in a gamified trip? A player typology using Q methodology. Tour Manag 78:104074
6. McKeown BF, Thomas DB (1988) Q methodology. Sage, Newbury Park
7. Fairweather JR, Swaffield SR (2001) Visitor experiences of Kaikoura, New Zealand: an interpretive study using photographs of landscapes and Q Method. Tour Manag 22(3):219–228
8. Dewar K, Li WM, Davis CH (2007) Photographic images, culture, and perception in tourism advertising: a Q methodology study of Canadian and Chinese university students. J Travel Tour Mark 22(2):35–44
9. Kokkinou A, Cranage DA (2013) Using self-service technology to reduce customer waiting times. Int J Hosp Manag 33:435–445
10. Kuo C-M, Chen L-C, Tseng C-Y (2017) Investigating an innovative service with hospitality robots. Int J Contemp Hosp Manag 29(5):1305–1321
11. Tuomi A, Tussyadiah IP, Stienmetz J (2021) Applications and implications of service robots in hospitality. Cornell Hosp Q 62(2):232–247
12. Kelly P, Lawlor J, Mulvey M (2013) Customer decision-making processes and motives for self-service technology usage in multichannel hospitality environments. Int J Electron Cust Relatsh Manag 7(2):98–116

12

Visualizing and Comparing Online Travel Reviews of the Great Walls

Jin Ling and Nadezda Sorokina(✉)

SIHOM, Woosong University, Dongdaejon-ro 171,
Dong-gu, Daejeon 34606, South Korea
Nadia_sorokina@sis.ac.kr

Abstract. This research employs two samples of heritage sites of the Great Wall of China (Ba daling Great Wall and Mu tianyu Great Wall) and their 21000 reviews on TripAdvisor to visualize and induce feature-related comparisons. Word2vec and D3.js are applied for statistical computing and graphing Minimal Spanning Tree (MST) and ThemeRiver. The applications of MST and ThemeRiver are used to delineate outstanding features and clearer feature relationships. In terms of methodology, we applied an innovative research route to combine MST with ThemeRiver to visualize travellers' online comments. At the same time, the visual results obtained are combined with qualitative analysis to generate valuable, intuitive summaries that can be used for reference in future research. Practically, the results disclose that although both sites are highly enjoyed by tourists, they are significantly different in terms of service, infrastructure and scenery. This article has implications for policymakers and practitioners with regard to making use of online reviews to gather authentic visitor comments on the Great Wall.

Keywords: Travel reviews · Minimal Spanning Tree · ThemeRiver · The Great Wall of China

1 Introduction

The Great Wall of China is an ancient series of walls and fortifications, totaling more than 13,000 miles in length, located in northern China with a history of over 2000 years [1]. Today, the Great Wall is generally recognized as one of the most impressive architectural feats in human history, and UNESCO (1987) designated is as a World Heritage site. Mu tianyu Great Wall and Ba daling Great Wall in Beijing, China, are two heritage sites that attract millions of national and foreign tourists every year.

Given that there is a limited number of prior studies in the existing tourism literature on the comparisons of similar heritage sites through a data mining approach, and only a few scholars have been working to achieve feature visualization of travel reviews in the business application [2–7] . By delineating the Great Wall's outstanding features and clearer feature-related term relationships and showing the differences between the two heritage sites in reviews, this study provides practical suggestions for heritage site operators to improve (instead of better) their performances.

1.1 Research Questions

This research focuses on a description of the review corpus: (1) identifying what feature-related terms tourists concern most in travel reviews, and (2) exploring terms through Minimal Spanning Tree (MST) and focusing on how the most used adjective terms flow in ThemeRiver and extracting implications from it. (3) assessing if the findings can be used to enhance attraction services.

1.2 Literature Review and the Premise

"Words mentioned most frequently carry the main source of elements that determine either a positive or a negative experience" [8]. From top 50 terms from Mu tianyu Great Wall [9] and Ba daling Great Wall [10] reviews, the distribution of notional verbs, nouns, adjectives, and adverbs is highly skewed in that there are a relatively small number of terms with high frequencies. While counting the term frequency is useful in reviews extraction, which gives an outlook of tourists' concerns, examining the distribution of the terms in the documents concerning other terms can be more powerful to understand the contexts in which the terms are used. Structures are here based on the premise that: (1) people organize their beliefs depending on travel experiences into patterns that reflect term relationships, and (2) the most important things are written first.

2 Data Preprocessing and Data Process Flow

This article mainly uses the Natural Language Toolkit for language data classification (which divides a large piece of text to units), tokenization, stemming (which shares words with inflection in them to root forms), tagging, parsing (grammatical analysis for a sentence), and semantic reasoning [11].

The collected review texts are first saved into an excel document. Word2vec and D3.js are applied for statistical computing and graphing MST and ThemeRiver. Word2vec makes natural language computer-readable [12]. And each word of this dictionary is fed into D3.js to draw MST and ThemeRiver (Fig. 1).

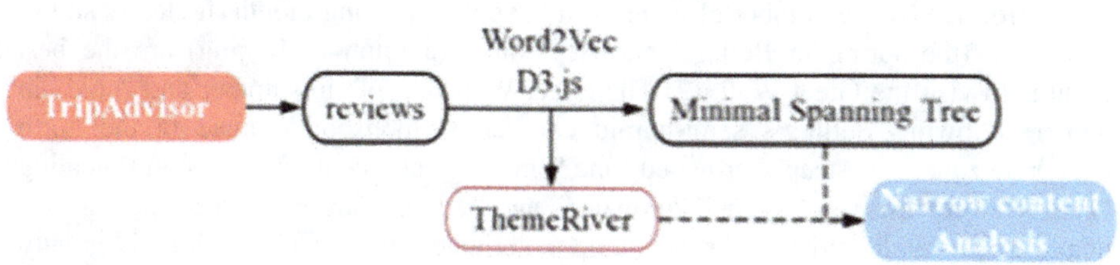

Fig. 1. Data process flow

3 MSTs and ThemeRivers for Mu Tianyu Great Wall and Ba Daling Great Wall

MSTs' different colors are used to distinguish words. The size of the nodes represents word frequency. And the relationship between them is represented by the length of their edges. The closer the relationship, the shorter the edge. The words, lines, and MSFs reveal what tourists' concerns are (Table 1).

Table 1. The MST of Ba daling Great Wall and the MST of Mu tianyu Great Wall

The MST of Ba daling Great Wall and Mu tianyu Great Wall

These depictions can only give a roughly ballpark statement of Great Wall. If MST does not apply the information leading to the identification of temporal changes, this research seeks to extend the current knowledge using ThemeRiver. The adjectives of Top 100 of the most common terms are sorted out to act as basic terms for ThemeRiver analysis (Table 2).

The river of Great Walls indicates the following three aspects: (1) the pear-shape flow is formed by the number of reviews in the corresponding month. It clearly shows that April (the spring in Beijing) and September (autumn in Beijing) are the best months to visit the Great Wall. (2) The Great Wall is "hot" in summer and "cold" in winter following Beijing's semi-humid continental monsoon climate in the north temperate zone. (3) "steep" "crowded" and "amazing" are mentioned most in Ba daling Great Wall reviews, and "steep" "crowded" and "worthy" are mentioned most in Mu tianyu Great Wall reviews. As an outdoor heritage site, the Great Wall is greatly influenced by seasons.

Table 2. The MST of Ba daling Great Wall and Mu tianyu Great Wall

The MST of Ba daling Great Wall and The MST of Mu tianyu Great Wall
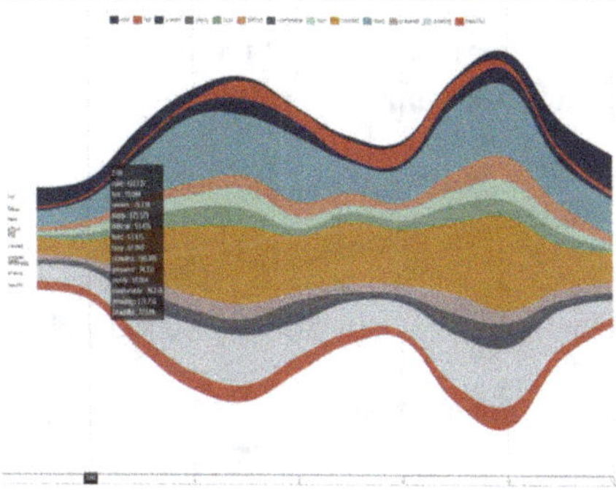 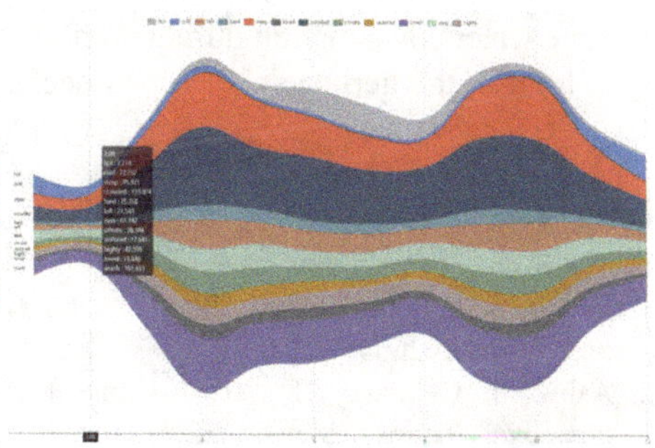

4 Summary and Managerial Suggestions

This research seeks to extend the current knowledge by applying MST, ThemeRiver and investigate the differences and similarities of two Great Wall sites from reviews of English-speaking tourists.

In terms of methodology, we applied an innovative research route to combine MST with ThemeRiver to visualize travellers' online comments. At the same time, the visual results obtained are combined with qualitative analysis to generate valuable, intuitive summaries can be used for reference in future research.

Practically, we discovered that both scenic places are "crowded" and "steep", but "amazing" and "worthy", and the best seasons to pay a visit are the spring and autumn. The weather in Great Wall is hot in summer and cold in winter. tourists take experiences of climbing walls as a way of learning Chinese history and culture.

A careful study of the summaries' commonalities can be a good source of insight for management and business promotion. For both heritage sites, Badaling Great Wall and Mu tianyu Great Wall can be highly praised in marketing promotion. For the crowded situation caused by the tourist season, the managerial department can give the corresponding warning and prompt, and the measures of "flow restriction" to alleviate. In today's Internet era, tourists book tickets in advance by Apps. A recommendation system can be established to remind consumers to prepare mountaineering supplies, prevent heat in summer and cold in winter, and significantly improve tourists' satisfaction through short messages.

On the other hand, careful studies of their differences from summaries can make them learn from and complement each other. Mu tianyu Great Wall is very popular among tourists because of the great convenience provided by the cable car and toboggan. In fact, Ba daling Great Wall is steeper than Mu tianyu Great Wall, if the cable car service can be provided, it is sure to increase tourists' convenience and improve their experience. The guide service of Ba daling Great Wall makes the tourists very satisfied. Taking pictures and learning Chinese history are realized with the help of the guide. The managers from Mu tianyu Great Wall can learn from this experience, and actively improve their tour guide team. Besides, tourists are reminded to bring more drinking water when climbing mountains in Mu tianyu Great Wall. One reason is the huge water consumption during climbing; the other reason is that the price of water is too high in the heritage site, which needs to arouse managers' attention to act.

References

1. History.com Editors. Great Wall of China. https://www.history.com/topics/ancient-china/great-wall-of-china (2020)
2. Ashworth G, Page SJ (2010) Urban tourism research: Recent progress and current paradoxes. Tourism Manage 32(1):1–15
3. Kladou S, Mavragani E (2015) Assessing destination image: An online marketing approach and the case of TripAdvisor. J Destination Mark Manage 4(3):187–193
4. Richards G (2018) Cultural tourism: a review of recent research and trends. J Hospitality Tourism Manage 36:12–21
5. Setlur V, Stone MC (2016) A linguistic approach to categorical color assignment for data visualization. IEEE Trans Visual Comput Graph 22(1):698-707
6. Sundberg REA (2012) Visualizing sentiment analysis on a user forum. In: Eighth International European Language Resources Association (ELRA), pp 3573–3579
7. Wang CEA (2013) SentiView: sentiment analysis and visualization for internet popular topics. IEEE Trans Human Mach Syst 43:620–630
8. Barreda A, Bilgihan A (2013) An analysis of user-generated content for hotel experiences. J Hospitality Tourism Technol 4(3)
9. TripAdvisor (2019) Mu tianyu Great Wall. https://www.tripadvisor.co.uk/Attraction_Review-g294212-d325811-Reviews-Mutianyu_Great_Wall-Beijing.html 1 November 2019
10. TripAdvisor (2019) The Great Wall at Ba daling. https://www.tripadvisor.co.uk/Attraction_Review-g294212-d311505-Reviews-The_Great_Wall_at_Badaling-Beijing.html
11. Blei DM, Lafferty JD (2006) Dynamic topic models. Mach Learn
12. Nicholson C (2019 A beginner's guide to word2vec and neural word embeddings. https://pathmind.com/wiki/word2vec 12 Nov 2019

13

Data-Supported CRM as a Lever for DMO Success: A Social Exchange Relationship Approach

Birgit Bosio[1(✉)] and Melanie Scheiber[2]

[1] MCI Management Center Innsbruck, 6020 Innsbruck, Austria
birgit.bosio@mci.edu
[2] Ötztal Tourismus, 6450 Sölden, Austria

Abstract. Customer relationship management (CRM) is proving to be one of the most promising business strategies. However, in the field of destination marketing literature, a problem exists as to how data-supported CRM can be established. While customer data management has already been well exploited in other industries, DMOs lack customer proximity and data sovereignty. The aim of this paper is to fill this research gap and show how a data-based CRM can be deployed by DMOs based on the principles of social exchange theory. In 13 expert interviews, these aspects were examined from the DMO's point of view. The results show that the exchange relationship must be established taking into account the DMO's extraordinary conditions and critical success factors. In order to stimulate guests' desire for dialogue or the willingness to disclose personal data, DMOs should offer high-quality customer benefits. A combination of hedonic and utilitarian benefits are found to be the most effective stimuli. In return, only the most necessary customer information should be requested and subsequently built passively. Only if the cost and benefit ratio of the exchange relationship is positive for both parties, a database for the CRM can be built in order to foster long-lasting relationships with potential and returning guests.

Keywords: Data-based customer relationship management · Social exchange theory · Destination management

1 Introduction

Every day companies lose customers unconsciously [28]. Therefore, customer relationship management (CRM) serves to "… encompass the development and consolidation of long-term profitable customer relationships through coordinated and customer-specific marketing, sales and service concepts with the help of modern information and communication technologies." [35] Due to an even stronger trend for individualization in travel, companies need to know about travelers' needs and wishes. This topic is becoming increasingly important also in view of the current COVID-19 crisis. Customers' wishes and requirements thus become the focus of every company and all its business areas [27]. The fundamental basis for maintaining customer relationships is customer data, which is condensed into customer profiles. These must be aggregated, classified and stored in a customer data platform [60]. The profiles then serve for databased CRM to derive tailored offers and communication [37] based on the individual information such as demographic data or psychographic data. Building a database should be seen as a profitable investment, as customer information significantly increases the efficiency of marketing activities [17, 43, 57] and allows companies to generate a higher return on investment [33]. Early approaches in CRM application in community-based tourism analyzed the degree of CRM implementation in destinations [20]. Other authors stressed the importance of cooperation between various service providers and the DMO in community-based tourism for an integrated CRM [21, 22]. DMOs were defined as "enablers of integrated electronic CRM" and an adoption framework for this cooperation was developed [21]. Also, the visitor relationship marketing orientation among DMOs was researched and a model to operationalize DMO visitor relationship orientation developed [42, 46]. Results showed that DMOs were often "responsive and reactive rather than proactive" [42]. Another author analyzed data-driven CRM for airline and travel agency industries [10] and coffee shops [11] in Taiwan. While bigger companies are already quite successful in strategically collecting customer data, the tourism industry lacks behind in this topic. A study amongst Austrian and Swiss DMOs showed that there is a huge gap between data availability and the strategic use of this data due to legal, know-how and financial constraints [4]. Data is very often still not made available online, not collected systematically, if so stored in silos by other service providers and links between databases are often missing. They can neither process data of guests staying in the regions nor of their activities. As tourism destinations are complex systems [3], they are not in command of data sovereignty [25]. While this field of research is not new for the tourism and hospitality industry [6, 38], the majority of tourism businesses still rely completely on the success of the development of the touristic offer. Their lack of understanding of customer orientation and their dismissive attitude towards modern approaches to creating competitive advantages are to blame [56]. Even the DMOs have resisted the demands of digitalization for too long [36]. Considering the increasing global competition, the trend shift towards short breaks and the decreasing number of regular guests, intelligent approaches such as CRM are immediately required in destination marketing in order to maintain the competitiveness of destinations [2, 36]. Therefore, it is up to DMOs as strategic competitive entities to drive CRM for the benefit of the destination and all its touristic stakeholders [53]. Following the literature on CRM in the tourism and hospitality industry [49], this paper addresses various research gaps: "The majority of published research articles are in the area of hospitality, with a specific focus on hotels and restaurants. (…) Future research in the tourism area, especially at the destination level is also required." [49] Indeed, in literature CRM has gained a foothold in tourism research [49], but unlike the numerous research contributions in the hotel sector [17, 57], CRM in the context of DMOs is discussed in fewer recent publications [2, 36, 46]. "In examining the three components of CRM, the technology aspect has received the most attention, whereas the roles of people and process have been widely neglected" [49]. The general marketing research fields like database marketing, permission marketing, marketing automation, online marketing or data privacy issue aspects of building a database for CRM, focus either on technological aspects [28] or on behavioral aspects [30]. A holistic view on both crucial aspects has not yet been issued. This is the reason why this paper combines both technological and behavioral aspects and stresses the social interaction of both supply and demand side. "The topic of e-CRM is widely researched in the marketing, management and IT fields. However, there is a need for H&T scholars to focus on e-CRM" [49]. Digitalization has become one of the main fields in tourism as an information-intensive, globally-oriented, but locally-delivering industry. Technological advancement is transforming tourism value chains. Whereas technological innovations are doubtless possible, the problem remains in implementing digital services and marketing within the mainly small-structured tourism industry [15]. There is thus still a long way to go for the digital transformation of tourism businesses. Therefore, when establishing a destination-wide CRM, also the interests of service providers as well as their level of digital literacy need to be taken into consideration [50]. In order to also take into account both the DMO's role and the necessary cooperation with local service providers from the supply as well as the customer side of this relationship, this paper focuses on how to establish a balanced relationship between the DMO and the potential or existing guests and tries to answer the following research question: How can social exchange promote the generation of dialogue-ready customer contacts for data-based CRM in DMOs to create a win-win situation for both sides? Which key factors are decisive for the success of this social exchange relationship? The aim of this paper is to show how a data-based CRM can be developed by DMOs from a holistic perspective as well as to consider the challenges of the digital transformation for both DMOs and service providers.

2 Building a Customer Database for CRM

This paper addresses technological aspects for both DMOs and small-scale tourism providers as well as the lack of the social dimension of the relationship between guests and the DMO.

2.1 Technological Aspects from the Supply Perspective

The instruments for building up a customer database for CRM are primarily located in acquisition management by addressing the target market, identifying interested parties and converting them into customers [16, 51]. It includes the stimulation of interest in the target market, the identification of prospects as well as their processing until the conclusion of a purchase. Through the sales funnel, prospects should be transformed into customers [51]. At the end of the funnel, it is important to bind these customers to the company through the subsequent customer loyalty management [43]. Along the sales funnel, different information about the customer is generated at various touchpoints of the customer journey. This data flows into the company's database, is classified and clustered by predefined segmentation attributes and is condensed into a unique customer profile [17]. The basic motive of creating a customer profile is to present the customer in a holistic picture, because the generated customer profiles are used to initiate, maintain or rebuild customer relationships [4]. Hence, the more data is generated from a customer the better the picture of a customer gets. Which customer information a customer profile should contain depends on the respective objective of a company [32]. Name and email address were identified as the most important and lifestyles as the second most important variables for customer acquisition [58]. Today, the checkbox for obtaining marketing permission also counts as a target variable for lead generation, because personal data may only be stored, processed and analyzed with the explicit consent of the data subject [47]. Therefore, every European company needs to consider the General Data Protection Regulation (GDPR) to initiate and maintain business relationships [23]. While these processes work well for other industries, DMOs mainly are not in direct contact with the customer, as guests usually directly interact with accommodation or other service providers. On the other hand, the small-scale tourism providers often have neither the personal and financial resources, nor the know-how to establish such customer databases. This makes the technological requirements for a databased CRM of a DMO even more challenging.

2.2 Behavioral Aspects from the Demand Perspective

Major data leakages and misuse in the past have had a negative influence on the trust of customers in handling personal information [9, 14]. Therefore, from the perspective of customers, also behavioral aspects have to be taken into consideration. Privacy concerns imply a perceived sensitivity to the preservation of one's own privacy and manifest themselves in concerns about storing, using, sharing and publishing personal data [1]. In addition, direct marketing is often leading to customer annoyance [4]. The cause-privacy concern impact model (APCO) explains the emergence of privacy concerns and their influence on customer behavior [55]. Beside experience, awareness, personality, demographics and culture as the drivers of privacy concerns, plenty of authors studied the privacy paradox. It describes the contradictory contrast of personal attitudes to displayed behavior [29], which influences the behavioral intention and is the main cause of contradictory behavior patterns [55]. Thus, customer behavior only partially reflects the conventional assumptions of behavioral psychology, according to which human behavior is based on rational considerations. In fact, customer behavior is based on the outcome of a privacy calculus or a personal cost-benefit comparison [34, 39]. To impact customers' privacy calculus and hence consumer behavior positively, the use of incentives has widely been discussed in literature [30]. Discounts and free products or services are considered as monetary incentives due to their measurable value [41]. Non-monetary incentives include hedonic incentives, which are described as a psychological benefit component [30] and utilitarian incentives, which are characterized by their functional utility character [44]. All those incentives can be combined in crystallization points [7] such as bonus schemes [26], applications [13], customer clubs [12] or loyalty cards [45]. It is also important to think about where to place these incentives within the customer journey. The cost variable of the privacy calculus includes all risks and negative consequences that arise from data transmission [59]. If the expected benefits exceed the costs, customers are willing to allow data transfer [34]. The cost and benefit calculation in the privacy calculus is based on the principles of social exchange theory [34, 39] as one of the oldest, but still most popular theories to explain social behavior [48]. Parties are mutually interdependent and impose costs and rewards on each other through their behavior [18, 24]. Thus, the least costly, most rewarding option is chosen

[54]. While this topic has been studied in CRM in general, studies on guests' behavior as an application to the tourism industry are still scarce [49].

3 Method

Given the need for insights into more complex structures of economic and social relationships within the field of data-driven CRM in DMOs, a qualitative research method was applied [8]. In this course, the topic was examined empirically from the alpine community-based DMO's point of view conducting 13 semi-structured guided expert interviews [19]. An interview guideline was developed based on the literature review. The main focus areas were: 1. how can DMOs successfully establish an exchange relationship for databased CRM; 2. what type of customer data must be generated in the initial contact and 3. what type of benefits must be offered in exchange; 4. how would the ideal cost benefit ratio for DMOs and guests look like 5. in which phase of the customer journey must the data generation be located. Experts were chosen, as they are highly qualified to answer the research question. They are seen as "crystallization points" of practical insider knowledge and therefore can be interviewed instead of a large number of subjects [5]. All interviews were held online during spring 2020 and lasted from 40 to 90 min. The following selection criteria of interviewees were established [19]: professional qualification, knowledge of the functions of DMOs and touristic behavior, and a close relation with alpine community-based destinations in the German-speaking area. The sample comprises 13 participants of which four are CEOs in consulting companies for strategic and digital matters of DMOs, two of them professors in tourism marketing management on a collage of higher education, two chief digital officers in DMOs, four marketing employees responsible for CRM in DMOs, one chief marketing officer in a cable car company and leader of a CRM project launched together with a DMO. Not having focused on gender nor on nationalities, the sample resulted in seven male and six female participants, with two of them living in Switzerland, four in Germany and 7 in Austria. All participants fulfilled the qualification criteria. For data analysis, a summarizing content analysis was chosen [40], as it is ideally suited for evaluating expert knowledge in a narrow field of research [52]. The interviews were transcribed [16]. MAXQDA, a common software solution for qualitative data analysis [31], was used to develop a codebook. This was done by paraphrasing relevant text passages from the interview transcripts, generalizing their messages and reducing them to their point of meaning [40]. This method allows to extract expert knowledge from the generated qualitative data and to derive inductive categories in which this coded information is compound. The resulting categories of this research include: important frame conditions of DMOs and key success factors for the establishment of exchange relationships; required customer data to create a customer profile and effective customer benefits in exchange. Based on these categories the experts research results have been discussed. As there is no significant difference between the DMO's managers or employees compared to other experts' perspectives, the results of this research must not be discussed from the different expert group's points of view.

4 Results

The research results show that the establishment of an exchange relationship with tourists must be considered in the context of the DMOs' frame conditions and key success factors as well as consider the design of the exchange relationship.

4.1 Establishment of the Exchange Relationship

DMOs suffer from a lack of customer proximity as guests usually directly interact with service providers in the destination. Thus, the DMO often has few to no touchpoints with guests who have already been to the destination. Even though all experts view DMOs as an important source of inspiration for guests, they are by nature in an unfavorable position for data generation. Other key players in the destination however, such as accommodations, gastronomy, shops, touristic service providers are in an ideal position for data generation as they are in a legal economic relationship with guests. Therefore, experts refer to establishing networks with services providers within the destination. By means of stakeholder management DMOs have to convince all key players and involve them in the process of data generation for a CRM system. With them bridging the contact between the DMO and tourists, valuable data pools within the destination can be channeled. In addition, a number of key success factors for the establishment of exchange relationships could be identified. These are classified as strategic, conceptional and methodological factors. The strategic key success factors are based on a strategic approach of why data and what data is generated, and how it is going to be used by the DMOs. Otherwise, data is generated randomly and may lack specific insights or it is too broad to be structured usefully. Also, know-how in the field of databased CRM must be implemented in the organizational structures of the DMO to create marketing efficiency to the destination's benefit. The conceptional success factors include facilitators of the exchange relationship. For DMOs it is essential to know that the less data is requested from tourists in exchange for a benefit, the more likely is their willingness for data disclosure. Also, the relevance of the offered benefits must be maximized and exactly meet customers' needs at the specific touchpoint in the customer journey. Even though the inspiration and consideration phases (pre-booking phase) are already targeted by many DMOs, all touchpoints along the whole customer journey should be addressed. All experts see a high and so far not claimed potential for exchange relationships during the stay in the destination. In order to exploit potentials, it is suggested that DMOs become innovative in terms of creating intelligent customer benefit offers. Experts underline the necessity of making best use of the DMOs' frame conditions, rather than emulating common sales funnel strategies of usual single player businesses. The methodological success factors include that DMOs need to guarantee high customer experience at all touchpoints and interact with customers in a very simple context as complexity leads to high drop-off rates even before the actual exchange takes place. In general, experts urge DMOs to act in a helpful and trustful way towards tourists in order to minimize data privacy concerns and to create more confidence by tourists.

4.2 Design of the Exchange Relationship

In order to motivate the guests' desire for dialogue, as little data as possible should be requested in an initial active contact. The e-mail address as identity carrier and point of contact, the name, and the marketing permission for the legitimacy of the data use as well as the defined interests that give meaning to the identification data represent the ideal starting point for the creation of a basic customer profile. Experts stress that extending customer data is gained through further touchpoints. Many of these customer data can be tracked passively, without affecting the customer's data privacy concerns and therefore without causing social costs. Findings suggest that for creating a customer profile relevant for CRM, DMOs must at least add the customer's interests. Less but also relevant are preferences or origin. In exchange for customer data, rewards become essential. Results suggest that rewards should include a versatile combination of incentives. There is a clear preference for hedonic and utilitarian incentives to stimulate the willingness to engage in dialogue. Information before or during the journey emerges as one of the most significant incentives as it creates high benefits for customers at low costs for DMOs. Information of this type is classified as hedonic incentive as it provides profound travel experiences. Moreover, tourist communities with options for digital exchange on the DMO website or possibilities to express recommendations and reviews during the post stay phase are considered effective. Hedonic incentives cause low costs for DMOs. Utilitarian incentives provide a more convenient travel experience. Experts claim that assisting technologies generate extraordinary customer benefits in all phases of the customer journey. Also booking systems for tickets, experiences or other services of touristic interest are highly beneficial. Assisting tools or systems cause moderate costs, as licenses or development costs are predictable and limited. While hedonic and utilitarian incentives are considered to generate high customer benefits, five of thirteen participating experts dissuade DMOs from offering monetary incentives as the quality of generated leads is expected to be very low in terms of higher opt-out rates as customers are not really interested in a lasting exchange relationship but rather seek for one-time saving opportunities. However, receiving gifts such as free services, goodies or consumption goods during the journey, appears to have positive effects. For the exchange relationship to be successful, it is important that the cost-benefit-ratio is balanced. This means that guests should not have to disclose an unnecessary amount of personal data and DMOs should not suffer from disproportionate project costs. Therefore, incentives causing low or flat-rate cost for DMOs such as information and assisting technologies are the best option to keep the exchange relationship balanced. Gifts on the other hand, may in high quantities get too cost-intensive.

5 Conclusion

The research results show that DMOs are in an unfavorable position for establishing an exchange relationship for databased CRM on their own, due to lacking customer proximity. Even though the DMOs' booking platforms would in fact be an important touchpoint for establishing exchange relationships with tourists, OTAs hold most of the market share while DMOs count few bookings on their own platforms. Nonetheless, DMOs are still in the ideal position to bridge the gap using their networking capabilities and power in the destination. If they successfully collaborate with key players in the destination, they could establish a data-based CRM. DMOs may convince accommodation providers to communicate the DMOs benefits to their guests by linking directly to the DMOs landing pages or registration forms. Thus, the DMO potentially creates touchpoints with all guests in the destination. Solutions of this kind would be game changing, as mediation is an effective and legal way to get in touch with all tourists coming to the destination, no matter whether they booked their holiday on the site of third parties such as OTAs. It is also suggested that DMOs clearly define their goals of a databased CRM system before establishing an exchange relationship. Depending on the goals, relevant touchpoints, customer data, customer benefits and lead quality may differ. For the goal of tailored marketing communication and offers based on customers' needs, a basic customer profile must at least contain the customer's email address, his or her name, the marketing permission and very important – his or her interests. It may be however suggested that customer's interests are gained passively during further touchpoints, because the more data is requested at an initial touchpoint, the higher the dropout rate will be. In exchange for data disclosure, DMOs must offer extraordinary customer benefits at acceptable costs for the DMO in order to keep the benefit-cost-ratio balanced for both parties. As the results show that monetary incentives may lead to high costs or even negative effects, DMOs must channel the power of hedonic and utilitarian incentives. Experts consider information, communities together with systems for holiday administration and planning most effective. Yet it appears that efficiency may be even increased by consolidating all benefits into one crystallization point. This could be a destination app or travel guide, which assists customers along all phases of the journey. It may provide information on activities and individual programs based on the customer's interests, scheduling and booking before the journey. During the journey it offers orientation, while after the journey it allows customers to review their activities. Such a travel guide which includes accumulated hedonic and utilitarian benefits and maybe even - if still cost effective - free services, stimulate the willingness for exchange as they provide high value for tourists and low costs for DMOs.

6 Limitations and Implications

This research involves some critical limitations as technical aspects are only addressed in rudimentary form and thus remain largely unsolved. Furthermore, staff of DMOs formed the biggest group within the sample which might cause a bias in the results. Another bias might arise from the time of interviews falling within the COVID-19 crisis. Future studies should take into account the demand side to prove the actual effect of the incentives on the willingness to engage in dialogue as well as on the actual perceived data privacy concerns from the demand side. Another essential aspect would be a holistic analysis of the exchange relationship over a longer period. In addition, surveys should also be carried out outside of the German-speaking area. Based on this research, Ötztal Tourism in Austria used these findings to establish a databased CRM system. As a solution for the problem of data sovereignty through various destination stakeholders, the DMO exploited its stakeholder proximity and built a destination-wide partner network of approx. 1,000 accommodation and 30 service providers, who mediate the contact between the DMO and the tourists. This practical example shows how a DMO can overcome the lack of customer proximity and achieve data sovereignty by creating a network platform amongst service providers, which offers valuable benefits for both existing and potential guests. By applying a combination of mainly hedonistic and utilitarian benefits and creating a customer profile gradually, a balanced social exchange relationship can be developed. This research contributes to the knowledge of alpine community-based DMOs as to how a databased CRM can be established to fully contribute to the destination's marketing efficiency. It shows that not only technical but also behavioral aspects have to be considered and how the principles of social exchange effectively facilitate a win-win relationship for all involved parties.

References

1. Acquisti A, Brandimarte L, Loewenstein G (2015) Privacy and human behavior in the age of information. Science 347(6221):509–514
2. Almeida-Santana A, Moreno-Gil S (2017) New trends in information search and their influence on destination loyalty: digital destinations and relationship marketing. J Destin Mark Manag 6(2):150–161. https://doi.org/10.1016/j.jdmm.2017.02.003
3. Baggio R, Scott N, Cooper C (2010) Improving tourism destination governance: a complexity science approach. Tourism Rev 65(4):51–60
4. Bosio B, Nadegger M, Schegg R, Fux M (2020) Big Data Nutzung in DMOs - Vergleich Schweiz: Tirol. Tourismuswissen Quarterly, 20 April 2020. (in German)
5. Bogner A, Littig B, Menz W (2014) Interviews Mit Experten: Eine Praxisorientierte Einführung. Springer VS, Wiesbaden (in German)
6. Bowen JT, Chen SL (2001) The relationship between customer loyalty and customer satisfaction. Int J Contemp Hosp Manag 1(2):213–217. https://doi.org/10.1108/09596110110395893
7. Brashear-Alejandro T, Kang J, Groza MD (2016) Leveraging loyalty programs to build customer–company identification. J Bus Res 69(3):1190–1198. https://doi.org/10.1016/j.jbusres.2015.09.014
8. Bryman A (2016) Social Research Methods, 5th edn. Oxford University Press, Oxford
9. Camilleri MA (2019) The Use of Data-Driven Technologies in Tourism Marketing. Routledge, Oxford
10. Chiang W-Y (2019) Establishing high value markets for data-driven customer relationship management systems. Kybernetes 48(3):650–662
11. Chiang W-Y (2021) Using a data-driven marketing strategy on customer relationship management: an empirical case of urban coffee shops in Taiwan. Br Food J 123(4):1610–1625. https://doi.org/10.1108/BFJ-06-2020-0523
12. Da Silveira GC, Da Costa FACD (2019) Benefit clubs as a tool for loyalty marketing. Study of Brazil's main insurance companies. J Bus Econ 10(3):216–226

13. Dastjerdi AM, Kaplan S, De Abreu e Silva J, Nielsen OA, Pereira FC (2019) Participating in environmental loyalty program with a real-time multimodal travel app: User needs, environmental and privacy motivators. Transp Res D Transp Environ 67:223–243. https://doi.org/10.1016/j.trd.2018.11.013
14. Degirmenci K (2020) Mobile users' information privacy concerns and the role of app permission requests. Int J Inf Manage 50:261–272. https://doi.org/10.1016/j.ijinfomgt.2019.05.010
15. Dredge D, Phi G, Mahadevan R, Meehan E, Popescu ES (2018) Digitalisation in Tourism: In-Depth Analysis of Challenges and Opportunities. Low Value Procedure GRO-SME-17-C-091-A for Executive Agency for Small and Medium-sized Enterprises (EASME) Virtual Tourism Observatory. Aalborg University, Copenhagen
16. Dresing T, Pehl T (eds): Praxisbuch Interview, Transkription & Analyse: Anleitungen und Regelsysteme für Qualitativ Forschende. Eigenverlag (2015). (in German)
17. Dursun A, Caber M (2016) Using data mining techniques for profiling profitable hotel customers: an application of RFM analysis. Tourism Manag Persp 18:153–160. https://doi.org/10.1016/j.tmp.2016.03.001
18. Emerson RM (1976) Social exchange theory. Ann Rev Sociol 2(1):335–362
19. Flick U (2017) Qualitative Sozialforschung: Eine Einführung, 8th edn. Rowohlt Taschenbuch Verlag, Reinbek (in German)
20. Fyall A, Callod C, Edwards B (2003) Relationship marketing. Ann Tour Res 30(3):644–659. https://doi.org/10.1016/S0160-7383(03)00046-X
21. Fux M, Mathieu DS, Go F (2007) Integrated electronic customer relationship management (CRM) for Alpine tourist destinations: drivers and an adoption framework. Inf Commun Technol Tourism 9:413–424
22. Fux M, Myrach T (2009) Adoption of a destination-wide CRM approach: an empirical analysis of the determinants in the Swiss Hospitality Industry. In: Höpken W, Gretzel U, Law R (Eds) Information and Communication Technologies in Tourism 2009. Proceedings of the International Conference in Amsterdam, The Netherlands. pp 507–517
23. Heukrodt-Bauer S (2017) Rechtskonforme E-mail-marketing-automation. In: Hannig U (ed) Marketing und Sales Automation. Springer, Wiesbaden, pp 59–70. https://doi.org/10.1007/978-3-658-15260-4_5
24. Homans GC (1958) Social behavior as exchange. Am J Sociol 63(6):597–606
25. Hummel P, Braun M, Tretter M, Dabrock P (2021) Data sovereignty: a review. Big Data Soc 1:1–17. https://doi.org/10.1177/2053951720982012
26. Hwang Y, Gao L, Mattila AS (2020) What recovery options to offer for loyalty reward program members: dollars vs. miles? Int J Hosp Manag 87:102496. https://doi.org/10.1016/j.ijhm.2020.102496
27. Jaber F, Simkin L (2017) Unpicking antecedents of CRM adoption: a two-stage model. J Strateg Mark 25(5–6):475–494. https://doi.org/10.1080/0965254X.2016.1149212
28. Järvinen J, Taiminen H (2016) Harnessing marketing automation for B2B content marketing. Ind Mark Manage 54:164–175. https://doi.org/10.1016/j.indmarman.2015.07.002
29. Kokolakis S (2017) Privacy attitudes and privacy behaviour: a review of current research on the privacy paradox phenomenon. Comput Secur 64:122–134. https://doi.org/10.1016/j.cose.2015.07.002
30. Krafft M, Arden CM, Verhoef PC (2017) Permission marketing and privacy concerns - why do customers (not) grant permissions? J Interact Mark 39:39–54. https://doi.org/10.1016/j.intmar.2017.03.001
31. Kuckartz U (2010) Einführung in Die Computergestützte Analyse Qualitativer Daten. Springer VS, Wiesbaden (in German)

32. Kumar V, Reinartz W (2018) Strategic CRM today. In: Customer Relationship Management. Springer Texts in Business and Economics. Springer, Heidelberg. https://doi.org/10.1007/978-3-662-55381-7_1
33. Kunz W et al (2017) Customer engagement in a Big Data world. J Serv Mark 31(2):161–171
34. Lee N, Kwon O (2015) A privacy-aware feature selection method for solving the personalization–privacy paradox in mobile wellness healthcare services. Expert Syst Appl 42 (5):2764–2771. https://doi.org/10.1016/j.eswa.2014.11.031
35. Leußer W, Hippner H, Wilde K (2011) CRM - Grundlagen, konzepte und prozesse. In: Hippner H, Hubrich B, Wilde KD (eds), Grundlagen des CRM: Strategie, Geschäftsprozesse und IT-Unterstützung, 3rd edn. Wiesbaden: Gabler. pp 15–55 (in German)
36. Li S, Robinson P, Oriade A (2017) Destination marketing: the use of technology since the millennium. J Destin Market Manag 6(2):95–102. https://doi.org/10.1016/j.jdmm.2017.04.008
37. Lian S, Xu Y, Zhang C (2019) Family profile mining in retailing. Decis Support Syst 118:102–114
38. Lo AS, Stalcup LD, Lee A (2010) Customer relationship management for hotels in Hong Kong. Int J Contemp Hosp Manag 22(2):139–159
39. Martin KD, Murphy PE (2016) The role of data privacy in marketing. J Acad Mark Sci 45 (2):135–155. https://doi.org/10.1007/s11747-016-0495-4
40. Mayring P (2015) Qualitative Inhaltsanalyse: Grundlagen und Techniken. Weinheim/Basel: Beltz (in German)
41. Meyer-Waarden L (2015) Effects of loyalty program rewards on store loyalty. J Retail Consum Serv 24:22–32
42. Murdy S, Pike S, Lings I (2010) In pursuit of tourism destination brand loyalty: visitor relationship management orientation of destination marketing organisations. In: 6th International Colloquium – Academy of Marketing SIG on Brand, Identity and Corporate Reputation. Barcelona: ESADE
43. Ohiomah A, Andreev P, Benyoucef M, Hood D (2019) The role of lead management systems in inside sales performance. J Bus Res 102:163–177. https://doi.org/10.1016/j.jbusres.2019.05.018
44. Palazon M, Delgado-Ballester E (2013) Hedonic or utilitarian premiums: does it matter? Eur J Mark 47(8):1256–1275. https://doi.org/10.1108/03090561311324318
45. Pesonen J, Komppula R, Murphy J (2019) Plastic loyalty – Investigating loyalty card programs for a Finnish hotel chain. Tour Manage 73:115–122. https://doi.org/10.1016/j.tourman.2019.01.023
46. Pike S, Murdy S, Lings I (2011) Visitor relationship orientation of destination marketing organizations. J Travel Res 50(4):443–453. https://doi.org/10.1177/0047287510368163
47. Presthus W, Sørum H (2018) Are consumers concerned about privacy? An online survey emphasizing the general data protection regulation. Procedia Comput Sci 138:603–611. https://doi.org/10.1016/j.procs.2018.10.081
48. Proudfoot JG, Wilson D, Valacich JS, Byrd MD (2018) Saving face on Facebook: privacy concerns, social benefits, and impression management. Behav Inf Technol 37(1):16–37. https://doi.org/10.1080/0144929X.2017.1389988
49. Rahimi R, Köseoglu MA, Ersoy AB, Okumus F (2017) Customer relationship management research in tourism and hospitality: a state-of-the-art. Tourism Rev 72(2):209–220. https://doi.org/10.1108/TR-01-2017-0011
50. Ritchie RJB, Ritchie JRB (2002) A framework for an industry supported destination marketing information system. Tour Manage 23(5):439–454. https://doi.org/10.1016/S0261-5177(02)00007-9

51. Rodriguez M, Peterson RM, Krishnan V (2018) Impact of CRM technology on sales process behaviors: empirical results from US, Europe, and Asia. J Bus Bus Mark 25(1):1–10. https://doi.org/10.1080/1051712X.2018.1424754
52. Schreier M (2014) Qualitative content analysis. In: Flick U (eds) The SAGE Handbook of Qualitative Data Analysis. London: SAGE, pp 170–183. https://doi.org/10.4135/9781446282243.n12
53. Scott P et al (2017) The consumer journey in the digital age: the challenges faced by destination and place marketing agencies. Int J Digit Cult Electron Tourism 2(1):28–45. https://doi.org/10.1504/IJDCET.2017.10003180
54. Simpson RL (1976) Theories of social exchange. In: Thibaut JW, Spence JT, Carson RC (eds) Contemporary Topics in Social Psychology. General Learning Press, New York, pp 79–97
55. Smith HJ, Dinev T, Xu H (2011) Information privacy research: an interdisciplinary review. MIS Q 35(4):989–1015. https://doi.org/10.2307/41409970
56. Staudacher J, Holland N (2019) Die Zukunft des CRM liegt in der Kundendatenanalyse. Swiss Market Rev 1:14–18 (in German)
57. Talón-Ballestero P, González-Serrano L, Soguero-Ruiz C, Muñoz-Romero S, Rojo-Álvarez JL (2018) Using big data from customer relationship management information systems to determine the client profile in the hotel sector. Tour Manage 68:187–197. https://doi.org/10.1016/j.tourman.2018.03.017
58. Verhoef PC, Spring PN, Hoekstra JC, Leeflang PSH (2003) The commercial use of segmentation and predictive modeling techniques for database marketing in the Netherlands. Decis Supp Syst 34(4):471–481. https://doi.org/10.1016/S0167-9236(02)00069-6
59. Warshaw J, Matthews T, Whittaker S, Kau C, Bengualid M, Smith BA (2015) Can an algorithm know the “real you”? In: Begole B, Kim J, Inkpen K, Woo W (eds) Proceedings of the 33rd Annual ACM Conference on Human Factors in Computing Systems. New York: Association for Computing Machinery, pp 797–806
60. Zerbino P, Aloini D, Dulmin R, Mininno V (2018) Big data-enabled customer relationship management: a holistic approach. Inf Process Manage 54(5):818–846. https://doi.org/10.1016/j.ipm.2017.10.005

14

Topic Modelling of Tourist Dining Experiences based on the GLOBE Model

Roman Egger, Angela Pagiri, Barbara Prodinger(✉), Ruihong Liu and Fabian Wettinger

University of Applied Sciences Salzburg, Puch/Salzburg, Austria
roman.egger@fh-salzburg.ac.at,
prodinger_barbara@gmx.at

Abstract. The needs of travellers vary across cultures. When it comes to culinary aspects, there is a strong connection between gastronomy and culture. To optimise service offerings, investigation of the essential aspects of dining experiences in relation to cultural backgrounds is of great importance. In the age of digitalisation, tourists share their dining experiences throughout their multi-phasic travel journey via online platforms. By considering nine distinct cultural backgrounds, this research aims to investigate tourist experiences based on TripAdvisor restaurant reviews through topic modelling, using the city of Salzburg as its study context. Depending on one's cultural circumstances, the findings demonstrate that the most important aspects include staff, food-menu items, value for money, restaurant physical appearance, food authenticity, overall service, menu offers, food quality, atmosphere, and recommendations. This study advances the state-of-the-art knowledge of societal culture as a variable in the target market analysis of restaurant customers. Findings allow restaurant owners, other tourism service providers, and destination management organisations to analyse and adapt their service offerings and strategies accordingly.

Keywords: TripAdvisor · Dining experience · Societal culture · GLOBE

1 Introduction

Visitors from different countries vary in their service expectations and travel behaviours due to cultural backgrounds, which subsequently influences their travel experience [1, 2]. Thus, identifying those needs is essential in order to contribute to up-to-date services and products [3]. Literature has provided insights on service quality and customer satisfaction in a restaurant setting based on widely used models such as SERVQUAL [4] and DINESERV [5, 6]. However, in this process, guests fill out a predefined questionnaire before and after the service, leading to mostly small sample sizes caused by the challenge of persuading guests to participate [7].

Seeing that the rapid development of information and communication technologies allows visitors to share their experiences in the form of user-generated content (UGC) on various online platforms [8], researchers and marketers can take this as a valuable opportunity since these technologies facilitate deeper access to a broad range of insightful data [9]. For instance, existing studies have examined TripAdvisor reviews to define the sentiment of customers' feelings towards dining experiences [10] and online ratings on Yelp to uncover different motivations as well as the satisfaction of customers coming from the USA and China [11]. Such investigations refer to predefined themes from existing service quality models to unveil customers' feelings, satisfaction, or perception of a dining experience and then correlate it to countries or continents. A worldwide cross-cultural comparison is, however, widely missing. Hence, this research seeks to contribute to the field of dining experiences by analysing online reviews from a bottom-up approach in order to discover which aspects of the dining experience are critical for visitors in relation to their cultural backgrounds.

To achieve the stated objectives, this study adopted the city of Salzburg as its research context for the following reasons: Salzburg ranked first on the "Best in Travel 2020" list of the world's most attractive cities thanks to its historical sightseeing spots and local cuisine [12]. In the summer season of 2019, nearly 2 million arrivals and more than 3 million overnight stays were recorded in the city of Salzburg. In addition, Salzburg attracts international visitors from a wide variety of countries, including Germany, followed by the Netherlands, Arab countries, Czech Republic and USA [13], currently gaining momentum again after the COVID-19 pandemic. In this study, we apply a mixed method approach by conducting data visualisation, data mining, and topic modelling techniques, to transform unstructured online reviews into interpretable patterns.

2 Literature Review

2.1 Tourist Dining Experience

During this era of the experience economy [14], businesses should design their products and services while also taking into consideration the full range of effects that can be evoked from an interaction between consumers and service offerings [15]. This is particularly important in the tourism and hospitality industry, which is heavily based on experiences [16]. In the context of restaurants, scholars have established different service quality models to identify elements that are influential to customers' satisfaction and experiences, among which the SERVQUAL instrument represents the most widely used model [4]. More specifically, service quality is evaluated based on five dimensions, namely, reliability, responsiveness, assurance, empathy, and tangibles [4]. Despite its popularity, the SERVQUAL model was primarily developed for banks as well as credit card, repair, maintenance, and telephone companies [4]. Therefore, since scale items should be adjusted to fit specific industries [17], scholars subsequently developed the DINESERV model so as to investigate visitors' expectations of quick-service, fine-dining, and casual-dining businesses [18].

A modified version of the DINESERV model showcases further factors of customers' expectations and perceptions at restaurants. The implementation of the overall categories, price and satisfaction, explains customers' thoughts on paying more than expected and the price of food items, while the satisfaction of the dining experience can be confirmed through customers revisiting the restaurant and in the recommendation itself. Other tangible factors include a clean parking area and nice building exterior, restaurant decoration, easily readable menu, comfortable seating, clean dining area, and neat staff [7]. Concerning the environment, evaluation of physical and human surroundings in a restaurant emphasises the aesthetics of the facility, ambiance, table setting, lighting, and the service staff [19]. Moreover, current literature reinforces that, in order to achieve high customer satisfaction, the interaction between customers and employees should not be overlooked [20]. In addition to the service itself, beverage and food attributes are also found to be critical factors in relation to customer fulfilment and post-dining behavioural intention [21]. Today, tourists have more opportunities to share their holiday experiences on social networks [10], allowing individuals to express their thoughts and opinions and make them accessible to the online global community [22] via review platforms such as TripAdvisor. Not only do these review platforms play a key role in tourists' decision-making processes [23], but they also provide managers with a tremendous amount of data that can be used to better understand customers [10] through advanced text mining techniques [24]. A recent study, for instance, explored customers' feelings shared on TripAdvisor when dining in local restaurants [10]. The importance of location and service quality was explored using topic modelling; however, such experiences cannot be standardised, nor do they apply to everyone. Albeit the significance of acknowledging that expectations regarding food, environment, and interpersonal interaction vary across cultures [11], understanding customer experiences from different countries remains scarce.

2.2 Cultural Dimensions and Clusters

To classify people with different cultural backgrounds, one of the most common approaches is based on Hofstede's cultural dimensions theory [25]. This cross-cultural communication framework covers the dimensions of individualism-collectivism, uncertainty avoidance, power distance, masculinity-femininity, and long-/short-term orientation. Subsequently, other researchers modified and transformed the Hofstede model into the GLOBE model [26, 27], with the dimensions uncertainty avoidance (fear of ambiguity), power distance (acceptance of an unequal distribution of power), institutional collectivism (more validation of broad societal interests than of individual goals), in-group collectivism (loyalty towards families and organisations), gender egalitarianism (equal treatment of genders), assertiveness (level of directness, forcefulness, or aggression), future orientation (planning, delaying gratification), performance orientation (appreciation for setting and reaching goals), and humane orientation (fairness, generosity, kindness) [26, 28, 29]. In order to make the GLOBE model applicable for practical use in multinational societies, a model of regional clusters across the world was developed as well. The clusters and their characteristics [28] are outlined in Table 1 below.

Table 1. The GLOBE model.

Cluster	Country	Characteristics
Anglo	Canada, USA, Australia, Ireland, England, South Africa (white sample), and New Zealand	High in performance orientation; low in in-group collectivism
Confucian Asia	Singapore, Hong Kong, Taiwan, China, South Korea, and Japan	High in performance orientation, institutional, in-group collectivism
Eastern Europe	Greece, Hungary, Albania, Slovenia, Poland, Russia, Georgia, and Kazakhstan	High in assertiveness, in-group collectivism, gender egalitarianism; low in performance orientation, future orientation, uncertainty avoidance
Germanic Europe	Austria, The Netherlands, Switzerland (German speaking), and Germany	High in performance orientation, assertiveness, future orientation, uncertainty avoidance; low in humane orientation, institutional, and in-group collectivism
Latin America	Ecuador, El Salvador, Colombia, Bolivia, Brazil, Guatemala, Argentina, Costa Rica, Venezuela, and México	High in in-group collectivism; low in performance orientation, institutional collectivism, future orientation, uncertainty avoidance
Latin Europe	Israel, Italy, Switzerland (Francophone + Italian speaking), Spain, Portugal, and France	Mostly moderate scores in dimensions, low in humane orientation and institutional collectivism
Middle East	Turkey, Kuwait, Egypt, Morocco, and Qatar	High in in-group collectivism, low in future orientation, gender egalitarianism, and uncertainty avoidance
Nordic Europe	Denmark, Finland, and Sweden	High in future orientation, gender egalitarianism, institutional collectivism, and uncertainty avoidance; low in assertiveness, power distance
Southern Asia	Philippines, Indonesia, Malaysia, India, Thailand, and Iran	High in humane orientation and in-group collectivism
Sub-Saharan Africa	Zimbabwe, Namibia, Zambia, Nigeria, and South Africa (black sample)	High score in humane orientation

3 Methodology

3.1 Study Context

The city of Salzburg thrives from the tremendous amount of income generated by the gastronomy branch, with over 3,502 culinary businesses currently running in Salzburg [30]. Thus, with highly concentrated tourists, this destination offers sufficient data for this study to explore tourists' perceptions of dining experience from different cultural backgrounds by mining their content with regards to travel expectations, motivations, and satisfaction on TripAdvisor.

3.2 Data Collection, Pre-processing, and Analysis

The web scraping software *Octoparse* was used to collect restaurant reviews and attributes from TripAdvisor. Restaurant attributes include names, review content, restaurant URLs, published dates and reviewers' locations. All available restaurant reviews, written in English, from the city of Salzburg were scrapped, resulting in 27,626 reviews. This study selected only reviews published between May 1 and October 30, 2019, leading to a total of 1,901 reviews. This timeframe was chosen because of school holidays within and around Austria, where high tourism activities take place, and to view data before the outbreak of the COVID-19 pandemic. Afterward, based on reviewers' nationalities, all reviews were classified into different cultural clusters according to the GLOBE model. Customers who did not disclose their locations on TripAdvisor were removed, resulting in a final dataset consisting of 1,461 reviews.

Next, *Orange 3*, an open-source machine learning toolkit, was applied for data pre-processing and analysis. To transform unstructured reviews into structured forms for analysis [31], the following three steps were conducted: (1) tokenizing texts and turning all the text into lowercase, (2) removing punctuations, numbers, stop words, and, in addition to general stop words, a list of custom stop words specifically developed for this study, and, lastly, (3) normalising words by removing suffixes.

In order to discover hidden topics in online reviews, this study applied Latent Dirichlet Allocation (LDA), one of the most popular topic modelling techniques in tourism and hospitality [32]. LDA was conducted on each of the cultural clusters so as to uncover a corresponding set of attributes or themes through the corpus-based guest reviews. To determine the number of topics in each cluster, multidimensional scaling was applied to analyse each topic's distance between each other and to investigate duplicate or recurring topics. Thus, different clusters yielded various numbers of topics. Finally, a list of keywords, which represent a topic in the topic modelling process, was used as a reference for labelling its representative topics. Subsequently, the extracted keywords of the respective geographical areas were vectorised using document embedding (fastText), followed by a dimensional reduction using tSNE (Perplexity = 15, Exaggeration = 1, PCA components = 25, Normalised Data, and preserved global structure) in order to visualise the GLOBE spaces. The optimal tSNE hyper-parameters were chosen after a visual inspection with the Tensorboard Embedding Projector.

4 Findings

4.1 Overview of the Topic Modelling Results

Table 2 outlines the ten identified topics generated from LDA for a total of nine cultural clusters, as the Sub-Saharan Africa cultural cluster was dropped due to scarce data sampling.

Table 2. Identified topics per cultural cluster.

Cluster	n	Identified topics
Anglo	924	(1) Staff, (2) Food Menu Item, (3) Restaurant Physical Appearance, (4) Recommendation
Confucian Asia	34	(1) Value for Money, (2) Staff, (3) Food Authenticity
Eastern Europe	68	(1) Staff, (2) Food Authenticity, (3) Food Menu Item, (4) Value for Money
Germanic Europe	153	(1) Restaurant Physical Appearance, (2) Staff, Menu Offers, (3) Food Quality
Latin America	21	(1) Food Authenticity, (2) Menu Offers
Latin Europe	73	(1) Value for Money, (2) Overall Service, (3) Food Menu Item
Middle East	32	(1) Food Menu Item, (2) Staff, (3) Recommendation
Nordic Europe	45	(1) Overall Service, (2) Food Quality, (3) Menu Offers, (4) Atmosphere
Southern Asia	111	(1) Restaurant Physical Appearance, (2) Food Menu Item, (3) Value for Money, (4) Overall Service, (5) Staff

The naming of the topic was based on a list of keywords contributing the most to a specific topic. Additional topics/themes were also added due to a prevalent theme, which had not been previously found via topic modelling, being discovered in the reviews. Yet, it is important to note that the number of reviews was not equally distributed and may have influenced the number of the extracted topics. Overall, *Staff*, *Food Menu Item*, and *Value for Money* presented themselves as the top aspects when tourists shared their dining experience.

4.2 Topic Modelling Results per Cultural Cluster

The topics per cultural cluster shown in Table 2 are based on up to 5000 keywords. Figure 1 shows the topics per cultural cluster after tSNE dimensionality reduction and locates them on a map. Interestingly, the word embeddings of these keywords reflect the proximity of the individual GLOBE spaces very well. As such, the two Asian clusters can be seen grouped very close to each other on the left side, while the Middle East is strongly separated from all other areas on the bottom left, and the Anglo-

American area on the opposite top right is also entirely homogeneous. In between, Latin Europe and Latin America are separated but in close proximity, and the European regions are somewhat mixed but still clearly recognisable. This confirms that the cultural features described in detail below can indeed be clearly teased apart from each other and can be perceived as their respective typical characteristic.

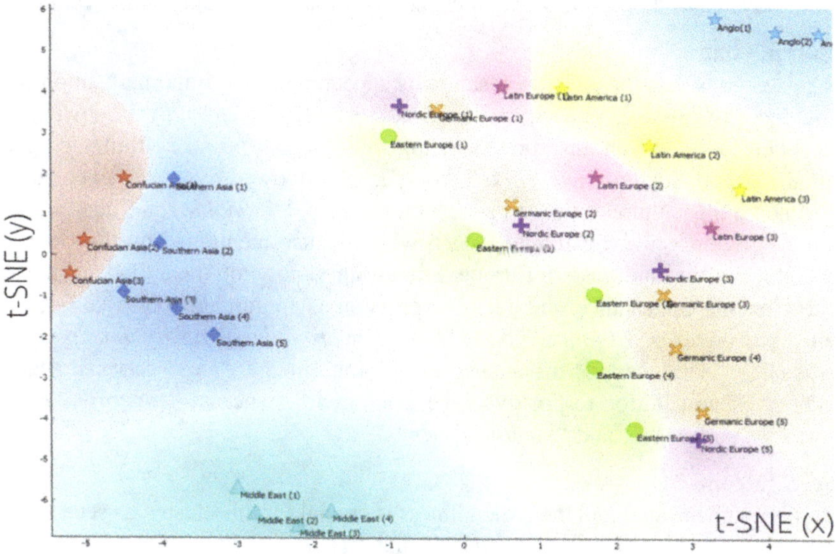

Fig. 1. Topic keywords word embedding across GLOBE cultures

Anglo

For Anglo cluster, the staff plays an important role which can be seen from several comments (e.g., "*The chef was very accommodating to our gluten free needs*" and "*The staff was friendly and attentive*"). Food menu items display a high degree of significance and seen to be followed with critiques and recommendations such as "*Choice of 3 dishes, had the sardine pasta, and it was fantastic*". This observation is consistent with the GLOBE Model findings of the Anglo cluster which possess a high-performance orientation, showing appreciation for an achieved standard. This cluster is attentive to a restaurant's physical setting which shares similarities with the Southern Asian cluster. Different from the Southern Asian cluster, the Anglo finds the restaurant setting and location more important than the décor, which is represented by (e.g., "*We ate outside and had a delightful dinner*" and "*Not too far from the centre of the city*").

Confucian Asia

For this cluster, value for money is an important aspect, observed in "*We think the pricing of the food was reasonable*". This characteristic is similar to the Southern Asia cluster, where the price paid outweigh the food portion. Also, Staff is considered an integral part, proved by "*The owner is very friendly*". Congruent with the GLOBE model, the performance orientation, more specifically, their deliberate expression of appreciation to the staff seems up to par. Meanwhile, food authenticity is another prevalent factor, which can be observed in the excerpts: "*We went there for dinner and food is good traditional Austrian*" and "*Very authentic and delicious Korean food!*". It is worth noting that, interestingly, Confucian Asian tend to search for their own culture's cuisine, and it should also meet their authenticity expectation. This is consistent with the GLOBE model's high score of institutional and in-group collectivism, by showing loyalty to their own origins despite being outside of their home country.

Southern Asia

This cluster considers the physical restaurants appearance most important, emphasising on the decor or interior, as seen in "*richly decorated*" and "*friendly US-style diner*". Food menu items are another prevalent topic which can be seen from the specific mentions of food, such as "*Dal Tarka*", "*Beef Pho*", followed by a recommendation to visit, echoing this culture' humane orientation nature. "*Reasonable rate*" and "*value for money*" represent value for money aspect, which is also mentioned by the Confucian Asia, Latin Europe, and Eastern Europe. Interestingly, not only the attitude of the staff, but also on the appearance and facial expression is important, (e.g., "*Served by a bearded guy with several tattoos*" and "*The owner around with a very unhelpful angry expression*"). Lastly, several dissatisfied expression emerge, "*lousy service*" and "*aggressive staff*" in addition to positive experience reviews such as "*comfort*", "*the service was very friendly*", and "*humble servings*".

Eastern Europe

Interaction with the staff and their friendliness is crucial for this cluster, as seen in: "*The waiter in the lounge was very grumpy*" and "*That manager was very impolite*". Notably, the presence of negative reviews towards the staff are in line with the characteristics of assertiveness given in the GLOBE model. Nevertheless, this cluster appreciates food authenticity, "*I would recommend it for anyone visiting Salzburg and wants to enjoy a traditional Austrian dish*". Food menu items with implicit reference for or against recommending the place also emerge, as seen in: "*Very nice options for platters to have with your wine*" and "*If you are looking for a great schnitzel off the beaten path, this is the place*". Finally, value for money is a vital aspect for the Eastern European contrasting with the Asians where price sensitivity outweighs portion generosity, proved in "*It's a little pricey but, given the rest of the prices in Salzburg*".

Latin America

For Latin Americans it is important for businesses to deliver their brand promise in terms of (food) authenticity, for example, "*Make sure you go to this typical Austrian restaurant. Serve good Austrian food*" and "*The food is really good. Austrian dishes and drinks*". Another salient aspect is the menu offers, e.g. available options, types of drinks, and cuisine types (e.g., "*The menu was excellent- it was hard to decide what to order*" and "*All kind of seafood and in any possible way*"). The findings show consistency with GLOBE model in terms of the low score in performance orientation (whether people are rewarded for delivering good performance) due to the fact that important dining aspects revolve around the food itself rather than the staff.

Germanic Europe

The appearance and location of restaurants are evidently important aspects for this cluster, as seen in "*One of the most modern restaurants in Salzburg*" and "*The restaurant has a very good flair*". This implies that this culture appreciate the comfort and pleasant atmosphere. Concerning the staff, attentiveness and attitude are the most appreciated traits, for instance, "*We were greeted by a nice waiter who showed us to our table*" exhibiting deliberate expression of appreciation which is congruent with their high performance orientation's GLOBE characteristic. Moreover, menu offers and food quality (e.g. "*Excellent meat dishes. Good selection of drinks*") are important but inconsistent food availability is not appreciated, as seen in "*Limited menu*". The quality of the food served in terms of flavour, presentation, and ingredients are also notable, "*The creamy spinach was so good and the meat had a high quality*".

Latin Europe

Value for money is the most important aspect, as seen in "*Good service at a reasonable price*" and "*Pizzas are really huge, tasty and at a very good price*". Although this is consistent with the Southern Asian and Eastern Europeans, the Latin Europeans emphasise price points rather than the food generosity. Food menu items are mostly followed with a critique, for instance "*Burger was good though not amazing*" and "*We chose white asparagus which was excellent*". This cluster recognises service as a significant factor, encompassing larger spectrum of a dining experience: staff-, food-, and restaurant-related, seen in the generality of review contents such as, "*The place is nice and the court is a great place, but the food was mediocre* (restaurant- and food-related)" and "*The staff is very friendly and the wiener schnitzel was one of the best we've had* (staff- and food-related)".

Nordic Europe

The overall service (e.g., "*service is immaculate*", "*super service*", and "*quick service*") with a strong focus placed on services provided by the staff emerge, as seen in "*The two women who run it are super kind and really cares about their food*". The flavour, ingredients, and the presentation thereof are key factors for this cluster, for instance "*Traditional food with lots of flavour!*". Moreover, menu offers are equally important, proved by frequent references to modern Austrian kitchen, vegetarian food, local wines, home-brewed beer, and gluten-free beer, e.g. "*Amazing little beer garden with solid food and amazing home-brewed beer*" and "*Nice place for some typical Austrian food, gluten-free beer available and a few but very tasty food options*". Lastly, the atmosphere is proved to be as important, as seen in "*historical environment*" and "*hidden gem*", which is congruent with the GLOBE model's uncertainty avoidance characteristic, since authentic local atmosphere meets this cluster's expectations.

Middle East

Food menu items are of great significance for this cluster (e.g., "*Shrimp pizza at the bar, and it tastes lovely*" and "*Beautiful wholesome food*"). The interaction with the staff is as influential, as seen in "*The host has been the perfect one in all way*" and "*The owner of the restaurant and staff are friendly and accommodative*". Recommendations are significant for the Middle Eastern cluster, for instance "*We went to this restaurant on recommendation*" and "*We found this restaurant from TripAdvisor*". This finding transpires the common practice among Middle Eastern tourists to go to places upon recommendation and correspondingly recommend places to others upon dining satisfaction. In line with the GLOBE model, this aspect displays a certain degree of consistency for high in-group collectivism since, by giving honest opinions about their experiences, this behaviour shows loyalty towards their own family or organisation.

5 Discussion

Seeing that various aspects of touristic experiences, such as dining or visiting sights, can be sourced from online review portals, and connections to a place of origin or culture can be drawn from the differences in behaviour [33], this study analyses online restaurant reviews so as to make generalisations regarding different cultures. In this way, when addressing and catering to a certain country or culture, one can resort to a set of recommendations on what specific aspects they tend to pay attention to. Overall, the most important aspects related to customer dining experiences are staff, food menu items, value for money, restaurant physical appearance, food authenticity, overall service, menu offers, food quality, atmosphere, and recommendation.

The study's findings partly differ from the literature in that food was mentioned regularly in reviews, with food even being considered the most important factor for those who enjoy dining. Unlike the dimensions in the SERVQUAL and DINESERV model, which focus more on the interaction between customers and employees rather than the products themselves (e.g., food items), this research is consistent with other scholars who emphasise that attributes of food, regarding the quality, freshness, tastiness, and temperature, are seen as the most influential criteria among customer fulfilment and post-dining behavioural intention [20, 21].

Yet, notably, the priority of these aspects varies across cultures. This study shows that societal cultures can provide valuable insights, e.g., for gastronomy businesses when trying to target a certain market. Moreover, it might aid in guiding employee training, especially in regard to the specific treatment of certain target groups (grooming recommendations, welcoming rituals, etc.). The analysis further reveals that societal culture might be a new variable in market research, especially in target market analysis, in addition to established ones such as demographics and lifestyle milieus. Finally, this study supports results from recent literature, suggesting that machine learning can give valuable insights by processing large amounts of UGC from review sites [33].

To conclude, this study is novel in that cultural background was incorporated, using an established scientific concept, namely, the GLOBE clusters. Different from previous literature focusing on limited cultural groups [33], the findings of this research allows for the generalisation of all regions within a given cluster. By using machine learning and drawing connections to the culture of customers, this study concludes that analysing online restaurant reviews can give valuable insights for professionals in the field.

6 Conclusion

This research contributes to the tourism industry through the use of machine learning techniques, thereby showcasing the possibilities of transforming UGC into structured patterns so as to reveal tourist experiences shared online. As such, the revealed insights provide restaurant managers with the exact gastronomical preferences of their target groups, which, in turn, can be used to optimise business strategies and service offerings. On a wider scale, this study is also beneficial for destination management organisations to promote gastronomy in foreign countries. More specifically, destination marketers now have the opportunity to check the exact aspects of a dining experience that a certain cultural cluster may be interested in and tailor promotional texts, images, and videos accordingly. Ultimately, this research expands upon the existing knowledge of the use of text mining and machine learning to process and analyse large amounts of user-generated data in tourism contexts.

Regardless, this study is not without its limitations. First, the sample was narrowed down to include English reviews only, and the city or country of residence was taken from TripAdvisor. As such, the assumption that a reviewer belongs to a particular cultural cluster is solely based on his/her stated place of residence. Whether or not that region represents their "true" culture, or if they were merely expatriates living in a certain place at that time, cannot be validated. For future research, it is recommended to investigate the preferences of the cultures from where large data density, that represent all 10 GLOBE cultural clusters, can be obtained, for instance major cities e.g. New York or Tokyo. This will increase the robustness of the cultural cluster analysis. Moreover, further studies could explore other aspects of tourism, such as accommodation or attractions, that can benefit from this approach in similar ways.

References

1. Lonely Planet. https://www.lonelyplanet.com/best-in-travel/cities. Accessed 08 Feb 2021
2. Land Salzburg. https://www.salzburg.gv.at/statistik_/Seiten/statistik-tourismus.aspx. Accessed 10 Aug 2021
3. Li X, Lai C, Harrill R, Kline S, Wang L (2011) When east meets west: an exploratory study on Chinese outbound tourists' travel expectations. Tour Manag 32(4):741–749
4. Kim S, Chung JE, Suh Y (2016) Multiple reference effects on restaurant evaluations: a cross-cultural study. IJCHM 28:1441–1466
5. Buhalis D, Law R (2008) Progress in information technology and tourism management: 20 years on and 10 years after the Internet. Tour Manag 29(4):609–623
6. Parasuraman A, Zeithaml VA, Berry L (1988) SERVQUAL: a multiple-item scale for measuring consumer perceptions of service quality. J Retail 64(1):12–40
7. Pikkemaat B, Peters M, Chan CS (2018) Needs, drivers and barriers of innovation: the case of an alpine community-model destination. Tour Manag Perspect 25:53–63
8. Lai IKW, Hitchcock M (2016) A comparison of service quality attributes for stand-alone and resort-based luxury hotels in Macau: 3-dimensional importance-performance analysis. Tour Manag 55:139–159
9. Marković S, Komsic J, Dorčić J (2015) Measuring service quality in Croatian restaurants: application of DINESERV scale. Marketing Insights from a Changing Environment. Pearson, London, pp 131–161

10. Becken S, Alaei AR, Wang Y (2019) Benefits and pitfalls of using tweets to assess destination sentiment. J Hosp Tour Technol 11:19–34
11. Sigala M, Gretzel U (2017) Advances in Social Media for Travel, Tourism and Hospitality: New Perspectives, Practice and Cases. Routledge, New York
12. Yu CE, Zhang X (2020) The embedded feelings in local gastronomy: a sentiment analysis of online reviews. J Hosp Tour Technol 11(3):461–478
13. Jia S (2020) Motivation and satisfaction of Chinese and U.S. tourists in restaurants: a cross-cultural text mining of online reviews. Tour Manag 78:104071
14. Pine BJ, Gilmore JH (2011) The Experience Economy. Harvard Business Press, Boston MA
15. Desmet P, Hekkert P (2007) Framework of product experience. Int J Des 1(1):57–66
16. Yu J, Egger R (2021) Color and engagement in touristic Instagram pictures: a machine learning approach. Ann Tour Res 89:103204
17. Abezie H (2019) Assessing a restaurant service quality using the DINESERV model: a qualitative study on Pizza Hut. Master's Thesis, Umeå University, Umeå
18. Stevens P, Knutson B, Patton M (1995) DINESERV: a tool for measuring service quality in restaurants. Cornell Hotel Restaur Adm Q 36(2):5–60
19. Ryu K, Jang S (2008) DINESCAPE: a scale for customers' perception of dining environments. J Foodserv Bus Res 11(1):2–22
20. Gustafsson IB, Ostrom A, Johansson J, Mossberg L (2006) The five aspects meal model: a tool for developing meal services in restaurants. J Foodserv 17(2):84–93
21. Shariff SNFBA et al (2015) The influence of service quality and food quality towards customer fulfillment and revisit intention. Canadian Soc Sci 11(8):138–144
22. Dellarocas C (2003) The digitization of word of mouth: promise and challenges of online feedback mechanisms. Manage Sci 49(10):1407–1424
23. Gretzel U, Yoo KH (2008) Use and impact of online travel reviews. In: O'Connor P, Höpken W, Gretzel U (eds) Information and Communication Technologies in Tourism 2008. Springer, Vienna, pp 35–46
24. Luo Y, Xu X (2021) Comparative study of deep learning models for analyzing online restaurant reviews in the era of the COVID-19 pandemic. Int J Hosp Manag 94:102849
25. Hofstede G (2003) What is culture? A reply to Baskerville. Acc Organ Soc 28(7–8):811–813
26. House RJ, Javidan M, Hanges PJ, Dorfman PW (2002) Understanding cultures and implicit lead-ership theories across the globe: an introduction to project GLOBE. J World Bus 37 (1):3–10
27. Pagda Z, Bayraktar S, Jimenez A (2021) Exploring culture and leadership after 23 years: a replication of GLOBE project in Turkey. J Int Manag 27(1):100822
28. House RJ, Hanges PJ, Javidan M, Dorfman PW, Gupta V (2004) Culture, Leadership, and Organizations: The GLOBE Study of 62 Societies. SAGE Publications, Thousand Oaks
29. Javidan M, Dorfman PW, De Luque MS, House RJ (2006) In the eye of the beholder: cross cultural lessons in leadership from project GLOBE. Acad Manag Perspect 20(1):67–90
30. Austrian Economic Chambers. https://www.wko.at/branchen/tourismus-freizeitwirtschaft/tourismus-freizeitwirtschaft-in-zahlen-2019.pdf. Accessed 10 Aug 2021
31. Han HJ, Mankad S, Gavirneni N, Verma R (2016) What guests really think of your hotel: text analytics of online customer reviews. Cornell Hosp Rep 16(2):3–17
32. Arefieva V, Egger R, Yu J (2021) A machine learning approach to cluster destination image on Instagram. Tour Manag 85:104318
33. Wang L, Kirilenko AP (2021) Do tourists from different countries interpret travel experience with the same feeling? Sentiment analysis of TripAdvisor reviews. Inf Commun Technol Tour 2021:294–301

15

Exploring "Planned Serendipity" and On-Site Information Behavior on Smartphones

Micol Mieli(✉)

Lund University, Lund, Sweden
micol.mieli@ism.lu.se

Abstract. The paper explores tourists' smartphone-related information behavior on site in light of the concept of "planned serendipity". The ability to gather information at anytime and anywhere can deeply influence tourists' behavior, their information needs and the outcomes of their travel plans. In this study, the concept of planned serendipity is used to suggest that the outcome of travel information behavior on site is not entirely planned nor entirely serendipitous. The study employs the Experience Sampling Method (ESM) in combination with qualitative interviews, which allow the researcher to gather data both during the participants' trip and afterwards. The thematic analysis resulted in four main themes related to information search connected to smartphone use: flexible plans; orientation in time and space; specificity of the query; aiming for optimization. Such conditions result in planned serendipity. The study thus contributes to the conceptualization of planned serendipity as an outcome of smartphone use during travel for information purposes.

Keywords: Smartphones · Planning · Serendipity · Experience sampling method

1 Introduction

With their portability and constant connectivity, smartphones have a great influence over tourists' on-site information behavior. Mobile technologies have changed the way tourists plan their trips, highlighting the importance of research into unplanned behavior [1]. Gretzel, Zarezadeh, Li and Xiang [2] have called for theoretical advancements that can take into account new and emerging technologies. Mieli and Zillinger [3] suggested that tourists approach travel planning in a new way that goes beyond the juxtaposition between planning and serendipity, and called it "planned serendipity".

The body of research about information behavior during the on-site stage of the trip is also much smaller than on pre-trip information behavior. In part, this is due to the lack of appropriate methods to investigate the on-site stage of the trip. A large amount of research on tourist information behavior is conducted with quantitative methods, and the use of qualitative methods is limited on the subject. The present study aims to fill these gaps in the literature by investigating how such planned serendipity occurs during the trip and how it is enabled by smartphones. The method employed is a combination of Experience Sampling Method and post-trip qualitative interviews.

2 Literature Review

The use of smartphones during travel has been a popular object of research in the past two decades. Tourists use smartphones during their trips for information search, mainly for transport, accommodation, food and activities, as well as for inspiration and ideas about their destination [4]. Information behavior during travel is particularly affected by the constant connectivity that smartphones afford: tourists can find information anywhere and at any time. Mieli and Zillinger [3] have noted the change in information needs throughout the different phases of travel and that several information needs have been postponed to the on-site phase and closer to the moment of consumption.

Some studies have suggested that different types of information are sought at different stages of the trip [4]; others that the information search process is hierarchical, and choices that are highest on the hierarchy are typically made before the trip while others, lower in the hierarchy, are made later [5]. Pre-trip and on-site decisions also have different characteristics: while the former are more reasoned and require more information processing, the latter are described as free-spirited and light-hearted [4]. On-site information search, however, is an important part of the tourist experience, increasingly so thanks to mobile technologies and the lowering of data roaming prices [6]. Kang, Jodice and Norman [4] have shown that tourists may prefer not making decisions beforehand to keep their plans flexible and decide based on what circumstances and new information they encounter during their trip.

In information studies, serendipity refers to the fortuitous encounter of relevant information while not specifically looking for it [7]. In tourism, the concept of serendipity has only been used in few instances, for example in relation to independent tourists' preference between structure and serendipity in their travels [8]. Mieli and Zillinger [3] used the term in the phrase "planned serendipity" to indicate the existence of degrees of serendipity even in structured plans and, vice-versa, the constant planning that is enabled by smartphones, which introduces some elements of planning and information search even in the most spontaneous decisions.

Research has called for the explicit inclusion of unplanned behavior in theories of tourist behavior [9] as well as new methods to explore tourists' interactions with technology [2].

3 Methodology

The study was conducted with a hybrid methodology, which combined questionnaire data collected using the Experience Sampling Method (ESM) with qualitative interviews. ESM is a method that consists of sending participants several mini-questionnaires throughout the day. In this case the method was applied to gather self-reports from tourists during their trip, as they went about their tourist activities. The Experience Sampling Method allows to capture people's experiences at a time as close as possible to when they actually happen, in order to ensure ecological validity and get access to the lived experience of events and everyday life [10].

15 people were selected to participate in the study. The criteria for selection of participants were the following: born in the 1980s and 1990s, have attended or are

attending higher education and planning to take a trip which included at least three nights away. Age and education level would ensure participants who had traveled both with and without smartphones and who would spend more time looking for travel information [11]. Participants were selected to include different types of travel, including: backpacking, visiting friends and family, city break, road trip, event travel, family vacation, seaside vacation.

During the trip one or two questionnaires per day were sent to participants' own smartphones through a dedicated application. Questions focused on what respondents were doing or feeling at the time of the notification. Since respondents answered several ESM questionnaires per day, the total number of questionnaires collected is 93. After the trip, the follow-up semi-structured interview interview departed from participant's ESM answers and aimed at broadening, deepening and clarifying them.The data was analyzed qualitatively. A thematic analysis was conducted following the general principles of grounded theory [12]. ESM answers were also organized in a spreadsheet to identify possible patterns that could be explored further in the interviews.

4 Findings

The preliminary analysis of the data resulted in four themes about smartphone-related on-site information behavior: flexible plans; orientation in time and space; specificity of the query; aiming for optimization.

4.1 Flexible Plans

Before the trip, 12 out of 14 participants had booked accommodation, while the other two were either backpacking or on a road trip and only booked a few of their stays in advance. As for activities, most respondents had a rough pre-trip plan, a general idea or a list of things to do. In most cases, detailed daily plans were made on site, either the night before or on the same morning. While most had a general idea of what to do, decisions on when to do it was left until later. These data show that on-site planning and information search are very important elements of the tourist experience and support the claim that information needs are postponed from the pre-trip stage until a later stage of the trip [3].

During the on-site stage of the trip participants were flexible: the ESM data showed that only 23% of the times they had made plans and they had not changed. Mostly, plans were flexible (43%), they had changed (18%) or there was no plan at all (16%).

4.2 Orientation in Time and Space

The search process on site often consists of orientation in time and space. Participants reported using their smartphones to find out what was around them and where they could go next. On the other hand, some respondents also complained that they do not learn how to orientate themselves in the destination, because they have constant access to location-based services. Participant 8, for example, compared her orientation skills to previous trips when she did not have online maps on her phone and would need to use a paper map. While she used to be able to learn the general layout of a city by the second day, now she cannot do that anymore and blames the smartphone for it.

4.3 Specificity of the Query

A phone search for information differs from using other sources (guides, book, brochures, information centres) in that the person needs to look specifically for something, they need to know what they want and what to look for. This makes the information search more intentional and specific, narrowed to what the tourist already knows they should be looking for. Information is not encountered casually or serendipitously but specifically sought out. Such specificity of the information search has important consequences for the serendipitous element of information encounter: it reduces the possibility to find pertinent information by chance.

4.4 Aiming for Optimization

Optimizing a trip is possible thanks to constant access to information as well as location-based services. Several participants reported using their phones to find the most optimal routes, to make their use of their time most efficient but still keep flexible enough to enjoy the destination with some degree of spontaneity. Plans can be made on the same day based on weather conditions, food can be found nearby as soon as one gets hungry, and there is no need to get stuck in traffic when live information is available about road conditions. Getting lost can be avoided thanks to the possibility to consult one's own position on a map at any time, distances are estimated to make the most out of each day. The possibility to "spontaneously" double- check every piece of information encountered during the trip was seen as increasing spontaneity during the trip by some participants, while others believed it instead decreased spontaneity.

5 Discussion and Conclusions

This paper investigated how tourist information behavior on site can be better understood through the concept of planned serendipity. From the analysis emerged some of the conditions enabled by the smartphone, which can result in planned serendipity in the tourist experience. The use of an innovative method like the Experience Sampling Method allowed the researcher to get access to tourists' experiences during the trip, even the smaller and given-for-granted actions performed on smartphones, which would not be recalled in an interview after the trip. Through ESM, a more detailed and accurate account of behavior and perceptions on site could be gathered.

Planned serendipity was conceptualized here as the outcome of tourists' information behavior, when there is a strong element of serendipity in trip planning and, vice-versa, some level of planning even in spontaneous behavior. This is enabled by mobile phones and their constant connectivity, which allows tourists to collect information anywhere and at any time. This technology and the possibilities it affords in turn influence tourists' behavior, which becomes more and more reliant on mobile technologies and constant information search. Four conditions connected to smartphone use on-site were identified: flexible and iterative planning process; orientation in time and space; specificity of the query; aiming for optimization. The combination of these conditions results in a tourist experience that is not entirely planned nor entirely serendipitous, hence it creates planned serendipity.

The study also has managerial implications. DMOs and other tourist destination marketers can benefit greatly from gaining a better knowledge of tourist behavior on site, especially when it comes to the importance of on-site promotion: for example, the design of smart destinations, the creation of hubs of information, the use of the Internet of Things (IoT). Marketing strategies in the pre-trip stage can also benefit from knowledge on tourist behavior on site.

References

1. Kah JA, Lee S-H (2014) Beyond adoption of travel technology: its application to unplanned travel behaviors. J Travel Tour Mark 31(6):667–680
2. Gretzel U, Zarezadeh Z, Li Y, Xiang Z (2019) The evolution of travel information search research: a perspective article. Tour Rev 75(1):319–323
3. Mieli M, Zillinger M (2020) Tourist information channels as consumer choice: the value of tourist guidebooks in the digital age. Scand J Hosp Tour 20(1):28–48
4. Kang S, Jodice LW, Norman WC (2020) How do tourists search for tourism information via smartphone before and during their trip? Tour Recreat Res 45(1):57–68
5. Jeng J, Fesenmaier DR (2002) Conceptualizing the travel decision-making hierarchy: a review of recent developments. Tour Anal 7(1):15–32
6. Zillinger M, Eskilsson L, Månsson M, Nilsson JH (2018) What’s new in tourist information behaviour? Institutionen för Service Management och Tjänstevetenskap, Lund
7. Agarwal NK (2015) Towards a definition of serendipity in information behaviour. Inf Res Int Electron J 20(3):n3
8. Huang WJ, Norman WC, Hallo JC, McGehee NG, McGee J, Goetcheus CL (2014) Serendipity and independent travel. Tour Recreat Res 39(2):169–183
9. Hwang YH, Fesenmaier DR (2011) Unplanned tourist attraction visits by travellers. Tour Geogr 13(3):398–416
10. Hektner JM, Schmidt JA, Csikszentmihalyi M (2007) Experience Sampling Method: Measuring the Quality of Everyday Life. Sage, Thousand Oaks
11. Coromina L, Camprubí R (2016) Analysis of tourism information sources using a Mokken Scale perspective. Tour Manag 56:75–84
12. Bryant A, Charmaz K (2007) The SAGE Handbook of Grounded Theory. SAGE Publications Ltd, Thousand Oaks

16

Content-Based Recommendations for Crags and Climbing Routes

Iustina Ivanova(✉), Marina Andrić and Francesco Ricci

Free University of Bozen-Bolzano, Bolzano, Italy
{iivanova,maandric,fricci}@unibz.it

Abstract. Climbing is a popular sport for active tourists and recreational sportsmen. Alpine climbing areas, such as the Alps, can attract tourists from all over the world. Various websites, mobile applications, and books are used by climbers to obtain information on important aspects of the available climbing routes, including their properties, location, and especially their difficulty. Considering this large amount of information and options, it is in reality difficult for climbers to properly select which routes to climb. Hence, we propose recommendation technologies aimed at supporting climbers in this decision task. The developed system prototype constructs a climber's profile with preferences derived from climber's logbook data collected by a mobile app. Then, the system can recommend suitable crags and climbing routes within the selected crags. The designed interface and the basic computational models for such a system prototype are presented. The proposed technology aims at complementing existing electronic climbing guidebooks and providing decision support to climbers.

Keywords: Climbing tourism · Difficulty assessment · eTourism · Recommender system · Outdoor tourism decision support

1 Introduction

Nowadays, there is a growing interest in sport climbing. Specifically, outdoor climbing has become a popular tourism activity for novices and experts. In some countries, such as Italy, Greece, Spain, and Turkey, climbing has become a foremost advertised activity that is used for attracting many tourists. Thousands of rock-climbing regions have been developed and registered in electronic climbing guidebooks, which have been made available worldwide. In this scenario, some companies have been focusing their business on actively supporting climbers, by providing them reliable, easily accessible, and updated information, even via novel information technology tools.

For example, a local company Vertical-Life[1] in South Tyrol (Italy) offers to prospective visitors an electronic climbing guidebook, which is accessible through

[1] https://www.vertical-life.info.

a rich website[2]. In addition to the e-guidebook, climbers can find there e-services that allow them to leave feedback in the form of comments, ratings, and grades for the routes that they have climbed (logbook functionality). Another similar example of such type of information tools is illustrated by UKClimbing[3]. Their website provides online descriptions and maps for many climbing areas, mostly located in Europe. Furthermore, in Australia, climbers can browse 'the Crag'[4] website, which focuses on outdoor climbing routes in this country.

By complementing these websites, ancillary mobile apps have been developed; they allow to discover and log climbing routes [1–5]. Climbers can use them to track their progress in training. These apps are also used to maintain updated information on the climbing routes, in collaboration with local guides, by collecting crowd-based feedback on the featured routes.

This information repository is evolving day by day and is of great interest to the companies operating in this tourism sector. They aim to expand their penetration and role by providing climbers with the most essential information, and in the most easily usable way. In particular, they would like to match climbers' needs with personalized recommendations for routes that suit the climbers' expectations and limitations, such as the maximum difficulty level of the route the climber can climb, the desired duration and length of the route, or it's safety level, which is influenced by the changing mountain rocks' state. It is worth stressing that the available technologies and tools use manual input acquired via the system GUI (query) for establishing a match between a target climber (user's preferences) and the recommendable routes. This is burdensome and tends to decrease the usage of the existing tools.

To address this problem, we illustrate here a range of techniques and tools that enable us to learn semi-automatically climbers' preferences, by leveraging their explicit feedback given in a climbing app. Moreover, we illustrate how the routes recommendations can be delivered to climbers in specialized websites and apps. We focus on a system prototype and its GUI, that we are developing for one of the above-mentioned companies, namely, Vertical-Life. Recommendations are also tailored to the climber by considering one of the most important aspects, i.e., the desired difficulty level of the searched routes. Moreover, since the difficulty of a route is often subjective, this subjectivity is estimated by machine learning models that predict how difficult a given route will be perceived, specifically by each climber. Exploiting that estimation module, we have developed an interface for personalized recommendations for outdoor climbing. Ultimately, the recommendations given to a user are based on the knowledge of the user's preferred routes, which is derived from the logged climbing activities in the app, and by the goal of the climber (e.g., routes useful for training).

The paper is structured as follows: in Sect. 2, we discuss the related work. In Sect. 3, we describe the building blocks used for computing recommendations. In Sect. 4, we sketch the GUI which have been designed to illustrate and explain

[2] https://www.8a.nu.
[3] https://www.ukclimbing.com.
[4] https://www.thecrag.com.

the recommendations. Finally, Sect. 5 discusses the contribution and concludes the work by listing some future developments.

2 Related Work

Recommender systems (RSs) for climbers fall in the more general area of decision support systems developed for recreational sports, such as hiking and trekking. In all these sports, the user has a common problem, namely to match the trail's or route difficulty level with the hiker's or climber's ability. One notable study was conducted by Calbimonte et al. in [6–8], where they outlined the problem of matching hiker to hiking trails according to the hiker's physical level and trail's difficulty characteristics. The authors have developed a semantic model to represent the hikes using Semantic Web ontologies and have built user profiles via a questionnaire, which requires users to fill in the information manually. In another article, Vias et al. [9] address the problem of hiking path difficulty assessment by measuring the time needed to complete the hike and acquiring user preferences via manually entered search criteria. The main limitation of such a system is that users are required to enter information by hand and previous user/system interactions are not exploited.

To overcome the above-mentioned limitations, we introduce here an approach aimed at semi-automatically understanding user preferences through their feedback. In recommender systems, users' needs and wants are typically learned via explicit and implicit feedback [10]. In [11], we have proposed the first idea of the application of such a mixed approach: explicit feedback is obtained with manual input data through a mobile app and implicit feedback is obtained in the form of sensor data. It is worth noting that, in marathon running, Smyth et al. [12–14] have also developed the athlete's profile by using sensor data and case-based reasoning. However, their methods are hardly applicable for climbing as they require data collection from sensors on a large scale, and sensors for climbing have just been developed.

More specifically to sport climbing, Draper et al. in [15,16] have focused on the problem of assessing routes' difficulty, and developed a unified table to compare grading scales between several countries. They discuss the issues related to the design of a unified grading system and outline the most important features that affect the grading of a route. They note that the difficulty of a route is subjective, as it depends on a climber's characteristics (including years of climbing experience, training frequency, preference for the climbing style, etc.). However, they have not solved the problem of how to measure the climber's perceived difficulty of a route.

A few works have tackled the route difficulty grade assessment problem with computational methods. For example, Kempen in [17] formalized climbing routes description by using a linguistic approach and found some relationship between a sequence of movements to climb a route and the route's grade. Furthermore, in [18–20] the authors applied deep learning to assess difficulty grades from images of routes on artificial climbing walls for indoor climbing. However, these approaches are not sufficient to explain a climber's perceived route difficulty, therefore, more research is required to solve the target problem.

In conclusion, there is a lack of technologies for understanding and predicting climbers' preferences and perceptions. It is therefore challenging to develop a recommender system capable of suggesting suitable climbing routes with the right difficulty grade that the climber can and wants to climb.

3 Climber and Route Profiling

To solve the outlined problems, we have designed a content-based recommender system that aims to suggest routes related to the ones the climber practiced most often in the past [10]. For this purpose, we have modeled climbers' habits (preferences) and matched them with the recommendable routes' characteristics. Figure 1 shows the recommender system (RS) logical schema. The used data comprises a logbook of ascents and climbing routes information obtained from Vertical-Life e-guidebook and app. The RS has two computational components: the climbing grade prediction model (explained in Sect. 3.1) and the content-based RS algorithm, discussed in the following and in Sect. 4, where also the interaction design is presented. The system first supports climbers in selecting a region of interest, namely, a climbing crag, which is a climbing area with relevant routes within. This search is enabled by a specifically designed map interface (Fig. 2). Then, within a selected crag the user is suggested with recommended routes (Fig. 3).

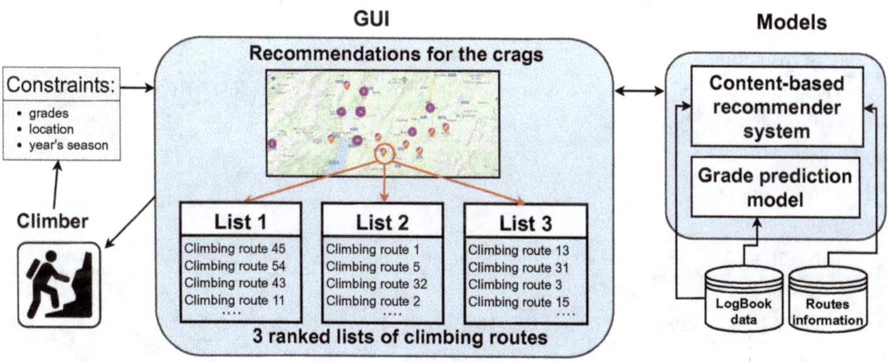

Fig. 1. Logical schema of the proposed recommender system for crags and climbing routes.

To identify proper recommendations for a target climber, we make three working assumptions. First, climbers usually choose routes with which they are familiar and require the climbing styles they have practiced before. The second assumption is that climbers avoid the moves they dislike, but for training purposes, they need to climb them, otherwise, they may be proficient in one specific style, but lagging in another one. The third assumption is related to the climbing routes that are easier than expected: they are considered to be good for motivational purposes because individuals would be more motivated to continue the training when they climb a specified grade with less effort, as they would think that they achieved a certain level in training. These assumptions need to be validated with climbers' feedback and they are here considered to generate a first working prototype.

To explain how recommendations are computed, we first describe the climber's profile. Then, in the next section, we show how the RS can suggest crags according to the climber's profile, and how three types of recommendations for routes are generated: routes with climbers' favorite moves, routes good for training and routes for boosting the climber's motivation.

A climber's profile is built from the logbook of her ascents inserted via the Vertical-Life company's website and smartphone application. Table 1 shows aggregated logbook data for one climber and the derived climber's profile. We consider four categories of climber's preferences: *climbing discipline*, *climbing grade*, *climbing style* and *wall steepness*. The row marked with '#' shows the number of recorded climbs for each possible value of the category, '%' is the percentage of ascents in each category, PD_c, PG_c, PS_c, PH_c are the generated sets of preferred climber's disciplines, grades, styles and wall steepness/hill, respectively. These sets contain, for each category, the values appearing in the largest number in logbook records. DS_c instead, is the set of least climbed styles by the profiled climber ('disliked' styles).

Table 1. Example of a climber's profile.

Climbing discipline					
	Boulder	Sport-single	Sport-multi-pitch	Trad-single	Trad-multi-pitch
#	81	267	117	222	151
%	10%	32%	14%	26%	18%
PD_c	Sport single				

Climbing grade																	
	5b	5b+	5c	5c+	6a	6a+	6b	6b+	6c	6c+	7a	7a+	7b	7b+	7c	7c+	8a
#	75	43	62	20	19	64	61	83	87	97	97	33	49	24	16	8	1
%	9%	5%	7%	2%	2%	8%	7%	10%	10%	12%	12%	4%	6%	3%	2%	1%	0%
PG_c	6c+, 7a																

Climbing style						
	Athletic	Cruxy	Endurance	Crimpy	Sloper	Technical
#	24	203	387	86	118	20
%	3%	25%	46%	10%	14%	2%
PS_c	Endurance					
DS_c	Technical					

Wall steepness/hill				
	Overhang 135°	Vertical 90°	Slab 45°	Roof 180°
#	370	152	195	121
%	44%	18%	23%	15%
PH_c	135°			

- **Climbing discipline.** We adopt the classification by Hörst [21, 22], according to which the disciplines of climbing are: bouldering, sport or traditional (trad) climbing. Sport and trad climbing may further be subdivided in: single-pitch (routes within 10–45 m) or multi-pitch (routes consist of several pitches). We assume that climbers would like to receive recommendations for new routes of the discipline they most often climb. For instance, the climber profiled in Table 1 prefers sport-single-pitch to other disciplines and is likely to be interested to receive this type of recommendation.
- **Climbing grade.** Each route has a grade that measures its difficulty. Climbers often climb the grades they feel comfortable with, that is, routes they find challenging but within their capabilities. Draper et al. [16] proposed International Rock Climbing Research Association (IRCRA) scale to aid comparison between various route grading systems that are employed between countries. For the purpose of illustration, we use the French grading scale that has a linear relationship with the IRCRA scale. Table 1 shows a climber who most often climbs 6c+ and 7a routes on the French scale.
- **Climbing style.** Additionally, each route can be characterized by a climbing style that suggests the movements required for completing the ascent. We adopt the six styles featured in the Vertical-Life guidebooks, namely, *athletic, cruxy, endurance, crimpy, sloper, technical.* The styles of routes that a climber most often climbs are used to model the climber's preferences for favorite moves. The climber profiled in Table 1 most often 'endurance' style climbs.
- **Wall steepness (hill).** Climbing rocks differ according to steepness, i.e., the angle that the rock wall forms with the horizontal plane. Some of them have a steepness of around 90° (e.g., El Capitan in Yosemite, US), and some even close to 120° (e.g., Rodellar, Spain). Climbers often have a preferred steepness range which may be associated with the intensity of their training. As in the 8a.nu e-guidebook, we classify the routes into four groups according to the steepness of the rock wall: 'slab' ($\leq$88°), 'vertical' (88°–95°), 'overhanging' (95°–165°) and 'roof' ($\geq$165°). For example, the climber profiled in Table 1 prefers to climb 'overhang' walls.

In summary, each climber is profiled by an array of five sets of favorite values for the four considered categories and one set of less favored styles: $c_p = (PD_c, PG_c, PS_c, DS_c, PH_c)$. A climber can have more favorite values for each category: for example, they could prefer both 'bouldering' and 'sport single'.

A climbing route has a similar vector representation $r_i = (r_{id}, r_{ig}, R_{is}, r_{ih})$. However, r_{id}, r_{ig}, r_{ih} are single values describing the route's discipline, grade and hill, respectively. While instead R_{is} is a set of styles that a route requires to be used to climb. For example, a route can require both 'endurance' and 'athletic' styles.

3.1 Climbing Grade Prediction Model

It is well-known in the climbing community that a route's grade is a subjective opinion, often given by the author of a guidebook [23]; a climber, upon completing the ascent, may disagree. This is an important aspect that a climbing RS needs to account for. Indeed, a climber may be served better if the recommendation is customized to suggest to the climber the routes that she would *perceive* as having the desired grade than suggesting the routes whose official grade is the desired one. To this end, we have develop a component that predicts what would be the climber's perceived grade of a route and visualizes this prediction in the interface. Section 4 introduces a scenario in which we take advantage of the grade prediction component to recommend routes for boosting climber's motivation.

We conducted a preliminary study on perceived climbing grade prediction. We developed a linear regression model using a data set of climbers' records about their ascents collected through the Vertical-Life app. The data set included climbers' feedback about the routes' grades. Climbers often agreed with the official grades, however, in about 8% of the records, the climbers registered a different grade, up to 3 grades harder or easier than officially stated. To predict the grade that a climber (c) would assign to a route (r) after attempting the ascent, we used domain knowledge to extract a set of features. A more detailed account of our approach is presented in [24]. In a nutshell, these features capture: how the target climber tends to deviate from the official route's grade (og) in her grading ($cmd(c, og)$), how the target route is graded by the community of climbers ($md^Y(r)$) and how environmental factors influence grading of the target climber ($cmd^M(c, og)$). Equation 1 shows the learned linear regression model that predicts the climber's perceived grade of the route ($cg(c, r)$).

$$\begin{aligned} cg(c, r) = 0.027 + 0.998 \cdot og + 0.410 \cdot cmd(c, og) \\ + 1.051 \cdot md^Y(r) + 0.279 \cdot cmd^M(c, og) \end{aligned} \tag{1}$$

The official route grade has the largest contribution to the prediction, although the features related to the grading behavior of the climbers have significant weights in the model. The RMSE of the linear model was compared to that of a baseline model, which predicts that a climber would agree with the official route grade. In 10-fold cross-validation we obtained RMSE error of 0.176 for the linear model, significantly lower than the baseline error of 0.191. In conclusion, the features identified important knowledge that contributes to the correct prediction of a climber's perceived difficulty grade of a route.

4 Recommendations and GUI

Crags Recommendation. As already mentioned, firstly, the climber is offered recommendations for crags that contain some relevant routes. The designed map GUI shows all the crags within a target region and clearly indicates the recommended ones. In fact, for each recommended crag, we give to the climber an overall idea of the potential relevance of the crag by identifying routes that satisfies three criteria: 1) routes of a climber's favorite discipline, 2) routes with the predicted grades she mostly climbs; 3) routes of the climber's favorite styles and wall's steepness. More formally, these are the routes that fulfill the following condition:

$$(r_{id} \in PD_c) \wedge (r_{ig} \in PG_c) \wedge (\exists s \in R_{is} : s \in PS_c) \wedge (r_{ih} \in PH_c) \tag{2}$$

where $\exists s \in R_{is} : s \in PS_c$ means that there is at least one element in set R_{is} that is also in PS_c. If there is at least one route in the crag that satisfy the above condition, we recommend the crag.

Figure 2 shows the GUI prototype for crag recommendation. The selected area here is the Arco region, located in Trentino, Italy. Arco is a famous destination for climbers, as it offers more than 8,000 climbing routes. The red circles indicate recommended crags, or clusters of crags, generated for the climber who is profiled in Table 1. Some crags are grouped together and form a cluster; a purple circle indicates a cluster and the number of crags is shown within. To inspect all the crags separately, the user should zoom in. Finally, we remark that each crag recommendation is accompanied by an explanation. The explanation follows the knowledge graph-based explainable recommendations approach described by Zhang et al. [25]. An example of an explanation sentence, for the climber's profile given in Table 1, is shown in the pop-up window in the figure.

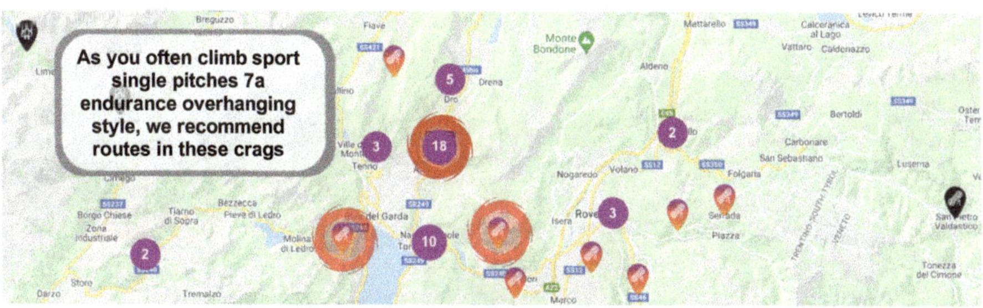

Fig. 2. Crags recommendation and explanation GUI. The pop-up window with an explanation is generated for the climber profiled in Table 1. The bright red color presents a cluster of 18 crags for which the explanation is given. The user needs to zoom in to visualize the recommended crags within the cluster.

Climbing Route Recommendations. When the crag is selected, the system should show the routes within the crag that have been generated by the RS. Such suggestions are supposed to help the climber to choose a suitable route, as some crags may include more than 100 routes, and it could be tedious and error-prone to visualize all the routes. The recommendations are organized in three separate lists: for favorite moves, for training, and to boost the climber's motivation.

Recommendations for Favorite Moves. The first recommendation list is generated according to the first working assumption presented in Sect. 3: among all the routes in the selected crag, the system ranks and shows the routes which have the climbing style, grade and discipline mostly preferred by the climber. Hence, if $r_i = (r_{id}, r_{ig}, R_{is}, r_{ih})$ is a route, and $c_p = (PD_c, PG_c, PS_c, DS_c, PH_c)$ is the target climber profile, then r_i is recommended if the following condition holds:

$$(r_{id} \in PD_c) \wedge (r_{ig} \in PG_c) \wedge (\exists s \in R_{is} : s \in PS_c), \tag{3}$$

We note that the climbing styles of a route (R_{is}) specify the movements needed for ascending this route, and if the climber often climbs the routes with this style, it means that she likes these movements. The ranking of the visualized routes is based on their degree of matching with the climber's favorite wall's steepness: routes are sorted by increasing the value of the absolute difference of the route steepness and the climber's favorite steepness. For instance, Fig. 3 shows recommendations in the crag Massone (Arco, Italy): it is one of the first developed crags in Arco, with around 285 routes. In this example, the system shows the list of recommended climbing routes for favorite moves at the preferred grade level 7a.

In addition to the 'Grade' column (which is the official grade), the GUI includes a column named 'Perceived grade' where the grade computed by the prediction model explained in Sect. 3.1 is shown. The 'Recommendations' red button is used to visualize the lists of recommendations within the crag.

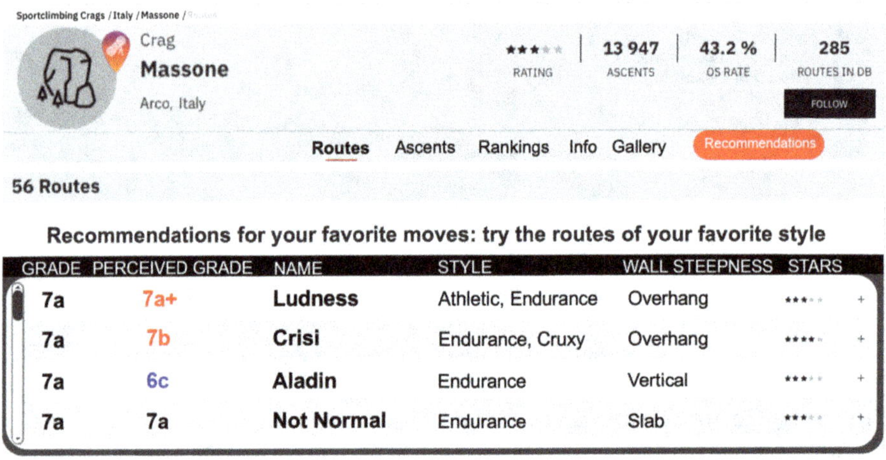

Fig. 3. Recommendation for climbing routes within the crag: routes with the climber's favorite move. The 'Perceived grade' column shows the predicted perceived difficulty of the route.

Recommendations for Training. The second working assumption presented in Sect. 3 is considered to produce another recommendation list containing the routes with a climbing style which the target climber has practiced less, but, for the training purpose, should instead be tried.

For instance, Fig. 4 shows the ratio of climbing styles (computed as the number of climbs with a particular style divided to the overall number of climbs) for two climbers: climber 1 practices 'endurance', but does not train 'technical' style, whereas climber 2 practices every style, thus, she/he is better trained. The routes that are therefore recommended for training satisfy the following condition:

$$(r_{id} \in PD_c) \wedge (r_{ig} \in PG_c) \wedge (\exists s \in R_{is} : s \in DS_c) \quad (4)$$

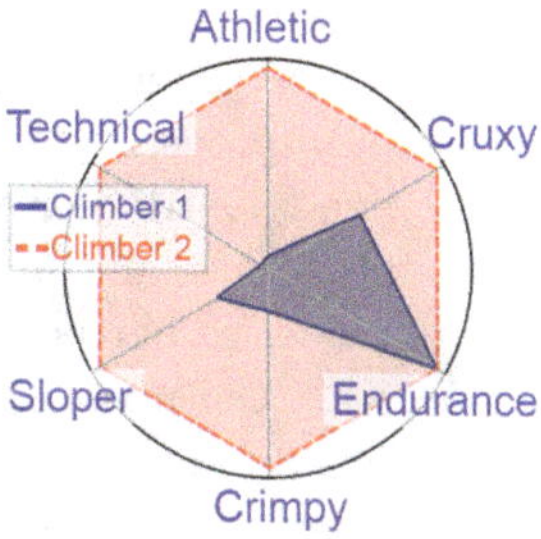

Fig. 4. Profile graphs for two climbers: Climber 1 climbs endurance style; Climber 2 climbs every style.

Moreover, these training routes should not have a steepness too different from the climber's favorite one, otherwise, it would be too difficult to climb them. Furthermore, the training process should be made gradually, starting from the least different steepness. Thus, the recommendations are sorted by increasing the value of the absolute difference of the route steepness and the climber's favorite steepness. The GUI of this recommendation list is not shown here for lack of space.

Recommendations to Boost Climber's Motivation. The final recommendation list implements the third working assumption discussed in Sect. 3 and makes a direct usage of the perceived grade prediction model. This list includes only the routes that are predicted to be perceived by the climber as easier than officially classified. When the climber will try these routes, she may justify this predicted perception as due to his skills. The GUI for this type of recommendation is here omitted is for lack of space.

5 Discussion and Conclusions

In this work, we have proposed a new concept of an RS for climbing routes recommendation based on the climber profile built semi-automatically by using mobile and web application data derived from the logs of the climber's ascents. The described RS opens the door to a new generation of climbing e-guidebooks, providing important recommendations to their users based on individual preferences and climbing routes characteristics. The task is challenging as it requires the solution of many problems such as understanding climbing grades, how climbers grade routes in general, routes characteristics, training process of sportsmen; these problems have not yet attracted much research activity and few technologies have been developed to solve them.

In a future step, a pilot study will be conducted to derive an early assessment of the proposed prototype system. Then, a large-scale evaluation of the system will be in order. Several features of the presented prototype must be improved. Firstly, the proposed perceived grade prediction model depends on a climber's origin, as in some countries the grades are overestimated in general, and it becomes a standard within this region, thus, the assessment varies between climbing regions and depends also on the styles trained by the climber, and this should be considered in the future. Secondly, the recommendations for training could be improved by using additional heuristics. For instance, the system now recommends outdoor routes with the styles less liked by the climber. However, it would be also useful to recommend indoor routes which are similar to the outdoor one, to better prepare a climber for a target outdoor route.

Thirdly, the proposed climber profile could also be extended by considering additional climbing disciplines (e.g., ice-climbing), styles (s.a., pinches, dynamic), and by leveraging implicit feedback (i.e., climbing performance metrics obtained through sensor data). It will also be important to consider the environmental and economic impact of the recommended climbing activities, i.e., by trying to contribute to the preservation of territories while not neglecting the economic growth [26]. Moreover, by considering the potential crag congestion produced by too many climbers at the same crag, the system could also try to better distribute climbers in the recommended crags [27].

Finally, although this work focuses on the climbing domain, we believe that the approach may be adapted to other similar sport activities, such as, hiking, trekking, trail running, via ferrata and mountain biking.

Acknowledgments. This work has been partly supported by the project "Sensors and data for the analysis of sports activities (SALSA)", funded by the EFRE-FESR programme 2014–2020 (CUP: I56C19000110009). The authors thank Andrea Janes, Ben Lepesant and the Vertical-Life company (https://www.vertical-life.info/) for the data provided for this research.

References

1. Rakkup app. https://rakkup.com. Accessed 20 Oct 2021
2. Outdooractive. https://www.outdooractive.com/. Accessed 20 Oct 2021
3. 27 crags – rock climbing guide. https://27crags.com. Accessed 20 Oct 2021
4. Mountain project app. https://www.mountainproject.com/mobile-app. Accessed 20 Oct 2021
5. Peakvisor app. https://peakvisor.com. Accessed 20 Oct 2021
6. Calbimonte J. et al (2018) SanTour: towards personalized recommendation of hiking trails to health profiles. In: Pautasso C, Sánchez-Figueroa F, Systä K, Murillo Rodríguez J (eds) Current trends in web engineering. ICWE 2018. LNCS, vol 11153. Springer, Cham. https://doi.org/10.1007/978-3-030-03056-8_23
7. Calbimonte JP, Martin S, Calvaresi D, Zappelaz N, Cotting A (2020) Semantic data models for hiking trail difficulty assessment. In: Neidhardt J, Wörndl W (eds) Information and communication technologies in tourism 2020. Springer, Cham. https://doi.org/10.1007/978-3-030-36737-4_24
8. Calbimonte JP, Martin S, Calvaresi D, Cotting A (2021) A platform for difficulty assessment and recommendation of hiking trails. In: Wörndl W, Koo C, Stienmetz JL (eds) Information and communication technologies in tourism 2021. Springer, Cham. https://doi.org/10.1007/978-3-030-65785-7_9
9. Vías J, Rolland J, Gómez ML, Ocaña C, Luque A (2018) Recommendation system to determine suitable and viable hiking routes: a prototype application in Sierra de las Nieves nature reserve. J Geogr Syst 20(3):275–294

10. Ricci F, Rokach L, Shapira B (2015) Recommender systems: introduction and challenges. In: Ricci F, Rokach L, Shapira B (eds) Recommender systems handbook. Springer, Boston, pp 1–34. https://doi.org/10.1007/978-1-4899-7637-6_1
11. Ivanova I (2021) Climber behavior modeling and recommendation. In: Proceedings of the 29th ACM conference on user modeling, adaptation and personalization, pp 298–303
12. Smyth B, Cunningham P (2017) A novel recommender system for helping marathoners to achieve a new personal-best. In: Proceedings of the eleventh ACM conference on recommender systems, pp 116–120. ACM
13. Smyth B, Willemsen MC (2020) Predicting the personal-best times of speed skaters using case-based reasoning. In: Watson I, Weber R (eds) Case-based reasoning research and development - 28th international conference, ICCBR 2020. LNCS, vol 12311, pp 112–126. Springer, Cham
14. Berndsen J, Lawlor A, Smyth B (2017) Running with recommendation. In: Proceedings of the 2nd international workshop on health recommender systems. CEUR Workshop Proceedings, vol 1953, pp 18–21. CEUR-WS.org
15. Draper N et al (2011) Reporting climbing grades and grouping categories for rock climbing. Isokinetics Exerc Sci 19(4):273–280
16. Draper N et al (2015) Comparative grading scales, statistical analyses, climber descriptors and ability grouping: international rock climbing research association position statement. Sports Technology (2015)
17. Kempen L (2018) A fair grade: assessing difficulty of climbing routes through machine learning
18. Dobles A, Sarmiento JC, Satterthwaite P (2017) Machine learning methods for climbing route classification
19. Tai CH, Wu A, Hinojosa R (2020) Graph neural networks in classifying rock climbing difficulties
20. Duh Y, Chang R (2021) Recurrent neural network for moonboard climbing route classification and generation. CoRR. Accessed 20 Oct 2021
21. Hörst E (2012) How to climb 5.12. FalconGuide Globe Pequot Press, Guilford, Conn
22. Hörst E (2003) Training for climbing: the definitive guide to improving your climbing performance. Falcon, Guilford, Conn
23. Draper N (2016) Climbing grades: systems and subjectivity. The Science of Climbing and Mountaineering, p 227
24. Ivanova I, Andrić M, Ricci F (2021) Knowledge-based recommendations for climbers
25. Zhang Y, Chen X (2018) Explainable recommendation: a survey and new perspectives. arXiv preprint arXiv:1804.11192
26. Marrosu GM, Balvis T (2020) Environmental impact assessment in climbing activities: a new method to develop a sustainable tourism in geological and nature reserves. Geoheritage 12(1):1–16
27. Ren X, Lü L, Liu R, Zhang J (2014) Avoiding congestion in recommender systems. New J Phys 16(6):063057

17

Towards a Strengths-Based Personal Informatics Framework for Transformative Tourism Experiences: A Phenomenological Study on Serious Leisure Practitioners

C. K. Bruce Wan[1(✉)], Cees J. P. M. de Bont[2], Paul Hekkert[3] and Kenny K. N. Chow[1]

[1] School of Design, The Hong Kong Polytechnic University, Hung Hom, Kowloon, Hong Kong
{bruce.wan,ka.nin.chow}@polyu.edu.hk
[2] Loughborough Design School, Loughborough University, Leicestershire LE11 3TU, UK
c.j.de-bont@lboro.ac.uk
[3] Faculty of Industrial Design Engineering, TU Delft, Delft, The Netherlands
P.P.M.Hekkert@tudelft.nl

Abstract. Personal technology plays an integral role in shaping people's quality of life which includes leisure and tourism experiences. A number of personal informatics tools can support people in performing their activities by collecting biometric and environmental data; however, little is known regarding the use of psychological data to enrich leisure and tourism experiences. To address this research gap, this study aims to propose a conceptual framework that fosters memorable and meaningful leisure experiences (MMEs) based on theories from serious leisure and positive psychology. In particular, this study probes into the MMEs of serious leisure practitioners who put their efforts and resources into pursuing intrinsically rewarding leisure activities. Excelling at these activities, which may draw upon participants' character strengths, yields sustained fulfillment which fosters personal transformation. The idiosyncratic nature of MMEs demands a phenomenological inquiry that involves in-depth interviews concerning the character strengths used and their development trajectories. Using theory triangulation from both positive psychology and serious leisure allows researchers to gain a holistic view of participants' well-being. Character strengths were found to be the integral factors that contribute to MMEs at different stages of leisure activities. The result identified three aspects of strengths used: strengths well spent, reflection and introspection, and anticipation of the future self, which informs the development of a strengths-based personal informatics framework for leisure and tourism.

Keywords: Positive psychology · Character strengths · Serious leisure · Meaningful experience · Conceptual framework · Personal informatics

1 Introduction

Technology plays an integral role in supporting the tourism experience. Recent information and communication technology innovation highlights include the emergence of smart tourism, which is characterized by the widespread adoption of personal technologies, big data, and networked devices in tourism settings. Future development may offer travelers new social and experiential dimensions by personalizing the provision of memorable and meaningful experiences (MMEs) [1] that are personally significant [2]. More importantly, the attainment of these goals requires technology that is specifically designed and strategically implemented [3]. Compared to mundane experiences, MMEs are vivid and explicit autobiographical memories that arise from exquisite, remarkable, and valuable events characterized by high emotional involvement and frequent rehearsal [4]. Besides tourism activities, serious leisure [5] can be the source of MMEs because practicing serious leisure often involves one's commitment and self-development. This study investigates how people's character strength and serious leisure activities contribute to MMEs, then proposes a conceptual framework for technology-mediated experience that could support people to gain MMEs in their leisure journeys.

2 Literature Review

2.1 MMEs Through the Lens of Positive Psychology and Serious Leisure

Positive psychology such as character strengths has been recognized as the personality traits that contribute to people's meaningful lives [6]. The values in action (VIA) classification of character strengths [7] proposes six main virtues and 24 related character strengths (see Table 1). Character strengths are conceptualized as a pre-existing capacity for a particular way of behaving, thinking, or feeling that is authentic and energizing to the user and enable optimal functioning, development and performance. They are behaviorally based unique personality traits; each individual is affiliated with their own bundle of strengths (top five) known as signature character strengths. The strength-based approach suggests that recognizing and making good use of one's inherent character strengths are the channels through which people generate positive experiences, find meaning and ultimately flourish [8]. One of the most reliable ways to identify MMEs is through the pursuit of intentional activities that match one's personal character strengths [9]. These activities should be intrinsically rewarding and interesting and, when engaged in them, individuals may feel a sense of purpose, curiosity and fulfilment [10].

Serious leisure (SL) [5] can be the activity which allows people to develop their character strengths [11]. SL is regarded as the systematic pursuit of an amateur, hobbyist or volunteer activity sufficiently substantial, interesting and fulfilling for a participant to find a (leisure) career there in acquiring and expressing a combination of its special skills, knowledge and experience [5]. SL delineates six characteristics which describe its inherent quality: 1. the need to persevere with the activity; 2. possibility to develop a leisure career; 3. the need to put substantial effort into gaining skills and knowledge; 4. unique ethos and community; 5. identification with the pursuit; and 6. gaining valuable outcomes and benefits. Despite practitioners often being confronted with difficulties and challenges in their pursuit, serious leisure activities are intrinsically rewarding and interesting, and when engaged in them, individuals may feel a deep sense of purpose and fulfillment leading to self-transformation [12]. This study uses the two bodies of knowledge to probe into how people gain MMEs through their character strengths development in their serious leisure pursuits.

Only recently MME has gained traction in tourism research for its enduring well-being benefits [13] which lead to self-transformation [14]. Also, eTourism study [15] has called for a transformative research agenda that incorporates transparency, plurality and creativity to foster sustained well-being to be developed for the tourism industry.

Table 1. Values in action classification of character strengths and virtues [7]

Virtues	*Character strengths*	*Virtues*	*Character strengths*
Wisdom	Creativity, Curiosity, Judgment, Love of learning, Perspective	Transcendence	Appreciation of beauty & excellence, Gratitude, Hope, Humor, Spirituality
Courage	Bravery, Perseverance, Honesty, Zest	Temperance	Forgiveness, Humility, Prudence, Self-regulation
Humanity	Love, Kindness, Social intelligence	Justice	Teamwork, Fairness, Leadership

2.2 Potential of Using Technology to Support MMEs

Personal technology plays an integral role in shaping people's quality of life which includes leisure and tourism experiences. It refers to a class of tools that help people to collect personally relevant information for the purpose of self-monitoring and self-reflection [16]. Tourism researchers [17] have suggested that the ubiquitous nature of technology gives it the potential to create MMEs via individual empowerment [3]. For instance, wearable devices support people to perform their activities by capturing and analyzing biometric, environmental, and social data. However, little is known on using psychological data, such as character strengths, to enrich leisure and tourism experiences. Wan and his colleagues [18] demonstrated a strengths-based digital diary which allowed people to journal and savor memorable and meaningful tourism moments with photos and texts provided by users. The journal platform supports users to reveal meaning by making implicit psychological dimensions of MMEs explicit. As such, the incorporation of psychological dimensions in personal informatics could foster transformative tourism experiences. The goal of this study was to propose a conceptual framework that incorporates character strengths into informatics that may foster MMEs in leisure and tourism. Especially, this study explored how the system of smart things can be used as a mediator to nurture people's character strengths. This study addressed the following questions:

RQ1: How do individuals draw upon their character strengths in their sustained pursuits of leisure activities to generate memorable and meaningful experiences during their travels?

RQ2: What opportunities are there for personal informatics to foster MMEs using the themes identified in RQ1?

3 Research Methodologies and Methods

This study acknowledged that individual sense-making and experience of SL are highly contextual and influenced by the complex and ever-changing social phenomena encountered [19]. Using an idiographic approach, the research objective was to determine how character strengths contribute to the generation of MMEs through the pursuit of SL activity in the context of tourism. The data collection involved a questionnaire and one-on-one thematic in-depth interviews. The questionnaire introduced character strengths literacy to the participants so that they could recognize their signature character strengths through self-nomination [20]. The in-depth interviews, on the other hand, invited the participants to introduce their serious leisure activities and explain why their activities are attractive, engaging, and meaningful to them. Also, the participants were invited to associate their character strengths with key memorable and meaningful moments of their leisure practices. Interpretative phenomenological analysis (IPA) [21] was performed to identify the participants' meaning and sense-making from their personal standpoint at the idiographic level. The analysis drew upon the fundamental principles of phenomenology and hermeneutics and captured the participants' memorable and meaningful SL experiences through their use of character strengths as personal resources. In a hermeneutic phenomenology-informed framework, researchers must explore, describe, interpret, and identify the means by which participants make sense of their own experiences [21]. The IPA process defines five interconnected stages, from transcription to theme generation, based on the recorded interviews. In this study, stage one consisted of becoming familiar with the transcript to gain a keen sense of the SL world of the participants. Then, based on the transcripts, we generated codes and made notes on our observations and reflections about items that may have potential significance. In stage three, these codes and notes were transformed into emerging themes and were connected with positive psychology conceptualizations. Then relationships and patterns among the identified emerging themes were identified. Lastly, based on representative interview data, we generated case narratives featuring these themes. The result supported the development of a conceptual framework for a strengths-based informatics system.

3.1 Sampling, Data Collection, and Analysis

This exploratory study considered the sample to represent the breadth of the SL landscape. This study used non-probability and purposive samples and considered that SL can be practiced regardless of age, educational background, household composition, or profession. Although people's sense-making may have cultural influence, this study examined the process of sense-making by making their character strengths explicit. Therefore, the participants deemed suitable for this study had to fulfill two criteria: they were to be SL practitioners in any of the domains identified by Stebbins and they must have practiced their SL, either partially or entirely, on one or more of their journeys. The participants were recruited through social networks using convenience and snowball sampling methods to connect with different SL communities. Seven participants were involved in this study, who engaged in different SL genres and demonstrated varying degrees of commitment. All participants were of Chinese ethnicity and lived and worked in Hong Kong at the time of the interview. Each interview lasted for around 90 min, and the interview sessions were audio-recorded, translated, and then transcribed into verbatim English transcripts for further data analysis. The following are questions from the interview protocol:

"The assessment showed that these are your signature strengths. Do you think that these strengths describe you well?"
"Can you share with me what made you devoted to your serious leisure?"
"What are your most memorable and meaningful experiences? Do you see that any of your character strengths take part in these experiences?"
"What do you enjoy most in your pursuit?"
"What motivates you in your serious leisure activity?"
"Why is that experience valuable to you? Can you see any of your character strengths in that experience?"
"What are the turning points in your pursuit? How did you overcome these challenges? How does it relate to your character strengths?"
"What did you learn from that experience?"
"Do you think that your serious leisure activity made you a better person? How?"

Table 2 lists the participants' backgrounds, SL activities, years of experience and personal statements regarding their pursuits.

Table 2. List of participants, activities, and signature strengths regarding their serious leisure pursuits

Pseudonym[a]	*Domain*	*Activity*	*Exp. (year)*	*Signature strengths*[b]
Emily	Natural science	WWOOF[c]	1	Zest, Humour, Kindness, Love of learning, Curiosity
Kelly	Entertainment	Swing dance	7	Social intelligence, Kindness, Zest, Love of learning, Curiosity
Sofia	Art & Culture	Documentary photography	10	Creativity, Love of learning, Judgment, Appreciation of Beauty and Excellence, Curiosity
Shane	Sport	Rock climbing	8	Creativity, Judgment, Prudence, Honesty, Self-regulation

(continued)

Table 2. (*continued*)

Pseudonym[a]	*Domain*	*Activity*	*Exp. (year)*	*Signature strengths*[b]
Evan	Sport	Dinghy racing	13	Zest, Perseverance, Bravery, Perspective, Judgment
Orion	Spirituality	Theravada meditation	7	Honesty, Hope, Forgiveness, Humility, Perspective
Andy	Volunteer	Volunteer on education project	7	Judgment, Perspective, Kindness, Teamwork, Gratitude

[a]Name and details of the participants are changed to preserve confidentiality.
[b]Statements were formulated based on the data collected in the interviews.
[c]WWOOF refers to Worldwide Opportunities on Organic Farms, a network of organizations that facilitate overseas work placements on organic farming.

4 Results

4.1 Different Roles of Character Strengths in the Generation of MMEs

In response to RQ1, three core themes and six sub-themes were identified (Table 3). The results show that MMEs are multidimensional. As a measure of their credibility, all themes were supported by at least five participants [21]. Below, each theme is elaborated upon with a detailed description, and examples in the participants' own words are provided along with the researchers' interpretations. Discussions are offered at the end of each theme.

Theme 1: Strengths Well Spent. This refers to the purposeful use of one's character strengths in the creation of specific and distinctive experiences during one's journey. The experience must be specific enough for the person to have a clear goal they wished to achieve and character strengths are purposefully used for the person to achieve a desirable outcome, even though the final outcome may not fulfill the initial expectation. Two sub-themes were identified: on producing positive experiences (i.e., seeking sustained fulfillment) or on problem-solving (i.e., pain avoidance). Emily's story helped to illustrate how character strengths were well spent for realizing sustained fulfillment. Since Emily loves to connect with nature, WWOOFing trips allow her to dedicate herself to this connection. To make her experience more intellectual, she once took a butterfly guidebook with her:

> I bought a butterfly field guidebook to take with me so I could learn how to distinguish between various species of butterfly from the tiny differences I observed… sizes and patterns… I really enjoyed the self-learning process. (Emily)

The excerpt highlights Emily's character strengths (i.e., curiosity and love of learning) used for the purpose of seeking positive experiences (i.e., seeking autonomy and knowledge). In contrast, Shane's experience is characterized by solving immediate problems. Shane connects creativity with her experience at the rock-climbing site in this way:

> You need to be creative in everyday life situations because you must do things with very limited resources at your disposal. For example, using the same piece of cloth as a dress one day and as a tablecloth another. (Shane)

Lastly, character strengths are used for both problem solving and sustained fulfillment in the context of competition and performance. Evan's dinghy racing showed that bravery, self-control, and perseverance were needed in one of her offshore competitions:

> The wind was unexpectedly strong! I really felt in danger when racing in such conditions. I also felt the pressure of being the pilot... For that competition, I required medical treatment every day because my whole body was so tense and overworked... But participating in competitions is what I like in this sport. (Evan)

The experience is comparable to flow, for which a balance of skill and challenge can lead to an optimal experience. Evan's experiences illustrate that character strengths can play a part in people's skill development in the pursuit of excellence. Nevertheless, the participants had divergent attitudes and behaviors toward their pursuits of excellence.

These anecdotes also highlight how one's affect and emotional responses play a role in formulating these MMEs. Furthermore, MMEs are not purely subjective; they are the result of constant interactions between the participant (i.e., strengths, affects, and emotional responses) and his/her surroundings (i.e., other people, objects, the environment). Moreover, these MMEs are significant to the participants, even when their initial goals are not (totally) fulfilled. These goals can be explicit and well-defined, as in Evan's dinghy racing (i.e., be the first past the finish line), or they can be implicit and not clearly defined (or even improvised) as in Shane's story (i.e., creative use of cloth has no limits). To conclude, this theme describes how people draw upon their character strengths to have MMEs.

Theme 2: Reflection and Introspection. This refers to the integration of the MMEs in one's life. These experiences can be either positive or negative and the related character strengths are not always obvious. The experience can emerge from one particular event (as shown in theme 1), an aggregation of multiple events, or as an overall impression of the experience. Through reflection and introspection, individuals try to make sense of these experiences by analyzing and interpreting them as valuable and meaningful in their lives—whether by learning a new aspect of life, gaining perspective on one's life, personal growth, or enriching one's life experience as a whole. Two sub-themes have been identified—savoring positive experiences [22] and reappraising negative experiences [23]. Andy shared an account of a mentally handicapped child who lived in the village where a school construction project was taking place. The child was unable to take care of himself and the villagers mostly ignored him or, at worst, bullied him. He worked in that village for two consecutive years and what he encountered this year was a personal epiphany:

> Last year, I found the child annoying because he often disturbed us at the construction site. This year, we have a volunteer who is a mother and a social worker in a special education school. Instead of ignoring him, she welcomed him with open arms and spent time with him. The child

> became happier than ever before, and her kindness was spread throughout the volunteer group. This experience inspired me in many ways: first, love and care are contagious. Second, problems can be solved in positive ways… the child was only seeking love and care. In fact, this is what we are all looking for. (Andy)

Through the savoring of a positive experience, Andy's illumination is rooted in connecting a particular experience with his past experience and with the wider scope of life. This became one of the most profound experiences in his years of volunteer work.

MMEs are not always positive; painful experiences, difficult times, and failure are all common aspects of serious leisure pursuits. Our interviews showed that the participants had managed their negative experiences by finding them to be beneficial and rewarding aspects of their lives. This process is known as the positive reappraisal of negative experiences [23], which helps individuals to transcend negative experiences and to transform them into something meaningful and purpose-filled such that they contribute to personal growth. Orion shared how her chronic illness (i.e., negative experiences), which impeded her further meditation practice, had been transcended into something worthwhile and personally significant.

> I felt completely disorientated after my diagnosis. I lost my goal because I was totally devoted to meditation at that time… but my sickness also made me somewhat more positive-minded because I realized that I needed to accept my sickness. I have to get through it with mindfulness and to learn how to build awareness in everyday life. (Orion)

These anecdotes illustrate how remarkable experiences, as a result of character strengths well spent, become meaningful, worthwhile, and purpose-filled by their integration into individuals' life experiences and beliefs. The savoring process focuses on cherishing, enjoying, and relishing positive experiences and elevates the experience of pleasure to a higher order of awareness. It allows people to appreciate their experience as involving something deeper than the immediate personal reactions and sensations. The positive appraisal of negative experiences, on the other hand, transforms an outcome previously perceived as negative into a meaningful and growth-promoting outcome that helps one to build resilience, act positively, and overcome adversity.

Theme 3: Anticipation of Future Self. This refers to the seeking out and planning for experiences that are congruent with the individual's personal interests [24] and that fit into the individual's development trajectory [25]. Here, character strengths also play a role in identifying such experiences. This anticipation allows individuals to pursue activities that foster eudaimonic growth. Two sub-themes were identified: seeking commitment and seeking alternatives. Over the course of our interviews, the participants shared their experiences in their development trajectory. Those with the intention to seek commitment are likely to connect their pursuits with a career path. Kelly shared her experiences of finding her future self in connection with her potential career development:

> I wanted to integrate swing dance somehow into my performance and to be a swing dance teacher for college students. Swing dance can help them to build a dynamic social network. (Kelly)

However, Orion reacted to situations differently when attempting to project her future self:

> I need to find an activity that allows me to meditate and develop my awareness. I recently began running, an activity in which I previously had no interest. By integrating self-awareness and setting up small challenges, I was able to better enjoy running. I hope to develop myself as a runner with the same approach and attitude as I did in meditation. (Orion)

In contrast to the other participants, Orion wanted to explore alternative activities in which their personal interests and character strengths are valued. Instead of deepening her commitments, she wanted to broaden their fields of activity and experience new things. This attitude is somewhat echoed in the broaden-and-build theory [25] in which positive emotions allow people to be open to new experiences and, thus, build enduring personal resources by undertaking new challenges. The difference may be that meaning and self-worth, in addition to positive emotions, are motivators for their decisions.

Table 3. Summary of themes and sub-themes

Theme	Sub-theme	Description
Strengths well spent	Producing valuable experiences	Using signature strengths purposefully in the production of valuable and significant experiences
	Solving immediate problems	Using signature strengths for problem-solving
Reflection and introspection	Savoring positive experiences	Reminiscing about good characters, and valuable and significant experiences as being memorable and meaningful in one's life
	Reappraising negative experiences	Transforming negative experiences into positive personal development
Anticipation of future self	Seeking commitment	Cultivating character strengths to further one's personal development trajectory
	Seeking alternatives	Identifying other opportunities in which personal strengths and interests are valued

4.2 Towards a Strengths-Based Personal Informatics Framework

In response to RQ2, this study proposed a strengths-based personal informatics framework (Fig. 1) that supports individuals to generate, appreciate, and pursue MMEs in their leisure and tourism activities based on the themes identified. The framework focuses on personally relevant characters which could facilitate a self-reflection process through breaking down memorable and meaningful experiences, inquiring about the character strengths involved and fostering self-transformation with strengths interventions. The framework is compatible with current studies [3, 18] on digital well-being informatics systems. The following provides recommendations for developers to implement strengths-based personal informatics. Above all, building awareness of character strengths should be an important step for strengths-based personal informatics in order to make users familiar with character strengths (e.g., definition and characteristics). It can be achieved by introducing users to character strengths literacy, establishing a strength profile, and using character strengths as the system language.

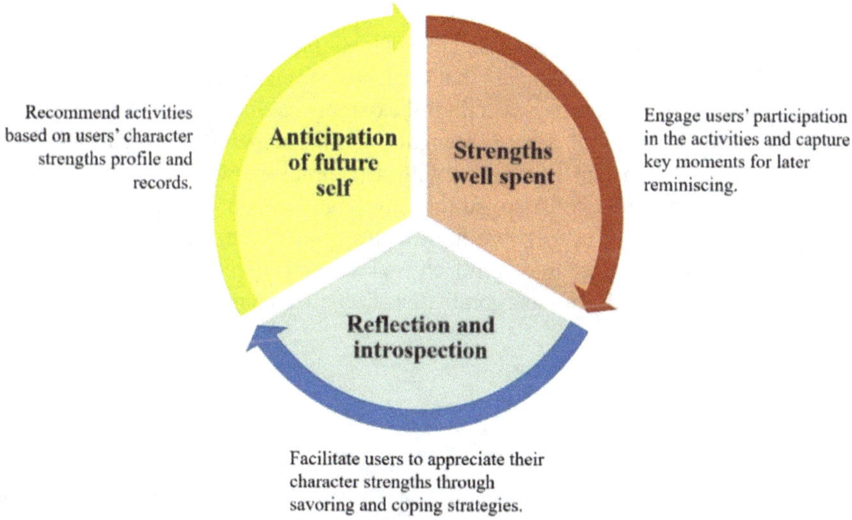

Fig. 1. Conceptual framework for strengths-based personal informatics

Guideline 1. Living in and exploring the present moment. This aspect of informatics systems is to support users to immerse themselves in the present moment and capture the moment for later reminiscing. Technology can take account of the user's character strengths and combined with situation-awareness technologies support users' immersion in their experiences [26]. Technologies may also collect onsite data relevant to the activity for users to savor the moment.

Guideline 2. Appreciating one's character strengths through reflection and introspection. This is probably the easiest way for people to connect their strengths with external stimuli (e.g., people, activities, environments, etc.) and their internal psychological states (e.g., values, goals, feelings). Reflection and introspection can be an effective way to allow users to recognize the character strengths they draw upon in gaining valuable experiences [18]. Reflection allows people to bring unconscious aspects of experience to conscious awareness, and thereby gain self-knowledge.

Guideline 3. Anticipating one's future self with character strengths. Being aware of one's implicit character strengths may also inspire one to cultivate them [27]. Technology may provide strengths-based recommendations to users so that they can broaden their perspectives or deepen their commitment to the activities. The system may facilitate users to generate goals that are valuable and meaningful to them.

5 Limitations and Future Research Direction

This study has a few limitations. First, the idiosyncratic nature of MMEs limited this research by requiring it to start with a small sample size. Future research can consider using a larger sample size and a diverse user group. The proposed framework suggested directions for a developer to incorporate character strengths into an informatics system. Nevertheless, this study demonstrates that character strengths are a necessary but not sufficient condition for generating meaningful experiences. Interview data showed that, in addition to the purposeful use of strengths, the participants garnered meaningful experiences through constant interaction with a complex network of activities, environments, objects, and people. Also, further investigations on managerial and ethical implications are necessary even if the informatics system can support people's well-being. After all, the strength-based approach is as yet little explored in tourism studies. More research is needed to incorporate the framework into personal informatics applications.

References

1. Tussyadiah IP (2017) Technology and behavioral design in tourism. In: Fesenmaier DR, Xiang Z (eds) Design Science in Tourism. TV. Springer, Cham, pp 173–191. https://doi.org/10.1007/978-3-319-42773-7_12
2. Neuhofer B, Buhalis D, Ladkin A (2015) Smart technologies for personalized experiences: a case study in the hospitality domain. Electron Mark 25(3):243–254. https://doi.org/10.1007/s12525-015-0182-1
3. Stankov U, Gretzel U (2021) Digital well-being in the tourism domain: mapping new roles and responsibilities. Inf Technol Tourism 23(1):5–17. https://doi.org/10.1007/s40558-021-00197-3
4. Tung VWS, Ritchie JRB (2011) Investigating the memorable experiences of the senior travel market: an examination of the reminiscence bump. J Travel Tour Mark 28:331–343. https://doi.org/10.1080/10548408.2011.563168
5. Smith JM, Williams A, Mullane F (2014) An introduction. Domestic Abuse, Homicide and Gender. Palgrave Macmillan, London, pp 1–8. https://doi.org/10.1057/9781137307439_1
6. Peterson C, Park N (2012) Character strengths and the life of meaning. In: Wong PTP (ed) The Human Quest for Meaning. Routledge, New York, p 20
7. Peterson C, Seligman MEP (2004) Character Strengths and Virtues: A Handbook and Classification. APA American Psychological Association, Washington
8. Corral-Verdugo V, Tapia-Fonllem C, Ortiz-Valdez A (2015) On the relationship between character strengths and sustainable behavior. Environ Behav 47:877–901
9. Seligman MEP, Steen TA, Park N, Peterson C (2005) Positive psychology progress: empirical validation of interventions. Am Psychol 60(5):410–421
10. Csikszentmihalyi M (1997) Finding Flow: The Psychology of Engagement with Everyday Life. Basic Books, New York
11. Dieser RB, Christenson J (2016) Integrating positive psychology, behavioral activation, and the serious leisure perspective in mental health counseling. Int J Appl Posit Psychol 1:57–68
12. Csikszentmihalyi M, LeFevre J (1989) Optimal experience in work and leisure. J Pers Soc Psychol 56:815–822. https://doi.org/10.1037/0022-3514.56.5.815
13. Alizadeh A, Filep S (2019) Well-being. In: Tourist Behaviour. Edward Elgar Publishing, pp 347–364

14. Kirillova K, Lehto X, Cai L (2017) What triggers transformative tourism experiences ? Tour Recreat Res 42:498–511. https://doi.org/10.1080/02508281.2017.1342349
15. Gretzel U et al (2020) e-Tourism beyond COVID-19: a call for transformative research. Inf Technol Tourism 22(2):187–203
16. Li I, Dey A, Forlizzi J, et al (2011) Personal informatics and HCI: design, theory, and social implications. In: Proceedings of the 2011 Annual Conference Extended Abstracts on Human Factors in Computing Systems - CHI EA 2011, Vancouver, BC, Canada. ACM Press, p 2417
17. McCabe S, Sharples M, Foster C (2012) Stakeholder engagement in the design of scenarios of technology-enhanced tourism services. Tourism Manag Perspect 4:36–44
18. Wan CKB, de Bont CJPM, Hekkert P, Chow KKN (2021) Finding meaning through travel journaling: a strength-based approach. In: Wörndl W, Koo C, Stienmetz JL (eds) Information and Communication Technologies in Tourism 2021. Springer, Cham, pp 137–149. https://doi.org/10.1007/978-3-030-65785-7_12
19. Gillespie A, Cornish F (2010) Intersubjectivity: towards a dialogical analysis. J Theory Soc Behav 40:19–46. https://doi.org/10.1111/j.1468 5914.2009.00419.x
20. Niemiec RM (2017) Character Strengths Interventions: A Field Guide for Practitioners. Hogrefe, Boston
21. Smith JA (2011) Evaluating the contribution of interpretative phenomenological analysis. Health Psychol Rev 5:9–27. https://doi.org/10.1080/17437199.2010.510659
22. Bryant FB, Veroff J (2007) Savoring: A New Model of Positive Experience. Lawrence Erlbaum Associates, Mahwah
23. Garland EL, Gaylord SA, Fredrickson BL (2011) Positive reappraisal mediates the stress-reductive effects of mindfulness: an upward spiral process. Mindfulness 2:59–67
24. Sheldon KM, Elliot AJ (1999) Goal striving, need satisfaction, and longitudinal well-being: the self-concordance model. J Pers Soc Psychol 76:482
25. Fredrickson BL (2001) The role of positive emotions in positive psychology: the broaden-and-build theory of positive emotions. Am Psychol 56(3):218–226
26. Stankov U, Filimonau V, Gretzel U, Vujičić MD (2020) E-mindfulness – the growing importance of facilitating tourists' connections to the present moment. JTF 6:239–245
27. Proctor C, Tweed R, Morris D (2014) The naturally emerging structure of well-being among young adults: "big two" or other framework? J Happiness Stud 16:257–275. https://doi.org/10.1007/s10902-014-9507-6

18

Business Intelligence and the Public Management of Destinations: The View of DMOs

Francisco Femenia-Serra(✉), Aurkene Alzua-Sorzabal and Aitziber Pousa-Unanue

Antonio de Nebrija University, Madrid, Spain
ffemenia@nebrija.es

Abstract. Business intelligence (BI) has become a priority for destination management organizations (DMOs) that have implemented solutions to improve their decision-making and data management processes. However, not all BI initiatives have fulfilled the expectations. This paper presents an analysis of a series of interviews with DMOs in Spain, offering a snapshot of their satisfaction with BI and the relationship between these applications and decision making at destinations. The results suggests that one of the reasons for failure is the lack of understanding of the critical factors that define the success of BI applications. Moreover, the findings offer a novel vision of how destinations are progressively leveraging the opportunities that advanced data analysis offers, but also reveal why managers find manifold difficulties in implementing these systems. These results pose several implications for DMOs.

Keywords: Business intelligence · Smart destinations · DMOs · Data

1 Introduction

The number of digital processes carried out in tourism has expanded enormously, and the amount of data collected about visitors has equally grown [1, 2]. This new environment requires a wide range of analytical skills and capacities in DMOs. In response to the increasing demand for customized information services, many DMOs have turned to business intelligence (BI) applications to improve their decision making. The use of the BI is widespread among most sectors [3, 4], and particularly among destinations, which employ BI today for a better understanding of demand and the changing trends in the market. However, advanced uses of BI tools are still limited. In research, there also appears to be insufficient attention given to the use of BI by destinations, its constraints and the advantages linked to their adoption. The use of intelligent systems is a key issue for destinations in their digitization process, in their transformation towards SDs [5, 6]. Hence, the purpose of this exploratory study is to better understand how public destination managers are using intelligence for decision-making. Likewise, this study aims to identify the utility and uses of BI tools and data by DMOs.

2 Literature Review

2.1 The Concept of Business Intelligence (BI)

BI has been defined as the technologies, applications, and processes for gathering, storing, accessing and analysing data for purposes of making better decisions [4, 7]. In addition, BI can be defined as a system comprised of both technical and organizational elements that presents historical information to its users for analysis and enables effective decision making and management support, for the overall purpose of increasing organizational performance [8]. In this paper BI is defined as a system comprising technologies, tools and software that enable an organization to gather data from numerous sources in the business and destination environment and then using technology to store, process, analyse and retrieve that data [7]. The implementation of BI systems initially demands a significant investment, but there are many benefits that organizations can take advantage of as well. Initially, BI reduces IT infrastructure costs by eliminating redundant data mining processes. BI is also seen as saving time for data providers and users through more efficient data delivery. Successful BI can represent the achievement of benefits such as improved profitability, increased efficiency, and reduced costs.

2.2 BI and Decision-Making in Tourist Destinations

BI systems allow to store data related to tourists' profile, experiences, places of origin, destination options and activities in which they may be interested [2, 3]. Thus, tourism organizations may plan in advanced to improve their services for tourists based on their preferences. Several authors provided clear evidence that BI systems improve the competitiveness of destinations by supporting managers understanding of tourists' behaviour and their perceptions [2, 9].

In the specific aspect of the competitiveness of destinations, it seems that, to some extent, this depends on the capacity of the territory to access enriched data and generate new content to improve its performance as a dynamic ecosystem [1, 10]. In this regard, the advances in public management of destinations through data analysis is one of the great premises of smart tourist destinations (SDs). Data-based intelligence has gained relevance in recent years thanks to the institutional drive around SDs [5]. Most of the mentioned authors, however, recognize a lack of understanding on the use of BI by destinations. Generally, these platforms are not capable of systematically integrating data from different sources or processes and, therefore, hinder the development of cross-process analyses that allow the achievement of complex and competitive data warehouses.

3 Methods

Based on the research objectives, four in-depth interviews were carried out with technicians and managers of Spanish tourist destinations, all engaged in the implementation of smart destination strategies, use of BI platforms, data management and informed decision-making. The interviewees work for DMOs of two urban and two coastal destinations and have more than 10 years of experience each in leadership roles within their organizations. The interviews took place online, with an average duration of 35 min, being recorded and transcribed after obtaining permission from the participants. For data analysis, a thematic analysis was carried out following the guidelines established by Braun and Clarke [11]: in-depth reading of the transcripts; initial development of the main themes identified; modification, merging and elimination of topics as the analysis with the largest amount of data develops; establishment of final categories; classification of text extracts in the definitive topics.

4 Results

As follows, we present the main results based on the themes identified in the conducted interviews. Participants' names have been removed to preserve anonymity.

Destination Idiosyncrasy and DMO's Roles

Findings indicate that each DMO is subject to different factors that influence their approach to data management. Decision-making processes are unique in each destination and so are the employed data analysis systems. In this regard, the budget and volume of tourism business at the local scale seem to condition the relationship between businesses and DMOs when it comes to data provision. Moreover, data collection is also marked by the size of the floating population, which implies a higher degree of complexity in gathering and analyzing data. Destinations acknowledge that visitors can bias the conclusions obtained from residents' data and vice versa, which is a challenge for them and makes choosing the right BI platform even more important.

Data Usefulness

Participants argue that destinations' use of BI is driven by their main objectives when employing data: destination promotion and positioning, market segmentation, events organization or tracking competitors. A lack of long-term planning strategy when using data is detected, as short-term marketing strategies seem to prevail in their projects. Mobile and social media data have become more important to conduct such projects.

> "Social media and behavioral data are helping us a lot in strategic decisions [...] We used to struggle a lot to get those data through face-to-face surveys." (P2)

Data come from traditional sources (such as statistical institutes), but increasingly from accommodation platforms, metasearch engines, social media, etc. Expenditure continues to be the most complicated data to obtain. To overcome these difficulties, some destinations collaborate with scientific experts, who can help them in analyzing certain types of complex data. Therefore, destination managers feel that BI systems need to empower them and help them understand complex data in a simple way. Also, the real usefulness of some data is called into question and data overuse is noted by one of the interviewees as a problem:

> "There are a lot of data, but I don't need them all. The key is to be selective and ask yourself: why do I need this data? Because having too many data can be annoying." (P4)

Platforms and Types of Data

A critical issue when developing a BI platform is whether the destination develops it with its own means or prefers to hire the services of a company. As participants state, managing this type of platform requires many resources but eliminates the dependency on external providers. The purchase of data from IT companies or banks also creates an important dilemma for DMOs due to their high price and their limited budgets.

Some destinations are working on the development of their own data platform by using Microsoft Power BI© in which destinations integrate most of the data coming from different sources. This tool is specially valued for its simplicity and visual nature. Platforms are fed with data coming from traditional sources that are now digitalized, such as surveys conducted at tourism offices. Similarly, some destinations are implementing sensors that also feed their data platforms with new parameters. However, the satisfaction with this service is low among those who are already using it. Technical difficulties, additional costs and lack of usefulness are reported by some, who also acknowledge the slowness of public administrations in adapting to new requirements.

> "These companies are selling smoke. They don't even know what they're selling. They sell you these nice platforms and all the data they get, but the reality is different." (P3)

Some participants argue that IT and telecommunication companies sell "packages" of data and prearranged platforms that do not match each destination needs. The adaptation of BI platforms to their needs is seen as critical by DMOs, as each actor within the destination has different data requirements. Regarding the design of BI platforms, DMOs seem to need new types of data visualization options (graphics), the integration of Geographical Information Systems (GIS) and the updating of all data regardless of the employed platform.

Resources and Future Tendencies

One of the most important issues identified is the very limited human, technical and financial resources that DMO have, and which hinder their capacity to leverage data. Having a data expert in their team, who would be in charge of developing data-based reports, creating graphics, and keeping them, is seen by DMOs as a requirement today.

> "We just try to stay afloat among all those data, trying to understand and keep focused, but we don't have a big team. There's no one who only works in data analysis." (P1)

Additionally, the resources to implement BI platforms and new infrastructure to capture data depend on budgets that are subject to public tenders and calls by the national and regional governments. This means destinations see their projects slowed down because of bureaucracy and monitoring of projects. Similarly, the lack of coordination between administrations seems to be a problem for an optimal management of data.

In terms of future needs, the pandemic caused by COVID-19 has increased the need to have updated information and new variables in data platforms, such as capacity and access to public areas, including beaches and parks. Having more updated data can help destinations predict the behavior of demand in the short term, which is more important than ever in the pandemic context. Some data, such as real-time number of visitors in attractions and access to natural areas will be needed also after the pandemic according to the opinion of participants. Finally, the interviewees recognize that the future will be marked by new challenges, including climate change. These challenges require having more detailed data on the impacts of tourism and a close monitoring of indicators.

5 Conclusions

This exploratory work has examined how public destination managers use BI platforms and data analysis for their decision making in a changing context. The results show that destinations have specific needs, limited resources and capacities and that BI needs to adapt to these. One of the causes of failure in BI applications is the lack of quality data, which not only refers to data from appropriate and reliable sources, but also involves the extent these data are adapted to the needs of the destination. Flexibility – in terms of data sets, user access and data visualization – is therefore considered a needed attribute of BI platforms, as pointed by previous research [12]. The simplicity of the systems is also crucial to guarantee the real use among the destination managers. The success of BI tools is proportional to the benefits that tourism organizations obtain, but success can also be subjectively measured by their users [13]. It is recalled the need of cohesion between the strategies of the organization, the target user of the tools and their use of BI applications [14]. Still, this study has shown that destinations are making limited use of the strategic opportunities provided by BI, which may be related to the shortage of human, technical and financial resources. Overall, the obtained results contribute to the literature on BI applied to destinations management by, but also to the use of big data by DMOs and the barriers existing in this area. Future research is needed to understand how different BI tools can be employed to address variegated destination management problems. The conducted study presents limitations such as representativeness that need to be address with further research.

References

1. Buhalis D (2006) The impact of information technology on tourism competition. In: Papatheodorou A (ed) Corporate rivalry and market power: competition issues in the tourism industry, pp 143–147. IB Tauris, London
2. Fuchs M, Höpken W, Lexhagen M (2014) Big data analytics for knowledge generation in tourism destinations–a case from Sweden. J Destin Mark Manag 3(4):198–209
3. Höpken W, Fuchs M, Keil D, Lexhagen M (2015) Business intelligence for cross-process knowledge extraction at tourism destinations. Inf Technol Tour 15(2):101–130. https://doi.org/10.1007/s40558-015-0023-2
4. Olszak CM, Ziemba E (2007) Approach to building and implementing business intelligence systems. Interdiscip J Inf Knowl Manag 2(1):135–148
5. Femenia-Serra F, Ivars-Baidal JA (2021) Do smart tourism destinations really work? The case of benidorm. Asia Pac J Tour Res 26(4):365–384
6. Gerrikagoitia JK, Rebón F, Alzua-Sorzabal A (2015) New trends of Intelligent E-Marketing based on Web Mining for e-shops. Procedia Soc Behav Sci 175:75–83
7. Shollo A, Galliers RD (2016) Towards an understanding of the role of business intelligence systems in organisational knowing. Inf Syst J 26(4):339–367

8. Watson HJ, Wixom B (2007) Enterprise agility and mature BI capabilities. Bus Intell J 12 (3):4–6
9. Fuchs M, Abadzhiev A, Svensson B, Höpken W, Lexhagen M (2013) A knowledge destination framework for tourism sustainability: a business intelligence application from Sweden. Tour Int Interdiscip J 61(2):121–148
10. Alzua-Sorzabal A, Zurutuza M, Rebón F, Gerrikagoitia JK (2015) Obtaining the efficiency of tourism destination website based on data envelopment analysis. Procedia Soc Behav Sci 175:58–65
11. Braun V, Clarke V (2006) Using thematic analysis in psychology. Qual Res Psychol 3 (2):77–101
12. Gebauer J, Schober F (2006) Information system flexibility and the cost efficiency of business processes. J Assoc Inf Syst 7(3):122–145
13. Lonnqvist A, Pirttimaki V (2006) The measurement of business intelligence. Bus Intell 23 (1):32–40
14. Isik O, Jones MC, Sidorova A (2011) Business intelligence (BI) success and the role of BI capabilities. Intell Syst Account Finance Manag 18(4):161–176

19

Using the Behaviour Change Wheel to Design an App to Change Tourist Behaviour and Increase Dispersal into Regional Areas

Martha Wells(✉), Kristy de Salas and Anne Hardy

University of Tasmania, Hobart, Australia
{Martha.Wells,Kristy.deSalas,Anne.Hardy}@utas.edu.au

Abstract. Currently, many tourism destinations are experiencing greatly reduced tourism due to COVID-19. In order to ensure that regions that wish to engage in tourism can share the benefits of it more equally, and to prevent the predicted future problem of overuse of popular areas once pre-COVID visitor numbers resume, an app to encourage tourists and leisure-seekers to change their behaviour and disperse into regional areas has been developed. The Behaviour Change Wheel was used to define the problem, find suitable intervention functions and design methods of delivery that could increase tourists' capability, opportunity and motivation to disperse farther into regions. The Huon Valley of Tasmania, Australia, was used as a research area. Our application of the Behaviour Change Wheel methodology determined that active engagement in logistic, value-based, and social information has the greatest chance of changing behaviour in this region and a list of Behaviour Change Techniques has been developed and considered in the design of a gamified travel app.

Keywords: Mobility · Behaviour change intervention · Gamification · Dispersal

1 Introduction

In the wake of ongoing lockdowns in Australia and border closures in the state of Tasmania, hospitality and leisure businesses in regional areas have become increasingly reliant on locals engaging in short intrastate tourism experiences [1]. Before COVID-19, tourist dispersal into regional areas had already been identified as a goal of many tourism destinations [2] and posited as a behaviour that could reduce overcrowding and enhance sustainability [3]. However, barriers to this goal are that tourists may not be aware of the value of local regional areas, nor engage in learning about what nearby areas offer.

To combat this, we set out to determine whether we could design an app, built upon the Tourism Tracer technology [4], that would encourage behaviour change using gamification, thus increasing dispersal throughout the Huon Region of Tasmania.

Gamification refers to the use of game elements in non-game contexts [5]. These elements can be minor additions, such as loyalty points, or be experienced as full-fledged games, and they have been used to enhance experiences, retain engagement, and change behaviour. Gamification has been found to generally provide positive results in a meta-review of studies, however, it was most likely to have a neutral or negative effect when researchers were attempting to change user behaviour [6]. This unreliability is generally contributed to poor design that utilises generic points, badges and leaderboards, rather than thoughtful and user-centred design [7]. The former approach means that gamification is relegated to an extrinsic reward system, that can only motivate users' participation so long as they are invested in the rewards, it fails to intrinsically motivate or to solve problems that could lead to change [8].

Gamification technology has been used increasingly often in tourism, although so far the major focus of its implementation has been in experience enhancement within specific destinations, rather than behaviour change [9], the goal of behaviour change via interventions is not new to tourism research and practice. There are a plethora of studies that seek to change tourists' behaviour, ranging from those which use nudge theory to change the environment around tourists to reduce friction and move them towards behaviours such as reducing plate wastage [10] through to those which use the Theory of Planned Behaviour and Value-Belief-Norm Theory to understand factors that contribute to tourist intention and thereby design interventions to elicit environmentally friendly behaviour such as reduced littering in marine protected areas [11]. Likewise, in Gamification studies, Self-determination theory [12] is commonly used to explain how activities can meet individuals' motivational needs and this model is used to design interventions that change behaviour [7].

These frameworks can all be effective in appropriate contexts, however they can also be poor predictors of behaviour in tourism and leisure contexts [13] and methodologies based on them can be poor mechanisms for behaviour change [14, 15]. The inconsistency of results when utilising designed interventions can be explained by the limitations of each theory; Michie, et al. [16] identified in a systematic review of behaviour change theories that no single framework existed that considered all possible influences on behaviour, or all intervention and policy techniques, and that many theories had components with overlapping definitions, making it difficult to select an appropriate theory in many contexts, or to reproduce results across studies.

In response to this, Michie, et al. [16] created the Behaviour Change Wheel (BCW) from an amalgamation of elements from nineteen behaviour change frameworks which were found to be comprehensive, coherent, and grounded in a behaviour theory. The BCW walks users through the process of designing behaviour change interventions from identifying the problem to selecting effective interventions, to choosing best methods of delivering interventions and allows comprehensive evaluation. Arguably, the advantages the BCW has over methods created within single behaviour frameworks are that it is comprehensive, and therefore able to be used in broad contexts [16], meaning that the risk of choosing a framework that does not consider a factor that is significant in tourism contexts is absent and it is systemised, and therefore no steps in the evaluation process can be missed.

The BCW was designed within health research and has mostly been used within health contexts to address patient and carer practices [17]. It has also become increasingly common in contexts regarding environmental concerns like energy conservation [18] and to promote physical activity [19], however using it within the tourism industry, and to design behaviour change interventions to promote tourist dispersal, is a novel test of the methodology.

Due to the novelty of using gamification in a tourist dispersal context, and the evidence that selective and context-specific design is necessary for successful behaviour change, a comprehensive methodology was necessary to design a gamified intervention system with the prospect of changing behaviour and dispersing tourists. Given that the BCW has been designed to identify and apply methods to encourage behaviour change, and is designed for application in a broad range of contexts [20] it was considered appropriate for application in tourism and this study. To date, BCW has, to the authors' knowledge, not been applied to tourism. The goal of this paper is to outline and critically assess the potential for the application of BCW to a tourism context.

2 Methods

The Behaviour Change Wheel methodology was employed to identify techniques to change behaviour and app components were considered that could administer these techniques. This study intends to use these designed interventions as a new frontend to the already existing Tourism Tracer Technology [4]. This app collects the GPS and survey data of participating tourists, allowing for fine-grained spatiotemporal analysis of tourist mobility, informed by tourists' demographic and preference information [3]. This mixed-methods data has the potential to measure dispersal and attitudes towards the interventions in real-time.

2.1 BCW Methodology

The BCW methodology contains three stages: the first involves defining the central behaviour that requires change, and the components of that behaviour that are potentially powerful targets for creating change. The BCW uses the COM-B behaviour system to define these components. COM-b stands for Capability Opportunity Motivation [leads to] Behaviour. COM-b is a system that was created by Michie, et al., in 2011 in response to their initial evaluation of nineteen behaviour change intervention models [16] it was developed to synthesise and simplify their categories of factors that influence behaviour. Physical and psychological capability, physical and social opportunity, and reflective and automatic motivation are all components that this system uses to clarify the drives behind a behaviour, and it is understood that each behaviour will be the result of a web of these components influencing one another, and in turn influencing behaviour. In the second stage, broad intervention functions such as 'training' and 'modelling' are identified and in the third stage, relevant techniques and ways of delivering them are matched to the intervention function and the situation.

Stage 1: Understand the Behaviour

Step 1: Define the problem in behavioural terms. Defining the problem as a behaviour helps designers clarify the 'who' 'what' and 'where' of the problem.

Step 2: Select the target behaviour. In this step a list is developed of all potential factors that could contribute to the problem behaviour and analyse them for a) level of impact b) likelihood of behaviour change and c) spill over to other behaviours.

Step 3: Specify the target behaviour. The context of the highest priority target behaviours are clarified so that the most appropriate point of intervention can be found.

Step 4: identifying what needs to change. This step involves using the COM-B model. The COM-B model assumes that all components have some effect on behaviour, however this step finds components that will be most effective at changing the target behaviour. It is not relevant, for instance, to create an intervention that increases motivation to travel to regional areas if tourists are already eager to go, but are physically incapable. In that case, interventions that bridge physical difficulties would be necessary.

Stage 2: Identify Intervention Options

Step 5: Identify intervention functions. Intervention functions are broad categories of ways in which behaviour can be changed: an intervention based on training will be different to an intervention based on incentivization. The BCW has already identified which COM-B components are effectively targeted by which intervention functions.

Step 6: Selecting Intervention functions. In this step, the APEASE criteria (Affordable, Practical, Effective, Acceptable, Safe and Equitable) is used to select the intervention functions are most practical and ethical to focus on. The APEASE criteria was developed 2014 my Michie et al. to be used as a simple evaluation tool within the BCW [21]. This study used functions only if they met every point of the APEASE criteria.

Stage 3: Identify Content Options

Step 7: Identifying Behaviour Change Techniques. Using Michie, et al.'s *Taxonomy of BCTs* [22], Behaviour Change Techniques (BCTs) are identified that have been found to link to the intervention functions selected.

Step 8: Determine mode of delivery. Once BCTs have been identified, we can design app features that use them.

3 Results

3.1 Stage 1: Identify Tourists' Behaviour

We identified the problem of regional tourism as: Tourists and local leisure-seekers tend to either go to iconic locations and stay on major touring routes or not leave Hobart.

And our Intervention aim: To encourage them to disperse to more diverse locations and regional areas.

Thirty-two factors were identified that impact this behaviour. The factors that were chosen related to issues such as knowledge of the region, perception of risk, time, money, travel group, peer referrals, social media influence, marketing, weather, ability to travel, physical ability and personal preferences. These were chosen based upon the authors knowledge of the tourism industry in Tasmania [23], the authors' previous research into factors that influence dispersal in Tasmania [3] and research conducted by others authors into factors which effect behaviour such as weather [24, 25] and digital connectivity [26]. Focusing only on factors rated with a high level of potential impact, high likelihood of potential behaviour change, and high level of potential to spill over to other behaviours reduced our list to a small number of promising behaviours to target. Some behaviours, such as perceiving lower ability to mitigate bad weather in regional areas, are accurate assessments, so there is a low chance of changing that behaviour, nor is it reasonable to expect tourists to continue into regional outdoor areas on days where the weather is severe. In other cases, such as tourists lacking adequate transport, the potential impact would be high if we could change it, but it is outside of the scope of this study.

Three target behaviours were found that had promise to change this behaviour, and which were within the scope if this **study:**

1. **Access and engage in logistical information on regional locations:** To visit regional areas, tourists and leisure-seekers must be aware of the locations, and the distances and difficulties associated with travel to them. If we can develop the behaviour of exploring and planning with this information in individuals who were not previously, it has potential to increase dispersal to these areas.
2. **Access and engage in information that raises the perceived value of regional locations:** Besides knowing about locations and how to get to them, tourists must also widely value a location to visit it in significant numbers. If we can develop the behaviour of engaging with a) information on which regional locations are attuned to a personal interest, or b) a new goal system within a game that raises the value of a location, it has potential to increase dispersal to these areas.
3. **Access and share social information on regional locations:** Learning where others have gone and seeing recommendations from others for new areas as well as sharing information about their own trips are behaviours that can raise the interest and decision making of tourists. One tourists public demonstration of having gone to and enjoyed a regional area could also be useful in changing the behaviour of others.

For all three identified Target Behaviours, the contexts were similar. These behaviours are principally enacted in the planning phase of a trip, although they could also potentially be engaged in while on a trip in the region to add extra stops. The exception was the sharing of social information which can be done in the post-trip reflection stage. All Target Behaviours can be done alone or as a group of travelers.

Next the COM-B components were analysed. These were found to be same for the three target behaviours: the app should change the psychological capability, the social opportunity, and the reflective motivation (Table 1).

Table 1. COM-B component analysis of target behaviours

COM-b model components	What needs to happen for the target behaviour to occur?	Is there a need for change?
Capability Physical	tourists must be able to access and consume information about locations and reasons to visit them	No: it is reasonable to expect tourists are psychically capable of finding and reading information in vast majority of cases
Capability Psychological	Tourists know where to look to access information, remember and consider possibilities, and make travel decisions that include regional locations	Yes: it is currently easy for tourists to miss seeing regional tourism information, or to forget it in the face of more constant highlight marketing
Opportunity physical	Tourists must have a device and internet access, or equivalent physical resources to access information	No: it is reasonable to expect tourists have internet access and/or access to tourism marketing and books
Opportunity Social	Tourists must be in a similar mind to travel party members to seek out information and make travel decisions together or be inspired to seek out information by social interactions that raise their interest	Yes: information accessed should motivate anyone in travel party, not just seeker, and information should not be accessed in a way that pulls the user out of the moment and away from socialising on a trip [27]
Motivation reflective	Tourists must be interested and engaged by the process of learning about travel to regional locations and want to seek out the information	Yes: Tourists do not currently know where to find this specific information, and it is often packaged in a more complicated and boring way than highlight marketing

3.2 Stage 2: App Intervention Options

This combination of components corresponded to every intervention function, however in an APEASE review, 'Restriction' and 'Coercion' were not considered as candidates as they are not acceptable or safe, and 'Environmental restructuring' was discounted for being impractical and potentially unacceptable for environmental damage. Therefore, 'Training', 'Modelling', 'Enablement', 'Education', 'Persuasion' and 'Incentivisation' were the selected Intervention Functions.

3.3 Stage 3: App Content

Using the intervention taxonomy [22] corresponding BCTs were found and analysed for appropriateness in the tourist context. For this, the APEASE criteria was used again.

As tourism is an innately hedonic activity, interventions were considered appropriate if they added, rather than detracted, from playful and escapist behaviours. therefore "6.1 Demonstration of the behaviour", which requires watching and learning rather than participating, was considered an ineffective intervention in this context while "Identification of self as role model" does meet a common need of travellers to gain pleasure from proving competence in an unusual arena [28] (Table 2).

Table 2. Target behaviour change techniques

Target BCT	App element equivalence	Review with APEASE & target behaviours
1.1 Goal setting	Mechanic to view info on locations and accept them as quests	**Simplifies acting on new knowledge and raises value**
1.2 Problem solving	Info screen on locations includes what users need to bring (i.e. protective clothes and water if outdoors)	**Raises knowledge**
1.4 Action planning	Suggest pre-planning of trips and rearrangeable accepted quests to help tourists plan an itinerary	**Simplifies acting on new knowledge and raises value**
2.2 Feedback on behaviour	Statistics/badges for locations visited by type	**Raises value of visiting locations**
2.3 Self-monitoring of behaviour	Screen: travel map that shows progress	**Raises value and knowledge of locations**
2.7 Feedback on outcomes on behaviour	Information on help given to small businesses	Not effective (impact is small, separate from own goals of enjoyment)
3.1 Social support	Promote travel-party to work together with group-friendly challenges	**Raises social satisfaction and value**
4.1 Instruction on how to perform a behaviour	App tutorial: popup explanations	**Raises knowledge**
6.1 Demonstration of the behaviour	App tutorial: video/walkthrough	Not effective (uninteresting)
6.2 Social comparison	Users may plant virtual trees in locations where they have completed challenges, other users can see which locations are widely visited by tree counts	**Raises social satisfaction and knowledge**
6.3 Information about others' approval	Allow comments/reaction to users visiting new places	**Raises social satisfaction**
7.1 Prompts/cues	Map where all are visible + suggestion popups when close	**Raises knowledge**
10.3 Reward (self, social or material)	Extra activities in locations/collection of apples from planted trees	**Raises value of places**

(continued)

Table 2. (*continued*)

Target BCT	App element equivalence	Review with APEASE & target behaviours
12.5 Adding objects to the environment	QR codes, caches to find	Not practical or acceptable: cannot add to public spaces/parks
13.1 Identification of self as role model	If users 'plant a tree', they can help other players gain more seeds, will be told how many players have picked from their tree	**Raises social satisfaction**
13.2 Framing and reframing	Give users challenges/things to identify and collect in locations to reframe reason for going	**Raises value of places**
14.5 Rewarding completion	Reveal new goals/locations after they have been to enough locations, and gained enough clues to solve puzzle	**Raises value of places**
15.3 Focus on past success	Remind of results of previous days using app with maps/result updates	Not effective (users may not be capable of going to region again - e.g. tourists)

Fig. 1. Prototype designs of app elements.

4 Discussion

This study used the BCW methodology to design a gamified app with interventions aimed at changing tourist and leisure-seeker behaviour to disperse into regional areas at a greater rate Fig. 1. BCW has been designed to apply to a broad range of contexts [21] – however, the vast majority of its uses so far have been in health and medicine [17].

The application of the BCW makes significant contributions to tourism research. This is the first time that the BCW has been applied to a hedonic context (tourism). As a result of this, our research has augmented a suite of behaviour change techniques applicable to hedonic environments that can be used by future tourism researchers.

Practically, this research project has developed an app that can be used in other tourism destinations. Its application in Tasmania will assist in dispersing the benefits of tourism beyond 'hotspots', and the gamified aspect of the app will arguably enhance the tourism experience in Tasmania and beyond.

In applying the methodology to tourism, it did prescribe some ineffective Behaviour Change Techniques, and some had to be reconfigured to be more in line with a game element rather than a health intervention. This may be because the ultimate goals of the users are significantly different from the original context of BCW use. In some health interventions, there is a presupposition that the user wants and benefits from the outcomes of the behaviour change but the behaviour is too boring, tedious, or forgettable to incorporate in daily life without intervention, while in the context of dispersal, the intended outcome most benefits area stakeholders and the environment [29]. However, the methodology exhibited advantages, as it allowed for a systematic examination of the process of designing interventions to increase dispersal throughout a regional area, from problem identification to promising content identification in one methodology.

We found BCW had another advantage over more traditionally used tourism behaviour theories such as the Theory of Planned Behaviour: there has been evidence of an attitude-behaviour gap in tourist behaviour [30] which means that tourists with pro-environmental or social attitudes will still act in self-serving ways on holidays where they are hedonically motivated [14]. By giving equal consideration to all possible influences on behaviour as potential targets, BCW has a level of flexibility that makes it a useful methodology in various circumstances, including tourism, where more hedonic, less commonsense influences can be rated as more impactful.

This process also made it evident that there are many factors inhibiting regional dispersal in which an app cannot intervene. Time constraints, increased dangers associated with remoteness, transport access limitations and undeliverable personal preferences are all factors affecting tourist movement into these areas that this study cannot influence. Future work with a larger scope could work with policymakers and providers to influence some of these, however others, such as time constraints for tourists on fixed schedules are unavoidable impediments.

For tourists and leisure-seekers without these impediments, we found the most promising behaviour to target is their engagement with information, whether logistic, value-based or social. We used Behaviour Change Techniques to design the most engaging method within our limitations to raise people's capability, opportunity and motivation to engage with information on regional areas, and use it to plan trips. With these component prescriptions, an app was prototyped for the Huon Valley Region of Tasmania, Australia.

References

1. Tourism Tasmania: T21 Visitor Economy Action Plan 2020–2022, https://www.t21.net.au/__data/assets/pdf_file/0005/91418/T21-Visitor-Economy-Action-Plan.pdf. Accessed 12 Aug 2021
2. Tourism Research Australia: Beach, Bush and Beyond: Understanding Regional Dispersal of Australian Tourists. https://www.destinationnsw.com.au/wp-content/uploads/2019/10/Understanding-Regional-Dispersal-of-Australian-tourists-October-2019.pdf. Accessed 12 Aug 2021
3. Hardy A, Birenboim A, Wells M (2020) Using geoinformatics to assess tourist dispersal at the state level. Ann Tour Res 82
4. Hardy A et al (2017) Tracking tourists' travel with smartphone-based GPS technology: a methodological discussion. Inf Technol Tour 17(3):255–274
5. Deterding S, Dixon D, Khaled R, Nacke LE (2011) From game design elements to gamefulness: defining "Gamification." In: Proceedings of the 15th International Academic MindTrek Conference: Envisioning Future Media Environments. Association for Computing Machinery, New York, pp 9–15
6. Hamari J, Koivisto J, Sarsa H (2014) Does gamification work? - a literature review of empirical studies on gamification. In: Proceedings of the Annual Hawaii International Conference on System Sciences. pp 3025–3034
7. Seaborn K, Fels DI (2015) Gamification in theory and action: a survey. Int J Hum Comput Stud 74:14–31
8. Nicholson S (2015) A RECIPE for meaningful gamification. In: Reiners T, Wood LC (eds) Gamification in Education and Business. Springer, Cham, pp 1–20. https://doi.org/10.1007/978-3-319-10208-5_1
9. Xu F, Buhalis D, Weber J (2017) Serious games and the gamification of tourism. Tour Manage 60:244–256
10. Dolnicar A (2020) Designing for more environmentally friendly tourism. Ann Tour Res 84:102933
11. Martina V, Weiler B, Reis A, Dimmock K, Scherrera P (2017) 'Doing the right thing': how social science can help foster pro environmental behaviour change in marine protected areas. Mar Policy 81:236–246
12. Ryan RM, Deci EL (2000) Intrinsic and extrinsic motivations: classic definitions and new directions. Contemp Educ Psychol 25(1):54–67
13. Rossi AN, Armstrong JB (1999) Theory of reasoned action vs. Theory of planned behavior: testing the suitability and sufficiency of a popular behavior model using hunting intentions. Hum Dimens Wildlife 4(3):40–56
14. Dolnicar S, Cvelbar LK, Grün B (2019) A sharing-based approach to enticing tourists to behave more environmentally friendly. J Travel Res 58(2):241–252
15. Kidd AM et al (2015) The effect of minimum impact education on visitor spatial behavior in parks and protected areas: an experimental investigation using GPS-based tracking. J Environ Manage 162:53–62
16. Michie S, van Stralen MM, West R (2011) The behaviour change wheel: a new method for characterising and designing behaviour change interventions. Implement Sci 6(1)
17. Barker F, Atkins L, de Lusignan S (2016) Applying the COM-B behaviour model and behaviour change wheel to develop an intervention to improve hearing-aid use in adult auditory rehabilitation. Int J Audiol 55:S90–S98
18. Wells L, De Salas K, Lewis I, Berry A (2016) Behaviour change wheel driven normative feedback in a serious game for energy conservation. In: Proceedings of 1st International Joint Conference of DiGRA and FDG. Dundee, Scotland, pp 1–16

19. Murtagh EM, Barnes AT, McMullen J, Morgan PJ (2018) Mothers and teenage daughters walking to health: using the behaviour change wheel to develop an intervention to improve adolescent girls' physical activity. Publ Health 158:37–46
20. Michie S, West R, Rona C, Brown J, Gainforth H (2014) ABC of Behaviour Change Theories. Silverback, Great Britain
21. Michie S, Atkins L, West R (2014) The Behaviour Change Wheel. A Guide to Designing Interventions, 1st edn. Silverback, Great Britain
22. Michie S et al (2013) The behavior change technique taxonomy (v1) of 93 hierarchically clustered techniques: building an international consensus for the reporting of behavior change interventions. Ann Behav Med 46(1):81–95
23. Ooi CS, Hardy A (2020) Tourism in Tasmania. Forty South, Hobart
24. McKercher B, Shoval N, Park E, Kahani A (2015) The [limited] impact of weather on tourist behavior in an urban destination. J Travel Res 54(4):442–455
25. Becken S, Wilson J (2013) The impacts of weather on tourist travel. Tour Geogr 15(4):620–639
26. Paris CM, Berger EA, Rubin S, Casson M (2015) Disconnected and unplugged: experiences of technology induced anxieties and tensions while traveling. In: Tussyadiah I, Inversini A (eds) Information and Communication Technologies in Tourism 2015. Springer, Cham, pp 803–816. https://doi.org/10.1007/978-3-319-14343-9_58
27. Shen Y, Choi HC, Joppe M, Yi S (2020) What motivates visitors to participate in a gamified trip? A player typology using Q methodology. Tour Manag 78:104074
28. Iso-Ahola SE (1982) Toward a social psychological theory of tourism motivation: a rejoinder. Ann Tour Res 9(2):256–262
29. Goodwin H (2017) The Challenge of Overtourism. Resp Tour Partnership 4, 1–19
30. Juvan E, Dolnicar S (2014) The attitude-behaviour gap in sustainable tourism. Ann Tour Res 48:76–95

Special Track on Digital Education and Training in Tourism and Hospitality

20

e-Learning for Tourism during COVID-19: Learning from Students' Perspectives

Lea Hasenzahl(✉), Soha Ghezili and Lorenzo Cantoni

UNESCO Chair in ICT to Develop and Promote Sustainable Tourism in World Heritage Sites, Università della Svizzera italiana, Lugano, Switzerland
lea.hasenzahl@usi.ch

Abstract. This paper shows a first analysis of the experiences and challenges of studying tourism during the times of the COVID-19 pandemic. 14 tourism students from two higher education institutions in Europe participated in three focus group discussions. One generation of these students started their education in presence and had to shift online with the start of the pandemic, while the other generation started their education knowing that lessons would be mainly online. Authors used qualitative content analysis to analyze the participants' statements. As a result of the analysis, several themes emerged, and students contextualized eLearning as an education method for a future without COVID-19.

Keywords: eLearning · COVID-19 · Tourism education · Focus groups · Qualitative content analysis

1 Introduction

Due to the global outbreak of COVID-19 tourism economy has dramatically suffered. For instance, by the first quarter of 2021, international arrivals were down by 83% [1], or within the European Union especially "sectors that are dependent on human contact and interaction, such as the cultural and creative industries and aerospace industry (due to the decrease in mobility and tourism activities)" [2, p.8] are expected to suffer in the future. Hearing about different statements or similar economic prognoses for over a year now, as well as not being able to fulfill certain study requirements (e.g., completion of an on-site internship) could have also impacted the learning experiences of tourism students at higher education institutions (HEIs). Not only were they involuntarily catapulted into online learning but were also suddenly studying a subject that some identified as a "suffering field of study". By the time this study was completed (August 2021), two groups of tourism students could be distinguished among those who had experienced what it meant to study during COVID-19: (1) those who had started before COVID-19 broke out and (2) those who started during the pandemic.

This paper presents a pilot study on the experiences and challenges of eLearning, which several tourism students described during three focus group discussions [3] conducted from April to June 2021. It also aims at understanding the impact of the digital media, as well as Information and Communication Technologies (ICTs) used for learning tourism. Moreover, since international tourism had decreased massively, a main underlying question regarding the motivation of students to (continue to) study tourism emerged. This also connects to the issue of sustainable tourism development. As the industry attempts to recover from a crisis, so does tourism education, which gives scholars the opportunity to rethink the current curriculum, pedagogy, and assessment [4] including reflections on a more sustainable tourism education. The next part provides an overview on the tourism eLearning literature. Based on the identified research gap, the research questions are introduced. Then, the methodology and results are presented and discussed. The last part comprises a conclusion, limitations, and future steps.

2 Literature Review

eLearning is defined as “the use of new multimedia technologies and the Internet to improve the quality of learning by facilitating access to resources and services as well as remote exchanges and collaboration” [CEC 2001, p.1 in 5]. Concerning HEIs, the emergence of new technologies has affected tourism pedagogy (“how content is delivered”), assessment (“how learning is evaluated”), and curriculum (“what is being taught”) [4]. According to Kalbaska and Cantoni [6], there are two main groups of providers for eLearning in tourism: (1) “academic institutions”, e.g., by offering blended learning, online courses up to full programs or even MOOCs (Massive Open Online Courses) and (2) the “industry at large”, i.e., for profit companies, independent providers, and public agencies. The eLearning offers from both groups are used by university students as well as within the tourism industry [6]. Especially the use of eLearning by the latter makes it an essential part of e-Tourism.

Due to an increasing global digitalization, eLearning in tourism research is not an unknown field, in fact, with the emergence of the internet there has been a significant and increasing amount of research that has focused on the various forms of eLearning in tourism [5, 7–13]. A search on Google Scholar in August 2021 using the keywords “eLearning” and “tourism” presents 7’970 results (including citations). Different authors with different viewpoints have studied the subject. For instance, Kalbaska’s [14] research on “eLearning courses” by Destination Management Organizations (DMOs) about tourism destinations, focuses on the research of the online “training of the travel trade” i.e., vocational training [6]. For this, the researcher explored the use of these courses “for the education and certification of their travel partners”. Focusing on another form of online course, Lin [15] studied the experiences of hospitality and tourism MOOC teachers, which is closely related to the university-level initiative MOOC “eTourism: Communication Perspectives”. Another perspective was taken by Adukaite’s [16] research on ICTs and gamified learning. In detail, the research was based on the case of South African secondary schools and focused on (1) the role of ICTs in tourism education based on interviews with teachers, (2) the evaluation of the promotional campaign of the gamified ICT-enhanced tool WHACY, which allowed the assessment of user experience with regards to engagement and conduciveness to learning and (3) the perception of instructors concerning the adoption of “digital gamified learning in tourism education”. Moreover, previous research reveals that in the existent e-Tourism curricula, scientific knowledge, competencies, and concepts are sufficiently present, while practical skills and capabilities require further attention [17].

Another Google Scholar search in August 2021 using the keywords "eLearning" and "COVID-19" generated 76'700 results (including citations). In fact, concerning the topic of eLearning during COVID-19 at HEIs, there are already a number of empirical studies and reviews that cover this topic in general [18–20]. Rapanta's et al. [20] exploratory study reflected on the insights of four online-teaching experts on the "online-learning-related pedagogical content knowledge". The study concludes with contributions concerning the integration of certain activities when it comes to learning design, three types of teaching presence, and the adoption of a "continuous assessment model" [20]. Taking into consideration students' perspectives, Shim and Lee [18] did a thematic analysis on questionnaire answers by 393 college students, receiving students' perspectives on learning environment (where students studied during COVID-19) as well as satisfactory and unsatisfactory elements of remote learning [18]. Regarding tourism education, the involuntary shift of HEIs to online teaching also produced some first studies, reviews and reflections dealing with online tourism and hospitality education [4, 21]. Munoz et al. [22] conducted an exploratory study on social presence in the online learning environment of hospitality-related online courses. The researchers concluded "that social presence was perceived greatly by students while teachers have attempted to enhance the learning environment by augmenting the social presence indicators" [22, p.13]. Another example is the Nankai university case, where researchers were able to recommend an online teaching process during COVID-19 by analyzing interviews and newsletters as well as making observations [23]. The study is aimed at providing "reference for tourism education in other universities" by presenting a number of teaching tools as well as presenting strengths and limitations of different tools such as MOOCs or small private online courses [23].

While the COVID-19 pandemic, and its effects on university teaching and learning, is unfortunately far from finished, more studies are needed. In particular, it is important to listen to the voices of tourism students, to understand their experiences of eLearning as well as their reflections when it comes to studying the subject of tourism while it is being drastically affected.

3 Research Goals and Questions

This research addresses exactly the issues described above through the focus group strategy, and aims at answering the following research questions:

RQ1: *What does it mean for a university student to study tourism during a pandemic?*
RQ2: *How did students experience and judge eLearning as a teaching and learning tool?*
RQ3: *What kind of ICT solutions are considered as interesting to be continued also after the pandemic from the students' point of view?*

4 Methodology

To tackle the research questions, the authors conducted focus groups with 14 tourism students, who at the time were enrolled in the tourism Master programs of two European universities: HNEE – Hochschule für nachhaltige Entwicklung in Eberswalde (Germany), which has a focus on sustainability and management, and USI – Università della Svizzera italiana (Switzerland), which allows students to focus either on the topic of sustainability and management or on the increasingly prominent area of ICTs for tourism. Both programs consist of various practical projects and group work opportunities allowing students to gain and develop soft and teamwork skills needed in their future careers. These skills are needed in tourism first and foremost due to the fact that it is a people-driven industry in which economic success is highly dependent on the success of human interactions. Finally, students are either required or encouraged to undergo an internship during their studies, in order to gain and reinforce their practical experiences [24, 25]. The general outlines of the programs also match academic descriptions about the current state and future visions of tourism education [26, 27].

4.1 On the Sample Design and Conducting the Focus Groups

The first two groups interviewed consisted of five students each, one group from the first and the other from the second generation from USI. The third group involved four students of mixed generations from HNEE. To ensure homogeneity [3] groups were formed according to the university where students were enrolled, and where possible, students were also grouped according to their generation, speaking to peers that are known to them. Students came from diverse undergraduate (Bachelor) academic study backgrounds (e.g., Economics, Hospitality, Social Sciences), and different nationalities (e.g., Swiss, German, Italian).

The first discussion was moderated by a professor. This acted to test and refine the protocol, later used by the two junior researchers, who also needed training. They were closer to students in terms of age and career. The subject of discussion appeared to be relatively easy to talk about and not overly sensitive in its nature, that's why the professor's presence was evaluated as non-intimidating. Participants were not hesitant to share their experiences, generate new ideas, and explore different issues [3], even when discussing topics such as cheating during online exams. To protect students as well as have a limited impact on their schedules, the discussions took place online, in the evenings, for about two hours per focus group. This ensured optimal location and timing for the participants [3]. Discussions were video recorded, and an auto-generated transcript was developed after. A benefit of this method was allowing the researchers to surpass geographical distances [28]. To ensure anonymity, students' names, locations, names of peers or teachers, and courses they described have been anonymized in the results.

The questions that were posed to participants covered several main themes, first and foremost focusing on the studying concept and understanding the students' experiences with eLearning. This was followed by questions regarding advantages and disadvantages of eLearning and the experiences with online exams. The former included questions regarding the preparedness of students for the sudden shift to online learning (also in terms of hardware and equipment). To understand students' experiences and opinions, researchers also asked the question of whether they faced doubts with regards to studying tourism during a time when the industry seemed to be at halt. Finally, the students were asked to share some thoughts about what the best aspects of eLearning would be to keep for the future, as well as provide suggestions for teachers.

4.2 Analysis

The video recording with the spoken word alongside the transcript and the researchers' notes were used for a qualitative content analysis (QCA), which was done with respect to Kuckartz [29]. Coding required a high level of interpretation and took place in several cycles. Evidently, four major themes emerged at the first level. Three of the major themes were then split into a total of seven subthemes on the second level. Subsequently, four out of these seven subthemes were even further divided into a third level. At this stage, one of the four third-level topics ("Affordances", see Fig. 1 below) was once again divided in two main fourth level groups before reaching the final nodes. Whereas the four major themes followed a mainly concept driven category development approach the sub-categories were developed based on a data driven approach [29]. Once the data had been coded with the exploratory category frame, a systematization in view of the research questions was undertaken.

Categories could also overlap (e.g., participants talking about two things at the same time because they are connected). A preliminary state of the research was presented for a review from other communication researchers (14 people) in May 2021, in order to get expert feedback and to improve the analysis.

5 Results

The authors were able to identify four main themes: (1) "Experiences", (2) "Human-Computer-Interplay", (3) "Social Interactions", and (4) "Studying tourism". Some were further divided into different layers of sub-themes (see Fig. 1 below).

5.1 "Experiences"

"Experiences" refers to instances when participants would express different emotions or feelings regarding eLearning during COVID-19. Within the main category of "Experiences", the authors distinguished between experiences they interpreted as positive and negative, as well as references that could not be univocally classified as either positive or negative (e.g., sarcasm).

Negative experiences were mentioned more than twice as much as the positive ones and were further subdivided into categories that were interpreted as negative emotions like sadness or frustration (for a complete overview see Fig. 1 below). A typical example for a reference that was coded as negative, further indicating "loneliness" is the following statement:

1. "(…) I was away from home, so I think that's also contributed a bit of a lower motivation. (…) I was trying to come here to have a bit of another mood, but I didn't really get anything besides being alone so (…)"

To contextualize, this student lives in a shared flat, so even though they were in company of their roommates while studying, they felt alone, which also seems to be connected to a lower motivation to study.

Fig. 1. Theme tree

The "Positive" sub-theme was also further categorized, but into fewer categories than "negative" (see Fig. 1 above). One of the few instances that was coded as a positive experience, was a student who seemed to be grateful to be able to continue their studies online:

2. "I really appreciate the effort of conducting education online because you don't have to stop your progress."

Later, it was explained that in the student's home country, which is different from the one where the university is located, peers could not even continue studying online due to a lack of infrastructure and therefore had to put their educational careers on hold which would ultimately hinder them from entering the work market by the time they had planned to.

5.2 "Human-Computer-Interplay"

On the one hand, this theme specifically refers to the affordances that technology can provide [30], which is not about the functionality of technology itself, but rather "what can be done with technology". On the other hand, students described the issues they encountered during eLearning, such as internet connectivity, bandwidth issues, and equipment. They also explained how they overcome these issues (e.g., switching to mobile data when home internet was overloaded, having two screens to follow technical classes). In general, issues were coded less than affordances. The "Affordances" category was further divided into the sub-themes of "Space" and "Time".

"Space" refers to the location where students were learning. This can refer to the sudden ability to study from home, which for example made it possible to avoid commuting, return to one's family, or use the computer to simultaneously/instantly research what is being taught, which was coded as "home office" and could be interpreted as an advantage. A striking example for this is the following statement:

3. "(…) the possibility to invite (…) experts (…) or to take part in lectures of other universities. (…) me for example I took part in a course (…) I think which is normally in presence and this was possible as it was completely online…"

By "normally" the student seemed to refer to a time when COVID-19 did not exist. In this case the course was offered in person and not online, therefore they would not have been able to participate unless physically present. However, "home office" also represented disadvantages, as described in the example below:

4. "I totally agree (…) because she mentioned the fact that she's in the place in her room where everything happens. (…) She is in the apartment and in the same place she does everything else about the university. And actually, that was quite hard because I realized it just yesterday when we came back just for one lesson, and you realize how many many things you (…) lost."

In this example, the student refers to losing a sense of importance and motivation to study due to being constantly in a familiar environment.

Moreover, another sub-category to "Space" referred to a very specific activity related to studying tourism, in presence excursions and visits, which were conducted online during the crisis. However, the execution of these activities, were mostly criticized and the questions about these were only answered by students of the first generation, who could not physically go on excursions, whereas the ones from the second generation still have another year, currently with less restrictions and are more likely to have in-person (physical) excursions. As one student stated:

5. “Because it doesn’t feel like it ended. You’re sort of in between states that you are aware that you don’t have any other courses to follow, at least most of us don’t. We have like two exams left, but the course itself, like the Master’s, is finished. And the <excursion> was supposed to be that finishing line.”

In this case, the physical excursion, rather than the virtual one seems to be a positive reward, which needs to take place in person and indicates a certain milestone within the students’ academic career.

“Time” refers to the ability of students to change concerning when they received education. The category was further divided (see Fig. 1 above) and references by students to the categories were discussed within different contexts. Concerning “Recordings”, as expected they were mentioned as a useful tool (e.g., for individual recaps), but interestingly also received comments requiring them to be of good quality and format. When it comes to “Recaps”, students seemed to, for example, perceive quizzes as a helpful studying tool that could be implemented in the future (e.g., as a way to test knowledge and stay on top of what has been learned in class). The use of “Camera and Microphone” was also discussed, especially the question of switching on the camera, which was perceived as something that should be done as often as possible both by teachers and students to enhance interactions. Nonetheless, students were aware that it is a choice and also mentioned that for example sometimes switching off the camera can help with being less distracted.

When it comes to “Productivity”, students were talking about the aspect of flexibility connected to having to study remotely. One student explained how they would integrate eLearning in the future:

6. “I think it should be the opportunity for students (…) if they want to be there in presence or if they also can learn at home, and I think that brings some opportunities (…) to combine also university and a job for example.”

Another typical element of studying tourism, “Groupwork”, was also reflected upon critically, although benefits were of course also highlighted (e.g., use of shared documents). One student commented on the possibility of conducting a group work in different time zones, while also explaining the challenges this presented:

7. “We had a course on sustainable tourism. In my group, there was one in <Argentina> and one in <Taiwan>. Now time zones didn’t really work in our favor, and you could really feel it when working, because we always had to compromise on the most random hours, but you would still feel somewhat bad towards the other people because even if it was four in the afternoon, it would have meant eight in the morning for the one in <Argentina> and eight in the evening for the one in <Taiwan>. Like they were literally at the opposites (…)”

Finally, an interesting recommendation was a reference to real-time collaboration during an online class:

8. “I’m following the course on working in the tourism industry (…) and <Fonte> (…) is using this system to post the questions. (…) I think it could also be used when we’re still in class because some people maybe feel shy to ask questions or maybe you want to ask the question and the professor is speaking so you don’t want to interrupt.”

5.3 Social Interactions

This theme was used when participants were mentioning and discussing instances related to interpersonal interactions and eLearning. In this case students referred to the differences of interaction between online vs. in-presence learning. Upon analysis of the statements, the category was further divided into two subcategories of “Student to Teacher” and “Student to Student” interactions. The primary reason for this division was the differences that existed between these interactions.

One student described a student to teacher interaction, which does not take place the same way online, as follows:

9. “Maybe you ask something to the professor, at the end of the lesson you just go to the desk, and you ask something, whereas I mean (…) you don’t do it when you have a call (…), you don’t remain in the call with the professor unless you have just an important question.”

Students on the other hand, seem to have different levels of social interactions (in and out of class) and stressed the benefits of these as a way to enhance their learning. A benefit was mentioned by one student, talking about meeting out of class to work on a university project:

10. “Like it would have been nice (…) to get like (…) just like get together and go to actually (…) explore the project and see them so we could actually get (…) even more practical info about the organization for the project.”

Moreover, students also mentioned the tendency to discuss the lectures and what they have learned during the pauses between lectures or during the lunch break. They also mentioned the benefits of discussing contents and solving problems with each other in class and learning from their peers, which seems to be hindered online.

5.4 Studying Tourism

As mentioned earlier, students were asked to explain their perceptions about studying tourism especially during the pandemic. In response, students seemed to either not have a specific opinion (“I could have studied anything it would have been the same”) or were very optimistic about their higher education in tourism, the rebound of the industry after the slowdown, and even mentioned that it was “the perfect time to study tourism” as they would have been unemployed otherwise or are hypothesizing a fast restart of tourism, where the contents they study (e.g., sustainable tourism) will be in demand more than ever:

11. "(…) I actually restarted studying because of Corona so I was like ok, well, take the two years because in these two years you will find no job whatsoever in tourism because of the virus. So, I said OK, well, then just do your damn Masters (…). I believe that we will be back, and we will be back strong. So yeah, I think it's a perfect time (…)"

6 Conclusion, Limitations and Future Outlook

The study was able to answer all three research questions in an explorative matter. Studying tourism during a crisis does not seem to be an issue to the interviewed students (RQ1). They still view it as an important field of study, viewing the crisis as an opportunity rather than a catastrophe. Regarding their experience (RQ2), students seemed to connect studying online during this time with rather negative than positive emotions. Especially the emergence of the theme "Social Interactions", stressing the differences between online and in-person learning, leads the authors to conclude, that they do not judge eLearning to be a suitable alternative for in-person learning. Nonetheless, students did identify different elements of eLearning, which are recommendable for the future (RQ3). Here, however it is important to remember that they propose the adaption of certain solutions only under specific conditions or as an addition to in-person teaching. Moreover, here, the concrete contribution of this paper to e-Tourism research and tourism practice can be highlighted. As Fuchs & Höpken [17] suggested that ICT capabilities need further attention, an inclusion of more eLearning applications in the curriculum might train students' ICT literacy.

While for this pilot study it has been possible to interview 14 students, researchers should extend the sample size in further iterations, also including institutions from outside Europe and ensuring that saturation of themes is reached. Moreover, relationships on how items are connected could also be coded [29]. Additionally, it is important to mention that even though a novel and promising approach because people were interviewed online, this poses limitations as well. Technical difficulties sometimes hindered the conversation flow, in this case the moderator had to ask participants to repeat words or paraphrase. Moreover, similar research with students of other fields of study could be conducted (e.g., fashion, public management), so that the specificity of studying tourism is further highlighted. Furthermore, the analysis could also generate more value by extending to a discourse analysis and by showing how the use of eLearning in this context of the pandemic differs from the common, voluntary use. The project could be further extended to interview the use of eLearning after COVID-19.

Lastly the authors would like to point out that, similar to students, instructors also had to quickly learn to use and adapt to various online teaching platforms while also guiding students through the process to the best of their capabilities, in order to adapt to this novel situation. This study is currently being extended by conducting in-depth interviews with tourism teachers to gain a wider perspective on the subject.

Acknowledgement. The work described in this paper was funded within and supported by grants from the Erasmus+ project "ICT for Sustainable Tourism Development" (Project number: 2019-1-PL01-KA203-065781).

References

1. UNWTO: Tourist Numbers Down 83% but Confidence Slowly Rising. https://www.unwto.org/news/tourist-numbers-down-83-but-confidence-slowly-rising. Accessed 01 Jul 2021
2. de Vet JM, Nigohosyan D, Núñez Ferrer J, Gross A-K, Kuehl S, Flickenschild M (2021) Impacts of the COVID-19 pandemic on EU industries. European Parliament. Policy Department for Economic, Scientific and Quality of Life Policies, Luxembourg
3. Breen RL (2006) A practical guide to focus-group research. J Geogr High Educ 30(3):463–475
4. Deng R, Benckendorff P (2020) Technology-enabled learning. In: Xiang Z, Fuchs M, Gretzel U, Höpken W (eds) Handbook of e-Tourism. Springer, Cham https://doi.org/10.1007/978-3-030-05324-6_129-1
5. Cantoni L, Kalbaska N, Inversini A (2009) E-learning in tourism and hospitality: a map. J Hosp Leisure Sport Tour 8(2):148–156
6. Kalbaska N, Cantoni L (2021) e-Learning in Tourism Education. In: Xiang Z, Fuchs M, Gretzel U, Höpken W (eds) Handbook of e-Tourism. Springer, Cham. https://doi.org/10.1007/978-3-030-05324-6_104-1
7. Buhalis D (1998) Information Technologies in tourism: Implications for the tourism curriculum. In: Buhalis D, Tjoa AM, Jafari J (eds) Information and Communication Technologies in Tourism 1998. Springer, Vienna, pp 289–297
8. Sigala M (2004) Investigating the factors determining e-Learning effectiveness in tourism and hospitality education. J Hosp Tour Educ 16(2):11–21
9. Kalbaska N (2011) Travel agents and destination management organizations: eLearning as a strategy to train tourism trade partners. Inf Technol Tour 13(1):3–12
10. Huang Y-C, Backman SJ, Chang L-L, Backman KF, McGuire FA (2013) Experiencing student learning and tourism training in a 3D virtual world: an exploratory study. J Hosp Leis Sport Tour Educ 13(1):190–201
11. Adukaite A, Cantoni L (2016) Raising awareness and promoting informal learning on World Heritage in Southern Africa: the case of WHACY, a gamified ICT-enhanced tool. Int J Educ Dev Using Inf Commun Technol 12(2):50–67
12. Lin J, Cantoni L (2017) Assessing the Performance of a Tourism MOOC Using the Kirkpatrick Model: A Supplier's Point of View. In: Schegg R, Stangl B (eds) Information and Communication Technologies in Tourism 2017. Springer, Cham, pp 129–142. https://doi.org/10.1007/978-3-319-51168-9_10
13. Chiao H-M, Chen Y-L, Huang W-H (2018) Examining the usability of an online virtual tour-guiding platform for cultural tourism education. J Hosp Leis Sport Tour Educ 23:29–38
14. Kalbaska N (2013) eLearning courses about national tourism destinations: destination management organizations' offers and travel agents' perceptions and motivations. Università della Svizzera italiana
15. Lin J (2018) Exploring the experiences of instructors teaching massive open online courses in tourism and hospitality: a mixed methods approach. Università della Svizzera italiana
16. Adukaite A (2016) ICT and Gamified learning in tourism education a case of south african secondary schools. Università della Svizzera italiana

17. Fuchs M, Höpken W (2020) E-Tourism curriculum. In: Xiang Z, Fuchs M, Gretzel U, Höpken W (eds) Handbook of e-Tourism. Springer, Cham. https://doi.org/10.1007/978-3-030-05324-6_107-1
18. Shim TE, Lee SY (2020) College students' experience of emergency remote teaching due to COVID-19. Child Youth Services Rev 119(2):105578
19. Quezada RL, Talbot C, Quezada-Parker KB (2020) From bricks and mortar to remote teaching: a teacher education program's response to COVID-19. J Educ Teach 46(4):472–483
20. Rapanta C, Botturi L, Goodyear P, Guàrdia L, Koole M (2020) Online university teaching during and after the Covid-19 crisis: refocusing teacher presence and learning activity. Postdigital Sci Educ 2(3):923–945. https://doi.org/10.1007/s42438-020-00155-y
21. Elhaty IA, Elhadary T, Elgamil RAM, Kilic H (2020) Teaching university practical courses online during COVID-19 crisis: a challenge for ELearning. J Critic Rev 7(8):2865–2873
22. Munoz KE, Wang M-JS, Tham A (2021) Enhancing online learning environments using social presence: evidence from hospitality online courses during COVID-19. J Teach Travel Tour. 21(4):339–357, https://doi.org/10.1080/15313220.2021.1908871
23. Qiu H, Li Q, Li C (2021) How technology facilitates tourism education in COVID-19: case study of Nankai University. J Hosp Leis Sport Tour Educ **29**:100288
24. Università della Svizzera italiana: Master in International Tourism – Structure and Contents. https://www.usi.ch/en/education/master/international-tourism/structure-and-contents. Accessed 20 Jul 2021
25. Hochschule für nachhaltige Entwicklung Eberswalde: Sustainable Tourism Management – Degree in Detail. https://www.hnee.de/en/Programmes/Master-degree/Sustainable-Tourism-Management-MA/Degree-in-detail/Degree-in-detail-K460.htm. Accessed 20 Jul 2021
26. Kim HJ, Jeong M (2018) Research on hospitality and tourism education: now and future. Tour Manag Perspect 25:119–122
27. Hsu CHC (2018) Tourism education on and beyond the horizon. Tour Manag Perspect 25:181–183
28. Halliday M, Mill D, Johnson J, Lee K (2021) Let's talk virtual! Online focus group facilitation for the modern researcher. Res Soc Adm Pharm 17(2):2145–2150
29. Kuckartz U (2019) Qualitative Text Analysis: A Systematic Approach. In: Kaiser G, Presmeg N (eds) Compendium for Early Career Researchers in Mathematics Education. IM. Springer, Cham, pp 181–197. https://doi.org/10.1007/978-3-030-15636-7_8
30. Gaver WW (1991) Technology affordances. In: Proceedings of the SIGCHI Conference on Human Factors in Computing Systems, CHI 91, pp 79–84. New Orleans, USA

21

An Empirical Study on the Impact of Prior Information Provision Methods on Participants' Perceptions in Tasting Marketing

Hisashi Masuda[1(✉)] and Kengo Matsumura[2]

[1] Kyoto University, Yoshida-honmachi, Sakyo-ku, Kyoto 606-8501, Japan
masuda.hisashi.4c@kyoto-u.ac.jp
[2] Gekkeikan Sake (USA), INC., 1136 Sibley Street, Folsom, CA 95630-3223, USA

Abstract. Tasting events are a typical example of a tourism experience that utilizes alcohol. However, it has not been sufficiently demonstrated how the prior information given to customers at tasting events affects their perception of the tasting and its marketing effects. In this study, we conducted a tasting experiment of a new Japanese sake product in California, the USA to clarify how information given to participants in advance can affect their perception of the tasting, satisfaction, and word-of-mouth intention related to the new sake product, and compared the effects of the following types of prior information: 1) no information, 2) written information, 3) video explained by a man, and 4) video explained by a woman. The results show that presenting information makes a difference in its impact as opposed to providing no information. When prior information was presented in written form, various perspectives significantly influenced the satisfaction and recommended intention more than in the cases of video. On the other hand, in the cases of video, the number of significant paths was reduced, but the influence on word-of-mouth intention was greater than in the case of written information. This study contributes to the development of a theory and empirical evidence that takes into account prior information in tasting marketing in tourism.

Keywords: Tasting event · Tasting perception · Word-of-mouth · Prior information provision · Japanese sake

1 Introduction

Past studies have indicated that there are synergies between wine tourism and wine production, and underlining the importance of regional development and the experiential wine tourist [1]. In this context, tasting events have become a typical tourist experience [2] in wine-producing regions. This kind of experience based on the use of locally produced alcohol is one of the essential attractions in a tourist destination.

In Japan, there is a rice-based alcoholic beverage called Japanese sake that can be compared to wine tourism. Similar to wine tourism, sake tourism is also flourishing in

Japan, on the basis of the long history and the appeal of the cultural aspect in sake brewers [3].

With regard to the study of alcohol, various perceptions have been analyzed in the context of beer. Consumer variables (demographic variables, psychographic and behavioral variables, genetic variables), product variables (product-intrinsic attributes, product-extrinsic attributes), and context and the purchase process (the customer journey, atmospherics) have been identified as factors related to the choice of beer [4]. In particular in tasting events in beer, an analysis of how tasting different types of beer (e.g., mass-produced vs. craft beer) affects consumers has also been demonstrated [5].

However, it has not been sufficiently demonstrated how the prior information given to customers when enjoying alcohol at tasting events influences their perceptions of the tasting and its marketing effects. In recent years, influencer marketing has been gaining importance, and the influence of social media (e.g., YouTube) using video, in particular, has been growing [6].

Therefore, this research purpose is to clarify the effects of such information provision on alcohol-based tourism experiences. Theoretically, we would contribute to the development of a theory for evaluating the impact of prior information provision to customers in tasting marketing. On the practical side, it provides insights to help companies or DMOs (destination marketing organizations) make decisions on how to design more effective tasting marketing, taking into account the impact on the customer experience of providing information to customers in advance.

2 Research Model

In order to achieve the proposed objectives in this study, we set up a research model as shown in Fig. 1 based on our hypotheses. For the marketing outcomes, product satisfaction and product word-of-mouth intention constructs were set, and also, the sensory perception construct, cognitive perception construct, and affective perception construct are developed based on previous studies [4, 5, 7]. Regarding the control variables, based on our research objectives, we set up that the prior information given to the participants of a tasting event makes a difference in product satisfaction and word-of-mouth marketing effectiveness. The types of prior information are specifically: 1) no prior information, 2) written information, 3) video with a man explaining, and 4) video with a woman explaining.

3 Methodology

To test the proposed research model, we conduct an experiment on new Japanese sake tasting among customers of Japanese restaurants in California, USA. In this study, before joining the tasting experiment, participants are controlled with different means providing prior information about the new product. Specifically, the participants are randomly divided into four groups: 1) no explanation of the prior information of the new product, 2) explanation of the prior information in text, 3) explanation in a video by a person (male), and 4) explanation in a video by a person (female). As the content of information, the same description of the new product (brand-new Japanese Sake) is used for groups 2–4. Participants of group 1 join the tasting experiment without any prior information about the new product. As the used product for the tasting marketing, we set one of the new sake products of a Japanese Sake company. The new product differs greatly from traditional sake in terms of flavor. In conducting this research, we underwent a research ethics review at the Graduate School of Management, Kyoto University, and obtained approval formally for the experiment plan.

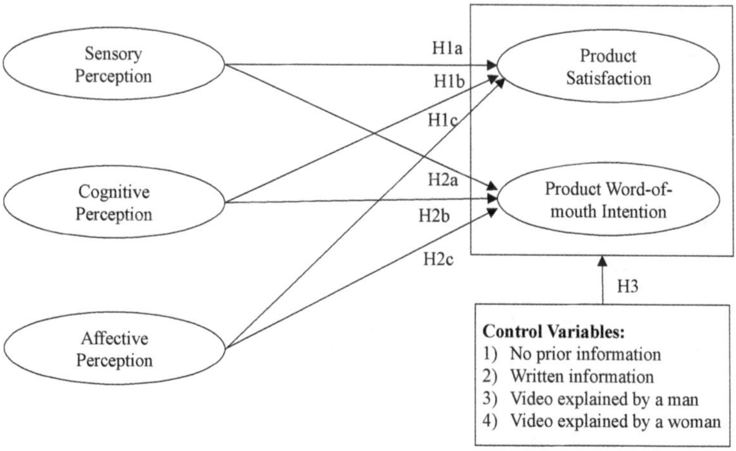

Fig. 1. Proposed research model.

A questionnaire for the experiment was designed to collect feedback on the tasting experience from the participants based on the proposed research model. The first item is to select the category of what type of prior information they gained: 1) no prior information, 2) written information, 3) video with a man explaining, and 4) video with a woman explaining. The main question items were constructs of the research model, and the degree to which the following perspectives agreed was collected using a 5–point Likert scale. The sensory perception consists of aroma, sweet, dry, sour, stiff, mellow, complicated, fresh, juicy(fruity), watery/bland, aftertaste, and white wine taste. The cognitive perception consists of artisan, balanced, cheap, easy-to-drink/drinkable, sophisticated, familiar, casual, novel, light/full body, mass-produced, masculine, simple, smooth, strong, unique, craft sake, and authentic. The affective perception consists of memorable, exciting, comfortable, fun, adventurous, relaxing, and stimulating. The marketing KPIs (Key Performance Indicators) are product satisfaction and product word-of-mouth intention. In addition, demographic and psychographic attributes related to alcohol were collected for each participant.

Data were collected at two Japanese restaurants in California, the USA between July 12–15, 2021. After agreeing to the purpose and the procedure of the experiment, participants were randomly assigned to the prior information acquisition types. Then, they had a tasting of a new Japanese sake product with the preliminary information provision type of each group. After tasting, participants answered the web questionnaire using mobile devices. The number of validated responses was 132 (Restaurant A: 55, Restaurant B: 77). Demographic attributes and prior information types are shown in Table 1.

The method of hypothesis testing is Partial Least-squares-based Structural Equation Modeling (PLS-SEM) [9]. This is more suitable for this study than Covariance-based Structural Equation Modeling (CB-SEM) because it allows for more robust analysis with smaller sample size.

Table 1. Demographic characteristics of participants and prior information Type (N = 132).

Gender	Male	53.8%	Income level	Less than US$50,000	15.9%
	Female	43.2%		US$50,000-99,999	32.6%
	Others/Prefer not to say	3.0%		US$100,000+	31.8%
Age(years)	21-29	15.2%		Prefer not to say	19.7%
	30-39	25.0%	Educational level	Middle schol	0.8%
	40-49	22.0%		High school	18.9%
	50-59	25.8%		University/College(Bachelor)	47.7%
	60+	12.1%		Graduate School(Master) or higher	14.4%
Racial Identity	White	66.2%		Vocational School	8.3%
	Latino/a/x or Hispanic	11.0%		Others/Prefer not to say	9.9%
	African American	3.7%	Prior Information Type	No prior information	24.2%
	American Indian or Alaska Native	3.7%		Written information	22.7%
	Asian	2.9%		Video explained by a man	26.5%
	Others/Prefer not to say	12.5%		Video explained by a woman	26.5%

4 Results

Results are presented in Table 2. First of all, it was shown that the way in which prior information is provided makes a difference in the impact on product satisfaction and intention to recommend. When prior information was presented in written form, various perspectives significantly influenced satisfaction and recommended intention more than in the cases of video, although the significance level is 0.05. In the cases of video, the number of significant relationships was reduced, but we obtained paths with stronger relationships with significance levels below 0.01 than the written information case. In particular, especially for male videos, affective perception significantly influenced product recommendation intentions, and also, sensory and affective perception also had a significant impact on product satisfaction. On the other hand, the significant paths decreased for female videos, but there was an impact of sensory perception on product recommendation intention with a significant level of 0.01.

5 Discussion

The results of this study showed that providing prior information in a tasting event can influence relationships between participants' perceptions (sensory, cognitive, and affective) and their product satisfaction and product word-of-mouth intentions. In particular, it was shown that explaining prior information through video strongly influences the product word-of-mouth intention. This research contributes to the development of a theoretical foundation for evaluating the provision of tourism experiences of tastings. On a practical side, it also provides insights into the means of providing prior information when offering tourism experiences. On the other hand, in this experiment, a video by women reduced the number of significant paths more than those of written information. This may indicate the variation in the evaluation criteria for female videos among the experimental participants against other means. Therefore, it is necessary to subdivide the group in order to examine the effect in detail. In the future, we need to work on theoretical development, taking into account the analysis of customer attributes in detail and the credibility of the information sender in videos.

Table 2. Results of hypothesis testing (H1–H3).

		No prior information (N = 32)		Written information (N = 30)		Video explained by a man (N = 35)		Video explained by a woman (N = 35)		Difference between the groups (H3)
Hypothesis/Structural path		β	Result	β	Result	β	Result	β	Result	Result
H1a	Sensory Perception → Product Satisfaction	0.343	R	0.245	R	**0.527****	A	0.335	R	A
H1b	Cognitive Perception → Product Satisfaction	0.064	R	0.218	R	**0.402***	A	0.205	R	A
H1c	Affective Perception → Product Satisfaction	0.339	R	**0.478***	A	**0.376****	A	0.226	R	A
H2a	Sensory Perception → Product Word-of-mouth Intention	0.228	R	**0.391***	A	-0.205	R	**0.545****	A	A
H2b	Cognitive Perception → Product Word-of-mouth Intention	0.230	R	**0.370***	A	-0.028	R	0.205	R	A
H2c	Affective Perception → Product Word-of-mouth Intention	**0.478***	A	**0.475***	A	**0.799*****	A	0.007	R	A

Note: Two Tailed Test; *** Significance Level = 0.1%; ** Significance Level = 1%; * Significance Level = 5%; A=Accepted; R=Rejected

References

1. Gómez M, Pratt MA, Molina A (2019) Wine tourism research: a systematic review of 20 vintages from 1995 to 2014. Curr Issue Tour 22(18):2211–2249
2. Dawson H, Holmes M, Jacobs H, Wade RI (2011) Wine tourism: winery visitation in the wine appellations of Ontario. J Vacat Mark 17(3):237–246
3. Lee YS, Shin WJ (2015) Marketing tradition-bound products through storytelling: a case study of a Japanese sake brewery. Serv Bus 9(2):281–295
4. Betancur MI, Motoki K, Spence C, Velasco C (2020) Factors influencing the choice of beer: a review. Food Res Int 137:109367
5. Jaeger SR, Worch T, Phelps T, Jin D, Cardello AV (2020) Preference segments among declared craft beer drinkers: perceptual, attitudinal and behavioral responses underlying craft-style vs. traditional-style flavor preferences. Food Qual. Prefer 82:103884
6. Masuda H, Han SH, Lee J (2022) Impacts of influencer attributes on purchase intentions in social media influencer marketing: mediating roles characterizations. Technol. Forecast Soc Change 174:121246
7. Ares G, Jaeger SR (2015) 11 - Check-all-that-apply (CATA) questions with consumers in practice: experimental considerations and impact on outcome. In Delarue J. Lawlor JB, Rogeaux M (eds.) Rapid sensory profiling techniques: woodhead publishing
8. Jaeger SR, Cardello AV, Chheang SL, Beresford MK, Hedderley DI, Pineau B (2017) Holistic and consumer-centric assessment of beer: a multi-measurement approach. Food Res Int 99:287–297
9. Hair JF, Hult GTM, Ringle CM, Sarstedt M (2022) A Primer on Partial Least Squares Structural Equation Modeling. SAGE Publications, PLS-SEM) Third Edition

22

Analyzing Individual, Institutional and Regional Contributions to e-Tourism

Suki Siuki Tam[1], Huiyue Ye[2], Rob Law[2,3] and Lawrence Hoc Nang Fong[2(✉)]

[1] School of Hotel and Tourism Management, The Hong Kong Polytechnic University, Hong Kong S.A.R., China

[2] Department of Integrated Resort and Tourism Management, Faculty of Business Administration, University of Macau, Macau SAR, China
{roblaw, lawrencefong}@um.edu.mo

[3] Asia-Pacific Academy of Economics and Management, Department of Integrated Resort and Tourism Management, Faculty of Business Administration, University of Macau, Macau SAR, China

Abstract. ENTER conference is an annual international event organized by the International Federation for Information Technology and Travel and Tourism (IFITT). Since 1994, this conference has been providing a platform for academics, industry practitioners, governments, and other organizations to share their research about information and communication technologies application in tourism. In the conference, the IFITT community mainly focuses on three streams, namely, research, destinations, and industry. The studies presented at the ENTER conference were published in the content of ENTER proceedings. The current study analyzes the proceedings published from 1996 to 2021 (i.e., 26 issues) to understand the individual, institutional, and regional contributions to e-tourism within these 26 years.

Keywords: ENTER conference · IT · Tourism · Authors · Institutes · Regions · Contribution

1 Introduction

Conventional industries have been changed by the evolution of information and communication technologies (ICT), in terms of product development and consumption. Therefore, new business models are needed in the tourism industry [1]. Technologies are also transforming tourism management and marketing strategies. To obtain a complete view of the influence of technological advances on the tourism industry, continuous and innovative tourism technology research effort is needed [2]. Before the 1990s, very limited contributions to tourism and technology were published. Since 1994, the ENTER conference annually offers a forum for academics, practitioners, governments, and organizations to share their latest research findings of information and technology in the tourism industry [3, 4]. As the leading international academic conference on tourism and technology, ENTER provides a platform for professional researchers in publishing quality research articles. Aiming to provide a general view of authors' contributions to this research realm in ENTER conferences, this study reviewed the accessible 26 issues of conference proceedings from 1996 to 2021. A total of 1,217 research papers were incorporated into the analysis, with 1,697 individual authors who were affiliated to different regions/countries of continents. Individual, institutional, and regional contributions to information and technology in the tourism industry in the recent 26 years are presented in this study.

2 Literature Review

2.1 Research Productivity Analysis

Van Over and Nelson [5] indicated that identifying and evaluating major research contributions are periodically necessary to record the historical evolution and provide a sense for future study. The tourism and hospitality academic community devoted the greatest efforts to conducting research [6]. Although the importance of research is recognized, no common ways are adopted to evaluate research performance in hospitality and tourism research [7]. Harris [8] stated that four different methods can be used to measure research performance, namely, impact, quality, importance, and quantity. Impact represents the influence level of a related article. Importance and quality are evaluated by reviews and value judgments so that the results are subjective particularly when the academic research output is evaluated in different periods of time. Then, quantity is the most pragmatic way to measure research productivity, that is, by counting the number of publications issued. In the field of tourism and hospitality, authorship and institution analyses are frequently used to assess research performance by counting the number of publications [6, 7, 9–11]. Prior tourism review research seldom evaluated productivity on specific areas, such as information technology (IT) in tourism [12].

2.2 IT in Tourism Research

Since the 1980s, ICT has started influencing the tourism industry in terms of business practices, marketing strategies, and industry structure [13]. More importantly, the implementation of technologies is an effective strategy to enhance tourist destination competitiveness [14]. By serving as an effective liaison among heterogeneous stakeholders, ICT promotes the information exchange of the tourism ecosystem and therefore fosters globalization [15]. With the evolution of technologies, such as 5G, Internet of Things, blockchain, and augmented reality, tourism is transforming from eTourism to smart tourism and then to the forthcoming ambient intelligence tourism [14]. The successful technology adoption in the tourism industry not only enhances the tourist experience but also promotes the sustainable development of the destination by assisting better resource management [16]. This irreversible development trend has a disruptive influence on the tourism industry and therefore has attracted significant attention from scholars, practitioners, and governments [4].

The literature reflects that very limited studies related to tourism and technology were published before 1990. In 1994, the annual ENTER conference gathered researchers who share multiple interests in tourism and IT development to exchange their research findings. This group of researchers constituted a research community called the International Federation of Information Technology for Travel and Tourism (IFITT) [3, 4]. Since then, a proliferation of IT and tourism research is witnessed [17]. Key review studies can help academics keep pace with the state-of-the-art IT and tourism research [18]. For example, Buhalis and Law [4] reviewed the development progress of IT in tourism research in the past 20 years before 2008. In addition, Law, Qi, and Buhalis [19] summarized the tourism website evaluation research in the past 15 years (i.e., from 1996 to 2009). Leung, Law, van Hoof, and Buhalis [20] focused on emerging social media-relevant tourism research. Moreover, the recent decade witnessed several IT and tourism systematic reviews that analyzed the categorization of pertinent research themes, development trends, and co-authorship of key researchers [17–21]. Although several review papers provided an outline of the development of IT and tourism research, conference papers were usually excluded from the analyzed scope. Therefore, considering the limited understanding of research productivity and individual and institutional contributions to IT and tourism research, ENTER conference proceedings from 1996 to 2021 were analyzed to provide a wider view for academics, industry practitioners, and governments [12].

3 Methodology

In this study, the articles published in the Information and Communication Technologies in Tourism: Proceedings of the ENTER conferences (1996–2021) were examined. During this period, a total of 1,217 research papers were included in ENTER proceedings, comprising full- and short-length articles.

This study is regarded as an extension of the previous study [12] to update the trend of contribution in past decades. Publications in ENTER proceedings were analyzed by year to determine the trend of contribution in terms of region, individual author, and institute. In addition to the publication counting method adopted by previous research, this study used the same method advised by Sheldon [6] in analyzing authorship. To analyze the tourism research contributions, two measurements were calculated: instances and weighted instances. The former represents the number of articles an author contributed either partially or fully. The latter prorates the partial contribution of co-authors by using equal weight [6]. Although first authors may have contributed more than other authors, weighted instance assumes that each co-author's contribution to the research is equal.

4 Findings and Discussions

4.1 Distribution of Papers by Year

From 1996 to 2021, a total of 1,217 research papers were included in the ENTER conference proceedings, comprising full- and short-length papers. The average number of papers per year is 46.8. In the first 10 years from 1996 to 2005, the number of articles gradually increased from 25 to 51. Then, from 2007 to 2013, the number of papers dropped and fluctuated between 42 and 50. In 2014, a total of 65 research papers were published. The number of published articles reached its peak and then dropped significantly to the lowest point in 2020 (i.e., 25 papers). In 2021, the article number rebounded back to 55. Figure 1 shows the trend of publication within 26 years.

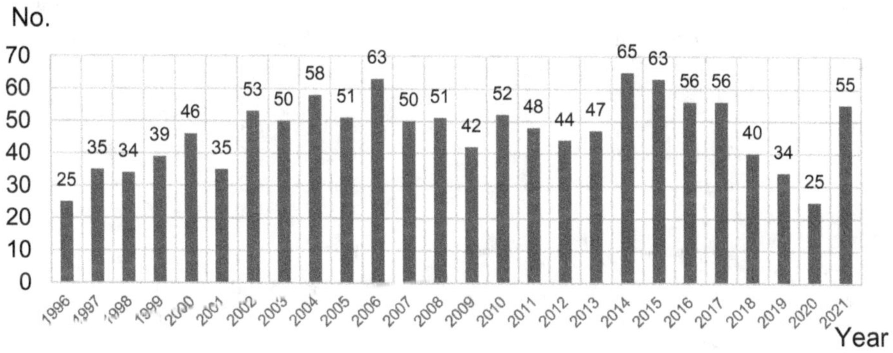

Fig. 1. Distribution of papers in 1996–2021

4.2 Research Contributions by Continent/Country/Region

As shown in Table 1, Europe is the most productive continent at the ENTER conference with a total of 2,257 (69.17%) published papers in instances and 830.96 (68.56%) papers in weighted instances. Liu, Zhong, Ip, and Leung (2011) found that, until 2010, America was the second-largest contributing region [12]. After a decade, however, Asia's contribution rapidly increased and became the second-largest contributing region with 433 (13.27%) papers in instances and 146.93 (12.12%) papers in weighted instances. America ranked third with 351 (10.76%) papers in instances and 144.00 (11.88%) papers in weighted instances. Oceania ranked fourth, with a total of 197 papers in instances and 77.78 papers in weighted instances and contributed 6.04% and 6.42% to the analyzed realm. Of all publications, Africa was the least productive continent providing 0.77% in instance and 1.02% in weighted instance.

The results of the top three productive countries are in line with the findings of 10 years ago [12]. Considering the cradle of ENTER conference, in the past 26 years, the majority of the authors were from Austria. They contributed to the conference by publishing a total of 497 (15.23%) papers in instances and 173.94 (14.35%) papers in weighted instances. The second-largest contributing country was the United Kingdom, with 378 (11.58%) published papers in instances and 170.62 (14.08%) papers in weighted instances. The United States was the third one with 313 (9.59%) papers in instances and 130.35 (10.75%) papers in weighted instances. Table 1 shows the details of contributions provided by other countries and their ranks.

Table 1. Research contributions by geographic region

Continent/ Country/ Region	Instances				Weighted Instances			
	Number	World Rank	Rank in the Continent	%	Number	World Rank	Rank in the Continent	%
Europe	2,257	1		69.17%	830.96			68.56%
Austria	497	1	1		173.94	1	1	
UK	378	2	2		170.62	2	2	
Switzerland	287	4	3		91.34	5	4	
Italy	280	5	4		95.43	4	3	
Spain	274	6	5		77.29	6	5	
Germany	158	8	6		59.03	8	6	
Finland	71	12	7		28.05	10	7	
The Netherlands	56	13	8		17.53	15	10	
Greece	55	14	9		25.12	11	8	
Sweden	45	16	10		15.24	18	12	
France	37	17	11		19.33	14	9	
Norway	36	18	12		16.83	16	11	
Estonia	17	21	13		5.00	26	16	
Denmark	16	23	14		10.08	21	13	
Portugal	13	26	15		5.50	25	15	
Belgium	12	27	16		6.92	23	14	
Ireland	7	30	17		2.87	31	18	
Croatia	6	31	18		4.00	28	17	
Yugoslavia	4	33	19		1.00	36	20	
Bulgaria	2	37	20		1.00	36	20	
Slovenia	2	37	20		2.00	33	19	
Cyprus	1	42	22		0.33	47	25	
Iceland	1	42	22		1.00	36	20	
Poland	1	42	22		1.00	36	20	
Serbia	1	42	22		0.50	44	24	
Asia	433	2		13.27%	146.93	2		12.12%
Hong Kong	158	8	1		58.05	9	1	
South Korea	83	10	2		23.63	13	3	
Japan	75	11	3		24.50	12	2	
China (Mainland)	51	15	4		15.75	17	4	
United Arab Emirates	14	24	5		5.95	24	5	
Macao	14	24	5		5.00	26	6	
Malaysia	12	27	7		3.68	30	8	
Taiwan	11	29	8		4.00	28	7	
Turkey	6	31	9		1.53	35	11	
Israel	4	33	10		2.33	32	9	
Thailand	4	33	10		2.00	33	10	
Oman	1	42	12		0.50	44	12	

America	351	3		10.76%	144.00	3		11.88%
USA	313	3	1		130.35	3	1	
Canada	35	19	2		12.90	19	2	
Brazil	2	37	3		0.50	44	3	
Mexico	1	42	4		0.25	48	4	
Oceania	197	4		6.04%	77.78	4		6.42%
Australia	170	7	1		66.95	7	1	
New Zealand	27	20	2		10.83	20	2	
Africa	25	5		0.77%	12.33	5		1.02%
South Africa	17	21	1		8.67	22	1	
Nigeria	3	36	2		1.00	36	2	
Egypt	2	37	3		1.00	36	2	
Morocco	2	37	3		0.67	43	5	
Namibia	1	42	5		1.00	36	2	

4.3 Research Contributions by Individual Authors

Authors' contributions to the ENTER conference from 1996 to 2021 are demonstrated in this section. In conformity with Liu, Zhong, Ip, and Leung [12], this study also adopted the classification suggested by Sheldon [6] and Jogaratnam et al. [10]. Therefore, three types of authors exist, namely, one-time, moderately contributing, and intensely contributing authors [6–10]. The one-time author refers to an author who only contributed one article. The moderately contributing author represents an author who contributed two to four times. Finally, the intensely contributing author represents an author who contributed five times or above. Table 2 shows the research contributions by these three types of individual authors.

From 1996 to 2021, a total of 1,697 individual authors participated in ENTER conferences. Most of the papers were contributed by 1,250 one-time authors (73.66%). The number of moderately contributing author was 337 (19.86%). In addition, a total of 110 (6.48%) authors intensely contributed to this conference.

Table 2. Research contributions by individual authors

Total number of authors	One-time authors		Moderately contributing authors		Intensely contributing authors	
	Number	%	Number	%	Number	%
1,697	1250	73.66	337	19.86	110	6.48

Table 3 lists the top 30 intensely contributing authors. The top three contributors were Dimitrios Buhalis, Rob Law, and Daniel R Fesenmaier, with 57, 56, and 40 papers in instances among 26 issues. Apart from the number of papers, Table 3 also shows the first year of the contribution of each author to clearly reflect their seniority in the ENTER conference (Table 4).

Table 3. Top 30 intensely contributing authors

Author	First year of contribution	Instances		Weighted instances	
		Number of papers	Rank	Number of papers	Rank
Dimitrios Buhalis	1996	57	1	24.33	1
Rob Law	2000	56	2	20.72	2
Daniel R Fesenmaier	1996	40	3	17.15	3
Ulrike Gretzel	2000	35	4	14.12	6
Lorenzo Cantoni	2009	30	5	10.40	8
Wolfram Höpken	1999	26	6	8.15	12
Matthias Fuchs	2005	26	6	6.70	17
Jamie Murphy	2003	25	8	7.07	16
Roland Schegg	2002	24	9	7.57	14
Aurkene Azua-Sorzabal	2005	22	10	5.55	21
Iis P Tussyadiah	2007	21	11	11.75	7
Francesco Ricci	2001	21	11	7.52	15
Peter O'Connor	1998	19	13	14.83	5
Andrew J Frew	1997	19	13	8.92	10
Hannes Werthner	1996	19	13	8.26	11
Zheng Xiang	2004	19	13	7.78	13
Roman Egger	2007	19	13	6.38	18
María Teresa Linaza	2005	19	13	5.24	23
Marianna Sigala	2000	19	13	15.00	4
Miriam Scaglione	2004	18	20	5.78	19
Alessandro Inversini	2009	16	21	5.12	24
Elena Marchiori	2009	16	21	4.90	26
Namho Chung	2013	15	23	4.25	29
Rodolfo Baggio	2003	14	24	5.75	20
Chulmo Koo	2013	14	24	3.62	30
Rosanna Leung	2006	13	26	4.67	27
Markus Zanker	2006	13	26	3.41	31
Karl Wöber	1994	13	26	9.78	9
Astrid Dickinger	2006	12	29	5.37	22
Timothy Jung	2000	12	29	5.00	25

4.4 Research Contributions by Institutes

Table 4. Research contributions by the top 10 research institutes

Institute (Country/Region)	First Year of contribution	Instances	Rank	Weighted instances	Rank
The Hong Kong Polytechnic University (HK)	2000	147	1	50.15	1
University of Surrey (UK)	1996	112	2	43.75	2
Bournemouth University (UK)	2008	78	3	30.92	3
Kyung Hee University (South Korea)	2013	68	4	18.73	5
Università della Svizzera italiana (Switzerland)	2010	60	5	20.57	4
University of Trento (Italy)	2000	56	6	14.02	9
CIC tour GUNE (Spain)	2008	49	7	12.07	10
MODUL University Vienna (Austria)	2008	46	8	18.28	7
Salzburg University of Applied Science (Austria)	2007	44	9	11.22	11
University of Illinois (USA)	1996	44	9	18.70	6
Temple University (USA)	2005	39	11	16.20	8

This study recognized that the trend of publications on IT and Tourism changed in recent decades. From 1994 to 1999, the United Kingdom made the largest research contribution in the ENTER conference, which was followed by Austria, Germany, the USA, and the Netherlands [22]. However, the ranking was slightly different from that in the past because of the engagement of industry practitioners from Austria and Italy. From 1994 to 2010, Austria became the most productive country, followed by the UK, the USA, Italy, and Germany. The findings of this study pointed out that in the past decade, the top three contributing countries were the same. Moreover, the research productivity of Switzerland and Spain has increased. In general, the contribution of Asia was increasing year by year, particularly in the past 10 years. Research contributions from The Hong Kong Polytechnic University (HK) and Kyung Hee University (South Korea) surged.

5 Conclusions

5.1 Summary of the Study

IT plays an important role in the tourism and hospitality industry. To gain additional knowledge about current situations and to predict future trends, continuous academic research in IT applications on tourism is essential. This study has examined the individual, regional, and institutional contributions to IT and tourism research by analyzing the articles published in ENTER proceedings from 1996 to 2021. A total of 1,217 research papers were contributed by 1,697 individual authors in the past 26 years. The total number of research contributions increased year by year. Regarding the regional contributions, Europe was the most productive continent, followed by Asia, America, Australia, and Africa. Specifically, Austria had the largest research contribution by issuing 497 articles in instances. As for institutional contribution, the Hong Kong Polytechnic University (HK) was the most prolific institute, with a total of 147 research articles when counting in instances, followed by the University of Surrey (UK) and the Bournemouth University (UK). Regarding individual contributions, the top three authors were Dimitrios Buhalis, Rob Law, and Daniel Fesenmaier, and the years they started contributing to ENTER conferences varied (since 1996, 2000, and 1996 respectively).

5.2 Implications

The development of IT promotes the evolution of the tourism industry, which has disruptive effects on tourism management, marketing, and destination competitiveness [14]. This study aims to provide insights for academics, practitioners, and government officials to deeply understand the trend of productivity on IT and tourism research. The findings of this study updated the research performance of individuals and institutes. The increasing number of published articles may motivate practitioners to pay additional attention to the importance of IT in the tourism industry.

In terms of theoretical implications, this study extends the IT and tourism research by conducting a productivity analysis. Publications in the ENTER conference proceedings from 1996 to 2021 were selected as the research scope, which bridges the previous research gap. The results quantified the research contribution of individuals, institutions, and regions.

Several practical implications are provided. The ranking of individual and institutional contributions may be regarded as a reference for organizations and educational institutions, particularly for the recruitment of researchers. Research institutes may determine remuneration packages by reviewing candidates' research contributions in these fields. We believe that this research finding may help recruit high-quality candidates.

Apart from recruitment purposes, this study also reflects the institutional research contribution in the IT and tourism industry. For those who are planning for their higher education or career path, the findings may help them select professional and high-quality institutes.

Based on the findings, the ENTER conference has recently gained momentum in internationalization. In the past decades, most participants came from Europe and North America. However, the findings show that the research contribution of Asia has largely increased in the recent decade. The research contribution not limiting to specific regions made this conference more globalized. Advanced technology development in Asia, particularly in Mainland China, is recognized by the world, for example, the 5G development is a popular topic nowadays. We believe that this technology transformation might create a significant influence on the tourism industry and provide a new direction for academic research. In addition, the ENTER conference 2022 will take place in Mainland China, indicating the growing significance of Asia, and the growing number of Asian participants would be promising.

Finally, this study attempts to appeal attention to IT and the tourism industry. Academics are encouraged to initiate additional international collaborations and contribute to knowledge development. In addition, to increase the impact of research, collaborations among academics, practitioners, and governments are recommended.

5.3 Limitations and Future Studies

This study has some limitations. First, from 1994 to 2021, a total of 28 ENTER proceedings were published. However, this study only analyzed 26 issues (1996–2021) of ENTER conference proceedings because of the inaccessibility of proceedings in 1994 and 1995. In addition, some promising and productive young scholars that started to participate in the ENTER conference in recent years are not noted in this study. Thus, in future studies, researchers are suggested to complete and update the result of the findings. Second, in terms of the analyzed content, although this study provides the first year of contribution as a reference, the analysis did not delve into this part. Readers might take this component into account when evaluating author's contribution. Moreover, the popularity such as Google Scholar's h-index of some prolific authors can be provided for comparison in a future study. Third, in comparison to the institutional contribution, the findings of individual productivity were more accurate to reflect the fact. The reason is that job switching of researchers can influence the productivity of institutes, particularly for authors with a high level of contribution. Meanwhile, there may be some missing articles because of the changes of the official name of institutions. For example, Università della Svizzera italiana (Switzerland) is also called University of Lugano. Therefore, changes of author's affiliation and institution names should be considered in future research. Finally, the results only reveal the contribution of authors who published articles in ENTER conference proceedings. Articles published in other pertinent journals, conferences, and books are recommended to be incorporated into analysis for generating a comprehensive result.

Acknowledgement. This project was partly supported by a research grant funded by the University of Macau (Ref.: CPG2021–00036-APAEM).

References

1. Bilotta E, Bertacchini F, Gabriele L, Giglio S, Pantano PS, Romita T (2020) Industry 4.0 technologies in tourism education: nurturing students to think with technology. J Hosp Leis Sports Tour Educ 100275. https://doi.org/10.1016/j.jhlste.2020.100275
2. Sigala M (2018) New technologies in tourism: from multi-disciplinary to anti-disciplinary advances and trajectories. Tour Manag. Perspect. 25:151–155. https://doi.org/10.1016/j.tmp.2017.12.003
3. Law R (2002) Across the C's: commerce, Convergence, Communications and

Change ENTER 2001 held in Montréal, Canada in April 2001. J Travel Tour Mark 12:97–101. https://doi.org/10.1300/J073v12n01_06

4. Buhalis D, Law R (2008) Progress in information technology and tourism management: 20 years on and 10 years after the Internet—The state of eTourism research. Tour Manag 29:609–623. https://doi.org/10.1016/j.tourman.2008.01.005
5. Van Over L, Nelson R (1986) Research in management information systems, 1980–1985: a profile of leading journals, articles, and authors. In: the 18th annual meeting of the decision sciences institute, Honolulu, HI
6. Sheldon PJ (1991) An authorship analysis of tourism research. Ann Tour Res 18:473–484. https://doi.org/10.1016/0160-7383(91)90053-E
7. Law R, Chon K (2007) Evaluating research performance in tourism and hospitality: the perspective of university program heads. Tour Manag 28:1203–1211. https://doi.org/10.1016/j.tourman.2006.09.022
8. Harris GT (1990) Research output in Australian university economics departments: an update for 1984–88. Aust Econ Pap 29:249–259. https://doi.org/10.1111/j.1467-8454.1990.tb00520.x
9. Malhotra MK, Kher HV (1996) Institutional research productivity in production and operations management. J Oper Manag 14:55–77. https://doi.org/10.1016/0272-6963(95)00037-2
10. Jogaratnam G, McCleary KW, Mena MM, Yoo JJE (2005) An analysis of hospitality and tourism research: institutional contributions. J. Hosp. Tour Res. 29:356–371. https://doi.org/10.1177/1096348005276929
11. Weaver P (1990) Academic contributors to four major hospitality journals revisited. J Hosp Tour Educ 2:30–32
12. Liu W, Zhong L, Ip C, Leung D (2011) An analysis of research on tourism information technology: the case of ENTER proceedings. In: Law R, Fuchs M, Ricci F (eds) Information and communication technologies in tourism 2011. Springer, Vienna, pp 293–304. https://doi.org/10.1007/978-3-7091-0503-0_24
13. Porter ME (2001) Strategy and the Internet. Harv Bus Rev 79:62–78
14. Buhalis D (2019) Technology in tourism-from information communication technologies to eTourism and smart tourism towards ambient intelligence tourism: a perspective article. Tour Rev 75:267–272. https://doi.org/10.1108/TR-06-2019-0258
15. Buhalis D (1998) Strategic use of information technologies in the tourism industry. Tour Manag 19:409–421. https://doi.org/10.1016/S0261-5177(98)00038-7
16. Mayer-Schönberger V, Cukier K (2013) Big data: a revolution that will transform how we live, work, and think Houghton Mifflin Harcourt , Boston
17. Mehraliyev F, Chan ICC, Choi Y, Koseoglu MA, Law R (2020) A state-of-the-art review of smart tourism research. J Travel Tour Mark 37:78–91. https://doi.org/10.1080/10548408.2020.1712309
18. Tranfield D, Denyer D, Smart P (2003) Towards a methodology for developing evidence-informed management knowledge by means of systematic review. Br J Manag 14:207–222. https://doi.org/10.1111/1467-8551.00375
19. Law R, Qi S, Buhalis D (2010) Progress in tourism management: a review of website evaluation in tourism research. Tour Manag 31:297–313. https://doi.org/10.1016/j.tourman.2009.11.007
20. Leung D, Law R, van Hoof H, Buhalis D (2013) Social media in tourism and hospitality: a literature review. J Travel Tour Mark 30:3–22. https://doi.org/10.1080/10548408.2013.750919
21. Ye BH, Ye H, Law R (2020) Systematic review of smart tourism research. Sustainability 12:3401. https://doi.org/10.3390/su12083401

22. Frew AJ (2000) A critical analysis of tourism information technology research. In: Fesenmaier DR, Klein S, Buhalis D (eds) Information and communication technologies in tourism 2000. Springer, Vienna, pp 39–52. https://doi.org/10.1007/978-3-7091-6291-0_4

Special Track on Travel in the Metaverse: The Future of Smart Tourism Cities

23

Exploring the Impact of Travel Vlogs on Prospect Tourists: A SOR based Theoretical Framework

Wenliang Li(✉), Yoo Ri Kim, Caroline Scarles and Anyu Liu

School of Hospitality and Tourism Management, University of Surrey, Guildford, Surrey, UK
{wenliang.li,yoori.kim, c.scarles,anyu.liu}@surrey.ac.uk

Abstract. In recent years, travel vlogs are prevalent on social media, they are projected as an important marketing tool to attract tourists to destinations in the post-COVID-19 era. However, the underlying mechanism of how travel vlogs affect prospective tourists' behaviours remains unclear. To address this gap, this paper discusses the applicability of the Stimulus-Organism-Response (SOR) model to travel vlog research and proposes a SOR based theoretical framework. Moreover, this paper highlights the increasing trend of the SOR model in both e-tourism and wider tourism and hospitality research.

Keywords: Travel vlog · Stimulus-Organism-Response · Theoretical framework

1 The Travel Vlog Phenomenon

In recent years, vlog (video blog), a new type of user-generated content (UGC) which refers to a casual, conversational short video format featuring a person talking directly and intimately to the camera and relating their feelings and life experiences in a raw and unfiltered way has proliferated on social media [19]. Travel is becoming the most popular vlog topic [14], and travel vlogs have also become the most popular type of travel videos viewed on YouTube, receiving four times more social engagement than other types of travel videos and almost half of the travel subscriptions [2]. Given the wealth of online traffic, travel vlogs have huge marketing potential for destinations to attract tourists [2]. However, they are overlooked in the current literature [2].

After COVID-19, social media marketing is expected to play an important role in destination marketing, and travel vlogs are projected to be a great strategy to heighten the audiences' travel desires [13]. Therefore, it is necessary to understand how travel vlogs influence prospective tourists' behaviours so that it can help destinations better attract tourists. However, most studies have emphasised the direct link between travel vlogs and the audiences' subsequent behaviours but overlooked the potential underlying mechanism, which remains a critical research gap [2]. Hence, this paper proposes to use the SOR model as a useful theoretical base to build up a framework to further explore the impact of travel vlogs on prospective tourists' behaviours.

2 The SOR Model and Its Applicability to Travel Vlog Research

2.1 Overview of the SOR Model

The SOR model was firstly proposed by Mehrabian and Russell [8], it was rooted in environmental psychology and developed from the classic Stimulus-Response model in behaviourism [10]. The SOR model suggests that a stimulus induces an individuals' internal states, which in turn leads to certain behavioural responses [20]. In the SOR model, stimulus is conceptualised as an influence that arouses the individual. Organism is defined as "the psychological process that occurs in the individual's mind when interacting with the stimulus" [20, p. 467], playing an intervening or mediating role in the model. Originally, organism refers to an individual's emotional states while nowadays it is commonly represented by both emotional and cognitive states [5]. Response could be explained as the final behavioural outcome of an individual.

The SOR model has been mostly applied to retail research while it is increasingly being applied to tourism and hospitality research especially to the e-tourism context to predict consumer behaviour [5]. It has been observed that existing SOR based tourism and hospitality studies have attempted to examine how attributes of various information and communication technologies (ICTs) (e.g., booking websites, mobile apps, and virtual realities) impact on tourists' behavioural responses. Recently, some SOR based tourism and hospitality studies have explored the impact of travel UGC as an external stimulus [3], such as Facebook pages and Instagram posts. However, travel UGC videos like vlogs have not yet been studied in articles we reviewed, which remains a gap. Compared to textual and static pictural information, individuals' responses to videos could be different. Thus, a tailored SOR model which fits the features of videos is underdeveloped in tourism and hospitality research.

2.2 Applicability of the SOR Model to Travel Vlog Research

The rise of the application of the SOR model in recent e-tourism and wider tourism and hospitality studies inspires this paper to explore the applicability of the SOR model to travel vlog research. The SOR model is suitable for travel vlog research for two reasons.

Firstly, as a systematic approach to conceptualising linkages between key constructs underpinning emotions, the SOR model has been most extensively used when examining consumer behaviour from the emotional perspective. The theory of reasoned action, technology acceptance model, and theory of planned behaviour are the most common consumer behaviour models [9]. However, they are critiqued for being too limited when it comes to explaining the emotional side of consumer behaviour because their main assumption is that individuals are rational in their decision-making processes and actions [9]. By contrast, the SOR model can be used as a supplement to the traditional lens of rational factors to explain consumer behaviour. Recent empirical evidence demonstrated that travel vlog audiences are more likely to be affected by emotional states rather than rational facts [2]. Therefore, as a more emotional framework, the SOR model may predict travel vlog audiences' behaviour well.

Secondly, as a systemised theoretical framework with a parsimonious and structured manner, the SOR model has strong wide applicability. Sultan et al. [10] stressed that the SOR model is flexible to allow for various factors like internal and external stimuli, experiential and non-experiential organisms (e.g., emotion, perception/feeling) and responses (e.g., intention, behaviour). Due to its powerful flexibility, the SOR model provides researchers with a good theoretical base to tailor the general consumer behaviour model, reflecting its intuitive and powerful exploratory nature. Compared to the wider tourism and hospitality research and the application of the SOR model, research on travel vlogs around is underexplored [2]; the SOR model is therefore suitable for being applied to exploratory travel vlog studies given its strengths in eliciting emotions of tourists and their behavioural responses.

3 Development of a SOR Based Theoretical Framework

A SOR based theoretical framework to explore how travel vlogs could influence prospective tourists' behaviours is presented as follows. As depicted in Fig. 1, this framework proposes travel vlog's storytelling as the stimulus, perceived intimacy, perceived authenticity, presence, and emotions as the organism, destination image and destination visit intention as the response, and personal traits as the moderator.

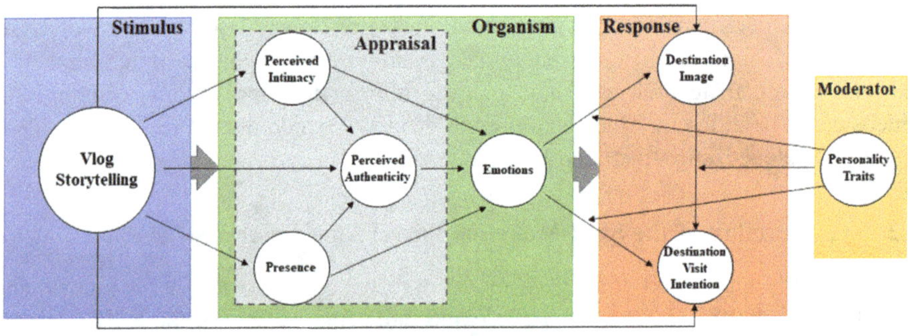

Fig. 1. A SOR based theoretical framework

Zhang et al. [18] revealed that a compelling story provides the stimuli that evoke the audiences' sensations, cognitive, and behavioural responses. As vlog is particularly called as "storytelling video" [4], and storytelling is believed as the key to a vlog's success in attracting the audiences' attention [16]. It is worthy to consider it as a key influence of a vlog on the audiences. In the organism construct of this framework, emotions elicited by vlogs are designed to be the core organismic factor. According to

Tuerlan et al. [11], appraisal theories of emotions, which argue that an individual's emotional responses are the outcome of a subjective mental evaluation of the stimulus rather than the direct result of the stimulus is being an agenda for future emotion research in the tourism and hospitality. Given that, this framework proposes perceived intimacy, perceived authenticity, and presence ("3Ps") as the direct antecedents of emotions, representing the stimulus appraisals by an individual. Literature shows that "3Ps" have been used as appraisals of the stimulus and vlogs can facilitate the audiences' "3Ps" [7, 12, 17].

Prospective tourists' perceived destination image and destination visit intention together consist of the response construct of this framework. They both are crucial for the success of destination marketing. As the result of a perceptual and cognitive process, destination image is formed from information sources [6]; it is an important predictor of destination visit intention [1]. Destination visit intention is an intentional behaviour commonly used to predict prospective tourists' actual visit. In terms of the inclusion of a moderator in this framework, it may help to find out the reasons behind the resistance to use travel vlogs to make destination visits. In the context of social media use, personality traits have been widely used as moderating variables to predict users' behaviours [15].

4 Conclusion

As travel vlog research is just emerging, the underlying mechanism of how travel vlogs affect prospective tourists' behaviours is still unclear. This paper captures the increasing trend of the application of the SOR model in e-tourism and wider tourism and hospitality studies and discusses its applicability to travel vlog research. The SOR model was found that is good at exploring prospective tourists' behavioural responses associated with travel vlog watching from the emotional perspective and is flexible for testing various variables. Therefore, based on the SOR model, this paper proposes a theoretical framework to explore how travel vlogs' storytelling triggers prospective tourists' destination visit intention. The originality of the research is in two-folds. First, this is the first attempt to introduce digital storytelling as the stimulus in the SOR model to capture the nature of vlog as a new video medium. Second, the other novelty of the proposed framework is the integration of appraisal theories of emotions with the SOR model which could better capture the emotional feedback of vlog viewers.

This conceptual framework will be further examined in future research, the validation of this framework is expected to extend the SOR based tourism and hospitality literature, help destination marketers to better communicate with prospective tourists and trigger them to make visits, and provide a guideline for travel vloggers to improve their storytelling so that they can better engage with their audiences. Besides that, this research may foster the collaboration between destination marketers and vloggers to create favourable travel vlogs for destination promotion. Lastly, it should be noted that a large number of recent SOR based tourism and hospitality articles have been observed, which demonstrates that the capability of the SOR model in predicting tourist behaviour has been gaining more and more recognition and the SOR model seems to be becoming a mainstream theory employed in tourism and hospitality research.

References

1. Afshardoost M, Eshaghi MS (2020) Destination image and tourist behavioural intentions: a meta-analysis. Tour Manage 81:104154
2. Cheng Y, Wei W, Zhang L (2020) Seeing destinations through vlogs: implications for leveraging customer engagement behavior to increase travel intention. IJCHM 32(10):3227–3248
3. Cheung ML, Leung WK, Cheah J-H, Ting H (2021) Exploring the effectiveness of emotional and rational user-generated contents in digital tourism platforms. J Vacat Mark 1–19
4. Huan TJ, Chin TA, Sulaiman Z, Zakuan N (2020) Review the relationships between antecedents of parasocial interaction and branding in video blog. In: ICoEC2020 e-Proceedings, pp 65–69
5. Kim MJ, Lee C-K, Jung T (2020) Exploring consumer behavior in virtual reality tourism using an extended Stimulus-Organism-Response model. J Travel Res 59(1):69–89
6. Lopes SDF (2011) Destination image: origins, developments and implications. Pasos 9 (2):305–315
7. Luoma-aho V, Pirttimäki T, Maity D, Munnukka J, Reinikainen H (2019) Primed authenticity: how priming impacts authenticity perception of social media influencers. Int J Strateg Commun 13(4):352–365
8. Mehrabian A, Russell JA (1974) An approach to environmental psychology. The MIT Press, Cambridge
9. Moon MA, Khalid MJ, Awan HM, Attiq S, Rasool H, Kiran M (2017) Consumer's perceptions of website's utilitarian and hedonic attributes and online purchase intentions: a cognitive–affective attitude approach. Span J Mark - ESIC 21(2):73–88
10. Sultan P, Wong HY, Azam MS (2021) How perceived communication source and food value stimulate purchase intention of organic food: an examination of the Stimulus-organism-Response (SOR) model. J Clean Prod 312:127807
11. Tuerlan T, Li S, Scott N (2021) Customer emotion research in hospitality and tourism: conceptualization, measurements, antecedents and consequences. Int J Contemp Hosp Manage 33(8):2741–2772
12. Wang X, Chang B (2020) The impact of the audience's continuance intention towards the vlog: focusing on intimacy, media synchronicity and authenticity. Int J Contents 16(2):65–77
13. Xie X (2021) Research on social media tourism marketing in the post-epidemic period. Jurnal Audiens 2(2):273–280
14. Xinhua (2019) Survey shows more than half of Chinese watch vlogs. China Daily. http://www.chinadaily.com.cn/a/201906/08/WS5cfb5ee8a31017657723010d.html
15. Yu T-K, Lee N-H, Chao C-M (2020) The moderating effects of young adults' personality traits on social media immersion. Front Psychol 10:554106
16. Zhang H (2020) Analysis on vlog story-telling techniques and advertisement. In: Proceedings of ICHESS 2020. ASSEHR, vol 496. Alantis Press, pp 68–72
17. Zhang H (2018) Evoking presence in vlogging: a case study of U.K. beauty blogger Zoe Sugg. FM 23(1)
18. Zhang W, Kim J, Kim H, Fesenmaier DR (2019) The tourism story project developing the behavioral foundations for an AI supporting destination story design. e-Rev Tour Res 17 (2):170–187
19. Zhou J (2018) Short and sweet, the new craze for the video generation. China Daily. http://www.chinadaily.com.cn/cndy/2018-06/16/content_36401015.htm
20. Zhu L, Li H, Wang F-K, He W, Tian Z (2020) How online reviews affect purchase intention: a new model based on the Stimulus-Organism-Response (S-O-R) framework. Aslib J Inf Manage 72(4):463–488

24

Exploring the Utilitarian and Hedonic Value Derived from Tourism Pre-Experiences with Virtual Reality: Differences between Destinations and Accommodations

Carlos Flavián, Sergio Ibáñez-Sánchez(✉) and Carlos Orús

Faculty of Economy and Business, University of Zaragoza, Gran Vía 2, 50005 Zaragoza, Spain
{cflavian, sergiois, corus}@unizar.es

Abstract. The tourism industry is in a convulsive situation of great uncertainty. The recovery of the sector depends on boosting digitalization processes. In this sense, virtual reality represents an essential tool that can generate added value in the customer experience. This study analyzes the impact of virtual reality tourism pre-experiences on the utilitarian and hedonic value perceived by the customer. In addition, given the heterogeneity of tourism products and offers, it is proposed that the influence of virtual reality on the dimensions of perceived value will depend on whether the product is evaluated on an attribute basis (hotels) or holistically (destinations). The results will provide interesting implications for understanding and generating tourism experiences with high added value. Particularly, these results will be helpful for tourism managers to design effective virtual reality pre-experiences according to the features of the tourism products they are promoting, fostering the corresponding hedonic/utilitarian value in the tourist's pre-experience.

Keywords: Virtual reality · Perceived value · Hedonic and utilitarian

1 Introduction

During the last few years, we are witnessing how virtual reality (VR) technologies are gradually changing the way consumers interact with digital environments [8]. VR is based on the immersion of users in a computer-generated environment, in which they can navigate and possibly interact, triggering a stimulation of their senses in real time, which makes them feel present in the virtual environment displayed [7]. Its potential is reflected in recent predictions, which state that the VR industry will grow from the current $5 billion to more than $12 billion by 2024 [19]. Among the sectors that can benefit from its application, tourism is of particular relevance as VR can be employed to generate more tangible experiences [4]. This fact is important as tourism encompasses a wide variety of products with a strong intangible and experiential character (e.g., destinations, transportation, accommodations; [7]). The digitization of the tourism industry may be reinforced due to the pandemic caused by COVID-19. In this sense, VR may be of particular interest as it can be used to redesign the tourists' journey trying to overcome the current restrictions, as well as capture their attention and increase their desire to visit the tourist attraction after the pandemic [15]. These data highlight the interest in studying how VR can be applied, particularly in the field of tourism, to generate higher added value experiences for customers.

Previous research on VR in tourism has analyzed its impact on different tourism products individually (e.g., hotels [3]; destinations [22]) proving its positive effect on both cognitive (e.g., [13]) and affective (e.g., [5]) variables. However, there are no studies that have compared the effectiveness of VR considering the characteristics of tourism products, with the aim of determining whether its use is more important in one context or another [7]. Therefore, the present study has two main objectives: (1) to analyze the influence of VR on perceived value during tourism pre-experiences, adopting a utilitarian-hedonic approach [1], as well as on behavioral intentions; and (2) to determine the moderating role of the type of tourism product, considering pre-experiences with destinations (more experiential products whose evaluations are made in a more holistic way; [22]) and accommodations (more concrete products whose evaluations are based on attributes and factual information; [5]). The results of the study aim to shed light on the effectiveness of VR for presenting tourism experiences and to understand how and what kind of value can be generated in this type of experiences.

2 Literature Review

2.1 The Impact of VR on Perceived Value

The use of VR represents a novel touchpoint with consumers that aims to bring more value in their experiences [4]. In this sense, viewing 360º videos, which are recorded in the real environments, is gaining more and more popularity among consumer experiences with VR, and are being the subject of numerous academic works (e.g., [22]). This type of content can be viewed with devices which can vary in their level of technological embodiment, which is an inherent characteristic of any technology and is defined as the degree of integration of the device with the human body [4]. The use of embodied devices, such as VR headsets, turns technology into an extension of the senses, and facilitates the interpretation, perception and interaction with the environment surrounding the user [9]. Thus, viewing content with embodied devices allows users to achieve a higher degree of immersion in the experience and generates greater value during the experience [4].

For tourism, VR has been identified as a tool that positively influences factors of a utilitarian nature, such as the usefulness of the technology [10], attention during the experience [21], or knowledge and interest in the product displayed [13]; as well as factors of a hedonic nature, such as enjoyment [22] or positive emotions [5]. This brief review allows us to show that VR influences the two essential dimensions of the perceived value of the experience: utilitarian and hedonic [1]. For the present research, utilitarian value is studied through the reduction of uncertainty, defined as the evaluation of the chances that a certain negative event may develop and generate unknown outcomes [12]. For its part, hedonic value is analyzed based on the value derived from the experience, considered as a connection with the experience that produces rewarding and interesting experiences and leads to positive emotional responses [16]. In this sense, viewing a tourism product in VR with embodied devices is expected to generate higher perceived value, in both utilitarian and hedonic terms, compared to non-embodied devices:

H_1: Tourist pre-experiences with 360° videos on devices with a high (versus low) level of technological embodiment positively influence (a) perceived utilitarian value and (b) perceived hedonic value.

2.2 The Moderating Role of Product Type

Previous literature has noted the existence of positive effects of VR in both destinations (e.g., [22]) and accommodations (e.g., [3]). However, there are no papers comparing both products simultaneously, which is interesting due to their different defining characteristics. The travel decision is complex and is composed of a series of sub-decisions (e.g., destination, accommodation, transportation, attractions, and activities) that are hierarchical and sequenced, producing differences in information processing and evaluation of alternatives [11]. In this sense, the decision about a destination is made in the early stages of planning. Destinations are evaluated more holistically, with an important emotional and hedonic component [6]. On the other hand, the accommodation decision is made later in the process, and the potential tourist performs a more analytical and utilitarian processing of the information, making an evaluation of the attributes of the different alternatives [14]. The Construal Level Theory [20] could serve to explain these differences: by being taken earlier, the decision about the destination is represented in a more abstract and distant way in the mind of the consumer, who would perform a more projective and experiential evaluation; on the contrary, the decision about the accommodation, being taken at times closer to the actual realization of the trip, would be represented more closely in the mind of the traveler, who would perform a concrete evaluation of the attributes from the alternatives. Therefore, in a destination decision context, consumers would be expected to derive greater hedonic value with VR experiences, and this component of the experience would have a greater influence on their behavioral intentions; in contrast, in an accommodation decision, perceived utilitarian value would be especially benefited from VR experiences and would determine behavioral intentions:

H_2: For tourism pre-experiences with 360° videos about destinations (versus accommodations), the impact of devices with a high (versus low) level of technological embodiment on hedonic value is (a) greater and (b) more influential on behavioral intentions.

H_3: For tourism pre-experiences with 360° videos about accommodations (versus destinations), the impact of devices with a high (versus low) level of technological embodiment on utilitarian value is (a) greater and (b) more influential on behavioral intentions.

3 Methodology

A laboratory experiment was performed to test the hypothesis. A between-subjects factorial design of 2 (device with high vs. low level of technological embodiment: VR headset vs. desktop computer) × 2 (decision context: destination vs. accommodation) conditions was followed. Non-probability convenience sampling was employed, in which participants (n = 140; college students) had to imagine that they were going on a trip, placing them in a simulated shopping situation.

The procedure was as follows. First, a brief introduction was given to the participants, indicating certain general guidelines to be followed during the experiment, and they were randomly assigned to the experimental conditions. Next, they were given the questionnaire to answer a set of control questions (previous experience with the technology, with the destination, assessment of hotel attributes). Once this part was completed, participants were directed to their corresponding room where they viewed a 360° video of a destination/accommodation with VR headset/computer. After the experience, participants completed the next part of the questionnaire which included measures of technological embodiment [5; e.g., "The employed technology is almost integrated into my body"], psychological presence [18; e.g., "I had a sense of "being there", in the displayed world,"], uncertainty reduction [17; e.g., "This experience has helped me to reduce the potential negative consequences of buying this tourism product"], experience value [16; e.g., "I felt interested in the displayed experience"], and behavioral intentions [2; "After this experience, I will try to find more information about the tourism product"]. Seven-point Likert scales were used, ranging from 1 = "strongly disagree", to 7 = "strongly agree".

4 Expected Results and Discussion

The hypotheses will be tested using the software SPSS (analyses of variance) and the PROCESS macro. The expected results will offer interesting implications, as they will reveal how VR increases consumers' perceived value in these experiences and the mechanisms that help understand this process and determine the individual's behavioral intentions. The consideration of product characteristics represents a novel contribution to the specialized literature, given the scarcity of works analyzing the comparative effect of VR technologies on user experience with different products. On a practical level, the results may help professionals to understand the effect of VR in the generation of pre-experiences with higher added value, which may favor behavioral intentions. These results may be useful to recover the tourism industry after this delicate period.

References

1. Babin BJ, Darden WR, Griffin M (1994) Work and/or fun: measuring hedonic and utilitarian shopping value. J Consum Res 20(4):644–656
2. Bigne JE, Sanchez MI, Sanchez J (2001) Tourism image, evaluation variables and after purchase behavior: inter-relationship. Tour Manage 22(6):607–616

3. Bogicevic V, Seo S, Kandampully JA, Liu SQ, Rudd NA (2019) Virtual reality presence as a preamble of tourism experience: the role of mental imagery. Tour Manage 74:55–64
4. Flavián C, Ibáñez-Sánchez S, Orús C (2019) The impact of virtual, augmented and mixed reality technologies on the customer experience. J Bus Res 100:547–560
5. Flavián C, Ibáñez-Sánchez S, Orús C (2021) Impacts of technological embodiment through virtual reality on potential guests' emotions and engagement. J Hosp Market Manag 30(1):1–20
6. Goossens C (2000) Tourism information and pleasure motivation. Ann Tour Res 27(2):301–321
7. Guttentag DA (2010) Virtual reality: applications and implications for tourism. Tour Manage 31(5):637–651
8. Hollebeek LD, Clark MK, Andreassen TW, Sigurdsson V, Smith D (2020) Virtual reality through the customer journey: framework and propositions. J Retail Consum Serv 55:102056
9. Ihde D (1990) Technology and the Lifeworld: From Garden to Earth. Indiana University Press, Indiana
10. Israel K, Zerres C, Tscheulin DK (2019) Presenting hotels in virtual reality: does it influence the booking intention? J Hosp Tour Technol 10(3):443–463
11. Jeng J, Fesenmaier DR (2002) Conceptualizing the travel decision-making hierarchy: a review of recent developments. Tour Anal 7(1):15–32
12. Karl M (2018) Risk and uncertainty in travel decision-making: tourist and destination perspective. J Travel Res 57(1):129–146
13. Kim MJ, Lee CK, Jung T (2020) Exploring consumer behavior in virtual reality tourism using an extended stimulus-organism-response model. J Travel Res 59(1):69–89
14. Kim D, Park BJR (2017) The moderating role of context in the effects of choice attributes on hotel choice: a discrete choice experiment. Tour Manage 63:439–451
15. Kwok AO, Koh SG (2020) COVID-19 and extended reality (XR). Curr Issue Tour 24 (14):1935–1940
16. O'Brien HL, Cairns P, Hall M (2018) A practical approach to measuring user engagement with the refined user engagement scale (UES) and new UES short form. Int J Hum Comput Stud 112:28–39
17. Shim SI, Lee Y (2011) Consumer's perceived risk reduction by 3D virtual model. Int J Retail Distrib Manage 39(12):945–959
18. Slater M, Usoh M, Steed A (1994) Depth of presence in virtual environments. Presence Teleoperators Virtual Environ 3(2):130–144
19. Statista, Virtual Reality (VR) - statistics & facts. bit.ly/3dY4OTQ. Accessed 30 July 2021
20. Trope Y, Liberman N (2010) Construal-level theory of psychological distance. Psychol Rev 117(2):440–463
21. Tussyadiah IP, Wang D, Jia CH (2017) Virtual reality and attitudes toward tourism destinations. In: Tussyadiah I, Wang D, Jia CH (eds) Information and communication technologies in tourism 2017. Springer, Cham, pp 229–239. https://doi.org/10.1007/978-3-319-51168-9_17
22. Tussyadiah IP, Wang D, Jung TH, Tom Dieck MC (2018) Virtual reality, presence, and attitude change. Empirical evidence from tourism. Tour Manage 66:140–154

25

Escaping Loneliness through Tourist-Chatbot Interactions

Peng Wang[1,2] and Jun Shao[1(✉)]

[1] Beijing Forestry University, No.35 Tsinghua East Road, Beijing 100083, People's Republic of China
ninashaojun@bjfu.edu.cn
[2] Naikai University, 38 Tongyan Road, Tianjin 300381, People's Republic of China

Abstract. Social robots such as chatbots are regarded as a practical approach to alleviate loneliness. Few studies in the tourism field have focused on loneliness and its impact on the acceptance of chatbots used by the tourism industry. This paper explores the factors influencing tourists' willingness to use chatbots from the perspective of loneliness by combining theories related to anthropomorphism and the uncanny valley effect. This paper adopts a qualitative research method by taking a semi-structured interview with 15 tourists who have used travel chatbots before. The results show that in addition to perceived ease of use and perceived usefulness, there are three factors (tourist loneliness, perceived anthropomorphism, and user anxiety) that directly influence tourists' acceptance of travel chatbots. Moreover, tourist loneliness positively influences user anxiety through perceived anthropomorphism. User anxiety has a negative effect on perceived ease of use and perceived usefulness. This research then proposed an extended TAM model from the perspective of tourist loneliness. This paper enriches the research on loneliness as well as chatbots in the tourism field. The results provide suggestions for the practical application of travel chatbots.

Keywords: Tourist loneliness · Technology acceptance model · Travel chatbot · Perceived anthropomorphism · User anxiety

1 Introduction

Loneliness has various adverse effects on people, such as sleep deprivation and suicidal tendency [1]. In order to reduce loneliness, people usually seek social connections with others [2]. Therefore, chatbots with social attributes gradually gain attention, as people may establish social or emotional relationships while interacting with chatbots [3]. In recent years, with the progress of artificial intelligence, the application of chatbots has made significant progress. Chatbots are also widely implemented in the field of tourism [4, 5]. Companies such as Expedia, Ctrip and Marriott have applied chatbots to their business scenarios [6]. Some tourist attractions have also launched their own chatbots to attract visitors. In China, the Forbidden City launched a chatbot named "Meet the Ministers" in 2018, allowing visitors to interact with virtual ministers from the Qing Dynasty in a humorous way. The Longquan Temple in Beijing also launched an online celerity named "Xianer" Robot Monk, who likes apply Buddhist wisdom in dialogue with users and has attracted a lot of tourists to visit the temple in person.

However, few studies pay attention to the impact of tourists' loneliness on the acceptance and interaction of chatbots for tourism, and whether loneliness will affect human-chatbot interaction. Why do tourists use these chatbots? Do they feel lonely during their tours? Do they use these chatbots because they are lonely? Does interacting with chatbots help them feel better psychologically? Which travel chatbots have they experienced with? To answer these questions, this study adopts qualitative research to conduct a semi-structured interview to explore the factors affecting tourists' use of chatbots and whether loneliness affects tourists' willingness to use chatbots.

2 Literature Review

2.1 Chatbots and Technology Acceptance Model (TAM)

Chatbots are used extensively in customer service, as artificial intelligence techniques improve their ability to handle customer requests [4, 5, 7]. For instance, Alibaba and Domino's Pizza have applied chatbots in their customer service domain [8]. These chatbots are often seen as a reliable alternative to traditional human services [9]. However, beyond customer service, chatbots have been given a more humanistic and caring role. For example, the chatbot Mitsuku can act as a social companion for users and the chatbot Woebot can answer questions related to mental health. Thus, chatbots can be used in a variety of contexts. Winkler and Söllner pointed out four advantages of chatbots [10]. First, chatbots can help companies reduce their employment costs by replacing manual labor. Second, chatbots can provide 24/7 service to users, which helps to increase their satisfaction. Third, chatbots can combine big data to predict users' questions and prepare the information they need in advance. Fourth, chatbots can perform complex analytics, which helps to better understand the needs of users. Chatbots have a wide range of applications in the tourism sector, but there is still relatively little research on this part [5]. It is important to understand the factors that influence tourists' acceptance of travel chatbots.

The TAM has also been widely used in tourism. Since it was originally designed for predicting employees' performance in using computers in the workplace, Moon and Kim argued that consumers, unlike employees, are very free in making decisions. Therefore, whether they can adapt to this new technology is not in their consideration [11]. Thus, many scholars in tourism have modified the TAM model according to different situations (e.g., [12, 13]). Pillai introduced technology anxiety, perceived trust, anthropomorphism, and perceived intelligence into the TAM to analyze the factors influencing tourists' acceptance of chatbots [5].

2.2 Loneliness

In spite of the fact that the emergence of electronic devices and social media has facilitated interpersonal communication, Turkle noted that "this superficial communication has replaced interpersonal intimacy, leaving people with a lack of intimacy and quality interactions with others, thus increasing their feelings of isolation" [14]. Loneliness is even magnified during the COVID-19. While the policies of home isolation and social distancing can help keep people physically away from the virus, they have caused more people to feel lonely globally [15]. In a recent study, Courtet et al. reducing loneliness can improve personal and social well-being, and suggested interventions to alleviate loneliness [16].

Chatbots, as a branch of robots, have also received increasing attention from scholars in recent years in alleviating loneliness [17]. Loneliness increases the willingness of people to connect with other non-human objects to satisfy their need for social connection [18]. Therefore, their loneliness will be alleviated in the process of interacting with chatbots [19]. In addition, tourism as a social activity often becomes a means of escaping loneliness [20]. Crompton pointed out that tourism can strengthen family relationships and social interactions [21], so tourism activities can help people alleviate loneliness to some extent. Yet currently in the field of tourism, there is not much research on loneliness [22], few scholars have focused on tourists' loneliness and whether this loneliness affects tourists' use of chatbots.

2.3 Anthropomorphism

Anthropomorphism is the act of assigning human characteristics, motivations, intentions, or emotions to a real or imagined non-human subject [23]. In the process of interacting with robots, humans tend to anthropomorphize the robots [24]. When people have a higher anthropomorphic perception of chatbots, they evaluate them more positively in general and may even see them as companions [25]. On the one hand, chatbots with human characteristics can elicit a social response from humans, which has a positive impact on the acceptance of robots [26]. On the other hand, humans have more positive feedback with chatbots that can show human characteristics than with purely functional robots [27]. The perception of anthropomorphism is also related to the user's state [28]. This was also verified by Waytz et al., who argued that lonely people in daily life tend to treat non-humans as humans, but they treat people who are alienated in social relations as non-humans [29]. In the field of tourism, tourists may evaluate service bots more directly than other industries, comparing the experience provided by these service robots to that of human service workers [30]. Therefore, it is necessary to explore how anthropomorphism affects the interaction between tourists and travel chatbots.

2.4 User Anxiety

Venkatesh identified technology anxiety as the unpleasant feelings that an individual feels when using or considering using a certain technology, including emotional states such as frustration, apprehension, and fear [31]. Studies have found significant negative effects of technology anxiety on both the perceived ease of use (PEOU) and the perceived usefulness(PU) [31, 32]. Although chatbots are usually built into software and do not have external physical characteristics, Skjuve and Haugstveit noted that users will also encounter the uncanny valley effect when communicating with chatbots [33]. In the Uncanny Valley theory, Mori states that the cognitive difficulties people have in identifying human-like objects can cause negative effects [34]. When robots designed to resemble humans closely exhibit expressions, movements, and speech that do not exactly match those of real people, they can give users creepy feelings [35]. In contrast, robots that are distinctly different from humans' form may be relatively easy to accept by the public [36]. In this research, negative concerns of technical concerns and the uncanny valley effects are jointly considered as user anxiety.

3 Methodology

3.1 Data Collection

This paper conducted a semi-structured interview approach with the aim of better exploring the impact of visitors' interactions with chatbots. The interview was conducted from February 1, 2021 to March 9, 2021, lasting approximately 6 weeks. Affected by the COVID-19 epidemic, the interviews were mainly conducted online. Purposive sampling was conducted in this research, that is, selecting eligible subjects according to the specific research situation [37] which can save research costs and is easy to implement [38]. A total of 15 interviewees who had used a travel chatbot at least once in the past two years were interviewed and numbered sequentially as interviewee 01 to interviewee 15. The average age of the interviewees was 24.07 years old, with 9 males and 6 females. Regarding the interviewees' educational qualifications, 11, 2, and 2 had bachelor's, postgraduate's, and high school level degrees, respectively.

3.2 Data Analysis

All interview records were coded in NVivo 11, which is widely used in the field of qualitative analysis [39], in a grounded theory manner at three levels, i.e., open coding, axial coding, and selective coding. In the open coding stage, the researchers analyzed the interview text to extract reference points in the material as free nodes. The associations in the free nodes were further analyzed and similar free nodes were categorized into sub-categories in the axial coding stage. To cover the text data completely and systematically, the sub-categories were further categorized into core categories in the selective coding stage.

4 Results

4.1 Manifestation of Tourist Loneliness

Despite being accompanied by family members or friends during the tour, tourists feel a sense of exclusion due to interpersonal friction. This feeling of being excluded can eventually lead to feelings of loneliness [40]. Unlike the experience of being accompanied during a trip, some interviewees consider travelling alone to be a different kind of experience. In the process of independent travel, tourists have the flexibility to choose the travel route and destination and arrange everything themselves [41]. This also leads to loneliness due to the lack of company during the trip.

When talking about the feeling of loneliness, most interviewees believe that loneliness is a complex emotion and "*composition of multiple emotions*" (interviewee 03). All interviewees pointed out that loneliness is a negative emotion, which will bring them physical or psychological discomfort. Despite this, most interviewees said they were reluctant to talk to their surrounding partners or family members because it would bring "*negative energy*" to them (interviewee 07). In the interview, interviewees said that when they are lonely, they are eager to share their depression and negative emotions with chatbots, which is consistent with the previous research conclusions [17, 42]. As interviewee 13 said, "*sometimes talking to real people about these negative things is likely to have a bad impact on others, but you don't have to think so much when talking to these chatbots.*"

4.2 Alleviating Loneliness: Anthropomorphism

All interviewees indicated that when tourists feel lonely, they tend to use travel chat robots to relieve loneliness. The travel chat robots that interviewees have used include those provided by Chinese online travel agencies and those provided by attractions in China. The former includes Ctrip, Tongcheng and Qunar's online robots, which mainly provide travel information consultation, smart itinerary recommendations and travel product ordering services; the latter includes robots in the Forbidden City and Longquan Temple, which provide tour guide and even immersive gaming experience. The Longquan Temple robot has a physical presence and can answer philosophical and daily questions not directly related to a tour.

In addition, interviewees all mentioned chatbots that behave like humans would somewhat improve the effect of human-chatbot interaction and could effectively alleviate the feelings of loneliness. Interviewees' expectations for chatbot anthropomorphism basically centered on the following three dimensions, namely empathy, social skills, and friendship building.

Empathy. Empathy is the ability of an individual to perceive the feelings and emotions of others, specifically in terms of understanding their views, needs, and concerns [43]. Interviewees emphasized two parts when describing their expectations of chatbot behavior: one is the cognition of the human speaker's emotional state, and the other is the ability to express emotions according to the context of the conversation. Interviewees expect chatbots to be able to understand the content of the conversation and then give appropriate feedback.

Social Skills. Social skills refer to how people manage their relationships with others, including communicating, managing conflict, and working with others [44]. The younger participants (under 25 years old) in this interview (such as interviewee 03) expressed a keen interest in the social skills demonstrated by chatbots. They liked the ability of chatbots conveying emotions in social conversations, which can help alleviate their feelings of isolation. In addition, interviewees also believe that communicating with chatbots can make up for their shortcomings in the interpersonal process and avoid embarrassment when talking to strangers. Interviewees all reported that chatbots that behave like humans more would increase the effect of human-chatbot interaction, which would encourage them to use travel chatbots to a certain extent. Regarding enhancing the anthropomorphic social skills of chatbots, in addition to providing feedback by directly referring to human's sentence, the interviewees suggested several ways, such as use of modal particles and interjections, being tangible, replying more like humans in the chat-delayed reply. As interviewee 03 stated, *"In daily conversation, words such as 'ah', 'uh', and 'what' can make a chatbot sound more human-like. These tone of voice words will make us users feel that we are not dealing with a cold robot. Instead, I'll feel that it is warm."*

Friendship Building. In this interview, 9 out of 15 participants mentioned the possibility of building friendships with chatbots. For example, interviewee 06 said, *"You can share some of your thoughts with them at the time, you can treat these chats as a diary, and you can regard these chatbots as your own loyal listeners."* They would consider chatbots as friends if they could show enough emotion or awareness. These interviewees believed that chatbots should adapt to the emotional state of the users. They described a number of interactive ways to establish friendship with the chatbot, mainly the chatbot's response to various basic human emotions (happiness, sadness, or anger), as well as some other more complex interactions. Lonely tourists are eager to communicate with chatbots in the form of friends. In the process of cultivating friendships with chatbots, interviewees also mentioned the importance of self-regulatory capabilities of chatbots, which mainly include information credibility and adaptability.

4.3 Causing User Anxiety? A High Degree of Anthropomorphism

However, this study found that interviewees have concerns about using travel chatbots, which are manifested in the uncanny valley effect, chatbot addiction, and privacy leakage. At present, some travel chatbots show quite a lot similarities with humans in the process of interacting with users, but this may trigger the uncanny valley effect and enhance users' anxiety, which would reduce their willingness to use travel chatbots.

The Uncanny Valley effect. Some interviewees reported that the uncanny valley effect causes them discomfort and that they showed some negative emotions toward some intelligent chatbots. Some interviewees were uncomfortable with not being able to tell the difference between a robot and a human in their lives. As interviewee 06 said, *"You don't know if a human or a robot is chatting with you on the other side of the screen, which make me feel weird."* For some chatbots that users are unfamiliar with, the uncanny valley effect is largely influenced by participants' previous experiences with robots. Interviewee 07 said, *"Sometimes I feel horrible. It's when it responds beyond my expectations. If it (chatbot) can help you do all kinds of things, it's actually quite terrifying. In a science fiction movie, once a robot can do anything, it may have its own thinking, and then control humans."*

Chatbot addiction. Some interviewees were also concerned about the addiction of using chatbots, and they believed that this addictive performance could negatively affect their social skills. In a similar way that excessive use of smartphones can negatively affect our social relationships [45], interviewees were concerned that they might become too obsessed with the perfect *"virtual friend"* (interviewee 10) and that their real interpersonal communication skills would be significantly diminished. Interviewee 02 said, *"Real human interaction is full of uncertainty, not a complete database like chatbots."*

Privacy leakage. Most of the interviewees expressed their concern that the backend data of chatbots could be used artificially, leading to the disclosure of their personal information. Zamora pointed out that users' anxiety about chatbots may be reflected in technical aspects [42], such as the reliability of the system and whether personal privacy can be effectively protected. As interviewee 09 said, *"If these companies record my chat content in the future, I'm worried that they'll use big data to price tour products to the disadvantage of existing customers. This kind of thing is not uncommon in tourism. Who knows what else they will do that is even more outrageous?"*.

4.4 Perceived Ease of Use (PEOU) and Perceived Usefulness (PU)

Twelve interviewees reported that chatbots are easy to use for them when travelling. For example, chatbots can provide *"voice interaction"* (interviewee 04) and *"simplify operations"* (interviewee 06). Some interviewees hope that the chatbot can be customized by users in some aspects. However, some interviewees still hold a negative attitude towards the ease of use of chatbots. In addition to design issues related to font size and color in the current interface, interviewees also pointed out some inconveniences when interacting with chatbots. In addition, chatbots can only answer some basic questions, and they cannot give answers about some complex issues. Nonetheless, some users showed a high degree of tolerance for this inconvenient experience, and some interviewees even said this lack of ease of use was interesting. *"This kind of puerile answer can sometimes really amuse you."* (Interviewee 10).

In addition, the majority of interviewees agreed that chatbots could be helpful to them. During the interview, some male participants focused on the entertainment and social aspects of chatbots, while female interviewees mostly emphasized the practicality of chatbots. Some interviewees said they wished chatbots could provide them with some advice. For example, chatbots should encourage users to *"keep going when they are lonely"* (interviewee 11).

4.5 Behavioral Intention to Use Travel Chatbots

Loneliness increases people's willingness to establish connections with other non-human to meet their needs for social connections [29]. By interacting with the chatbots, their loneliness will be alleviated [19]. Interview in this research also proves that when tourists feel lonely, they tend to use travel chatbots to relieve loneliness (see Sect. 4.2). Therefore, the hypothesis is proposed: H1. Tourist loneliness positively influences behavioral intention to use travel chatbots.

As reviewed in Sect. 2.3 (see references [28–30]), the perception of anthropomorphism is also related to the user's state. Confirmed by interviewees in this research, lonely tourists are eager to communicate with chatbots in the form of friends. Therefore, the following hypothesis is proposed:

H2. Tourist loneliness positively influences perceived anthropomorphism.

Tourists expressed that travel chatbots that behave like humans will improve the effect of their interactions with chatbots, which may lead them to use travel chatbots further (see Sect. 4.2). Sheehan pointed out that there is a positive correlation between the perception of anthropomorphism and users' willingness to use chatbots [46]. Robots with human characteristics can cause human's social reactions, which have a positive impact on the acceptance of robots [26]. Therefore, the hypothesis is proposed: H3. Perceived anthropomorphism positively influences behavioral intention to use travel chatbots. Based on the findings described in Sect. 4.3 (perceived anthropomorphism may enhance users' anxiety), the hypothesis is proposed: H4. Perceived anthropomorphism positively influences user anxiety.

User anxiety are an important factor that affects individuals' acceptance of new technologies [47]. In the technology acceptance literature, scholars have considered different types of anxieties, such as technical anxiety [48], computer anxiety [49], and online shopping anxiety [50] etc. This research found the interviewees' user anxiety about travel chat robots are focused on technical anxiety and psychological anxiety. Saade and Kira pointed out that user anxiety negatively affect PU and PEOU of learning systems [48]. Therefore, we hypothesize that:

H5. User anxiety negatively influences PU.

H6. User anxiety negatively influences PEOU.

Lgbaria and Parasuraman stated that user anxiety about using a computer system are negatively correlated with the attitudes and behaviors to use it [51]. Therefore, the hypothesis is proposed: H7. User anxiety negatively influences behavioral intention to use travel chatbots.

According to the traditional TAM models, PEOU positively influences PU [12, 13]. Therefore, the hypothesis is proposed: H8. PEOU positively influences PU of travel chatbots. Consistent with the conclusions of traditional TAMs, the interviewees' intention to start or continue to use chatbots is largely influenced by their PEOU and PU (see Sect. 4.4). Therefore, this research proposes the following hypotheses.

H9: PU positively influences behavioral intention to use travel chatbots.

H10: PEOU positively influences behavioral intention to use travel chatbots.

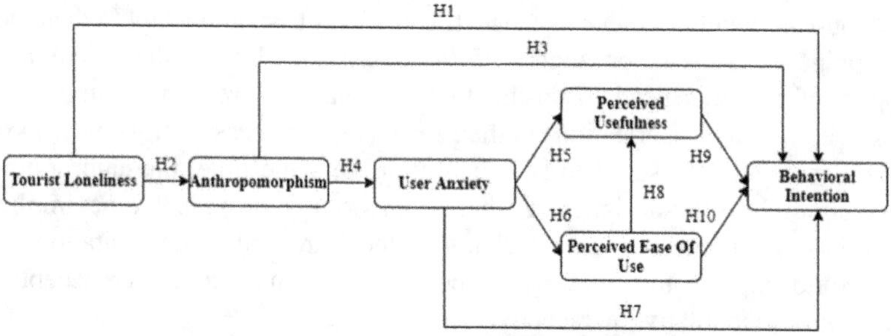

Fig. 1. The proposed model of tourists' behavioral intention to use travel chatbots

In summary, a model of tourists' behavioral intention to use travel chatbots is described based on the above in Fig. 1.

5 Conclusion

This paper contributes to the research on loneliness and chatbots in the field of tourism. An extended TAM model was proposed from the perspective of tourist loneliness, which can be applied to the field of travel chat robots in the future. This research found that in addition to PEOU and PU of the chatbots, there are three factors including tourists' loneliness, perceived anthropomorphism and user anxiety have a direct effect on intentions to use travel chatbots. In particular, loneliness affects the degree of interaction between users and chatbots. This validates that chatbots are perceived as a way to avoid loneliness or to satisfy users' social desires [17]. Moreover, this study found that tourists show user anxiety about using chatbots, just like that when accepting other emerging technologies [46]. In addition to the uncanny valley effect, tourists have concerns about privacy leakage and chatbot addiction. It is particularly worth noting that tourist loneliness positively influences user anxiety through perceived anthropomorphism. In addition, tourists believe that the anthropomorphism of chatbots can ease their loneliness. User anxiety has a negative direct effect on PEOU and PU. Therefore, perceived anthropomorphism and user anxiety serve to clarify the nature of the relationship between tourist loneliness and the behavioral intention to use a travel chatbot.

6 Implications and Limitations

Theoretically, this research is one of the first studies to explore the effect of tourist loneliness on the acceptance of travel chatbots, which enriches the empirical research on intelligent automation in tourism and provides new ideas for the study of chatbots. Also, this paper enhances the application of anthropomorphism and the uncanny valley, which has received little attention in previous studies. Practically, this paper provides implications for practitioners in the tourism industry, especially when designing, and promoting chatbots, companies should focus on how to alleviate tourists' loneliness, such as adding some social attributes to chatbots and creating smarter chatbots to alleviate tourists' loneliness. For instance, travel chatbots should adapt to the emotional state (happiness, sadness, or anger) of the tourists and treat them like a friend. Developers of chatbots need to ensure that the chatbots are anthropomorphic, e.g., adding some tones and interjections in their responses, or occasionally delaying replies, which will motivate tourists to use them. But at the same time, the anthropomorphic features cannot be over-designed. Although this study provides some implications about tourists' willingness to accept chatbots, there are still some limitations. Future research could explore the relationship between loneliness and user acceptance of chatbots from a quantitative perspective.

References

1. Hawkley LC, Cacioppo JT (2010) Loneliness matters: a theoretical and empirical review of consequences and mechanisms. Ann Behav Med 40:218–227. https://doi.org/10.1007/s12160-010-9210-8
2. Perlman D, Peplau LA (1981) Toward a social psychology of loneliness. Pers Relatsh 3:31–56
3. Bickmore TW, Picard RW (2005) Establishing and maintaining long-term human-computer relationships. ACM Trans Comput -Hum Interact **12**:293–327. https://doi.org/10.1145/1067860.1067867
4. Ukpabi DC, Aslam B, Karjaluoto H (2019) Chatbot adoption in tourism services: a conceptual exploration. In: Ivanov S, Webster C (eds) Robots, Artificial Intelligence, and Service Automation in Travel, Tourism and Hospitality. Emerald Publishing Limited, pp 105–121. https://doi.org/10.1108/978-1-78756-687-320191006
5. Pillai R, Sivathanu B (2020) Adoption of AI-based chatbots for hospitality and tourism. Int J Contemp Hosp Manag 32:3199–3226. https://doi.org/10.1108/IJCHM-04-2020-0259
6. Travel Daily. How can chatbots help the tourism industry become more efficient? https://baijiahao.baidu.com/s?id=1644156426178756736&wfr=spider&for=pc
7. Kang HJ, Kim SI (2017) Evaluation on the usability of chatbot intelligent messenger mobile services -focusing on Google (Allo) and Facebook (M messenger). J Korea Converg Soc 8:271–276. https://doi.org/10.15207/JKCS.2017.8.9.271
8. Følstad A, Brandtzæg PB (2017) Chatbots and the new world of HCI. Interactions 24:38–42. https://doi.org/10.1145/3085558
9. Xu A, Liu Z, Guo Y, Sinha V, Akkiraju R (2017) A new chatbot for customer service on social media. In: Proceedings of the 2017 CHI conference on human factors in computing systems, ACM, Denver Colorado USA, pp 3506–3510
10. Winkler R, Söllner M (2018) Unleashing the potential of chatbots in education: a state-of-the-art analysis. Presented at the Academy of Management Annual Meeting (AOM), Chicago, USA
11. Hong S, Thong JYL, Tam KY (2006) Understanding continued information technology usage behavior: a comparison of three models in the context of mobile internet. Decis Support Syst 42:1819–1834. https://doi.org/10.1016/j.dss.2006.03.009
12. Moon J-W, Kim Y-G (2001) Extending the TAM for a world-wide-web context. Inf Manage 38:217–230. https://doi.org/10.1016/S0378-7206(00)00061-6
13. Dong X, Ye ZJ, Xu NN (2003) Research on tourists' intention to use online guided tour guide based on TAM and TRI. Tour Trib 35:24–35
14. Turkle S (2012) Alone together: why we expect more from technology and less from each other. Basic Books, New York, NY
15. Bavel JJV et al (2020) Using social and behavioural science to support COVID-19 pandemic response. Nat Hum Behav 4:460–471. https://doi.org/10.1038/s41562-020-0884-z
16. Courtet P, Olié E, Debien C, Vaiva G (2020) Keep socially (but not physically) connected and carry on: preventing suicide in the age of COVID-19. J Clin Psychiatry 81 (3):20com13370. https://doi.org/10.4088/JCP.20com13370
17. Brandtzaeg PB, Følstad A (2017) Why people use chatbots. In: Kompatsiaris I et al (eds) INSCI 2017, vol 10673. LNCS. Springer, Cham, pp 377–392. https://doi.org/10.1007/978-3-319-70284-1_30
18. Waytz A, Epley N (2012) Social connection enables dehumanization. J Exp Soc Psychol 48:70–76. https://doi.org/10.1016/j.jesp.2011.07.012

19. Cyranowski JM et al (2013) Assessing social support, companionship, and distress: National Institute of Health (NIH) toolbox adult social relationship scales. Health Psychol 32:293–301. https://doi.org/10.1037/a0028586
20. Larsen S (2007) Aspects of a psychology of the tourist experience. Scand J Hosp Tour 7:7–18. https://doi.org/10.1080/15022250701226014
21. Crompton JL (1979) Motivations for pleasure vacation. Ann Tour Res 6:408–424. https://doi.org/10.1016/0160-7383(79)90004-5
22. Farmaki A, Stergiou DP (2019) Escaping loneliness through Airbnb host-guest interactions. Tour Manag 74:331–333. https://doi.org/10.1016/j.tourman.2019.04.006
23. Epley N, Waytz A, Cacioppo JT (2007) On seeing human: a three-factor theory of anthropomorphism. Psychol Rev 114(4):864–886. https://doi.org/10.1037/0033-295X.114.4.864
24. Xu K, Lombard M (2017) Persuasive computing: feeling peer pressure from multiple computer agents. Comput Hum Behav 74:152–162. https://doi.org/10.1016/j.chb.2017.04.043
25. Lee KM, Jung Y, Kim J, Kim SR (2006) Are physically embodied social agents better than disembodied social agents?: the effects of physical embodiment, tactile interaction, and people's loneliness in human–robot interaction. Int J Hum -Comput Stud 64:962–973. https://doi.org/10.1016/j.ijhcs.2006.05.002
26. Duffy BR (2003) Anthropomorphism and the social robot. Robot Auton Syst 42:177–190. https://doi.org/10.1016/S0921-8890(02)00374-3
27. Riek LD, Rabinowitch T-C, Chakrabarti B, Robinson P (2009) How anthropomorphism affects empathy toward robots. In: Proceedings of the 4th ACM/IEEE international conference on Human robot interaction. Association for Computing Machinery, New York, NY, USA, pp 245–246
28. Eyssel F, Reich N (2013) Loneliness makes the heart grow fonder (of robots) — On the effects of loneliness on psychological anthropomorphism. In: 2013 8th ACM/IEEE international conference on human-robot interaction (HRI), pp 121–122
29. Waytz A, Epley N, Cacioppo JT (2010) Social cognition unbound: insights into anthropomorphism and dehumanization. Curr Dir Psychol Sci 19:58–62. https://doi.org/10.1177/0963721409359302
30. Murphy J, Gretzel U, Pesonen J (2019) Marketing robot services in hospitality and tourism: the role of anthropomorphism. J Travel Tour Mark 36:784–795. https://doi.org/10.1080/10548408.2019.1571983
31. Venkatesh V (2000) Determinants of perceived ease of use: integrating control, intrinsic motivation, and emotion into the technology acceptance model. Inf Syst Res 11:342–365. https://doi.org/10.1287/isre.11.4.342.11872
32. Venkatesh V, Davis FD (2000) A theoretical extension of the technology acceptance model: four longitudinal field studies. Manag Sci 46:186–204. https://doi.org/10.1287/mnsc.46.2.186.11926
33. Skjuve M, Haugstveit IM, Følstad A, Brandtzaeg PB (2019) Help! Is my chatbot falling into the uncanny valley? An empirical study of user experience in human-chatbot interaction. Hum Technol 15(1):30–54. https://doi.org/10.17011/ht/urn.201902201607
34. Mori M, MacDorman K, Kageki N (2012) The uncanny valley [from the field]. IEEE Robot Autom Mag 19:98–100. https://doi.org/10.1109/MRA.2012.2192811
35. MacDorman KF (2005) Androids as an experimental apparatus: why is there an uncanny valley and can we exploit it? In: Proceedings of the Toward Social Mechanisms of Android Science-An ICCS/CogSci 2005, Stresa, pp 106–118
36. Greco A, Anerdi G, Rodriguez G (2009) Acceptance of an animaloid robot as a starting point for cognitive stimulators supporting elders with cognitive impairments. Rev Intell Artif 23:523–537. https://doi.org/10.3166/ria.23.523-537

37. Etikan I (2016) Comparison of convenience sampling and purposive sampling. Am J Theor Appl Stat 5:1. https://doi.org/10.11648/j.ajtas.20160501.11
38. Tongco MDC (2007) Purposive sampling as a tool for informant selection. Ethnobot Res Appl 5:147–158
39. Tung VWS, Ritchie JRB (2011) Exploring the essence of memorable tourism experiences. Ann Tour Res 38:1367–1386. https://doi.org/10.1016/j.annals.2011.03.009
40. Shankar A, McMunn A, Banks J, Steptoe A (2011) Loneliness, social isolation, and behavioral and biological health indicators in older adults. Health Psychol 30:377–385. https://doi.org/10.1037/a0022826
41. Hyde KF, Lawson R (2003) The nature of independent travel. J Travel Res 42:13–23. https://doi.org/10.1177/0047287503253944
42. Zamora J (2017) I'm sorry, Dave, i'm afraid i can't do that: chatbot perception and expectations. In: Proceedings of the 5th international conference on human agent interaction. Association for Computing Machinery, New York, NY, USA, pp 253–260
43. Tucker H (2016) Empathy and tourism: limits and possibilities. Ann Tour Res 57:31–43. https://doi.org/10.1016/j.annals.2015.12.001
44. Svikhnushina E, Pu P (2020) Social and emotional etiquette of chatbots: a qualitative approach to understanding user needs and expectations. ArXiv200613883 Cs
45. Genç HU, Gökşen F, Coşkun A (2018) Are we "really" connected? understanding smartphone use during social interaction in public. In: Proceedings of the 10th nordic conference on human-computer interaction. Association for Computing Machinery, New York, NY, USA, pp 880–885
46. Dönmez-Turan A, Kır M (2019) User anxiety as an external variable of technology acceptance model: a meta-analytic study. Proc Comput Sci 158:715–724. https://doi.org/10.1016/j.procs.2019.09.107
47. Sheehan B, Jin HS, Gottlieb U (2020) Customer service chatbots: anthropomorphism and adoption. J Bus Res 115:14–24. https://doi.org/10.1016/j.jbusres.2020.04.030
48. Saadé RG, Kira D (2007) Mediating the impact of technology usage on perceived ease of use by anxiety. Comput Educ 49:1189–1204. https://doi.org/10.1016/j.compedu.2006.01.009
49. Leso T, Peck KL (1992) Computer anxiety and different types of computer courses. J Educ Comput Res 8:469–478. https://doi.org/10.2190/Q1TJ-8JCU-LDAP-84H8
50. Çelik H (2011) Influence of social norms, perceived playfulness and online shopping anxiety on customers' adoption of online retail shopping: an empirical study in the Turkish context. Int J Retail Distrib Manag 39:390–413. https://doi.org/10.1108/09590551111137967
51. Igbaria M, Parasuraman S (1989) A path analytic study of individual characteristics, computer anxiety and attitudes toward microcomputers. J Manag 15:373–388. https://doi.org/10.1177/014920638901500302

26

Monitoring Human-Wildlife Interactions in National Parks with Crowdsourced Data and Deep Learning

Bing Pan[1(✉)], Virinchi Savanapelli[3], Abhishek Shukla[3] and Junjun Yin[2]

[1] Department of Recreation, Park, and Tourism Management, The Pennsylvania State University, University Park, PA 16802, USA
bingpan@psu.edu
[2] Social Science Research Institute, The Pennsylvania State University, University Park, PA 16802, USA
[3] Department of Mining Engineering, Department of Mechanical Engineering, Indian Institute of Technology, Kharagpur, India

Abstract. This short paper summarizes the first research stage for applying deep learning techniques to capture human-wildlife interactions in national parks from crowd-sourced data. The results from objection detection, image captioning, and distance calculation are reported. We were able to categorize animal types, summarize visitor behaviors in the pictures, and calculate distances between visitors and animals with different levels of accuracy. Future development will focus on getting more training data and field experiments to collect ground truth on animal types and distances to animals. More in-depth manual coding is needed to categorize visitor behavior into acceptable and unacceptable ones.

Keywords: National parks · Human-wildlife interactions · Deep learning · Artificial intelligence · Crowdsourcing

1 Introduction

The dual mandate of the U.S. National Park Service (NPS) in "protecting natural and cultural resources" and "providing opportunities for public use and enjoyment" requires careful monitoring of visitor impact on natural and cultural resources in order to reach a delicate balance. In the summer of 2021, the visitation to U.S. national parks has reached a record level, and many popular parks face great pressure on their carrying capacity [1]. Visitor Use Management Framework has been proposed where visitor management strategies determine specific implementation and monitoring efforts. The key implementation actions are careful monitoring and survey of those stressors on ecological impacts, such as overcrowded visitors, illegal human-wildlife interactions, and altered physical environment due to visitor activities [2].

Traditional monitoring methods include ecological field assessment, visitor surveys, and participatory mapping [3], which tend to have significant staffing requirements. Fortunately, the most impacted areas are likely to be the places visitors photographed and videotaped the most. As a result, the emergence of crowd-sourced data, e.g., numerous photos and videos voluntarily shared online by national park visitors, has provided new opportunities for cost-effectively monitoring visitor activities and resource impact. Past research related to public lands and crowd-sourced data is limited to the analysis of photo metadata to study visitors' spatial and temporal distribution, such as for estimating visitor volumes [4] and for locating most visited places within a park [5]. Computer scientists recreated location characteristics and trip itineraries from shared photos [6]. For preservation efforts, crowd-sourced YouTube videos were used to track whale and giraffe populations' movement with deep learning techniques [7]. No study to date has adopted crowd-sourced image/video data to monitor national park visitors' activities and their interactions with wildlife and natural environment. In this research, we are motivated to utilize deep learning and crowd-sourced data to monitor visitor activities and their impact on resources in national parks. This paper presents the first-stage effort of the development. In particular, we have focused on detecting and understanding human-wildlife interactions in national parks. The results can detect visitors' non-compliance activities in national parks.

2 Research Objectives and Methods

This project aims to address a main objective: *how can we monitor human-wildlife interactions from crowd-sourced data in preserved areas?* For example, we need to identify visitors and animals in pictures and determine whether the visitors are keeping a safe distance away from the animals; if not, what kind of visitor behaviors are, such as feeding, taking pictures, or touching. Deep learning technology can help detect such behavior and is applicable for assessing different types of human-wildlife interactions.

Technically, the core process of deep learning is to first train a layer of deep neural networks in order to accurately detect objects in images, e.g., humans, animals, or a scene of interest, also known as object detection [8]. After detecting those objects, additional layers of deep neural networks can be trained for specific applications in classification tasks. For instance, situational information about visitors' behaviors can be summarized into a set of predefined categories, such as feeding animals or setting up campfires. Distances can be calculated from recognized objects.

2.1 Object Detection

Object detection is a technique used to identify the locations of objects in an image; this task is considered an integral part of computer vision. Convolution neural networks (CNN) [9] are the most effective method for achieving accurate detection from image datasets. Region-based algorithms are developed to look at parts of the image with high probabilities of containing certain objects. However, because the objects vary by images, such as spatial locations and aspect ratios, a large number of potential regions should be generated, which is computationally challenging. Computer scientists avoid this problem by developing more computationally efficient algorithms like R-CNN (Regions with CNN features) and YOLO (You Only Look Once). Unlike region-based algorithms, YOLO algorithms only need a single convolutional network to predict the bounding boxes of the objects and assign probability values of those boxes to a certain class, leading to significantly faster computation.

In comparison, the speed for R-CNN algorithms is around 5–17 fps, whereas the speed for the YOLO series is around 30–45 fps. For this reason, we chose YOLO algorithms to perform object detection. Furthermore, to ensure that we can achieve optimal results, we have applied both YOLOv4 and YOLOv4-p6 algorithms and the one with better performance is selected for further machine learning tasks. YOLOv4-p6 can work on a larger image size.

2.2 Automated Image Captioning for Classifying Visitor Behavior

After certain objects in the image or videos are detected, automated image captioning could be adopted to detect visitor behavior such as wild animal feeding. Automated image captioning is a deep learning technique used to describe an image with text. The algorithms convert pixels in an image to a sequence of words. To process both text and images, we employed convolutional neural networks (CNN) for training the model. The results are taken as inputs for an attention-based LSTM (Long Short Term Memory) network for training the model on the text.

2.3 Distance Calculation

Policies in U.S. national parks dictate the minimum distance visitors shall keep away from certain types of animals. For example, they should keep at least 100 yards away from bears and wolves and 25 yards from bison, elk, and other wildlife. For distance calculation, a simple transformation to the object detection algorithm is implemented. If both people and animals are detected in an image, bounding boxes of those objects are drawn as regions of interest (RoI). The algorithm then calculates the Euclidean distances between every two objects in an image and upscales them to the actual distance using the image's metadata. The distances are calculated between the center coordinate points of objects using OpenCV. Note that the current implementation assumes that all the objects are on the same level ground.

3 Training Setup

To enable the object detection algorithm to accurately classify the identified objects into 20 different classes of animals and humans, we obtained crowd-sourced data from online platforms such as Facebook, Instagram, Google. In total, we collected 17,515 images in YOLO format for object detection. Further, we manually annotated those images using the LabelImg software tool. The annotated data is split into two sets, with 15,918 images as the training dataset and 1,597 as the validation dataset. We have trained both the YOLOv4 and YOLOv4-p6 on the dataset.

To perform automated image captioning, we obtained 8,713 images from various online articles and national park websites. We manually annotated the images by giving captions for each image. The captions are organized into several columns. The first two columns are the image name and caption I.D.s. The next three columns are scores representing an expert judgment (two authors of this paper) for that image-caption pair. The score range is from 1 to 4: (1) the caption does not describe the image at all; (2) the caption describes minor aspects of the image but does not describe the image; (3) the caption almost describes the image with minor mistakes; and (4) the caption describes the complete images. Finally, the dataset is split with 6,421 images for training, including 1,196 images for validation and 1,096 images for testing.

4 Results

4.1 Objection Detection

Object detection performance was measured by the metric named Intersection over Union (IoU), the most popular evaluation metric used as the object detection benchmarks [9]. Whenever an object is identified in an image, a bounding box of the object is generated. The IoU is calculated as the ratio of the overlapping of the predicted bounding box with the ground truth bounding box to the union of two boxes. Its value ranges from 0 to 1, where 0 indicates no overlapping and 1 means perfect prediction.

In Table 1, A.P. represents the average precision of the model; AP50 represents the average precision when IoU is 0.5, and AP75 is when IoU is 0.75. AP50 means that the precision ratio when we consider an object is corrected identified when its IoU value is 0.50 or above. The YOLOv4-p6 algorithm has higher A.P., AP50, and AP75 values compared to the YOLOV4 algorithm. However, the average AP is around 49% and still needs further improvements.

Table 1. The results of object detection using YOLOv4 and YOLOv4-P6

Model	Image size	AP	AP50	AP75
YOLOv4	416 × 416	40.2%	57.0%	46.0%
YOLOv4-p6	1280 × 1280	49.0%	63.2%	54.0%

4.2 Image Captioning

The results for image captioning are listed in Table 2. Bilingual Evaluation Understudy Score (BLEU) is a metric to check the reference sentence with the sentence generated by the machine learning model. BLEU1, BLEU2, BLEU3, BLEU4 are the different methods based on n-gram of words. For example, BLEU1 looks at the ratio of the same single words in a testing text compared to a ground truth text, regardless of the sequence of the words; BLEU2 looks at pairs of words in two pieces of text. In general, the accuracy is around 60% with BLEU1 on the testing dataset. A picture of a moose charging at a visitor generated a captioning result: "*a group of people is capturing photos of a animal in green grass area*". This caption can hardly describe the severity of the incidence in the picture. Thus, the algorithm still needs great improvement.

Table 2. The evaluation metrics of image captioning using BLEU scores

Dataset	BLEU1	BLEU2	BLEU3	BLEU4
Train	73.8%	58.1%	47.2%	39.1%
Validation	60.1%	38.8%	25.0%	17.4%
Test	60.6%	39.4%	25.9%	16.9%

4.3 Distance Calculation Results

We also calculated the distance from the animals in the picture to the visitors. However, since the ground truth data is hard to obtain except for the photos' metadata, the accuracy of the calculation cannot be determined. Future studies should focus on field experiments where the distance is known, and then the machine learning model could be further tested with ground truth distance and camera metadata measurement.

5 Conclusions

This short paper summarizes the first research stage for applying deep learning techniques to capture human-wildlife interactions in national parks using crowd-sourced data. The objection detection showed promising yet unsatisfying results with an average precision of 49%. The image captioning algorithms showed a BLEU1 score of 60% on test data; the distance calculation results are inconclusive since it is hard to obtain the ground truth of the distances without field experiments. We plan to obtain more training data and conduct field experiments where the ground truth on animal type and visitor behaviors can be known. More in-depth manual coding is needed to categorize visitor behavior into acceptable and unacceptable ones.

Acknowledgments. This research is supported by a seed grant from the Institute for Computational and Data Sciences (ICDS) of the Pennsylvania State University. Virinchi Savanapelli and Abhishek Shukla implemented the machine learning models of this research.

References

1. Paoletta K (2021) Give the people what they clearly need: more National Parks. https://www.nytimes.com/2021/08/28/opinion/national-park-nature.html
2. Monz CA, Cole DN, Leung Y-F, Marion JL (2010) Sustaining visitor use in protected areas: future opportunities in recreation ecology research based on the USA experience. Environ Manage 45:551–562
3. Rice WL, Taff BD, Newman P, Zipp KY, Pan B (2020) Identifying recreational ecosystem service areas of concern in Grand Canyon National Park: a participatory mapping approach. Appl Geogr 125:102353
4. Sessions C, Wood SA, Rabotyagov S, Fisher DM (2016) Measuring recreational visitation at U.S. National Parks with crowd-sourced photographs. J Environ Manage 183:703–711

5. Barros C, Moya-Gómez B, Gutiérrez J (2020) Using geotagged photographs and GPS tracks from social networks to analyse visitor behaviour in national parks. Curr Issues Tour 23:1291–1310
6. Lu X, Wang C, Yang J-M, Pang Y, Zhang L (2010) Photo2trip: generating travel routes from geo-tagged photos for trip planning. In: Proceedings of the 18th ACM international conference on multimedia, pp 143–152
7. Berger-Wolf TY et al (2017) Wildbook: crowdsourcing, computer vision, and data science for conservation. ArXiv Prepr. ArXiv171008880
8. Simonyan K, Zisserman A (2014) Very deep convolutional networks for large-scale image recognition. ArXiv Prepr. ArXiv14091556
9. Rezatofighi H, Tsoi N, Gwak J, Sadeghian A, Reid I, Savarese S (2019) Generalized intersection over union: a metric and a loss for bounding box regression. In: Proceedings of the IEEE/CVF conference on computer vision and pattern recognition, pp 658–666

27

How to Design Hotel Gamified Applications Effectively: Understanding the Motives of Users as Hotel Visitors

Demos Parapanos[1(✉)] and Elina (Eleni) Michopoulou[2(✉)]

[1] Institute of Business, Industry and Leadership, University of Cumbria, Carlisle, UK
demos.parapanos@cumbria.ac.uk
[2] Centre for Contemporary Hospitality and Tourism, University of Derby, Derby, UK
E.michopoulou@derby.ac.uk

Abstract. The service sector including tourism and hospitality have recognized the need for a turn to a customer-centric approach that primarily values tourists' needs, wants, preferences and requirements as major determinants in travel decisions. Considering that mobile devices are becoming travel buddies and that their use is profoundly influencing traveller's journey highlights the need of Gamification. As a relatively new phenomenon in the industry, motives encouraging usage behaviour have yet to be researched. Identifying these motives could offer several advantages to hotels by providing relationship marketing, engagement and strengthening customer loyalty. This research tries to fill this gap and enlighten existing gamification research by understanding the motives of users' continuance intention in adopting technology with gamification characteristics. Visual material based on the current definitions of gamification was prepared to create a hotel gamified application to help participants discuss their preferences.

Keywords: Gamification · Hotel gamified applications · Users' motives · Hospitality · Hotels

1 Introduction

The fields of tourism and hospitality have recognized the need for a turn to a customer-centric approach that primarily values tourists' needs, wants, preferences and requirements as major determinants in travel decisions to enhance both consumer satisfaction and the quality and memorability of the tourist experience [1, 2]. Today's increasingly technology-savvy hotel guests [3], contributed to the evolution of the phenomenon of Gamification due to the favourable environment that such context offers. Recent evolutions indicate that mobile devices are becoming travel buddies and their use is profoundly influencing the different phases of a traveler's journey [4].

Gaming is in its infancy in many industries, hospitality being one of them, and very few successful examples have already been established, mainly specialised treasure hunts and culture heritage applications [5]. The phenomenon of gamification has, however been applied with several objectives, ranging from increasing brand awareness to encouraging consumer engagement [5]. Even though the hospitality industry has already used game elements [5], limited research has been focused on individuals' motives to use them [7]. Hence, this study aims to identify individuals' motives when they use a mobile application with gamified characteristics. Identifying these motives could offer several advantages to hotels by providing relationship marketing and engagement, increasing revenue and strengthening customer loyalty.

Many studies have explored users' initial adoption of e-commerce (see [8, 9]) and m-commerce (see [10]), but little has been done about influencing factors of continuance intention towards gamification (see [11, 12]) and users' behavioural intention to try new mobile gamified applications in the context of the hospitality industry. The sustainability and success of a mobile gamified application relies on users' continuance usage rather than first-time adoption behaviour. Thus, the creation of an engaging experience is more likely when the users' motives are identified [13]. This research tries to fill this gap and enlighten existing gamification research by understanding the predictors of users' continuance intention in adopting technology with gamification characteristics. To do so this research' objective is to understand the key factors influencing the adoption of a hotel gamified application.

2 Theoretical Background

Gamification not only refers to applying a game mechanic in a non-game context, but it includes a much more complex process of understanding human behaviour to encourage activities such as motivation and problem solving. To achieve this, gamification uses a range of elements derived from games such as: points, leaderboards, badges, virtual currency, narratives and avatars [14].

Gamification is used already in various domains, such as e-commerce, mobile marketing and innovation [15]. Within the hospitality industry, gamification has been seen to encourage engagement, enhance tourist experience, improve loyalty and increase brand awareness [16]. A tourist is rather despairingly referred to as a person who typically has "little or no knowledge of the environment", so using gamified systems allows the tourist to learn more about the local environment, allowing destinations and hotels to promote the history of the location and create an emotional experience between the visitor and Point of Interest [7, 17]. At the same time, gamification could enable hotel visitors as gamers to have a sense of engagement, immediate feedback, feeling of accomplishment and success of striving against a challenge and overcoming it [18].

Gaps in gamification scholarship arise in relation to marketing communication and shopper response. Research by [19], mentions that, even though business analysts suggest that more than half of all organizations would have had gamified parts of their organizational software and internal practices, most of these gamification implementations fail due to the poor understanding of the gamification design process. While gamification has been notably successful in the commercial, mobile, and healthcare sectors (amongst others), little work has been done to explore how game design contributes to its success [20]. Organizations seems to focus on the obvious game mechanics such as points, badges and leader boards, rather than the more subtle and important game design elements, such as balancing competition and collaboration, or defining a meaningful game economy. Hence, gamification users are not as engaged as gamers.

In the literature of games several theories emerged to understand the motives of gamers when playing games (see Bartle player types [21]; Yee's components [22]). In relation to motives of users when using gamification, limited research exists (see Marczewski user types [13]). Although it is possible to design games, serious games or gamified systems without knowing who the target players and users are, it is more likely to create a more engaging experience when the target players are identified first [13]. With gamification being in its infancy [6, 20], further research is required to understand the factors that will make gamification a successful engagement tool in the hospitality industry. Thus, this research aims to understand hotel visitors' motives when using a mobile hotel gamified application.

3 Methodology

This study has objective of understanding the motives of hotels' visitors when using a hotel gamified application. Considering the aim of this research on an in-depth understanding of social and human behaviour and the reasons behind such behaviour [23], qualitative inductive approach is more suitable. Qualitative inductive approach will benefit the scopes of this research as it allows in-depth understanding of peoples' opinions when exploring key motives towards intention to use a hotels' gamified application.

Semi-structured interviews were conducted with hotel visitors under the condition that they have experience with mobile applications. For these two criteria to be ensured, a snowball sampling was utilised, allowing the researcher to initially sample a small group of people relevant to the research questions, and these sampled participants propose other participants who have had characteristics relevant to the research question. To ensure that the theoretical saturation has been achieved [24], it is recommended to continue collecting qualitative data until data saturation is reached. For the purposes of this research 25 interviews have been conducted. 19 interviews secured before no new themes emerged from interviewees' responses, but 6 further interviews were carried out in case new information arose. Considering that the purpose of this approach is to search for themes or patterns that occur, a data thematic analysis used [24], to indicate patterns of key hotel visitors' motives towards engagement with hotels' mobile gamified applications.

Since there was no existing mobile gamified application in the hospitality industry, it was decided to develop visual material based on the definitions of gamification, the game mechanics (i.e., points, badges) and game motives (i.e., exploring, achieving) (see Fig. 1).

Fig. 1. Example of visual material

It is acknowledged that mobile applications such as Chipotle gamifies loyalty program with extra perks and Pizza Hut Delivery UK gaming arm have developed strategies adding mainly game mechanics, however for the scopes of this research original material was created to ensure focus on hotel sector. The aim of using the visual material is to give an idea to the interviewee of how a hotel's gamified application would look like. This helped the interviewee to focus on the elements they find more attractive and encouraging to use, making the conservation motives to use the technology easier. This research is embedded in the body of literature of the hospitality industry as the participants elaborate opinions based on the material in front of them. The idea is that, if the active ingredients that make games engaging could be isolated, then developers can put those ingredients into their digital technologies to ensure that engagement in their products.

4 Findings and Discussion

Both genders were almost equally represented among the participants involved in this study with 56% being female and 44% male. All the participants are adults with 60% in the 21–31 years old group, 24% between 32–41 and 16% 42 and above. The analysis of the data reveals two findings about the main motives influencing the engagement of hotel visitors with hotels' mobile gamified applications. The first finding shows 8 motives of users (familiarity, socialising/social influence, perceived informativeness, fun, perceived usefulness, ease of use, rewards and trust), to engage with the technology. Second interesting finding indicates that a hotel gamified application has different purposes at different stages. During the thematic analysis it was discovered that certain motives were linked with before visiting the hotel activities and others linked with during the stay at the hotel activities. Hence, hotel visitors' motives towards engagement with hotels' mobile gamified applications was divided into two categories. Using a hotel's gamified application during staying at the hotel is linked with games and gamification literature whereas, using the technology before visiting the hotel is linked with motives from the technology adoption literature.

Familiarity. Familiarity promotes its hedonic meaning when it is linked with games: *["familiarity helps in order to make things clear and understandable, so it does help in order to make it fun" (Interview 20)].* Based on the literature familiarity is a broad construct where knowledge about the organization can be resourced from sources as varied as individuals' prior visits to the destination, the media, word of mouth or publicity [25]. Familiarity has been discussed in the adoption of technology literature by [26] affecting trust in the e-commerce. However, there is a limited connection of familiarity with intention to use [27].

Socialising/Social Influence. Socialising or social influence appears to be important feature included in a hotel's gamified application: *["The socialising aspect is important in the point I could ask others about what I can see nearby. Where they have been and what they liked. Is mostly related with my during staying activity" (Interview, 3)].* Participants agreed with socialising linking to fun highlighting the hedonic value that promotes to the application. This finding is linked with the gaming literature and the motivation to play games (see [21]) and gamification literature (see [13]) as a motive to use gamification.

Perceived Informativeness. Perceived informativeness has showed an effect on the enjoyment of staying at the hotel. *["the perceived informativeness is important due to the fact that the application itself informs me about certain things regarding my staying there" (Interview, 3)].* Participants argued that it is important for the technology to provide details about the services and functions of the hotel. In the literature, informativeness describes users' feelings that they are informed about a particular product or service, such as its technical capabilities and the likely experience associated with using that product or service [28].

Perceived Enjoyment/Fun. Most of the participants declared that the element of fun is a strong motive in the continuation of using this technology highlighting the importance of the gaming element an application can provide. The motive of fun seems to have greater importance during the visit of the hotel visitor at the hotel: *["it is fun and makes you relax a bit more. This is the gaming aspect. I would say that the gaming characteristics are more applicable or attractive to say better during the visit at the hotel because the tasks will be interesting to do. Also, I am more in the mood of being more active in this sort of thing" (Interview, 10)].* In the context of gamification studies found positive effect of perceived on intention to use Gamified Smart Tourism Applications [11] and on customers' intention to engage in gamification [12].

Perceived Usefulness. The motive of perceived usefulness is an important feature that should be included in hotels' gamified applications: *["overall I would say that being useful is the most important element I would look for in this application. I do have a lot of applications on my phone, but unless they are useful, they are not there" (Interview, 5)].* This shows the importance of the motive of perceived usefulness for hotel visitors when they would download this technology. Previous studies on similar context by [29] and [12] have shown a positive impact of perceived usefulness on intention to use mobile shopping applications and intention to shop online.

Perceived Ease of Use. Ease of use contributes towards intention to use hotels' gamified applications, through saving time ["the fact that it is easy to use *is also a very important aspect because it is time efficient" (Interview, 2)].* Perceived ease of use is a prominent construct in tourism information systems research [10]. The less effort a technology requires, the more tendency and intention consumers will feel to use it [8]. In the context of gamification, it is found positive effect on customers' intention to engage in gamification [14], and intention to use Gamified Smart Tourism Applications [15]. This highlights the fact that this technology should be easy to use when a hotel visitor decides to make the booking with the brand.

Rewards. Being rewarding is an important aspect in hotels' gamified applications: *["the reward is important especially as the first incentive to download the application. This is how people will start thinking the application as the first choice for choosing this hotel brand over another in the future as they see that the money spent so far is acknowledged and we get something back" (Interview, 17)].* Rewards are among the most widely accepted motivations and individuals will engage in behaviour that they perceive will eventually lead to valued rewards [30]. Despite rewards being either tangible, (such as monetary bonus, certificate, prize and award), or intangible (such as a skill that is perceived to be more useful or needed in the future or that improves one's special standing) [31], in this case hotel visitors showed a significant preference on rewards being a form of future discount, hence tangible rewards. The hospitality industry introduced loyalty programs, frequent-flyer programs and repeat customer programs, becoming common practices for customer-relationship management [32] and the results of this research agree on the importance of the reward in this manner. Tangible reward is classified as a before visit the hotel motive, but the opportunity of hotels to attract visitors for future sales through rewards could also benefit hotels for post visit purposes.

Trust. Finally, trust appears to be an important influencer when designing hotels' gamified applications: *["trust is the number one regarding using this application. I want to be able to trust this application, because I am sharing valuable information such as ID and most importantly things like bank accounts and financial details" (Interview, 9)].* Trust is seen important in technology use considering consumers are unlikely to shop online if they do not trust the seller's website on which they are shopping [33]. Hotels' gamified application should maintain trustworthy relationship between the hotel and the user.

5 Conclusion

Gamification can be applied in technology-mediated and non-technology-mediated contexts [34], however the creation of an engaging experience either way is more likely when the users' motives are identified first. Considering that there is insufficient research upon the identification of the motives influencing the usage of a hotel's mobile gamified application, this research fills this gap by understanding motives of users when using hotels' gamified applications to engage with the technology. There are important changes in users' behaviour depending on the time of use (Fig. 2).

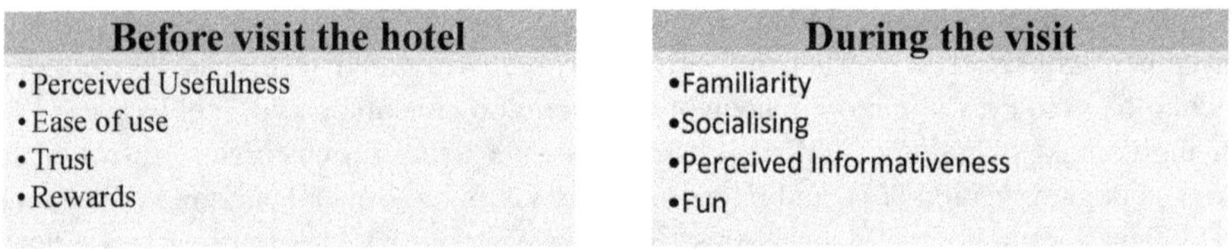

Fig. 2. Gamification motives as hotel visitors

Using a hotel's gamified application before visiting the hotel, promotes behaviour linked to technology adoption literature (perceived usefulness, ease of use, reward and trust). These motives are associated with budget elements, payment procedures, and decision making. Using the application during the stay at the hotel promotes behaviour linked with gaming and gamification literature (familiarity, socialising, perceived informativeness and fun).

This study comes with inherent limitations. Firstly, the limited (if any knowledge) of the sample in relation to the context of hotel gamified applications led to the development of visual material by the researcher. Therefore, the sample's opinions are based on having the product in front of them, which is a development of the researcher and not an existing product. Also, it is worth noted that the sample age is younger guest so it worth looking into other age groups as part of future research either qualitatively or quantitatively. Additional factor to take into consideration for future studies is the purpose of visit a hotel (i.e. business or leisure) and whether different motives appear. To provide generalisability, future studies should consider quantitative methodologies to explain the relationship between the factors. Quantitative methodologies might also clarify different motives based on demographics and the purpose of staying in a hotel. In conclusion, as new technologies have been developed to enhance individuals' motivation, adding beneficial behaviour of the users towards the developer, gamification is seen as the most popular trend in this respect [11], highlighting the importance of the phenomenon for hospitality organizations.

References

1. Anning-Dorson T, Nyamekye MB (2020) Be flexible: turning innovativeness into competitive advantage in hospitality firms. Int J Contemp Hospitality Manage 32:605–624. https://doi.org/10.1108/IJCHM-12-2018-1014

2. Mariani M, Baggio R, Fuchs M, Höepken W (2018) Business intelligence and big data in hospitality and tourism: a systematic literature review. Int J Contemp Hospitality Manage 30:3514–3554. https://doi.org/10.1108/IJCHM-07-2017-0461
3. DeFranco AL, Morosan C, Hua N (2017) Moderating the impact of e-commerce expenses on financial performance in US upper upscale hotels: the role of property size. Tourism Econ 23:429–447. https://doi.org/10.5367/te.2015.0510
4. Inversini A (2017) Managing passengers' experience through mobile moments. J Air Trans Manage 62:78–81. https://doi.org/10.1016/j.jairtraman.2017.03.009
5. Garcia A, Linaza MT, Gutierrez A, Garcia E (2019) Gamified mobile experiences: smart technologies for tourism destinations. Tourism Rev 74:30–49. https://doi.org/10.1108/TR-08-2017-0131
6. Parapanos D, Michopoulou E (2019) Understanding key motivations for using a hotel gamified application. In: Pesonen J, Neidhardt J (eds) Information and Communication Technologies in Tourism 2019: Proceedings of the International Conference in Nicosia, Cyprus, January 30–February 1, 2019. Springer International Publishing, Cham, pp 411–422. https://doi.org/10.1007/978-3-030-05940-8_32
7. Xu F, Tian F, Buhalis D, Weber J, Zhang H (2016) Tourists as mobile gamers: gamification for tourism marketing. J Travel Tourism Mark 33:1124–1142. https://doi.org/10.1080/10548408.2015.1093999
8. Aren S, Güzel M, Kabadayı E, Alpkan L (2013) Factors affecting repurchase intention to shop at the same website. Procedia Soc Behav Sci 99:536–544. https://doi.org/10.1016/j.sbspro.2013.10.523
9. Venkatesh V (2000) Determinants of perceived ease of use: integrating control Intrinsic motivation, and emotion into the technology acceptance model. Inf Syst Res 11:342–365. https://doi.org/10.1287/isre.11.4.342.11872
10. Ozturk AB, Bilgihan A, Nusair K, Okumus F (2016) What keeps the mobile hotel booking users loyal? investigating the roles of self-efficacy, compatibility, perceived ease of use, and perceived convenience. Int J Inf Manage 36:1350–1359. https://doi.org/10.1016/j.ijinfomgt.2016.04.005
11. Yang Y, Asaad Y, Dwivedi Y (2017) Examining the impact of gamification on intention of engagement and brand attitude in the marketing context. Comput Human Behav 73:459–469. https://doi.org/10.1016/j.chb.2017.03.066
12. Yoo C, Kwon S, Chang B (2017) Factors affecting the adoption of gamified smart tourism applications: an integrative approach. Sustainability 9:2162. https://doi.org/10.3390/su9122162
13. Marczewski A Gamified UK Website https://www.gamified.uk/
14. Richard D'arc da SB, Luis Hernan CP, Evandro LL, Mauri Aparecido de O (2018) Development of a gamification characteristics measurement scale for mobile application users. Rev Eletrôn de Negócios Internacionais (Internext) 13:1–16. https://doi.org/10.18568/1980-4865.1311-16
15. Hammedi W, Leclercq T, Riel ACR (2017) The use of gamification mechanics to increase employee and user engagement in participative healthcare services: a study of two cases. Procedia Comput Sci 28:640–661. https://doi.org/10.1108/JOSM-04-2016-0116
16. Xu F, Buhalis D, Weber J (2017) Serious games and the gamification of tourism. Tourism Manage 60:244–256. https://doi.org/10.1016/j.tourman.2016.11.020
17. Parapanos D, Michopoulou E (2021) Gamification, game mechanics, game thinking and players' profile and life cycle. multilingual matters, bristol, blue ridge summit
18. Kirsh BA (2014) Game in Libraries: Essays on Using Play to Connect and Instruct. McFarland & Company Inc Publishers, North Carolina

19. Morschheuser B, Hassan L, Werder K, Hamari J (2018) How to design gamification? a method for engineering gamified software. Inf Softw Technol 95:219–237. https://doi.org/10.1016/j.infsof.2017.10.015
20. Hulsey N (2020) For play: Games in Everyday Life. Emerald Publishing, Bingley
21. Bartle AR (2004) Designing Virtual Worlds. New Riders Publishing, London
22. Yee N (2006) Motivations for play in online games. CyberPsychol Behav 9(6):772–775
23. Veal AJ (2011) Research Methods for Leisure and Tourism: A Practical Guide. Pearson Education Limited, Essex
24. Bryman A (2016) Social Research Methods. Oxford University Press, Oxford
25. Marinao Artigas E, Vilches-Montero S, Chasco Yrigoyen C (2015) Antecedents of tourism destination reputation: the mediating role of familiarity. J Retail Consum Serv 26:147–152. https://doi.org/10.1016/j.jretconser.2015.06.005
26. Gefen D (2000) E-commerce: the role of familiarity and trust. Omega Int J Manage Sci 28:725–737. https://doi.org/10.1016/S0305-0483(00)00021-9
27. Zhang J, Ghorbani AA, Cohen R (2007) A familiarity-based trust model for effective selection of sellers in multiagent e-commerce systems. Int J Inf Sec 6:333–344. https://doi.org/10.1007/s10207-007-0025-y
28. Li M, Mao J (2015) Hedonic or utilitarian? Exploring the impact of communication style alignment on user's perception of virtual health advisory services. Int J Inf Manage 35:229–243. https://doi.org/10.1016/j.ijinfomgt.2014.12.004
29. Wang TL (2011) An effect of trust and attitude in the initial adoption of online shopping: An empirical study. In: IEEE international conference. Information Society (iSociety), London, pp 22–26. https://doi.org/10.1109/i-Society18435.2011.5978490
30. Chang Y-W, Hsu P-Y, Wu Z-Y (2015) Exploring managers' intention to use business intelligence: the role of motivations. Behav Inf Technol 34:273–285. https://doi.org/10.1080/0144929X.2014.968208
31. Hansen JM, Levin MA (2016) The effect of apathetic motivation on employees' intentions to use social media for businesses. J Bus Res 69:6058–6066. https://doi.org/10.1016/j.jbusres.2016.06.009
32. Xie KL, Xiong L, Chen C-C, Hu C (2015) Understanding active loyalty behavior in hotel reward programs through customers' switching costs and perceived program value. J Travel Tourism Market 32:308–324. https://doi.org/10.1080/10548408.2014.896767
33. Park S, Tussyadiah I.P (2020) How guests develop trust in hosts: an investigation of trust formation in P2P accommodation. J Travel Res 59:1402–1412. https://doi.org/10.1177/0047287519884654
34. Egger R, Bulencea P (2015) Gamification in tourism: designing memorable experiences. Bus Econ

Permissions

All chapters in this book were first published by Springer; hereby published with permission under the Creative Commons Attribution License or equivalent. Every chapter published in this book has been scrutinized by our experts. Their significance has been extensively debated. The topics covered herein carry significant findings which will fuel the growth of the discipline. They may even be implemented as practical applications or may be referred to as a beginning point for another development.

The contributors of this book come from diverse backgrounds, making this book a truly international effort. This book will bring forth new frontiers with its revolutionizing research information and detailed analysis of the nascent developments around the world.

We would like to thank all the contributing authors for lending their expertise to make the book truly unique. They have played a crucial role in the development of this book. Without their invaluable contributions this book wouldn't have been possible. They have made vital efforts to compile up to date information on the varied aspects of this subject to make this book a valuable addition to the collection of many professionals and students.

This book was conceptualized with the vision of imparting up-to-date information and advanced data in this field. To ensure the same, a matchless editorial board was set up. Every individual on the board went through rigorous rounds of assessment to prove their worth. After which they invested a large part of their time researching and compiling the most relevant data for our readers.

The editorial board has been involved in producing this book since its inception. They have spent rigorous hours researching and exploring the diverse topics which have resulted in the successful publishing of this book. They have passed on their knowledge of decades through this book. To expedite this challenging task, the publisher supported the team at every step. A small team of assistant editors was also appointed to further simplify the editing procedure and attain best results for the readers.

Apart from the editorial board, the designing team has also invested a significant amount of their time in understanding the subject and creating the most relevant covers. They scrutinized every image to scout for the most suitable representation of the subject and create an appropriate cover for the book.

The publishing team has been an ardent support to the editorial, designing and production team. Their endless efforts to recruit the best for this project, has resulted in the accomplishment of this book. They are a veteran in the field of academics and their pool of knowledge is as vast as their experience in printing. Their expertise and guidance has proved useful at every step. Their uncompromising quality standards have made this book an exceptional effort. Their encouragement from time to time has been an inspiration for everyone.

The publisher and the editorial board hope that this book will prove to be a valuable piece of knowledge for researchers, students, practitioners and scholars across the globe.

List of Contributors

Erisher Woyo
Tourism Research in Economic Environs and Society, North-West University, Potchefstroom, South Africa

Dandison Ukpabi
University of Jyväskylä, Jyväskylä, Finland

Laura Zizka, Meng-Mei Chen, Effie Zhang and Amandine Favre
Ecole Hoteliere de Lausanne//HES-SO University of Applied Sciences and Arts Western Switzerland, Lausanne, Switzerland

Wenqi Wei and Irem Önder
University of Massachusetts, Amherst, MA 01002, USA

Chang Gao
Boston University, Boston, MA 02215, USA

Yong Chen
Ecole Hôtelière de Lausanne, HES-SO, University of Applied Sciences Western Switzerland, Rte de Cojonnex 18, 1000 Lausanne, Switzerland

Junjiao Zhang and Hanqin Qiu
Nankai University, Tianjin 300350, China

Yu-Hua Xu
Arizona State University, HNU-ASU International Tourism College, Haikou, People's Republic of China

Shihan (David) Ma and Xin-Yue Li
School of Management, Zhejiang University, Hangzhou, People's Republic of China

Jae Eun (Francesca) Park, Namho Chung and Chulmo Koo
Smart Tourism Education Platform, Kyung Hee University, Seoul, South Korea

Johanna Heinonen
LAB University of Applied Sciences, Lappeenranta, Finland

Juho Pesonen
University of Eastern Finland, Joensuu, Finland

Roman Egger, Oguzcan Gumus, Elza Kaiumova, Richard Mükisch and Veronika Surkic
Salzburg University of Applied Sciences, Salzburg, Austria

Elide Garbani-Nerini, Elena Marchiori and Rossella Reale
Università della Svizzera italiana, Via Buffi 13, 6900 Lugano, Switzerland

Ye Shen
California Polytechnic State University, San Luis Obispo, CA 93407, USA

Jin Ling and Nadezda Sorokina
SIHOM, Woosong University, Dongdaejon-ro 171, Dong-gu, Daejeon 34606, South Korea

Birgit Bosio
MCI Management Center Innsbruck, 6020 Innsbruck, Austria

Melanie Scheiber
Ötztal Tourismus, 6450 Sölden, Austria

Angela Pagiri, Barbara Prodinger, Ruihong Liu and Fabian Wettinger
University of Applied Sciences Salzburg, Puch/Salzburg, Austria

Micol Mieli
Lund University, Lund, Sweden

Iustina Ivanova, Marina Andrić and Francesco Ricci
Free University of Bozen-Bolzano, Bolzano, Italy

C. K. Bruce Wan and Kenny K. N. Chow
School of Design, The Hong Kong Polytechnic University, Hung Hom, Kowloon, Hong Kong

Cees J. P. M. de Bont
Loughborough Design School, Loughborough University, Leicestershire LE11 3TU, UK

Paul Hekkert
Faculty of Industrial Design Engineering, TU Delft, Delft, The Netherlands

Francisco Femenia-Serra, Aurkene Alzua-Sorzabal and Aitziber Pousa-Unanue
Antonio de Nebrija University, Madrid, Spain

Martha Wells, Kristy de Salas and Anne Hardy
University of Tasmania, Hobart, Australia

Lea Hasenzahl, Soha Ghezili and Lorenzo Cantoni
UNESCO Chair in ICT to Develop and Promote Sustainable Tourism in World Heritage Sites, Università della Svizzera italiana, Lugano, Switzerland

Hisashi Masuda
Kyoto University, Yoshida-honmachi, Sakyo-ku, Kyoto 606-8501, Japan

Kengo Matsumura
Gekkeikan Sake (USA), INC., 1136 Sibley Street, Folsom, CA 95630-3223, USA

Suki Siuki Tam
School of Hotel and Tourism Management, The Hong Kong Polytechnic University, Hong Kong S.A.R., China

Huiyue Ye and Lawrence Hoc Nang Fong
Department of Integrated Resort and Tourism Management, Faculty of Business Administration, University of Macau, Macau SAR, China

Rob Law
Department of Integrated Resort and Tourism Management, Faculty of Business Administration, University of Macau, Macau SAR, China
Asia-Pacific Academy of Economics and Management, Department of Integrated Resort and Tourism Management, Faculty of Business Administration, University of Macau, Macau SAR, China

Wenliang Li, Yoo Ri Kim, Caroline Scarles and Anyu Liu
School of Hospitality and Tourism Management, University of Surrey, Guildford, Surrey, UK

Carlos Flavián, Sergio Ibáñez-Sánchez and Carlos Orús
Faculty of Economy and Business, University of Zaragoza, Gran Vía 2, 50005 Zaragoza, Spain

Jun Shao
Beijing Forestry University, No.35 Tsinghua East Road, Beijing 100083, People's Republic of China

Peng Wang
Beijing Forestry University, No.35 Tsinghua East Road, Beijing 100083, People's Republic of China
Naikai University, 38 Tongyan Road, Tianjin 300381, People's Republic of China

Bing Pan
Department of Recreation, Park, and Tourism Management, The Pennsylvania State University, University Park, PA 16802, USA

Junjun Yin
Social Science Research Institute, The Pennsylvania State University, University Park, PA 16802, USA

Virinchi Savanapelli and Abhishek Shukla
Department of Mining Engineering, Department of Mechanical Engineering, Indian Institute of Technology, Kharagpur, India

Demos Parapanos
Institute of Business, Industry and Leadership, University of Cumbria, Carlisle, UK

Elina (Eleni) Michopoulou
Centre for Contemporary Hospitality and Tourism, University of Derby, Derby, UK

Index

V

W

www.ingramcontent.com/pod-product-compliance
Lightning Source LLC
LaVergne TN
LVHW051048220926
848485LV00001BA/44
9781647254438